Borderlands

THE ARCHAEOLOGY OF THE ADDENBROOKE'S ENVIRONS,
SOUTH CAMBRIDGE

By Christopher Evans,
with Duncan Mackay & Leo Webley

With contributions by
J. Alexander, K. Anderson, G. Appleby, P. Blinkhorn, S. Boreham, M. Brudenell,
A. Challands, A. Dickens, N. Dodwell, M. Edmonds, A. Hall, C. Haselgrove,
M. Knight, T. Legge, S. Lucy, A. McLaren, A. Popescu, K. Roberts, R. Standring,
C. Swaysland, S. Timberlake and D. Webb

Principal illustrations by Andrew Hall

Cambridge Archaeological Unit

Published by
the Cambridge Archaeological Unit
Department of Archaeology, University of Cambridge,
Downing Street, Cambridge, CB2 3DZ
www-cau.arch.cam.ac.uk

Distributed by
Oxbow Books, Oxford, OX1 2EW

ISBN: 978-0-9544824-7-3

This book is available direct from
Oxbow Books, Oxford, OX1 2EW, UK
(Phone: 01865-241249; Fax: 01865-794449)

and

The David Brown Book Company
PO Box 511, Oakville CT 06779, USA
(Phone: 860-945-9329; Fax: 860-945-9468)

or

via the Oxbow Books website
www.oxbowbooks.com

Front cover image: Fox's 1923 Roman Map greatly enlarged; back cover, detail of the same.

Page design, copy editing and typesetting by Dora Kemp.
Printed in Great Britain by Short Run Press, Exeter.

CONTENTS

Figures

Tables

Foreword

New Archaeologies of the Cambridge Region

The publication of this volume marks the first of what is intended to be a series of CAU studies concerned with the archaeology of Cambridge's hinterland. Effectively its suburban 'envelope' or even the 'Land behind Cambridge' (cf. Adams 1965), over the last 15 years this area has seen an enormous quantity of fieldwork, and sufficient developer-funded projects have been undertaken that the amassed material now warrants publication. From the cumulative results, a new sense of local/sub-regional patterning is emerging. Accordingly, we refer to this series of volumes as *New Archaeologies of the Cambridge Region* in direct reference to Fox's groundbreaking landscape study that first appeared some 85 years ago (1923). Not only does this title reflect a general historiographic directive towards fieldwork-study (e.g. Evans & Appleby forthcoming 2009), but, moreover, Fox had an active connection with the South Cambridge landscape with which this volume is concerned (see Scott-Fox 2002). Acknowledging his own predecessors, Fox's approach to his 'Cambridge Region' was well summarized in his 1947 'Reflections' paper:

> Since Mr O.G.S. Crawford wrote his pioneer paper on the 'Distribution of Early Bronze Age Settlements in Britain' in 1912 … *the importance of the study of the pattern* which the find-spots of a given class of group of ancient structures or artefacts make on the map, in relation to the geological structure, the contour, the soil character and the water supply had been current among archaeologically minded students of the past in this country (1947, 1–2; emphasis added).

The second volume in our series will cover the City's western hinterland, and will also include what few recent investigations there have been within Cambridge's Roman upper town on Castle Hill (Evans & Lucas forthcoming). There is, in fact, a certain irony in this. Whereas the Roman town proper saw a considerable body of excavation by John Alexander and his colleagues during the 1960s and '70s (Alexander & Pullinger 2000), it has seen very little development (and excavation) over the last 15 years or so, Indeed, huge swathes of Roman Cambridge were destroyed with little or no excavation during the '80s. Conversely, since 1990 and the advent of developer-funded fieldwork, it is the City's surrounding 'green space' environs that have hosted the brunt of excavation. Consequentially, a much firmer understanding of Cambridge's later prehistoric and Roman hinterland is emerging, to the extent that it now arguably out-strips our appreciation of its (walled) 'core'.

The emphasis on Archaeologies' plural in the series' entitlement must be stressed; this is not a matter of there being a new local 'story', but rather *enquiry towards pattern*, which is certainly not the same thing (see e.g. Gardiner & Williamson 1993). The sheer quantity of excavation that has now occurred within the area means that there can no longer be *an* over-arching local narrative and, given the relentless pace of development, any we now propose will surely be shortly outmoded. Yet this does not imply that sites should simply be treated as individual case-studies. Given the landscape-scale of a number of local development projects, for the first time archaeology is beginning to achieve a sound grasp of prehistoric and early historical settlement densities, the real *fabric of the past*. Put simply, there clearly is a vastly greater quantity of archaeology and more sites than anyone could ever have envisaged in the 1960s–80s, let alone in Fox's time. Appropriate to these 'new knowledges', our approach in this series is to present together inter-related groups of sites so that, if only as an interim measure, at least some level of coherent landscape/settlement research is ensured.

In further acknowledgement of Fox's seminal study, Cambridge does not exist in any kind of isolation as a quasi-historical locale to permit a 'stand-alone story'. On the one hand, there is the matter of the area's specific interrelationships with broader extra-regional (material) cultural phenomena, be these its situation relative to the Late Iron Age Aylesford-Swarling zone or to the Anglo-Scandinavian Danelaw. On the other hand, for much of the time-frame we are concerned with, Cambridge simply did not exist as a place. Our 'focus' was only a spot/dot among many: somewhere vaguely at the junction of the middle/lower reaches of the River Cam, and in the borderland swathe between the (later) County's southern downlands and the Fens. We are, therefore, fully aware of the arbitrary nature of Cambridge's hinterland as a study framework. Be this as it may, fieldwork (wherever) requires context, and 'enquiry'/projects are invariably contingent; all of which broaches the question, to what extent do we choose our 'research' landscapes and to what extent do we simply make the best of the situation we are drawn into?

Finally, aside from reminding us of the need for a robust extra-site scale of research-study, does Fox have any relevance today or should his 'bicycle-driven' survey work only be considered a charming interlude in the history of region's archaeology? Arguably his geographic-imperative — *the active framework of landscape* — is something that is today too often ignored in site-only-focused studies (although the recent interest in the claylands of the Midlands and Eastern England bucks this trend: e.g. Clay 2002; Mills & Palmer 2007). After all, it was the character of landscape that determined the possibilities of early settlement, be it the availability of potting clays or water resources, and, moreover, it was only the geographic/environmental 'mix' of landscapes that fostered long-term settlement traditions and, ultimately, provided whatever basis there is for *a regional archaeology*.

Christopher Evans, Cambridge, 2008

ACKNOWLEDGEMENTS

The Long Run

One of the few constants throughout more than a decade of fieldwork has been Roger Cutting, Capital Planning Manager of Addenbrooke's Hospital. It was he who first realized the need for coherence in its sponsored archaeological works and, over the years, it has only been a pleasure to work with him.

The Hutchison Site excavations were funded by the University of Cambridge, with support from Cancer Research-UK amongst others, and we are grateful for the full co-operation and encouragement throughout of Timothy Warren (University Estates Management and Building Services) and Dr John Tooze of those respective organizations. The excavations greatly benefited from the development programme's management by the Davis, Langdon & Everest team, variously Stuart Axcell, Will Bidewell and John Pearson, and was also further facilitated by Steve Edwards at Laing O'Rourke (and the site's ground crews). Nick Champion of the University's Press Office much abetted the smooth running of the site's press liaison and helped with its open days.

The subsequent Addenbrooke's/Trumpington Meadows Environs fieldwork was variously directed by Matt Brudenell, Duncan MacKay, Ricky Patten and Adam Slater, with Katie Anderson overseeing much of the fieldwalking. The success of 2020 Lands and Clay/Glebe Farm evaluation fieldwork was due in no small part to the cooperation of Jo Clark and John Oldham of Countryside Properties Ltd and, latterly, Annie Bingham of Scott Wilson (with Tim Bowes of WS Atkins acting on behalf of Cambridgeshire County Council as regards the Southern Relief Road-line works). The owner of most of the land in the area, Anthony Pemberton of Pemberton Farms, put up with our intrusions into his fields with admirable patience and good grace, and has since been generous with sharing his local knowledge.

Similarly, for the Trumpington Meadows investigations, the CAU would like to thank Mick Sullivan and Steve Brown of RAGT, Ed Skeates (Grosvenor) and Mr Charles Leeks, the local metal-detector who kindly allowed us to review his material. Equally, for the Bell School Paddocks Site we would like to thank Richard Bailey and Simon Smith of SSR for facilitating the work, and also Ian Sinclair and The Bell Education Trust. Both the Trumpington Meadows and the 2008 Clay Farm 'Green Corridor' investigations (and also the Barrington Quarry fieldwork) were managed by Alison Dickens.

Of the other case-study evaluation surveys, anticipating the construction of 'Northstowe' the Longstanton fieldwork was funded by Gallagher Estates (latterly with English Partnerships) and we are grateful to David Hunt and Andrew Lawson of Gallagher for their exemplary co-operation throughout; James Meek, Sally Randell and Alan Thomas of WSP Environmental greatly facilitated its organization and contributed to its success. The Barrington Quarry work was funded by CEMEX UK and co-ordinated by Robert Masefield of RPS Planning Transport and Environment. The 2002 Granham's Farm investigations were commissioned by David Wood (Leafdome) on behalf of the Mandarin Oriental Hotels Group.

The CAU's many fieldwork projects here described have greatly benefited from the long participation of Rog Palmer (aerial photography), Tony Johnston and Oxford Archaeotechnics (geophysical surveys), Adrian Challands (magnetic susceptibility) and Steve Boreham of the Dept. of Geography, University of Cambridge (palaeo-environment/-topography and geology).

The fieldwork programmes have been variously monitored by Andy Thomas and Kasia Gdaniec, Development Control Archaeologists of Cambridgeshire County Council, and we have also been grateful for their advice. Equally, the long-term intellectual input of Colin Haselgrove, J.D. Hill, Gavin Lucas, Richard Reece and Jeremy Taylor is here duly acknowledged, and J.D., Gavin and Jeremy have read and kindly commented upon various portions of this volume. Evans gratefully acknowledges discussion with Dr Kate Pretty, that went far to elucidate just what conditions were like during the 1967 New Addenbrooke's excavations. Val Rigby and Geoff Dannell's comments on the F.566 grave assemblage were invaluable, as were also Prof. Iain Davidson's concerning his 1969 work at the Trumpington Plant Breeding Institute; David Hall provided insights relating to the area's post-Roman agriculture, as did Rosemary Jefferies concerning the Hutchison's kilns. Otherwise, for the provision of background context, we would like to thank Imogen Gunn for facilitating archive access in the University Museum of Archaeology and Anthropology, and also Pam Smith for lending a copy of Lethbridge's unpublished Autobiography; Alice Lyons, Elizabeth Popescu and Judith Roberts generously provided information concerning the County Council's Duxford cemetery site. The final text has only benefited from the comments and editorial skills of Jo & Grahame Appleby and Sam Lucy.

Covering so much amassed fieldwork, it is unfortunately impossible to name the many Unit site assistants who have participated, but certainly their sustained efforts are here gratefully acknowledged. Throughout, the sites' finds were processed with the utmost efficiency first by Norma Challands and, later, by Gwladys Monteil. The illustrations within this volume variously reflect the skills of Marcus Abbott, Matt Brudenell, Mike Court, Iain Forbes, Vicki Herring and Jane Matthews; however, in the main, they show the hand of Andrew Hall, who also is responsible for much of this book's illustrative design and 'look'. Dave Webb undertook much of the photography included herein, and all of the studio shots.

Finally, by way of dedication, John Alexander seems the only choice: with good humour, charm and grace, at a time when almost no funding was available, in the 1950s–70s he, more than any other individual, mobilized the archaeology of the Cambridge region.

At that time there were many blank spaces on the earth, and when I saw one that looked particularly inviting on a map (but they all look that) I would put my finger on it and say, When I grow up I will go there (Conrad, *Heart of Darkness*, 1902).

My route sometimes took me to villages along the border. But this happened infrequently. For the closer one got to a border, the emptier grew the land and the fewer people one encountered. This emptiness increased the mystery of these regions. I was struck, too, by how silent the border zone was. This mystery and quiet attracted and intrigued me. ... I wanted one thing only - the moment, the act, the simple fact of *crossing the border* (Kapuscinski, *Travels with Herodotus*, 2007)

CHAPTER 1

Framing Contexts and the Study of Pattern

Christopher Evans

Today, coming into Cambridge from the south by train, the distinct silhouette of Addenbrooke's Hospital announces that you have arrived at the city. At least from the south, the Hospital has a comparable long-distance iconic-landmark status as once did the roof-line of King's College Chapel (prior to the city's twentieth-century expansion and 'high builds'), which can be readily appreciated in Loggan's seventeenth-century views of Cambridge (Fig. 1.1).

Emerging from the shadow of the high Shelford Downs on your journey north, just before the Hospital you pass through typical rural, gently rolling farmland. It is a green and pleasant plain, nestled at the foot of the downlands, and clearly marks the border between the city and the South Cambridgeshire countryside. As outlined below, this is destined to radically change through mass future development in the area. Yet, as will be demonstrated, this sense of

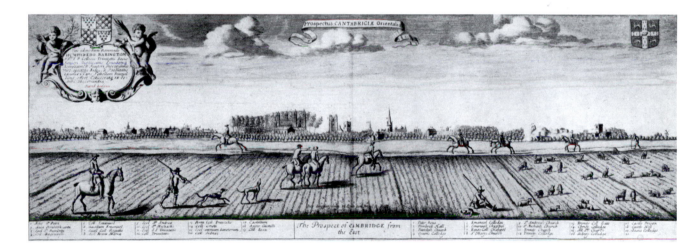

FIGURE 1.1. *Cambridge Approached: Top, Loggan's 1690 prospect of the town from the east (with King's College Chapel lurking behind the trees in the left-centre); below, Cambridge from the south with Addenbrooke's Hospital right.*

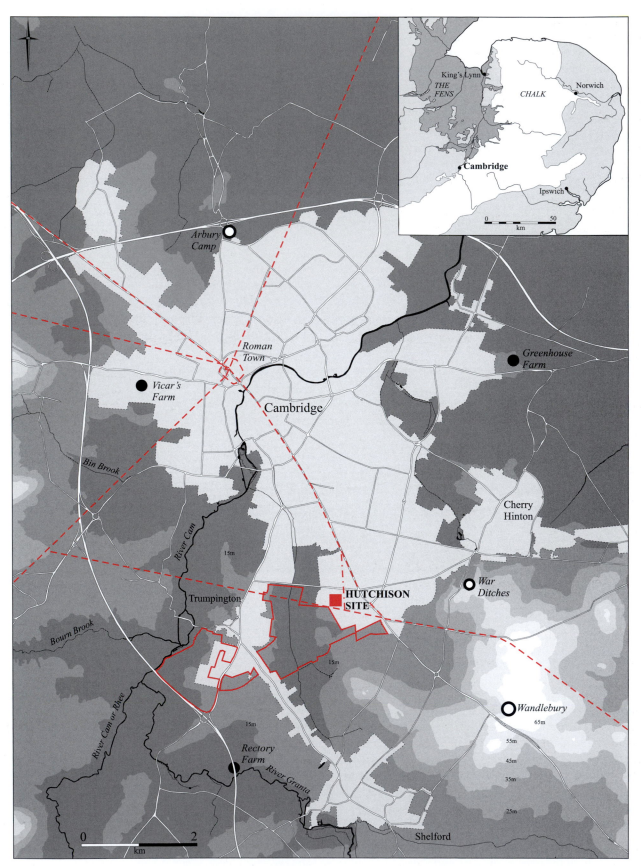

FIGURE 1.2. *Location Map, with broader environs survey area outlined in red and Roman roads in dashed line. (Reproduced by permission of Ordnance Survey on behalf of HMSO. © Crown copyright 2008. All rights reserved. Ordnance Survey licence number 100048686.)*

pristine rural idyll was not always so, and certainly in late prehistoric/Roman times this was a much busier and more 'lived-in' landscape.

This volume will, in the main, be concerned with the Cambridge Archaeological Unit's (CAU) large-scale excavations on the northwest side of Addenbrooke's Hospital at the Hutchison Site in 2002/03, undertaken in conjunction with the construction of the new Cancer Research UK Cambridge Research Institute (Li Ka Shing Centre) and a new multi-storey car park. Having all periods between the Mesolithic and Middle Saxon times variously represented, the crux of its sequence was its later Iron Age and Early Roman phases and, as such, it directly reflects upon crucial issues relating to Conquest Period dynamics and the vexed processes of Romanization. Yet, no matter how large, *no site is an island* (see Evans & Hodder 2006b). Accordingly, the remainder of this chapter will be given to the exploration of both the wider landscape setting and the historiographic background of the fieldwork, the Hutchison Site itself only being presented in the second chapter.

In order to more fully appreciate the implications of the site's sequence, broader framing is needed. Therefore, Chapter 3 will include an outline of the CAU's surveys and evaluation trial trenching campaigns that have since occurred across the fields west of the hospital and stretching down to the River Cam/Granta (Fig. 1.2). This represents the results of four development projects, variously relating to both the hospital's planned expansion and anticipating the city's forthcoming housing allocation. Whilst each has arisen out of separate development proposals, from the outset the Unit has considered them as part of a unified programme of landscape investigation and, consequently, has now been able to apply standard sampling methodologies across some 200 ha. The results of this major survey programme deserve presentation both in their own right and for the degree to which they illuminate the Hutchison's archaeology. This being said, over the course of the next decade, much of this area is slated to see large-scale construction-related excavation, which will certainly both nuance and correct facets of the landscape's interpretation arising from the survey data alone. It is for this reason that, in relating the results of the landscape investigations, we will largely restrict ourselves to matters of broad patterning and otherwise only detail a few outstanding 'exemplars', particularly those resonating with the Hutchison's sequence.

In publishing this survey-phase data, we recognize that this is something of a departure from most current practice in Britain, where nothing less than 'total excavation' is now usually the norm.

Yet, through the influence of 'New Archaeology' and in an attempt to begin to tackle issues of past-settlement densities, the 1970s and '80s saw a spate of major survey projects, with the Fenland Project, Raunds and Stansted surveys only the most obvious regional examples (Hall & Coles 1994; Havis & Brooks 2004; Parry 2006). In this case, the publication of the Addenbrooke's environs surveys attests to the CAU's commitment to formal sampling methodologies and, moreover, the acknowledgement that survey/evaluation fieldwork should be considered as 'knowledge projects' in their own right and not just means by which to discover sites in direct anticipation of their excavation (see e.g. Evans 2000a). This is particularly true when it is considered that surface techniques — variously fieldwalking and test-pitting procedures — can reveal a range of landscape activities that often lack any significant sub-soil/feature-based trace. This applies particularly to the registering of pre-Middle Bronze Age activity/occupation.

It is a nice conceit to think that, with this volume's series directly referencing his *The Archaeology of the Cambridge Region* (1923), Fox himself would have fully approved of this publication of survey results alone (Fig. 1.3). Through the current spate of 'great' developer-funded fieldwork projects in the region, archaeologists are beginning to engage (in-depth) with landscapes on a scale that were previously only susceptible to 'landscape-school' survey techniques (e.g. various by Fox, Taylor, Williamson and others). Yet these should not become diachronic approaches, with archaeologists now only practising machine-stripping techniques and ignoring the wealth of data caught up in overlying top-/sub-soil horizons.

Excavating New Addenbrooke's — 1967 & 2007

The immediate area was firmly put on the region's 'archaeological map' with Mary Cra'ster's 1967 excavations in the Hospital's grounds. Undertaken entirely on a voluntary basis, the work arose due to the observation of ditch sections by workmen during the course of the 'Stage 2' of the Hospital's construction. The fragmentary character of the plan in her 1969 report reflects the conditions of fieldwork (Figs. 1.4, 1.5 & 1.12:1), and discussion with one team member suggests dire rescue circumstances, with only limited cleared exposure amid machine-churned ground (K. Pretty pers. comm). Its main feature was a rectangular ditched enclosure, with rounded corners, some 340 ft across (*c.* 103 m). Its 'V'-shaped ditch was 7 ft (2.10 m) across and four feet deep (*c.* 1.20 m: Cra'ster 1969, figs. 1–3). A few pits were exposed within its interior (apparently unexcavated) and it was remarked that

Figure 1.3. *Fox, Landscape and Modernism - Scene-setting or 'framing' helps to appreciate Fox's …* Cambridge Region *(1923) achievement (upper left). Five years after the end of WWI, 1923 saw, for example, Hitler's Munich Putsch, the official establishment of the USSR and Britain assuming control of the Palestine Mandate; in archaeology, on February 16th of that year Carter opened the inner chamber of Tutankhamen's tomb, and excavation continued on the Peking Man Site at Zhoukoudian, China; Hasek published* The Good Soldier Svejk *and Milne* The House at Pooh Corner. *Otherwise, in the arts, W.B. Yeats was awarded the Nobel Prize for literature, Duchamp finally completed his great assembly piece,* The Bride Stripped Bare by Her Bachelors, Even *('The Large Glass'; lower right) and Le Corbusier issued his manifesto work,* Vers une Architecture *('Toward an Architecture'; lower left), celebrating the design of mass-produced machine age. In short, it was a time of transition, marking the passing of the pre-War 'old world' order and the cusp of Modernism. In many respects this is also true of Fox's study, as it represents a new codification of what were essentially 'casual' antiquarian findings. In terms of the era's cultural-political geography, the volume could be considered as symptomatic of a growing interest in a more domestic 'homeland' with the Nation's imperial drive beginning to wane. A world at home with Heywood Sumner's Arts & Crafts-style New Forest kilns illustrations (upper right), Fox's* The Personality of Britain *of 1932 and Jacquetta Hawkes's* A Land *(1951) would be an even stronger expression of the same (though*

with accompanying illustrations by Henry Moore, the latter is very much a more 'modern' vision of such). Yet, with its chapter-introductory quotations largely drawn from Kipling (and also Housman and Browne) and an emphasis upon past invasions, the Cambridge Region *can still seem an imperial-inspired product, and — as opposed to the 'shock of the new' — with today's eyes appears as if it belongs to a 'long' nineteenth century. This, of course, simply reflects that there will always be something inherently absurd about so benchmarking an era to a single date: time/events will always have innumerable connections leading both forward and back. In the case of Fox's map analyses, their roots must ultimately lie in John Evans's Society of Antiquaries County Mapping initiative of the 1890s (e.g. J. Evans 1893). Conversely, the impact of modernism in landscape study could be considered as occurring as late as the 1960s with the influence of Locational/Central Place Theory (see e.g. Clarke 1972); in other words (and after Le Corbusier), the sense of landscape as being a 'machine' — or, better, 'uniform plane' — for living in.*

many more probably went unnoticed. A quantity of domestic refuse was recovered from the ditch's basal fills and there can be little doubt that the enclosure was occupied as such. The pottery recovered was of 'Iron Age A' type and thought to be comparable to the assemblage from Barley (Cra'ster 1961).

Aside from the main enclosure, a series of parallel ditches ran along its southern side (Cra'ster 1969, fig. 2 'B' & 7). These were not firmly dated and only one seems to have been fully excavated (Cra'ster 1969, fig. 4). This produced pottery of the same general type as the main enclosure, but also yielded a fine, La

Tene-style, decorated pot (Fig. 1.4). The only definite settlement evidence *per se* was found outside of the main enclosure and south of the parallel ditches (also location 'A' on Cra'ster's 1969 plan). There the remains of sub-circular building ('hut'), as defined by postholes and a prepared floor, were recovered.

The finds from the site are held by the University of Cambridge Museum of Archaeology and Anthropology, and the pottery was reviewed in the course of this study (Acc. No. 1968.345, 348, 349, 351, 352 & ZZZ015). The assemblage relates to a Middle/later Iron Age ceramic tradition (J.D. Hill pers. comm.)

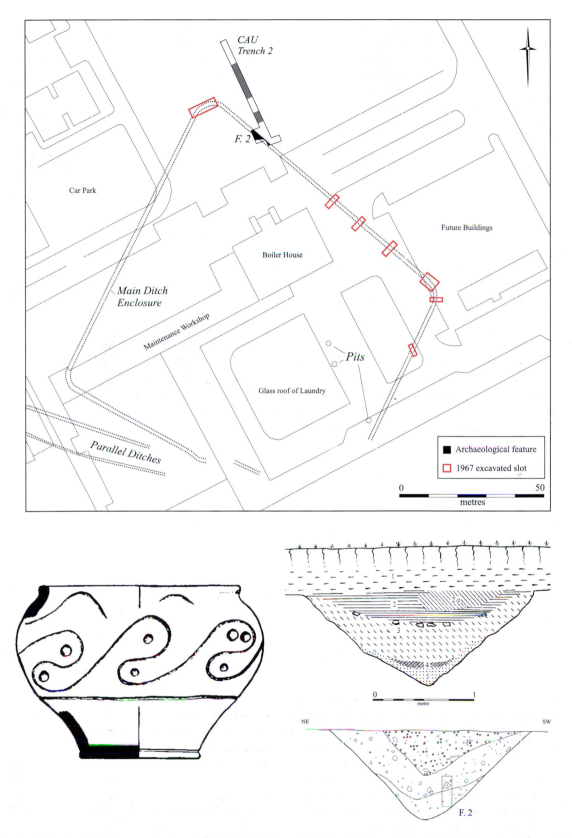

FIGURE 1.4. *Addenbrooke's Excavations — 1967 & 2007: Top, Cra'ster's plan with the CAU's trenches imposed; lower left, the '67 La Tène-style pot; lower right, enclosure ditch section (top, Cra'ster; below, CAU; after Cra'ster 1969 and Hutton & Evans 2007). (Reproduced by permission of Ordnance Survey on behalf of HMSO. © Crown copyright 2008. All rights reserved. Ordnance Survey licence number 100048686.)*

FIGURE 1.5. *Cra'ster's Excavations: archive photographs of the 1967 excavations (Cambridge Museum of Archaeology and Anthropology).*

and is probably of third-/second-century BC date, though the La Tène decorated pot could be later and suggests occupation into the first century BC. (Note that the assemblage includes a few Romano-British sherds and a piece of roof tile, which apparently derive from the upper profile of the main enclosure ditch.) The bone from the excavations cannot be located and may have been discarded. This is indeed unfortunate as it precludes radiocarbon dating of the site's assemblages. The material was, however, studied for Cra'ster's report and of the 107 pieces recovered, 57% were cattle and 38% sheep/goat; three horse (3%) and two pig (2%) bones were also noted (1969, appendix). In short, there seems nothing particularly noteworthy in this as a faunal assemblage, apart perhaps from the frequency of pig — held to be a marker of site status (e.g. see Davis in Evans 2003a and in Malim 1997) — which is very low.

In March of 2007, anticipating the construction of a multi-storey car park, the CAU were fortunate enough to be able to return to further investigate the northern apex-end of Cra'ster's enclosure (Hutton & Evans 2007). The machine treads in the foreground of the resultant Figure 1.6 photograph, which had evidently been impressed into the natural during the '60s construction, attest to the extreme rescue conditions on-site at that time. In the end, our programme only entailed evaluation fieldwork, with two trenches being excavated. Removal of former car park hard-standing showed that its construction has caused substantial truncation of the white chalky marl natural/geology, and there were swathes of deeper lateral downcutting. The one, northern, trench (1) only included a slight gully that might be deemed of 'archaeological origin'. At its extreme southern end, the other trench (2) just clipped the eastern edge of ditch features. Seeming to exactly match the location of Cra'ster's enclosure, we duly opened a cutting on its western side (this being despite the fact that this immediate area was not intended to see any significant ground disturbance) and there, exactly where the 1969 plan indicated, was Cra'ster's ditch. As a reasonable solution to the current development's limited impact upon it, our excavations were, essentially confined to digging a metre-wide segment across it. Although clearly having undergone substantial construction-related truncation in the 1960s, the ditch still proved robust: with a broad, 'V'-shaped profile, it was 2.05 m wide and 0.75 m deep. The fill within its lower half was relatively sterile and consisted of clean, weathered marl-derived light-mid grey/brown clay silts. In contrast, its upper profile was much more distinct: a dark grey/brown clay silt, blackened with charcoal and with frequent stone/flint inclusions, that was obviously occupation-related.

For such a limited cutting across the enclosure's perimeter, the finds assemblages were modestly impressive. Aside from four undiagnostic worked flints, nine sherds of handmade pottery of the Iron Age were recovered. Reported upon by Brudenell, these were rendered in sandy fabrics typical of the Middle/later Iron Age assemblages of southern Cambridgeshire and directly comparable to Cra'ster's material; the absence of any wheel-turned wares, vertical combing or 'late' handmade forms would suggest a date of the third–first century BC. In addition, some 280 animal bones were recovered and, of the 127 that were identifiable, all but one (probably from 'sheep/goat') were cattle. Again in keeping with Cra'ster's results, the vast majority of this material derived from the feature's upper profile (the sherds found in its basal deposits, though, indicate that there was no substantial chronological interval between the two fills; i.e. the enclosure's ditch could not have been dug much before the third century BC). This patterning was also true of the feature's three bulk plant-remain samples. Whilst that from its basal fills was essentially sterile (apart from only a few charcoal fragments), those from the upper fill yielded cereal grains and chaff (spelt and possibly both barley and emmer) and, also, 29 wild plant seeds; the latter variously deriving from waste ground or grassland and arable field (i.e. an 'open land' mix).

While to some extent the 2007 investigation did no more than confirm the broad details of Cra'ster's findings (certainly serving as a testimony to the accuracy of her surveying) and attest to the degree of the site's subsequent construction-related truncation, it also hinted at the density of the enclosure's occupation. If the finds generated from our cutting were representative of the densities around its perimeter as a whole, then it would have contained in excess of 3500 sherds of pottery and some 100,000 animal bones.

Despite the fact that only an incomplete plan of the enclosure was retrieved and little of its interior could be examined in detail (understandable given the limited resources at hand), Cra'ster's Addenbrooke's site has long been held to be 'special' — but is this still the case? Its status has basically hinged upon the deep 'V'-shaped profile of its boundary ditch and, more importantly, the recovery of a La Tène-style decorated vessel that was unique in the region at that time and suggestive of high status and/or distant trade connections. It must also be remembered that the work occurred at a time when earthmoving machinery was only occasionally used on sites, and to recover a *convincing* near-complete plan of a prehistoric enclosure in its entirety was itself rare. In addition to just how few (and those small-scale) excavations had been carried out (Mucking, for example, only commenced in 1968), aerial photography was then also still in its infancy. All this resulted in the fact that prehistoric to early historic land-use/settlement densities were grossly underestimated, and helped to fuel the *Rescue* ethos of the day (i.e. sites as something rare); put simply, today there is a lot more past! As will be apparent in the discussion below, we now know from the area's cropmark plots that the Addenbrooke's landscape appears to include a number of enclosures directly comparable to Cra'ster's. Moreover, although in 2007 we retrieved no other La Tène-decorated pottery sherds (unsurprisingly, given the narrowness of our cutting), in recent years, whilst not commonplace, such wares regularly occur in excavations of Iron Age settlements within the region, although in frequencies of only one or two sherds in many (Hill & Horne, in Evans 2003a, 180). When their fabrics have been analysed, however, it has been shown that they were atypical of their respective assemblages; this and their distinctive decorative style suggests some manner of specialist manufacture. The crucial point in relationship to issues of Late Iron Age/Conquest Period prestige goods systems, is that specialist production and the striving for something 'beyond' the immediately local were already well-afoot earlier in the Iron Age.

Histories and resonance

Returning to Cra'ster's site after a 40-year interval provides this volume with a sense of resonance and research history (i.e. taking us back to 'origins'). We were conscious that this neatly wrapped up a phase of our own fieldwork within the Hospital's grounds and, indeed, delayed the publication of this volume in its anticipation. Beyond this, as is clear in Webb's photograph, this work also allowed us to appreciate and demonstrate the scale and manner of the Hospital's building programme during the '60s (Fig. 1.6). Look at the white chalky marl deposit that runs across the background. Clearly a cut-fill relating to the truncation of the Iron Age ditch, it attests to the 'open-cast mine'

FIGURE 1.6. *Addenbrooke's Investigation 2004 & 2007: left, looking east towards the hospital along one of the 2020 Lands evaluation trenches, note the depth of dumped chalk marl sealing the groundsurface; right, Cra'ster's enclosure ditch as exposed in the recent CAU excavations; note the machine-treads impressed into the levelled top of the lower chalk geology in the foreground and the 'big pit' truncation of the ditch behind (i.e. chalk backfilling of construction cut).*

type mode of the Hospital's construction (i.e. it was essentially built in a 'big pit').

Prior to our work at the Hutchison Site, the Unit had undertaken limited-scale trenching programmes within the main core of the Hospital's grounds on two occasions during the 1990s, and each time encountered comparable, deeply dumped, sterile marly deposits with no trace of archaeology whatsoever (Regan 1996; Robinson 1995). Something was clearly wrong in terms of how its construction was commonly remembered (although in fairness, Cras'ter had noted that it involved downcutting by 20 ft; 1969). Accordingly, when in 2002 plans for Addenbrooke's long-term expansion were first mooted, we approached Roger Cutting of the Hospital and suggested that they commission a major Desktop Study that both covered the area of its future development and thoroughly reviewed the building history of its established 'core'. The results of these researches will feature below. For our immediate purposes, most pertinent was Palmer's appraisal of the aerial photographs. Documenting the many stages of the hospital's construction, those of the '60s-phase

clearly revealed mass, area-wide, truncation relating to its system of building-connecting tunnels. Equally significant, they show the dumping of extracted material across the field immediately to the west and beside the Cambridge/London railway line (Fig. 1.8). Having distinctly groomed, 'rolling' contours, its deep-sealing accounts for the lack of any subsequent aerial photographic register across it (evident within Figure 1.6, when we trenched that plot in 2004 it was found to have been made-up by 1–2.00 m with chalky marl dumps; see Chapter 3 below).

That the manner of the Hospital's 'big pit' construction seemed largely to have been forgotten primarily attests to the extent to which the personnel of so vast an institution as Addenbrooke's change over such a period (and the lack of lodging of detailed building plans in public records). In the course of undertaking the Hospital's environs researches, other recent 'overlooked histories' also came to light. As shown in Figure 1.7, one is that the Cambridge and Ely Agricultural Show regularly, and on occasion the Royal Agricultural Show (1922, 1951 & 1960–61), took

FIGURE 1.7. *The Royal Show, 1960–61: looking west across the area of Clay Farm fields to Trumpington (top right) and, in the central background, with the huts of the PoW Camp still standing (see Fig. 1.8; photograph provided courtesy of Anthony Pemberton).*

place on the Clay Farm fields bordering Trumpington and west of the railway line from the 1920s (Brown 2003). Extending over as much 60 ha, with its many thousands of participants, this mass-event serves to warn us against assuming any sense of a timeless countryside continuum and, again, tells us that at times these were intensively utilized lands.

Interestingly enough, while obviously resulting from topsoil truncation/disturbance, evaluation fieldwork in the Clay Farm area showed little below-ground trace of the fair. The same is certainly not true of another neglected history, that being the WWII defences and other related facilities on the south side of the City. That a pillbox stood on that side of its grounds was widely known. This war-time background became more striking when we received both USAF and RAF imagery for the area (see *Defence and Fieldwork* Inset below). Apparent on these aerial photographs are, in fields to the west, both the barrow-like rings of an anti-aircraft battery and also a prisoner of war camp (Camp 45; Fig. 1.8); throughout the area runs the town's Anti-tank Ditch. Part of the 'GHQ' (General Headquarters) defensive line that ran

from Bristol to London and then north to Cambridge and up to Richmond (Foot 2006), the latter today skirts the southern side of the hospital's grounds (Figs. 1.9 & 1.12). The scale of this defensive perimeter was brought home to us when in 2002, during the course of evaluation fieldwork up on Shelford Down, we excavated — albeit largely by machine — a length of another of its circuits (Whittaker *et al.* 2002). 4.00 m wide and 2.00 m deep, with a distinctly asymmetrical profile, this clearly would have posed a formidable barrier (Fig. 1.9). In fact, when the scale of the town's wartime defensive network is appreciated, it becomes somewhat unnerving for archaeologists to realize just how quickly such a vast series of earthworks could become lost from popular memory.

Cambridge is by no means distinct in this, and the results of the Council for British Archaeology's 'Defence of Britain' survey (e.g. Foot 2006) have generally come as a surprise for all but wartime enthusiasts, with a comparable example being London's three great anti-tank circuits. Equally, although much further afield, when undertaking field survey with Caroline Humphrey in Inner Mongolia within the steppe-like

FIGURE 1.8. *Landscape Lost: Top, Mosaic of Ordnance Survey photographs from 1967 (OS67145: 144 & 176) showing the hospital's 'big pit' open-area construction technique and the dumping of the resultant spoil in the field immediately to the west/left. Below left, anti-aircraft position located in the northwestern Clay Farm fields south of Long Road (TL 450555), which was constructed around August 1940 and significantly expanded by April 1944 when it was photographed by a US Air Force training flight. Appearing to include both searchlights and anti-aircraft gun emplacements, the site is protected by a nearby pillbox and permanently staffed from nearby billets. A metal-detector survey recovered a cap badge of the Royal Artillery and rifle ammunition from adjacent to the billets (see Chapter 3, Inset). Bottom right, the buildings of the PoW Camp in the Trumpington Meadow fields as of May 1953 (TL 439538; copyright English Heritage [NMR] RAF photography).*

FIGURE 1.9. *The Defensive Perimeter: the (pre-) Addenbrooke's landscape with the GHQ line indicated right. The trench was rapidly constructed from June 1940, being completed around southern Cambridge by the end of August 1940 when it was photographed by a Luftwaffe reconnaissance sortie. Below, the Anti-tank ditch as excavated at Granham's Farm, Shelford in 2002 (see Fig. 3.17 for location; Whittaker et al. 2002).*

environs of the medieval Mergen Tibetan-Mongolian monastery, a similar sense of lost military-landscape 'trace' or knowledge was experienced. Located at the foot of the Mona Uul mountains and close to the Mongolian border, the area had been heavily fortified during the period of the Sino-Soviet conflict of the 1960s (Evans & Humphrey 2002; 2003). Some of the resultant features were obvious, such as tunnel-linked bunker systems, and were generally acknowledged by all for what they were. However, for other settings, such as completely overgrown small embanked rings, there was much more ambiguity. Appearing to all intents and purposes to be 'ancient', we at first speculated whether they might be old house sites or even some manner of small henge-like monuments (see Evans & Hodder 2006a concerning the lingering impact of the 'intellectual baggage' we all bring to projects). When we queried our local colleagues and informants about the nature of these they all readily agreed, 'yes, they were very old'. It was only much later, when our 'eye' was properly into the local land-scape, and when the scale of its various '60s trench and fox-hole systems was appreciated, that we recognized these ring settings for what they were: recent artillery emplacements.

More directly relevant to the core themes of this volume is the fact that archaeology was actually exposed when Cambridge's anti-tank ditch was dug on the south side of the hospital. This included a Late Neolithic Grooved Ware pit (Frere 1943) and, in 1945, a later prehistoric settlement was summarily investigated when pottery and a bronze razor were recovered (along with animal bones and residual flints: Figs. 1.12:2 & 4.1; Collins 1948; see also Fell 1949). The latter material, originally assigned to the Iron Age ('A'), has recently been reviewed by Brudenell and, with its pottery entirely burnt-flint tempered, has been reattributed to the later Bronze Age. (The renowned German archaeologist, Gerhard Bersu — who later as a refugee in Britain excavated the site of Little Woodbury in Hampshire — during WWI had the job of inspecting military trenches for archaeological findings: Evans 1989.)

Concerning the town's former defensive pe-rimeter — following Dunkirk's evacuation in 1940, the GHQ was considered the 'stop line' should a German invasion penetrate the 'coastal crust' — and *borders* more generally, another resonance arises, that being the fact that Cambridge straddles the northern limits of the Aylesford-Swarling zone (e.g. Birchall 1965). Belying its inelegant title, this is one of the major boundaries in southern British archaeology. It was *the* divide in the cultural geography of later Iron Age southeastern England and marks the limits of

direct Roman Gaulish influence during the later first century BC and the first half of the first century AD. The Aylesford-Swarling zone is reflected in the uptake of new modes of pottery (wheelmade manufacture) and burial (cremation rite), changes in dress/grooming and the adoption of coinage (see Hill *et al.* 1999). As will be explored below, this is directly reflected in the Hutchison Site by the occurrence of Iron Age coinage and the frequency of brooches and wheelmade pottery (see Evans 2003b).

The kind of oddities that the acculturation proc-ess of early first-century AD 'contact' generated are illustrated in Figure 1.10. One of these is a Late Iron Age sherd recovered during evaluation fieldwork along the north side of Cambridge Airport and just south of the Greenhouse Farm Site, with which its source-settlement must be continuous (Cooper 2003; Gibson & Lucas 2002). The piece is from the base of a handmade vessel made in direct imitation of imported, wheelmade, Roman Samian platters. Whereas the imported vessels of this type are often stamped with their makers' names (i.e. spelt out), in this case the stamp is illiterate/geometric and, instead of writing, there are only impressed circles and lines (what we don't as yet know is whether this was still a true and/or specific maker's symbol, or just a generic 'imitation-gesture'; see Webley, Chapter 2 and Fig. 2.30:4).

The other example is a Late Iron Age inhuma-tion from a 2005 site excavated in the grounds of the Babraham Research Campus in the south of the county (Armour 2007). There, within the area of a major Roman farmstead (including a 36-interment second- to fourth-century cremation and inhumation cemetery) two isolated inhumations lay together, side-by-side, on one side of the settlement. Both were mature and lay supine. Whilst the male was without accompanying grave goods, his female counterpart had a Colchester-type brooch on her breast and two pottery vessels by her head: a beaker and a pedestal tazza (Fig. 1.10:1–3). The 'classic' interment-rite of the period was cremation (often with the same type of goods as in this grave) or, otherwise, the deposition of disarticulated remains, and to the best of our knowl-edge a grave good-accompanied inhumation from this time within the area is unique (the Early Roman burial practice was predominately cremation, but inhuma-tion was also practised; Fox, though, records two other possible such Iron Age inhumations in Suffolk: 1923, 97, see also e.g. Hey *et al.* 1999).

Before proceeding, there are further themes that require emphasis. One, completely in keeping with our 'Fox-directive', is that of the *geographical possibilities of land*: in this case the area's 'inland

Figure 1.10. *Iron Age 'Singularities': Top, stamped Late Iron Age pot base (with detail of geometric stamp right) from Cambridge Airport investigations (Cooper 2003); bottom left, the Babraham Research Campus Late Iron Age inhumation, with its grave goods beside it (Armour 2007).*

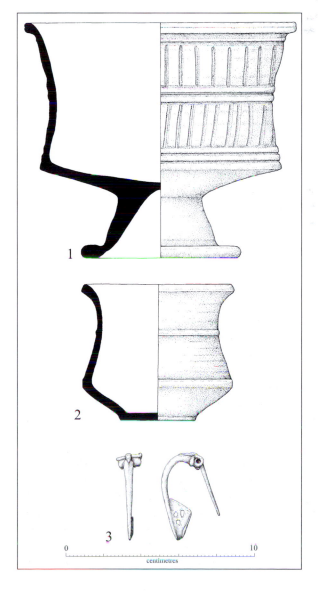

FIGURE 1.11. *The Addenbrooke's Landscape — Geology and Contour Plan. (Reproduced by permission of Ordnance Survey on behalf of HMSO. © Crown copyright 2008. All rights reserved. Ordnance Survey licence number 100048686.)*

locale' would obviously have impinged upon its early settlement history. Falling *c.* 2.5 km east of the River Cam/Granta, the situation of permanent water sources would have had a significant bearing. Prior to the Bronze Age when deep pit-wells seem to first have been regularly dug, settlement of any duration would have had to rely on spring-lines along the foot of the chalk Downs. To wit (and as a further instance of the area's historical nuancing/connections), in the fields south of the hospital lies the *Nine Wells* spring (Fig. 1.11), from which in 1610 (at the instigation of the University's Vice-Chancellor, Andrew Perne) water

was diverted to provide the town with a clean supply; the Cambridge carrier, Thomas Hobson (1545–1631), of both 'Hobson's Choice' and '… Conduit' renown, was a member of its overseeing committee.

Similar are questions of long-term landscape continuities, particularly the potential 'fossilization' of alignments. Comparable to Taylor's analysis of the lingering influence of Roman boundaries at Duxford or Williamson's of the present-day survival of Iron Age field systems in Essex (Taylor & Fowler 1978; Williamson 1987), in this case there is considerable ambiguity as to what degree the area's cropmark-fieldsystems — largely a Roman-landscape 'artefact' — actually had their origins in prehistory. How can we possibly account for continuities stretching over a millennium or more? Here, as highlighted in Chapter 3, the evaluation fieldwork in the Bell Language School paddocks on the Hospital's southern margins provides remarkable evidence of the actual 'mechanism' of such long-term landscape determinants.

Finally, lurking in background are underlying issues of general 'landscape character'. The south of the County still presents a traditionally 'pretty' village-based landscape and *the village* sits centrally in studies of its past, with Parker's *The Common Stream* (1975) being the most obvious example (see also Taylor 1997 and Oosthuizen 2006). Moreover, due to the obvious upstanding earthwork-survival of their monuments, the County's southern downs were a focus of early fieldwork, being a landscape that could be easily read. Yet, while its downland could potentially have had an appeal comparable to Hardy's Wessex, the weight of the region's romantic projection has, rather, lain with the Fenland marshes (Evans 1997). This has been despite Lethbridge's efforts to infuse its 'downland-scape' with mysticism (e.g. 1957; as outlined below, the University's 1990s excavation at Wandlebury firmly dispelling the existence of his putative chalk figures there, they proving instead to be the result of tree-rooting: French 2004). In this capacity, in his unpublished autobiography Lethbridge relates discussing (with his friend Manny Forbes) the folklore associations of Nine Wells and its potential connections with 'Nine Maiden's Holes/Wells' (and, thereby, 'the great Earth Goddess'). Stating that they lay close to the 'the celebrated Iron Age tombs at Chronicle Hills', he continued:

> These indicated that some important pre-Roman, we might perhaps call it 'Belgic' family, had once lived in the neighbourhood. No one as yet appears to have found one of the houses of the people of this kind; although there may be one near Lord's Bridge, not far from Barton (Lethbridge n.d.).

This statement tells of the sense of scale that was implicit in the early constitution of the County's past. The Chronicle Hills barrows lie some 6 km distant from Nine Wells, but somehow their direct associative-connection was considered valid; there simply being no idea of just how densely settled was the region's prehistoric landscape. Equally, almost single-handedly, Lethbridge engendered a local landscape mysticism. Claims that the Cambridge Region was the true site of Troy can be considered only the most extreme example of his legacy today (e.g. Wilkens 2005), and it could be argued that promotion of the Gog Magog Hills area as some manner of an extraordinary ritual nexus would essentially amount to only a more polite version of the self-same (see below).

Fieldwork context and landscape setting

The area lies in the plain at the northern foot of the County's downlands and below the rise of White Hill (*c.* 35 m OD; Figs. 1.11 & 1.13). The geology consists essentially of Lower Chalk (chalk marl with gravel). However, terrace gravels locally outcrop southeast of the Hospital and immediately west of the Babraham Road/Worts Causeway junction, and extend continuously as a north–south band just west of the railway line. The topography is unremarkable and generally lies between 13 and 20 m OD. However, within the area of the Hospital proper, landscaping in the course of its construction has had a significant impact, resulting in both levelling and make-up of the ground surface. Fortunately, Cra'ster produced a contour map for the Hospital core area (Cra'ster 1969, fig. 1). While only showing variation between 42 and 62 feet (*c.* 13–19.00 m), it indicates that the '67 Iron Age enclosure lay across the crown of a distinct east-west oriented rise which must continue west from the area of Wort's Causeway/Red Cross. Aside from attesting to the immediate landscape sensitivity of the enclosure's layout, this relief also hints at what 'topography' has been lost through the construction of the Hospital; certainly no trace of the rise survives today.

Palmer's cropmark plan shows that a network of fieldsystems extends across much of the area (Fig. 1.12). Across its south-centre and extending eastward, these are generally of north–south/east–west orientation; across the north-centre and to the northwest they lie on a more northwest–southeast axis. Throughout, a number of discrete sub-rectangular-/-square ditched compounds have been plotted, some of which may be comparable to Cra'ster's enclosure (Fig. 1.12:1; see also Inset, Chapter 3; note that in order to ease presentation, the map's enumerated listings have been minimalized and stray evidence omitted: see Evans 2002 for its full gazetteer). Moreover, as is apparent in Figure 1.13's topographic rendering, to the south these cropmark boundaries even continue up the flanks of White Hill Down. The most elaborate cropmark is the probable villa complex (6.8 ha), with associated settlement and roads/trackways, in the southeast corner just north of Great Shelford and beside the railway (Figs. 1.12:3 & 2.56). The area's only Scheduled Ancient Monument (SAM CAM 57), the date of this site has been confirmed through fieldwalking, when first- to fourth-century AD pottery was recovered (Bradford 1978).

Two other cropmarks are also immediately striking: the triple circuit sub-rectangular enclosure

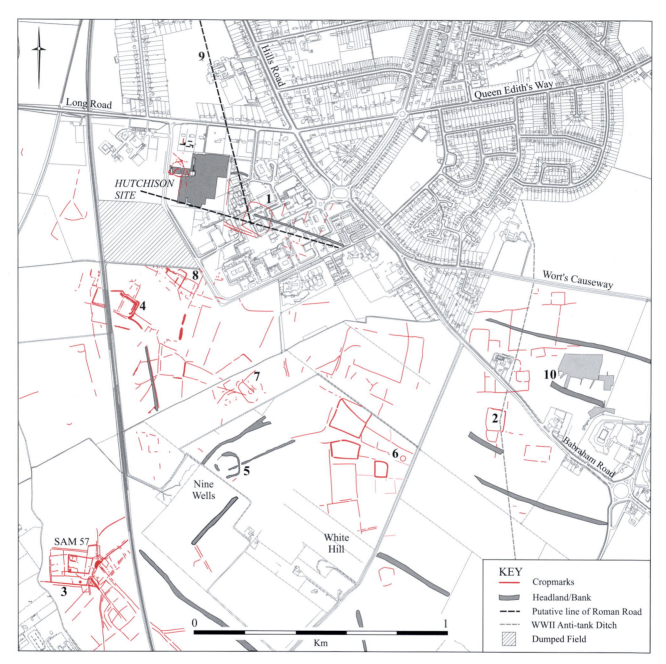

FIGURE 1.12. *The Addenbrooke's Landscape — Cropmark Plot. (Reproduced by permission of Ordnance Survey on behalf of HMSO. © Crown copyright 2008. All rights reserved. Ordnance Survey licence number 100048686.)*

bisected by the railway west of the hospital (70–90 × 180 m: Fig. 1.12:4) and, just below White Hill and near Nine Wells, a *c.* 100 m diameter embanked ring (Fig. 1.12:5). While the former has subsequently been trench-investigated and will accordingly feature in Chapter 3, below, the same is not true of the latter. It has been inspected in the field, but no surface finds were present by which to potentially date it. Therefore, on the basis of its size and plan-form alone, it can only be broadly attributed to prehistoric times. It is possibly a henge, but is more likely of Bronze or Iron Age date

(potentially even a Later Bronze Age Ringwork comparable, perhaps, to those at Mucking or Springfield Lyons: e.g. Priddy & Buckley 1987, 50–51). Although somewhat more tenuous, it is worth noting the higher density of small paddock settings that lie just northeast of the triple-circuit enclosure and immediately south of the made-up field (Fig. 1.12:8), as these are suggestive of settlement.

Finally, two *c.* 20.00 m diameter 'circles' also warrant notice at this stage. One lies relatively isolated in the centre of the area and is probably a ring-ditch

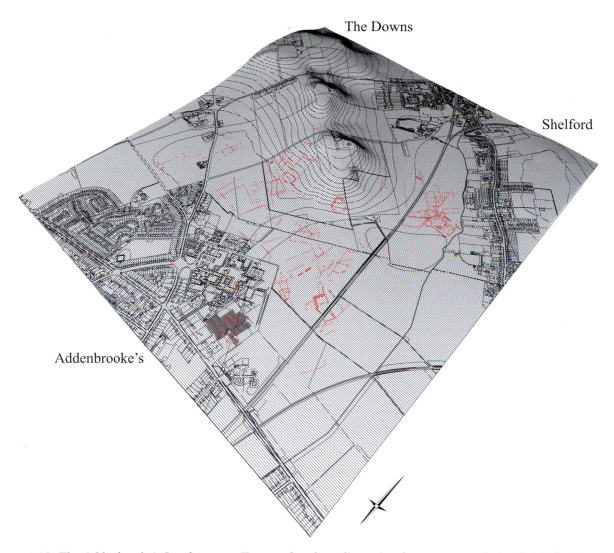

The Downs

Shelford

Addenbrooke's

FIGURE 1.13. *The Addenbrooke's Landscape — Topography: three-dimensional computer rendering (with the Hospital in the left-centre foreground) looking southeast towards the high downland of the White Hill (note the height to which cropmarks extend up the latter's flanks). (Reproduced by permission of Ordnance Survey on behalf of HMSO. © Crown copyright 2008. All rights reserved. Ordnance Survey licence number 100048686.)*

monument (Fig. 1.12:6). The other is sited further to the west and might be of the same attribution, but it lies centrally within a sub-square compound and may conceivably, therefore, indicate a large roundhouse (although at *c.* 5.00 m it does seem too large for such a categorization).

Falling, as they do, adjacent to the flanks of Cambridgeshire's southern chalk downlands (i.e. the County's own 'Wessex'), the hospital grounds are framed by some of the county's most celebrated early excavations. This would have to include Hartley's work with the University Field Club (1955–56: Hartley 1957) on the Iron Age hillfort at Wandlebury (Fig. 1.2). Aside from noting that the more recent, 1994–97, excavations there have shown that its defences are probably of Middle Iron Age date and that they were

preceded by 'open' Early Iron Age settlement (French 2004), lying some 3 km south of the Addenbrooke's area its sequence need not be further rehearsed. More pressing, as they reflect upon the southern approaches of the town's Roman road system and the early pottery production of that period, are, respectively, the excavations at Perse School to the north and those at the War Ditches 2 km eastward:

Perse School (TL 46265583; Fig. 1.12:9)
Walker first undertook excavations in the area of the School in 1909 when the line of the north–south Roman road to Cambridge — the *Via Devana* running north to the town — was unearthed and pottery, tile, a coin and a brooch were recovered (Walker 1910). Subsequently, when the field was levelled in 1911, a

brooch, coins, bronze objects, a pot and tessarae were recovered. Further excavation of the road occurred in 1953 as a result of school building. Its flanking ditches were found to be 14.5 yds (*c*. 13.25 m) across, but no evidence of metalling was recovered (RCHM[E] 1959, 5–6). Late second-century pottery was forthcoming from a nearby pit and a coin of Severus (AD 193–211) was found. Pottery and tile were also recovered when digging a school building-related foundation trench in 1970. Somewhat surprisingly, evaluation fieldwork at the Perse School along the projected line of the road in 1996 produced no significant archaeology (Leith 1996). Similarly, a number of subsequent evaluations further to the north, across the road's line in the grounds of Homerton College and in a development adjacent to the Hills Road/Cherry Hinton bridge have all also failed to recover any definite evidence of its route.

War Ditches (TL 48405550; Figs. 1.2 & 1.14)
Lying on the lower chalk, the enclosure has now all but been quarried away. It was thought to have been circular (*c*. 150 m diameter) and enclosed by a steep sided 'V'-shaped ditch 3.00 m deep with a flat base (see Fig. 2.46:4&5). The first serious investigation of the site was by Hughes (1904a) at the turn of the century (Fig. 2.46:6; see Taylor 1999, fig. 3). The 'accepted' interpretation of the site is that the enclosure was constructed in the third–fourth centuries BC and in the first century BC the 'massacred remains' of the site's last defenders were interred in, and the smouldering rubble of its defences shovelled into, the upper profile of the ditch by Belgic invaders; it was later occupied in Roman times and remains of Early Roman pottery-making were found (Taylor 1977, 40). However, as remarked upon by M.W. Thompson, '… the site, now largely quarried away, has been reluctant to yield up its secrets' (1990, 70), and when, in 1939, Lethbridge excavated there he found only Bronze Age material in the ditch's primary fills. This, and the fact that he could not locate the circuit on its eastern side, led him to speculate that it was 'an unfinished work or something of a different character' and that it was never a 'completely symmetrical fort' (1948, 119). Aside from recovering six skeletons (and a skull) within the ditch, Lethbridge also recovered an Early Roman kiln (Fig. 2.46:3).

In an *addendum* to his 1948 report, Lethbridge noted that the area east of the chalk pit had then been stripped of topsoil anticipating the quarry's expansion. The University Field Club intermittently undertook excavations across this swathe between 1949–62, with White only publishing part of this in 1964 (a & b; Lethbridge also seems to have done some further work, that essentially went unpublished; see Wright

1950, 104). Aside from exposing the full circuit of the main enclosure and excavating the overlying Roman settlement, the Field Club also then dug two barrows in the north of the area; the results of this work feature in Chapter Two's Inset, *War Ditches — Squaring (and losing) the Circle*.

Other more minor investigations over the last 15 years within the immediate area include the County Council Unit's trenching along the then-proposed route of the City's Southern Relief Road (Kemp 1993). While in three of their 12 trenches they recovered second- to third-century Roman pottery and Middle Iron Age sherds, generally the results can only be counted as minimal. Equally, no dating evidence was forthcoming from the apparently fieldsystem-related ditches exposed within the Council Unit's trenches in 2000, within the ground of Long Road Sixth Form College, just northwest of the Hutchison Site (Abrams 2000). Located somewhat further northeast (*c*. 6 km), evaluation fieldwork by the same organization at Glebe Road revealed a scattering of Middle Iron Age settlement features (Connor 2000).

Otherwise, in recent years there have been three excavations in the wider area (located somewhat further afield) that have a direct bearing on our investigations:

Fulbourn Hospital (TL 498566)
Evaluation fieldwork by the CAU in 1993 identified evidence of prehistoric settlement on the site (Gdaniec 1993). Subsequently, in 1996, a 0.36 ha site was excavated by the Oxford Archaeological Unit (Brown & Score 1998; see Fig. 4.2). Although only limited evidence of settlement *per se* was forthcoming, this revealed part of a large 'open' Middle–later Bronze Age enclosure system with accompanying posthole fence-lines. Worthy of note is the fact that the system's ditches were relatively large: in the main, 1.80–3.60 m across and 1.15–1.50 m deep.

Babraham Road Park-and-Ride (TL 47255460; Figs. 1.12:10, 4.1 & 4.2)
The site was excavated by the County Council Unit in 1998 (see Hinman 1999b; 2001) and three main periods of activity were distinguished. The first, of later Neolithic–Early Bronze Age attribution, was of mixed character: three inhumation burials, a scattering of Grooved Ware-associated pits and two deep circular shafts/pits (1.80 m+ deep). The main features of the second period were two aligned, earlier–Middle Bronze Age ditches (interrupted by a *c*. 5.00 m entrance). Associated with timber beam slot-like settings, the ditch boundaries were robust (2.5 m wide and 1.20 m deep) and yielded a radiocarbon date of 1755–1415 cal. BC.

The final, Late Iron Age, period consisted of a series of unusually shallow, flat-based, trench-like linear ditches that are without ready parallel. Stressing the environs' ceremonial/symbolic landscape context throughout and the fact that the site lay centrally within a 'natural amphitheatre' defined by the Downs along its southern side (and, also, its proximity to the Nine Wells spring-head), its director has emphasized the site's ritual associations (Hinman 2001); pending full publication, such arguments are difficult to evaluate.

Trumpington Road Park-and-Ride (TL 44255427; Fig. 3.1) In 2001 the County Council Field Unit excavated a *c.* 1.7 ha site on the southwest side of Trumpington (see also Davidson & Curtis 1973 for earlier work in the area). Whilst it included a few Neolithic pits, the main period of use was during the Iron Age. This extended to a number of finds-rich Early Iron Age pits, many including human remains (they also yielded great quantities of pottery comparable to the material from Wandlebury); there were also a number of later Iron Age pits and sub-rectangular enclosures, also of that attribution. Producing a substantive assemblage of brooches, its excavator interpreted the site largely within a ritual paradigm, rather akin to that same organisation's Babraham Site (Hinman 2004; full publication still awaited).

More thoroughly outlined in Chapter 3 below, a number of excavations occurred in the lands west of the area down by the riverside, relating to the construction of the M11 Western Bypass in the 1970s (e.g. Cra'ster 1982). These included the discovery of a probable timber causeway at Lingey Farm (Pullinger *et al.* 1982) and a series of prehistoric to Romano-British site complexes, particularly those identified during the work at Edmundsoles (Millar & Millar 1982) and Rectory Farm, Great Shelford (see Inset, Chapter 3; e.g. Trump, Legge & Alexander 1975) and the Obelisk Kilns, Harston Site (Pullinger & Young 1982).

Finally, something must be said of the Roman roads in the immediate Addenbrooke's area, for as shown on Figure 1.12, the established (RCHM[E] 1959) 'story' would have a major crossroads situated immediately east of the Hutchison Site. The projection of these routes was primarily determined by the presumption that *de facto*, Roman roads were consistently straight; recent work shows this not to have been the case and, moreover, that their recognition is often difficult as they were usually only ditch-flanked within contemporary settlements. In this instance, the putative road junction was determined by the projection of Cambridge's *Via Devana* route south from where it had been exposed by Walker at the Perse School (see above; RCHM[E] 1959,

xxxiii, 5; cf. Fox 1923, map IV) and its meeting with the road running southeast to Colchester (there Worstead Street). However, locally the line of the latter has largely been a matter of informed supposition and not direct evidence. Essentially, its route at this point has been based upon the line of Wort's Causeway, which has been equated with the Roman road (RCHM[E] 1959, 6). This route is thought to have led to a bridgehead or ford at Grantchester and from there to have continued westwards to join Akeman Street northeast of Barton (Margary 1955, fig. 9, no. 241). The problem with this interpretation is that Wort's Causeway is known to have been upcast by William Worts in 1763 (Walker 1910). While it may have incorporated the earlier Roman route, it could originally have been a medieval headland and a number of headlands are plotted in the vicinity on a parallel alignment (Fig. 1.12). In other words, Wort's Causeway itself need not directly mark the line of the Roman road.

Computer plotting of Cra'ster's site against these putative routes (something that has not been attempted before: cf. Browne 1974, map 26) would have the Roman roads meeting within the '67 enclosure. While, from this, the very existence of these routes at this point could be questioned, given that Cra'ster's site does align so closely to (at least) the east–west Colchester road/Worstead Street (as does also much of the broader 'landscape grid') it is likely that they either kink along their length or that their position has not been accurately projected. The east–west road may, in fact, have lain further south than has been plotted and its line could well be indicated by the parallel ditches on the southern side of Cra'ster's enclosure. If so, then the headland immediately south of Wort's Causeway would be a better candidate for the road's route. Fortunately, as outlined below, the Hutchison Site provided relevant evidence for both of these 'ways': entirely negative in the case of the northward *Via Devana*, but with a firm 'fix' finally achieved for the east–west route towards Colchester.

The problems of establishing the area's Roman road-lines provide contrast with Fox's introduction to the period in *The Archaeology of the Cambridge Region*:

> The situation of the writer, passing from the Early Iron to the Roman Age, may be likened to that of a traveller who, traversing a countryside inadequately surveyed and utilizing in his journey such boggy paths and rutted droveways as appear to lead in the direction he wishes to go, suddenly reaches a broad metalled highway with guideposts and milestones.
>
> Prehistoric trackways have, in fact, been left behind; and before us stretches the exact alignment of the Roman Road (1923, 158).

'War Ditches' — defence and fieldwork
with ROBIN STANDRING

During WWI army trench-digging was usually referred to as 'fieldworks', with soldiers thus engaged in 'spadework'. Archaeology's borrowing of this terminology (e.g. Woolley 1953) should remind us of the military careers of a number of leading practitioners. With Pitt Rivers, Wheeler and Frere being among the most renowned, their military experience not only exposed them to the organization of mass-labour but also surveying techniques (see also e.g. Hingley 2000). Although he never saw combat, to the above list should also be added Cyril Fox (1882–1967; see Scott-Fox 2002; Fox 2000).

Through the influence of the pathologist, Louis Cobbett (also a keen amateur archaeologist), in 1903 Fox started work with the Royal Commission investigating Bovine Tuberculosis at their experimental facility at Blythwood Farm near Stansted. With its closure in 1907, he moved with Cobbett and the Commission's other investigators to continue their researches at the Cambridge University School of Agriculture and became the Superintendent of their Field Laboratory on Milton Road. It was while at Cambridge that, encouraged by Cobbett, Fox's archaeological landscape interests developed greatly. In 1907 he had enlisted, on a part-time basis, with the Essex Imperial Yeomanry and it was experience with the force that allowed him to develop his scouting and map-reading skills.

With the outbreak of the War in 1914, through the University's Officer Training Corps he was gazetted as a 2nd Lieutenant (later promoted as Acting Captain). However, due to a weak chest, he was only posted to Home Service and spent the war years training young officers in various reconnaissance

techniques (while still serving as the Superintendent of the University's Field Laboratories). With the end of the war, in 1919 he enrolled at Magdalene College and, at the ripe age of 37, began his formal archaeological studies. In the following year, on presenting an undergraduate dissertation on the archaeology in the Cambridge region, extraordinarily, he found himself up-grading to PhD-level, completing his thesis, *Archaeology of the Cambridge Region* in 1922.

Prior to its publication in the following year, Fox had published two papers; one in 1922 was concerned with Anglo-Saxon sculpture and, four years earlier in *Buzz*, his first issued work was a study of Cambridge's 'Ancient Military Earthworks' (1918). Ranging from the district's Iron Age dykes to Cromwellian defences, he considered them 'silent, but certain witnesses of forgotten wars' and, as regards Wandlebury, concluded 'if East Anglia should ever again lie under the curse of war, Cambridge — and the dominating ridge on which Vandelbury [*sic*.] stands — will loom large in future military history as it has done in the past' (Fox 1918; Scott-Fox 2002, 23).

Cambridge saw extensive military activity during WWI. Much of this was temporary by nature and included the requisitioning of buildings and the construction of marshalling stations and camps on the common land and hutted hospitals in Cherry Hinton and near the current University Library (Osborne 2002). Many WWI activities in Britain left few long-lasting structural remains and there are relatively few contemporary aerial photographs with which to identify these 'hidden'-activity sites. A notable exception is the construction of 'fieldworks' or practice trenches: trench systems, which may have been designed for practising manoeuvres, live firing, or engineering training. Once infilled and returned to agriculture,

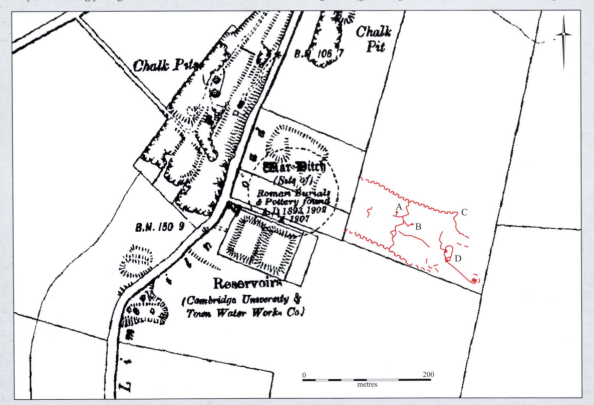

FIGURE 1.14. *War Ditches: Cropmark register of WWI 'practice trenches' plotted upon 1925 OS map.*

these may show as cropmarks on modern photographs, such as those at Leverington Heath in Suffolk (Hegarty & Newsome 2007); outside the lowland zone, some such fortifications still survive as impressive earthworks (see Driver 2007).

Recent research on modern air photos of southern Cambridge has located one such set of practice trenches at Lime Kilns Hill in Cherry Hinton, beside the *War Ditches* Ringwork (Fig. 1.14; see above and Chapter 2, Inset). Typologically, they closely match the static trench systems known from northern France, styles which have been illustrated in the extensive mapping of training areas from both World Wars at Salisbury Plain (McComish *et al.* 2002). The Lime Kilns ditches appear to be an 'edited highlight' of a larger system having a front-line and a support trench with saw-toothed or 'crenellated' edges (Fig. 1.14:A) and connected by zigzag communications trenches (Fig. 1.14:B), both being designed to limit blast injuries and the progress of enemy soldiers. The ends or corners of the trench system (Fig. 1.14:C) are characterized by a redoubt which allowed an all-round field of fire, closely paralleling seventeenth-century fortifications. The well-developed command centres and dugouts (Fig. 1.14:D) may have facilitated observation of the training. Whether Fox was actually involved in the execution of the trenches may never be known, although his biography does note his Service commendation for training troops in 'fieldcraft' (Scott-Fox 2002). (Interestingly, in a 1963 letter to Mary Cra'ster, then curator of the University Museum of Archaeology and Anthropology [held in the museum's archives], Lethbridge wrote concerning the background of the Field Club's post WWII involvement at the War Ditches Site. He criticized the standard of their fieldwork and suggested that some of the postholes they found there might actually have derived from WWI military activity: see Chapter 2, Inset.)

This 'hidden' feature is only periodically visible as a cropmark, the best example being from air photo coverage of the warm spring in 2002. Whilst no national overview has been made of these types of monuments (cropmarks or earthworks), the majority of well-preserved examples are recorded from military training areas where they have not been subject to intensive agricultural activity. Other examples that have been subject to study include an extensive network preserved in Pullingshall Wood in Buckinghamshire (Dawson 2007). At Cambridge, however, these features must have been comparatively short-lived, probably being constructed in 1915/16 with the introduction of mass-conscription, and being infilled shortly after 1918 so that the land could return to agriculture.

Though, in fairness, he himself admitted that the 'way' of roads (and, by extension, *books*) is often not straightforward:

> The analogy must not be pressed too far as to imply that our difficulties are over; even Roman roads only survive in broken segments, and we may yet lose direction before reaching our goal (Fox 1923).

Text and structure

Having now scene-set and laid-out the Hutchison Site's immediate landscape background, this effectively represents the first of this volume's 'framing contexts'. The second, outlined and presented in Chapter 3, is the wider evaluation-survey landscape running west down to the riverside and Trumpington Meadows. Beyond this, however, in order to further explore site-/settlement-type parallels and elucidate key themes, the results of other fieldwork projects will also be included. While, for the sake of this volume's geographic-directive, this '*miscellanea*' will largely be drawn from the southern Cambridgeshire area, where necessary other examples will also be drawn in from further afield within the region.

When the CAU's accumulated reports on the broader Addenbrooke's/Trumpington Meadows landscape are taken into account, they represent many hundreds of pages of amassed 'grey literature'. Listed below, they testify that this volume cannot extend to 'close' feature-specific reportage; if wishing for such detail, the relevant reports should be consulted.

Anderson, K. & C. Evans, 2005. The Archaeology of Clay Farm, Trumpington, Cambridge: Preliminary Investigations. (Cambridge Archaeological Unit Report 699.)

Armour, N., 2001. An Archaeological Evaluation at Downing College Sports Field, Long Road, Cambridge. (Cambridge Archaeological Unit Report 452.)

Brudenell, M., 2004. Land Adjacent to the Bell Language School, Cambridge: an Archaeological Evaluation. (Cambridge Archaeological Unit Report 646.)

Brudenell, M. & A. Dickens, 2007. Trumpington Meadows, Cambridge: an Archaeological Evaluation of a Bronze Age, Iron Age and Romano-British Riverside Landscape. (Cambridge Archaeological Unit Report 753.)

Cessford, C. & D. Mackay, 2004. Cambridgeshire Guided Busway; a Series of Archaeological Evaluations. (Cambridge Archaeological Unit Report 591.)

Dickens, A., 2002. Clay Farm, Trumpington, Cambridge, Archaeological Desktop Assessment. (Cambridge Archaeological Unit Report 506.)

Evans, C., 2002. The Archaeology of the Addenbrooke's Environs: a Desktop Essay. (Cambridge Archaeological Unit Report 497.)

Evans, C., D. Mackay & L. Webley, 2004. Excavations at Addenbrooke's: the Hutchinson Site. (Cambridge Archaeological Unit Report 609.)

Evans, C., D. Mackay & R. Patten, 2006. The Archaeology of Clay and Glebe Farms, South Cambridge. (Cambridge Archaeological Unit Report 708.)

Hutton, J. & C. Evans, 2007. NCP Car Park, Addenbrooke's Hospital, Cambridge: Archaeological Investigations. (Cambridge Archaeological Unit Report 778.)

Mackay, D., 2002. Addenbrooke's Electricity Substation: an Archaeological Evaluation. Cambridge: (Cambridge Archaeological Unit Report 469.)

Mackay, D., 2004. Elective Care Facility, Addenbrooke's Hospital, Cambridge: a Second Archaeological Evaluation. (Cambridge Archaeological Unit Report 606.)

Regan, R., 1996. An Archaeological Evaluation for Smith Kline Beecham, Addenbrooke's Hospital, Cambridge. (Cambridge Archaeological Unit Report 189.)

Robinson, M., 1995. Addenbrooke's Island: an Archaeological Evaluation. (Cambridge Archaeological Unit Report 148.)

Slater, A. & A. Dickens, 2008. Further Evaluation at Clay Farm, South Cambridge: the 2008 Green Corridor Evaluation. (Cambridge Archaeological Unit Report 826.)

Timberlake S., 2007. Addenbrooke's Hospital Water Main Diversion: an Archaeological Investigation. (Cambridge Archaeological Unit Report 794.)

Tipper, J., 2003. Elective Care Facility, Addenbrooke's Hospital, Cambridge: an Archaeological Evaluation. (Cambridge Archaeological Unit Report 578.)

Wait, G.A., 1992. Archaeological Investigations: New Addenbrooke's, Centre for Brain Repair, 1992. (Cambridge Archaeological Unit Report 74.)

Whittaker, P., 2002a. An Archaeological Evaluation at 28–30 Long Road, Cambridge, Cambridgeshire. (Cambridge Archaeological Unit Report 483.)

Whittaker, P., 2002b. An Archaeological Evaluation at Strangeways Laboratory, Worts Causeway, Cambridge. (Cambridge Archaeological Unit Report 487.)

In the text that follows the calibration of all radiocarbon dates is to two sigma.

Finally, a note concerning the volume's 'Insets'; those in Chapters 2 and 3 outline two of the region's more major unpublished sites, or, in the case of the first, components thereof: the War Ditches (1949–51) and Rectory Farm, Great Shelford (1975–80). In both instances, the Unit has had access to and been able to appraise the excavation archives. Yet, for neither are their summaries meant to be the 'final word' and both warrant further research. Admittedly this policy of including 'old sites' could be questioned given how much current fieldwork goes unpublished. However, it reflects the CAU's general commitment to the historiographic context of fieldwork (e.g. Evans & Appleby forthcoming 2009) and is considered an act of 'site rescue' in its own right.

Chapter 2

The Hutchison Site, Addenbrooke's

Christopher Evans, Duncan Mackay and Leo Webley

The *c.* 3 ha site was situated on the northwest side of the grounds of Addenbrooke's Hospital (TL 46255535). Though to all intents and purposes the area of excavation was essentially flat, with its geology bedding between 16.80 and 17.70 m OD, the highest ground lay in its southeastern corner (Fig. 2.2). This correlates with a slight ridge whose line can be reconstructed from Cra'ster's earlier survey work within the Hospital's grounds. The character of the natural changed markedly across the site: the western third had a sandy matrix with marl 'interruptions', whereas the eastern portion was marly grey clay beds. As will be demonstrated, these variations in the sub-soils clearly influenced activities occurring across the site, and also provided the constituent elements

for its main industrial processing (i.e. sand and clay for pottery production).

The site had been subject to fieldwork evaluation in the late summer of 2001 (Armour 2001). The procedures applied varied according to the differing conditions of its ground cover. Across the western third — an intensively utilized Hospital car park — there was good aerial photographic coverage, which yielded a large sub-square/polygonal cropmark enclosure with associated ditch lengths (Fig. 2.2; see Palmer, in Hall 2001; Armour 2001). The eastern two-thirds of the area lay under the groomed playing fields of Downing College. Because of their on-going needs — respectively parking and 'playing' — only limited sondages and test pits could be dug within their

FIGURE 2.1. *Site Panorama: Main picture, taken from the top of Addenbrooke's Nurses' Hall of Residence, mosaic-photograph looking west across the main area of excavation (with the Downing College Sports Pavilion still left 'stranded'); lower right, recording of evaluation trench in front of the pavilion.*

546125/255504

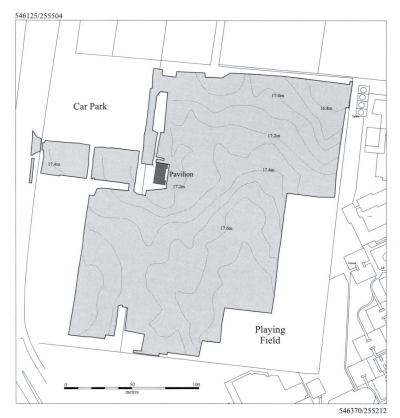

546370/255212

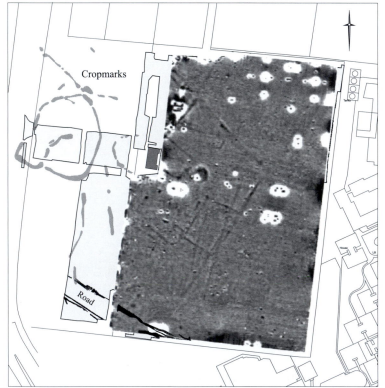

FIGURE 2.2. *Stripped surface contour plan (above) and geophysical and cropmark plot (below; respectively after Oxford Archaeotechnics and R. Palmer). (© Crown copyright and/or data base right. All rights reserved. Licence number 100048686.)*

interior swathes, and any significant evaluation trenching had to be restricted to their perimeters. In an effort to off-set this, in 2001 the playing field was subject to geophysical survey by Oxford Archaeotechnics (Fig. 2.2). This revealed what seemed to be two distinct networks of linear features: in the main, a northwest–southeast oriented system of regular paddocks and also other, more dispersed, linears on a more true north–south orientation. Aside from a scatter of geophysical 'spot anomalies', a distinct large circular feature clearly registered in the middle of the field which was encircled by a distinct ring of high-value resistivity.

On the whole, the results from the evaluation succeeded in characterizing the site's archaeology. Against a background Mesolithic/Neolithic 'presence', evidence of later Bronze Age occupation was detected. The main paddock fieldsystem was identified and determined to be of first century AD, Late Iron Age/Early Roman attribution, though it was also recognized that the larger cropmark enclosures on the western side of the area were potentially of earlier, Middle/later Iron Age date. Given the results, the most important trench in terms of expanding or informing the scope of the final area of excavation was 13, sited along the western margin beside Robinson Way (see Fig. 2.4). Accordingly, its findings are fully incorporated within the report below.

Generally the evaluation demonstrated that the playing field part of the site carried 0.40–0.70 m topsoil cover, and locally a 0.10–0.15 m thick, paler sub-soil was detected within its lower profile (as were traces of ridge-and-furrow cultivation). Whilst no horizontal strata as such were found to survive, at the eastern end of Trench 1 a robust spread of cobbles locally extended across the truncated surface of the natural (see Fig. 2.4). During the course of the excavation itself this was found to equate with road metalling that lay within the profile of a 'hollow-way'.

The excavations occurred between late September 2002 and March of the following year. Portions of the site had to be relinquished by phased stages to dovetail with the concurrent building works, with the result that at any one time we never commanded its extent as a whole. Late in the programme, watching brief recording also occurred along

FIGURE 2.3. *Feature Base-plan. (Reproduced by permission of Ordnance Survey on behalf of HMSO. © Crown copyright 2008. All rights reserved. Ordnance Survey licence number 100048686.)*

the line of a new access road running east from the site; its results are reported herein. Information arising from those evaluation trenches that eventually fell outside of the final area of excavation is also summarized within this text. Equally relevant are the findings from a single evaluation trench dug along the western side of the adjoining plot, immediately to the northeast of the site (*The Addenbrooke's Sub-Station Site*: Mackay 2002), and also the evaluation in the rear gardens of

28–32 Long Road (*The Addenbrooke's Day-Care Centre Site*: Whittaker 2002a; see Fig. 2.3). In other words, all of these findings are considered as part of a unified programme of investigation.

In the course of the main excavations some 1264 features were exposed, with 4717 contexts recorded (there being 1279 excavation 'interventions'; e.g. individual ditch segment slots or discrete feature excavations). The site, indeed, proved to be prolific with more

FIGURE 2.4. *Base-plan, showing excavation segments/'interventions'.*

than 43,000 finds recovered in total, including some 21,917 sherds of pottery and 12,500 animal bones. Features were metal-detected prior to their excavation, though earlier topsoil trials had demonstrated that metal-detecting was unfeasible within this higher level due to the frequency of lost sport-shoe studs. Upon the discovery of the site's kilns, relevant swathes were, in addition, subject to magnetic susceptibility sampling (see Fig. 2.4).

Aside from localized patches of metalling across the southern part of the site, no horizontal strata as such survived its long history of arable usage. The construction of the car park had clearly resulted in some degree of truncation across the western third of the site. When this was broken-out and its underly-ing hardcore stripped off, the 'geology' was cleanly exposed (i.e. the sub-soils were truncated). This being said, its construction had clearly been carefully executed, with a geotextile membrane laid over much of the area. There was little additional compression of feature-fills and only very localized evidence of any machine-rutting. As is clear from the site's base-plan, while across the southern part of the site the density of postholes is much less in the west than the east, the point at which they stop does not coincide with the edge of the car park but is well shy of it. Moreover, a distinct cluster of postholes did survive in the north-western corner of the main car park swathe (south of the access road area): in other words, truncation did not determine their distribution/survival.

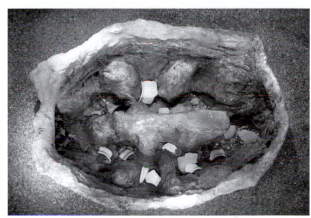

FIGURE 2.5. *Public Initiatives: left, site open-day poster; right, kiln (F.1117) as reconstructed within the Li Ka Shing Centre's lobby.*

Public and display initiatives

As Figure 2.1 bears witness, the playing field's handsome sports pavilion was left standing throughout the excavations, allowing it to serve as office facilities. As a consequence, the archaeology within its footprint was never formally recorded. On the plus side, however, it proved an invaluable work space and allowed us to mount displays therein during the site's Hospital open-days and school-party visits.

When touring the site near the end of our programme, Dr John Tooze of Cancer Research UK decided that some of the site's key features should be incorporated into the design of the new building. In the end, pragmatics tempered ambition and only one of its Early Roman kilns was chosen (F.1117: Fig. 2.5). Nevertheless, this first involved painstaking labours on the part of Jon Price to cast it and, then, for Andy Hall and his CAU team to paint it and reset finds for its permanent display in the Li Ka Shing Centre's front

lobby. Miraculously it was there on schedule for HRH the Queen's opening of the building in February of 2007 (but then without its notice-board and, looking for the world like a bizarre abstract sculpture; what Her Majesty made of it can only be guessed).

Phasing structure

Leaving aside the site's twentieth-century intrusions, seven main phases of usage/occupation were identified:

1. Neolithic and Middle Bronze Age activity;
2. Late Bronze Age settlement;
3. Later Iron Age occupation;
4. Conquest Period occupation;
5. Later Roman fieldsystems;
6. Middle Saxon settlement;
7. Medieval ridge-and-furrow agriculture.

The excavation results are presented by the site's phases. Specialist studies are integrated within the appropriate sections, with only the results of the environmental analyses standing alone within the latter part of the text. A full gazetteer of feature descriptions was included within the 2004 archive report (Evans *et al.* 2004).

Prehistoric activity

Only two Neolithic features, both small pits (F.176 & F.468: Fig. 2.6), could be identified, with no other features dated to before the Middle Bronze Age. Modest quantities of Mesolithic to Early Bronze Age worked flint were, however, recovered in residual status within later features. A particular concentration of Early Neolithic (and, possibly, some Mesolithic) flint — including a leaf-shaped arrowhead — occurred in and around pit F.468, but otherwise the material seems fairly evenly distributed across the site (though see *Concluding Discussion* below). The impression gained is of only transient or low intensity landscape-use during earlier prehistory.

Middle Bronze Age (Phase 1)

Five features contained pottery of the Deverel-Rimbury tradition, dating them to the Middle Bronze Age (*c.* 1500–1000 bc: Fig. 2.6). In the eastern area of the site, F.120 and F.150 were oval postholes or small pits, *c.* 0.50 m across and 0.1 m deep, while pit F.157 was larger, measuring 1.5 × 0.95 × 0.32 m. Removed some distance to the north of these was an isolated pit or posthole F.342 (0.36 × 0.33 × 0.10 m), which was distinct from the other Middle Bronze Age features, containing pottery with a different fabric (see Knight below). Finally, in the northwestern part of the site was a series of intercutting 'hollows', F.727, 4.75 m across and up to 0.56 m deep. The distribution of finds among the Middle Bronze Age features shows differential patterning, with most of the pottery (>1 kg) coming from the two small pits F.120 and F.150 in the southeast, while most of the bone came from the F.727 complex. The absence of worked flint from any of the features is notable, and could indicate that a full range of 'domestic' activities was not taking place.

The small number of features datable to this period indicates a fairly modest level of activity. The distribution and nature of the activity mirrors that of the Late Bronze Age, with 'settlement' features clustering in the southeastern part of the site. While the Middle Bronze Age usage can thus be seen as a direct precursor of the Late Bronze Age settlement, the fact that Deverel-Rimbury and post-Deverel-Rimbury pottery were never found together in the same feature does imply a degree of chronological distinction between the two phases.

Late Bronze Age (Phase 2)

An extensive swathe of features extending across much of the site can be dated to the Late Bronze Age (*c.* 1000–800 bc) by the presence of pottery in the Post-Deverel-Rimbury (PDR) tradition. These consist of 21 pits greater than 0.5m diameter, 32 smaller pits or postholes, a possible cremation pit, a large area of quarry-pitting, and a small ring-gully (Fig. 2.6). The main concentration of settlement evidence lies in the south and southeast of the site, with two small pits to the north (F.647 and F.721), while the quarrying and ring-gully lie in the otherwise unoccupied northeast. It is likely that many more of the small pits and postholes in the southern and eastern areas of the site actually related to this phase, but these yielded no datable material. Significant amounts of PDR pottery were found as residual material in later features, suggesting that the Late Iron Age and Roman enclosure systems had obliterated many earlier features.

Although there is an abundance of postholes, with particular clusters lying in the south and southeast of the site, it is difficult to recognize individual structures and no roundhouses can be identified. Any houses that did exist may have been overlain by the Late Iron Age and Roman enclosure systems or, alternatively, could lie outside the excavated area, as the limits of the settlement swathe were not reached to the east and south. The only buildings that can be discerned are three rectangular 'four-posters', Structures 1–3; such structures are usually interpreted as raised granaries.

Structure 1 - Located at the southeastern edge of the site, this measured 2.25 m north–south by 2.75 m east–west, formed by postholes F.142–F.144 and F.146. The postholes range from 0.22–0.32 m in diameter and from 0.09–0.28 m deep with mid brown silt fills (F.143 held 12 g of PDR pottery).

Structure 2 - Set a short distance to the northwest of Structure 1, this measured 1.75 × 1.75 m. With grey-brown silt fills, the four postholes (F.160, F.161, F.163 and F.164) ranged from 0.30–0.43 m diameter and from 0.09–0.28 m deep. No artefacts were recovered, but the structure falls within an area of dense Late Bronze Age settlement activity.

Structure 3 - Located in the western part of the site, this measured 2.25 × 2.25 m. The four postholes (F.582–F.585) range from 0.20–0.36 m in diameter and from 0.04–0.12 m deep, with fills of dark grey-brown sandy silt. No finds were recovered. Due to its location, the period attribution of this structure is not certain, but it has been tentatively assigned to the Late Bronze Age by analogy with Structures 1 and 2.

In addition, two other 'four-posters' (one actually being a five-post setting) were possibly apparent (marked A & B on Fig. 2.6), though these are of much more dubious status.

FIGURE 2.6. *Neolithic and Late Bronze Age Features (top), with contemporary artefact distributions below.*

Despite the lack of recognizable settlement structures other than granaries, some zoning in the character of activity is apparent. A plot of the dimensions of the pits suggests a division into three size-categories, suggesting functional distinctions (Fig. 2.7). Most of the pits were not more than 1.3 m diameter, nor greater than 0.35 m deep. However, two were larger at 2.25–2.40 m diameter and 0.60–0.95 m deep (F.45 and F.970), and there was one 'shaft-like' pit measuring 1.1 m diameter and over 1.0 m deep, whose base was not reached (F.369). While the densest concentration of pits occurred in the southern and southeastern parts of the site, these all fell into the smallest category. All of the pits in the two larger categories lay in the 'peripheral' areas to the west and north. It can also be noted that the two features with by far the largest assemblages of PDR pottery (>1 kg each) were both large 'peripheral' pits (F.45 and F.369), which complicates the issue of where the settlement 'core' lay. In both of these the pottery deposit lay above a lens of charcoal. None of the pits seem to closely resemble the large 'pit-wells' that are regarded as a type-feature of settlements of this period (e.g. Evans 1999).

A possible cremation, F.166, is located close to the densest area of occupation at the southeast of the site. It consists of an oval pit, 0.60 × 0.48 m and 0.22 m deep, containing 282 g of burnt bone (unidentifiable, apart one probable human premolar) along with a single pot sherd and a few small pieces of burnt flint.

Set some distance apart from the settlement swathe, in the northeastern part of the site were some features of a different nature, possibly relating to raw material extraction and agricultural activity respectively. The former was represented by a substantial complex of irregular, intercutting quarry pits (F.650–F.660, F.696–F.699, F.701–F705), covering an area of *c.* 35 × 20 m and varying from 0.1–1.0 m deep. These quarry pits were presumably created for marl/clay extraction for the purposes of potting, building construction and so forth. While, based on their extraction

function, it is tempting to associate these with the site's intensive Early Roman pottery production, this seems unlikely as the pits collectively contain 473 g of PDR pottery but no later material. It is highly unlikely that large hollows could have been open along the edge of such a substantial Roman site without refuse collecting or being dumped within them. (Nevertheless, given this cluster's 'arrangement', and particularly the fact that their southern edges lay roughly parallel with the later fieldsystem, this still leaves room for some suspicion that they relate to the ensuing Conquest Period settlement; see below.)

Also in the northeastern part of the site, Structure 4 (F.27) was a small circular ring-gully with an internal diameter of *c.* 3 m, a width of 0.46–0.60 m and a depth of 0.17–0.22 m. It had a single silt-fill with some charcoal and produced two small fragments of PDR pottery. This feature was far too small to be a levelled barrow or a mortuary ring-ditch, and is more likely to be a drainage gully surrounding an agricultural feature such as a hayrick. While its date must remain uncertain due to the paucity of finds, a parallel is provided by a *c.* 2 m diameter ring ditch recently found associated with a Late Bronze Age/Early Iron Age fieldsystem at Deeping St James, south Lincolnshire (Denison 1996). A similar small ring-setting has also been found associated with the Colne Fen, Earith, Bronze Age fieldsystem and, more recently and importantly there, another encircled a satellite cremation and conjoined with a major, mortuary-related, ring-ditch complex (see Evans, with Appleby, Lucy and Regan forthcoming; see also Germany 2007, 41, 113–15, figs. 28 & 71).

Of somewhat ambiguous status, it is possible that the northnortheast–southsouthwest oriented ditch (F.31 & F.976) and its western return (F.32) were related to this occupation. Of very minor, 'gully-like' proportions, the only datable find from it was a small piece of iron. This may, though, have been intrusive; that the ditch was cut by the line of the later Roman road (and possibly any Late Iron Age precursor) could suggest its 'early' attribution. Given this, as shown on Figure 2.6, it is also just possible that the F.177 (*et al.*) ditch and its northwestward return, which are ascribed below to the site's later Iron Age layout, could actually have related to this later Bronze Age system (the main problem with this attribution being its sympathetic relationship with that phase's Enclosure I, which was certainly Iron Age).

Artefact studies
Worked flint
(ANDREW MCLAREN & MARK EDMONDS)
A total of 564 struck flints were recovered during the excavation. These are listed by type and quantity in

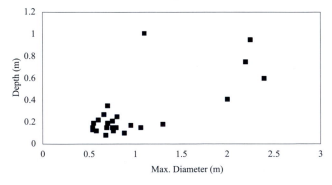

FIGURE 2.7. *Late Bronze Age Pit Dimensions (pits over 0.5 m diameter only).*

Table 2.1. An appraisal of this material was conducted to assess its chronological composition and to characterize the technologies represented. Typological and technological characterization indicates a chronologically mixed assemblage reflective of the multiple phases of site usage. Diagnostic tool types and chronologically specific reduction strategies indicate a moderate earlier to later Neolithic/Early Bronze Age component, with a few pieces perhaps dating to the Mesolithic. Aside from pit F.468, most of these earlier pieces were recovered as residual material from demonstrably later features. In addition, the presence of haphazardly worked cores and retouched implements in features dated securely to the later Bronze and Iron Age provides robust evidence for the continued, albeit limited, exploitation of flint during these periods.

Struck flints were recovered from all parts of the site and in features ranging from the Middle Bronze Age to the Saxon period. Only one noteworthy concentration was identified during excavation: F.468, an Early Neolithic pit, produced 121 struck flints, 21.5% of the site total. No other significant concentrations were identified; small (1–3) to moderate (5–15) numbers of struck flint were fairly evenly distributed across the site.

The assemblage consists entirely of struck nodular flint. Examination of remnant cortical surfaces indicates an exclusive reliance on locally occurring secondary gravel deposits. The raw material quality is generally high, though thermal flaws were noted in several pieces. Broadly speaking, the assemblage is in good condition; the majority of artefacts appear fresh with clean, sharp edges. This said, several artefacts exhibit edge and/or surface damage/wear consistent with post-depositional trampling and abrasion. Given the relatively high degree of lithic residuality on this site, this is unsurprising. Of the 563 flints examined, 16 (2.8%) have been burnt to varying degrees. Partially and wholly recorticated/patinated pieces form a significant component of the assemblage.

Three major approaches to flint-working can be distinguished in this assemblage and each relates to a broad phase of activity on the site. The first dates to the Mesolithic/Early Neolithic and is characterized by a high degree of control over the knapping process. Mesolithic and Early Neolithic reduction strategies focused on the production of regularly shaped blades and narrow flakes for immediate use or secondary modification. These were struck from well-prepared and -maintained cores. In typological and technological terms, these periods are definitively represented by a multi-platform blade core ([156]: Fig. 2.8:4), a triangular-sectioned and heavily worn fabricator ([1156/7]: Fig. 2.8:6), a finely made leaf-shaped arrowhead ([3314]: Fig. 2.8:5), a classic end-scraper made on a blade ([3314]: Fig. 2.8:1), three micro-denticulated blades ([3314]: Fig. 2.8:2 & [1375]), one micro-denticulated flake ([3314]), four utilized blades ([3314] & [230]), as well as several blades and flakes displaying carefully prepared striking platforms and/or evidence of soft hammer percussion. Recovered blade(lets) vary considerably in form and size; one at 7 cm in length is considerably larger than the others and may be earlier Mesolithic in date.

The second approach to flint-working evident in the assemblage dates broadly to the Late Neolithic/Early Bronze Age. This is characterized by the expedient reduction of cores alongside controlled secondary modification of flake blanks. Several of the recovered flake cores may well be the product of later Neolithic and Early Bronze Age core-reduction strategies, which typically involved the use of hard hammer percussion, frequent core rotation and little to no core preparation. Scant attention appears to have been given to the morphology of the flakes being produced

TABLE 2.1. *Struck flints.*

Type	Quantity	% of Total
Waste flake	330	58.61%
Waste blade(let)	20	3.55%
Unmodified utilized flake	4	0.71%
Unmodified utilized blade	3	0.53%
Flake shatter	70	12.43%
Blade(let) shatter	15	2.66%
Angular shatter	46	8.17%
Blocky fragment	7	1.24%
Misc. retouched flake	14	2.49%
Misc. retouched angular shatter	1	0.18%
Single platform flake core	8	1.42%
Multi-platform flake core	11	1.95%
Multi-platform blade core	1	0.18%
Opposed platform flake core	1	0.18%
Discoidal core	4	0.71%
Core fragment	9	1.60%
Core rejuvenation flake	2	0.36%
Piercer	2	0.18%
End-scraper	2	0.36%
Thumbnail scraper	1	0.18%
Side- and end-scraper	1	0.18%
Scraper fragment	1	0.18%
Notched flake	2	0.36%
Fabricator	1	0.18%
Serrated blade	3	0.53%
Serrated flake	2	0.36%
Flake knife	2	0.36%
Leaf-shaped arrowhead	1	0.18%
Total	**564**	**100%**

during the reduction process, the sole aim being to remove a series of otherwise usable flakes. Given these comments, the presence of four discoidal cores in this assemblage is of particular interest (e.g. Fig. 2.8:10). Often referred to as a specialist form of core, discoidal cores are typically assigned to the Late Neolithic and are thought to have been associated with the production of thin flake blanks for arrowhead and knife manufacture. That one or more of the discoidal cores recovered may have been utilized for this purpose cannot be discounted. However, it is worth stressing that such pieces may simply be worked-out bifacial cores.

Diagnostic retouched implements attributable to this period include two knives made on flakes ([141] & [156]: Fig. 2.8:8), a piercer ([156]: Fig. 2.8:7) a fine thumbnail scraper ([891/2]: Fig. 2.8:9) and the two remaining scrapers ([3314]: Fig. 2.8:3 & [582]), both of which display relatively fine semi-invasive retouch. A semi-invasively flaked scraper fragment from [521] is most likely of a similar date. Some of the miscellaneously retouched and utilized flakes may also date to this period. Isolating material of later Neolithic/Early Bronze Age date amongst the remaining debitage from the site is problematic. With regards to waste flakes, all one can say is that the technological characteristics of the vast majority of excavated flakes are in keeping with the patterns identified for later Neolithic and Early Bronze Age flint-working practices and a proportion must date to these periods (e.g. Ford *et al.* 1984). With very few exceptions, recovered waste flakes follow the well-established metrical trend

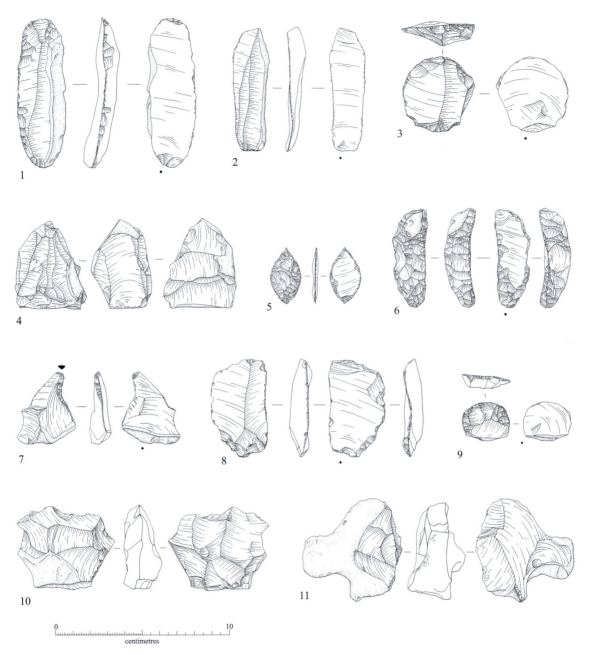

FIGURE 2.8. *Worked Flint: 1) End-scraper on soft hammer blade, with abrupt to semi-abrupt unifacial retouch and edge-damage along left lateral margin merging to invasive retouch across distal end - Mesolithic–Early Neolithic; 2) Micro-denticulated soft-hammer blade, with denticulations along left lateral margin - Early Neolithic; 3) End-scraper on tertiary hard hammer flake, with abrupt to semi-abrupt unifacial retouch across distal end; trimmed platform - Late Neolithic–Early Bronze Age; 4) Multi-platform blade core made on gravel cobble; multiple removals - Mesolithic–Early Neolithic; 5) Leaf-shaped arrowhead on tertiary flake, with fine invasive unifacial retouch across dorsal surface, and marginal semi-abrupt retouch on ventral surface - Early Neolithic; 6) Finely flaked fabricator on secondary flake, with triangular-section; heavily worn - Mesolithic–Early Neolithic; 7) Piercer on secondary hard hammer flake, with moderate edge-damage across tip - Late Neolithic–Early Bronze Age; 8) Knife on tertiary hard hammer flake, with moderate unifacial edge-damage along feathered right lateral margin; abrupt to semi-abrupt unifacial 'backing' retouch along left lateral margin - Late Neolithic–Early Bronze Age; 9) Thumbnail scraper on small, hard hammer flake, with fine semi-abrupt unifacial retouch on both lateral margins and across distal end - Early Bronze Age; 10) Discoidal core made on gravel cobble; multiple removals - Late Neolithic–Early Bronze Age; 11) Multi-platform flake core made on gravel cobble, with several incipient cones indicative of unsuccessful flake detachments; multiple removals - Late Bronze Age?*

of being broad and squat. Almost all display pronounced bulbs of percussion and unprepared striking platforms. Hinge terminations are also common. Although all stages of the reduction sequence are represented, secondary flakes are easily the most dominant form. This is almost certainly a product of knapping relatively small flint nodules from the gravels.

The final approach to flint-working identified in the assemblage dates to the later Bronze/Iron Age and is characterized by an extremely basic and *ad hoc* approach to core reduction and secondary flake modification. The general technological characteristics of British later Bronze and Iron Age flint assemblages are now well-established (see Ballin 2002; Butler 2005, 179–92; Young & Humphrey 1999); so too is the trend towards less technical competence and fewer formal tool types over time (e.g. Ford 1987; Ford *et al.* 1984). Studies have also highlighted important changes in the character of stone artefact procurement and deposition from the Middle Bronze Age onwards (Edmonds 1995, 184–6; Herne 1992). To date, two broad models have been offered to account for the processes highlighted above (Edmonds 1995, 178–89; Ford *et al.* 1984; Herne 1992, 66–74; Young & Humphrey 1999). Ford *et al.*'s (1984) pioneering study emphasized *functional substitution* as the driving force behind technological change in Bronze Age lithic assemblages. More recently, authors such as Herne (1992), Edmonds (1995) and Young & Humphrey (1999) have argued for a greater appreciation of the role of the changing social value of flint in the decline of lithic utilization in Britain. The course of the Bronze Age, they suggest, witnessed an erosion of the central role of flint artefacts in the negotiation and maintenance of social relations and its movement towards a purely functional and utilitarian role in domestic contexts.

Identifying material of later Bronze and Iron Age date amongst this assemblage is difficult given the presence of diagnostically earlier material. Nevertheless, the presence of crudely worked flints in direct association with later Bronze pottery at The Hutchison Site provides compelling evidence for the continued, albeit limited, production and use of struck flints during these periods. Some of the recovered cores (e.g. those from [1088]: Fig. 2.8:11) and [316]) and miscellaneous retouched flakes would fit comfortably with the known technological characteristics of later Bronze Age/Iron Age flint-work, as would the piercer recovered from [2657] and notched flakes from [1818] and [1324]. More generally, later Bronze and Iron Age flint-work betrays a lack of knowledge of, or perhaps concern over, the knapping process. None of the potential later Bronze and Iron Age cores identified display any form of core preparation, be it platform faceting or overhang removal. Moreover, these cores display extensive platform crushing, frequent hinging/stepping on core faces, as well as multiple incipient cones on striking platforms, a product of numerous unsuccessful attempts at flake detachment. In keeping with these patterns, the striking platforms of potential later Bronze/Iron Age waste flakes frequently display incipient cones and/or crushing. Awkward striking platform angles are also common, as are hinge terminations. Retouched implements attributable to this period display a comparable level of technical finesse. Retouch is typically abrupt and haphazardly executed.

A cursory examination of this assemblage has revealed that we are dealing with flint-working residues generated over a long period of time. Diagnostic retouched forms and technological characteristics suggest the presence of Mesolithic through to Iron Age flint-work. A brief review of the depositional context of diagnostically earlier flint-work demonstrates that much of this material was incorporated as residual debris into the fills of later features. Consequently, it is difficult to make any definitive statements about the scale, duration or spatial patterning of Mesolithic,

Neolithic or Early Bronze Age activities on the site. Perhaps the only observation worthy of note in this regard concerns the concentration of early material recovered in F.468. What exactly this concentration represents remains unclear. This material aside, we are dealing with a relatively low density scatter of pre-Middle Bronze Age material across the site and this is perhaps suggestive of small-scale and short-lived episodes of activity.

Moving forward in time, the presence of crudely worked flints in features dated securely to the later Bronze and Iron Age on this site is of particular interest given recent debate on this subject (see, e.g. Young & Humphrey 1999; Humphrey 2003; 2004). Critically, the majority of British lithic specialists would now accept the continued production and use of struck flints into the Iron Age in Britain. There is a growing consensus that the displacement of lithic technology by metallurgy in Britain was a long and complex process. It is no longer acceptable to talk about an across-the-board cessation of flint-working in Britain; rather, it is a process that must have occurred at different times in different places in response to a diverse array of economic, environmental, social and technological factors.

Early Neolithic and Middle Bronze Age pottery (MARK KNIGHT)

The assemblage comprised 296 sherds, with a total weight of 1845 g (MSW: 6.23 g), recovered from eight different contexts. Two main types were identified: Early Neolithic (40.5% by number or 32% by weight), as represented by thin-walled carinated forms with flint inclusions; and Middle Bronze Age (59.5% by number or 68% by weight), thick-walled bucket forms with mainly shell inclusions. The condition of the assemblage was fair and included several sherds over 5 cm in length and breadth, but also many small fragmented pieces.

Early Neolithic (Fig. 2.9)
This included 120 sherds with a combined weight of 590 g (MSW: 4.92g; Table 2.2). The fabrics varied between being 'coarse' and flint-rich (Fabric 1), and 'fine' and relatively flint-poor (Fabric 2). Sherds belonging to the latter type also tended to retain applied slips and were decorated. Feature sherds included three rims, four neck/shoulder fragments and seven decorated pieces. Close to 50% of the assemblage appeared to be burnt (as indicated by the uniform

TABLE 2.2. *Mildenhall-type assemblage.*

Feature	Context	Sherds	Weight	Fabric
468	3314	108	563 g	1 & 2
176	899	12	27 g	1 & 2
Totals	**2**	**120**	**590 g**	**2**

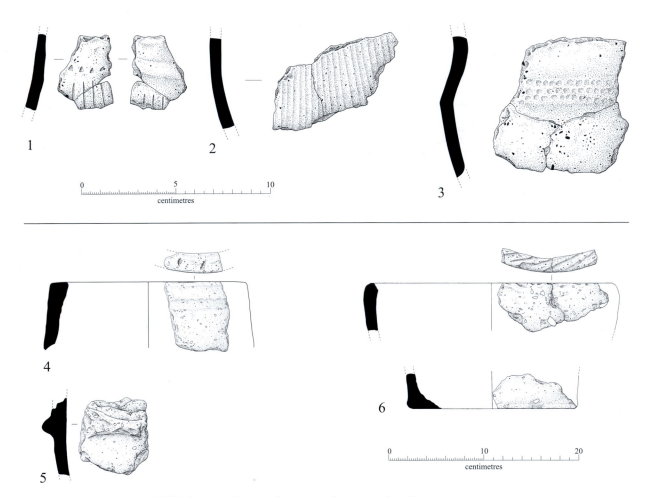

FIGURE 2.9. *Neolithic and Middle Bronze Pottery: (respectively 1–3 and 4–6).*

TABLE 2.3. *Deverel-Rimbury assemblage.*

Feature	Context	Sherds	Weight	Fabric
150	77	22	313 g	3
342	1441	18	52 g	5
157	1740	14	136 g	3
727	2831	1	16 g	4
727	2838	7	35 g	4
120	3284	114	703 g	3
Totals:	**6**	**176**	**1255 g**	**3**

plain out-turned rim pieces were also present and, in total, F.468 appeared to contain the remnants of at least six vessels.

F.176 yielded only 12 sherds. Three of these came from a fine bowl form decorated with a single row of triangular stab-marks; these underlined a band of diagonally incised lines which, once again, filled the neck-zone (Fig. 2.9:1). The remaining fragments belonged to a separate vessel made from the coarser of the two fabrics, making two the total number of vessels within this pit.

The character of the assemblage from both contexts can be described as typical Mildenhall pit-type assemblages (fragmented, burnt and unburnt sherds, decorated and plain, etc.) as previously excavated at the type-site Hurst Fen, Mildenhall (Clark 1960) or more recently at Kilverstone, Thetford (Garrow *et al.* 2005).

Middle Bronze Age (Fig. 2.9)
The assemblage comprised 176 sherds, with a total weight of 1255 g (MSW: 7.13 g: Table 2.3), recovered from six different contexts. In all, three separate fabrics were identified. Only 7.4% of the total number were feature sherds (five rims, seven base-angles, one applied shoulder cordon). Decoration was equally rare and, with one possible exception, confined to rims. Without exception, all of the sherds came from thick-walled vessels (between 10 and 15 mm).

F.120 produced the largest group and included the fragments of at least two vessels. The first (dia. 0.26 m) has a flattened, simple rim decorated along the top with incised diagonal lines (making a twisted rope or cable effect: Fig. 2.9:6). The second vessel (dia. 0.28 m) is represented by a simple rounded rim decorated with

light colour and 'dry' texture).

F.468 produced 108 sherds of which three were rims, four were decorated and three came from the neck/shoulder parts of the vessels. Diagnostic forms were represented by three sherds, which conjoined to form a weak shoulder from an upright carinated bowl that was decorated immediately above the shoulder with three rows of impressed dots. Faint vertical incised lines were just visible above the dots filling the neck-zone. The rim profile was missing, but in profile the upper part-neck became thicker towards the outside, thereby suggesting an externally thickened rim was once present (Fig. 2.9:3). Upper body fragments from a similar vessel were decorated with vertical (fine) fluting (Fig. 2.9:2). Three separate small and a diagonal fingernail impression. Other sherds from this context included two large base-angle fragments (*c.* 0.20 m dia.) and a possible body sherd with a fingertip decoration.

F.150 included a large rim fragment (simple flattened) above a slight shoulder (Fig. 2.9:4). The top of the rim had two diagonal, widely spaced fingertip impressions. The diameter of the rim equalled *c.* 0.30 m. A base-angle fragment from the same context had a diameter of *c.* 0.26 m.

F.157 was dominated by a large body sherd with a plain, applied shoulder cordon (Fig. 2.9:5).

F.342 contained small flint-tempered fragments, three of which were base-angles.

F.727 [2831] had a single, burnt body fragment.

F.727 [2838] comprised seven sherds, one of which was a simple, rounded rim fragment (dia. *c.* 0.24 m).

The Middle Bronze Age assemblage represents the fragments from at least seven large, thick-walled, bucket-shaped vessels of the Deverel-Rimbury tradition. It includes biconical and straight forms both with simple rims. Apart from one flint-tempered vessel, the dominant inclusion is shell. Decoration consists of diagonal-incised lines or fingertip/nail impressions and one vessel had an applied cordon.

Although small, the assemblage includes vessel forms, rim types and decorative traits found amongst other East Anglian and East Midland Deverel-Rimbury assemblages (Longworth *et al.* 1988). For instance, the rims decorated with distinctive diagonal slashes also occur on vessels at Grimes Graves, Norfolk (Longworth *et al.* 1988), Fengate, Cambridgeshire (Pryor 1974) and Ardleigh, Essex (Erith & Longworth 1960).

Fabrics
Neolithic
1) Hard with abundant small medium large burnt flint.
2) Hard sandy with moderate small burnt flint and small quartz.

Middle Bronze Age
3) Moderately hard with abundant small, medium and large shell and rare small flint.
4) Moderately hard with frequent to abundant very small and small shell.
5) Very hard with abundant small, medium and large flint.

Late Bronze Age pottery
(MATT BRUDENELL)

The excavations produced a large assemblage of Late Bronze Age Post-Deverel Rimbury (PDR) pottery, dating to *c.* 1100–800 BC, with 1049 sherds (8156 g) recovered from a total of 143 features. By weight, 21% of the pottery was recovered from Iron Age, Roman and later features (273 sherds, 1695 g), mainly fieldsystem ditches and enclosure boundaries in the central area of the site. Only 54 features contained non-residual PDR pottery (Fig. 2.6). Most of these were postholes and small- to medium-sized pits clustered in the northeast and southwest corners of the excavated area — zones with relatively little later activity. For this analysis, all sherds were examined and recorded in line with the guidelines of the Prehistoric Ceramic Research Group. Sherds weighing less than 1 g (classified as crumbs) were excluded from the quantification.

Fabric series
Burnt-flint tempered fabrics
F1: Moderate–common, coarse, poorly sorted calcined-flint inclusions.
F2: Moderate–common, very coarse, poorly sorted calcined-flint inclusions.
F3: Moderate–common, medium calcined-flint inclusions.
F4: Sparse, medium-coarse, moderately well-sorted calcined-flint inclusions.
F5: Moderate–common, fine–medium well-sorted calcined-flint inclusions.
F6??: Sherds with calcined-flint inclusions but which are too small to ascribe to a specific group.

Burnt-flint and quartz-sand tempered fabrics
QF1: Moderate–common fine sub-angular quartz sand, with sparse, medium, moderately–well-sorted calcined-flint, and rare coarse–very coarse calcined-flint.
QF2: Sparse, medium–coarse, moderately–well sorted calcined-flint inclusions, with moderate sub-angular quartz-sand.
QF3: Moderate–common fine sub-angular quartz sand, with moderate–common medium–coarse calcined-flint.

Burnt-flint and grog tempered fabrics
GF1: Moderate–common, coarse–very coarse calcined-flint and sparse–moderate medium–coarse grog.
GF2: Moderate medium grog with rare coarse grog, and sparse medium coarse calcined-flint.
GF3: Moderate medium–coarse grog and rare coarse calcined-flint.

Shell tempered fabrics
S1: Moderate–common fine–medium well-sorted shell.
S2: Moderate coarse–very coarse fossil shell.

Form series
Cups (Class V)
1. Small vessels less than 10mm in diameter, with straight-sided, ovoid or slightly convex bodies, and either tapered, slightly hooked, or internally bevelled rims.

Bowls (Class III & IV)
2. Biconical bowls, with a well-defined angular or rounded shoulder and inward sloping neck.
9. Round-bodied bowls with out-turned rims.

Jars (Class I & II)
10A. Straight-sided, near-cylindrical jars. A separate neck-zone is occasionally identifiable. Rims are usually direct with flat, rounded or slightly tapered lips. Related to Form 13.
11. High-shouldered jars with pronounced or rounded shoulders, relatively long inward sloping necks and short upright or out-turned rims. Closely related to Form 12.
12. High-shouldered jars with rounded shoulders and near upright or concave necks. Closely related to Form 11.
13. Plain neckless jars with ovoid/convex bodies and high rounded shoulders. Rims are normally in-turned, hooked or rounded. Related to Form 10A.
14. Angular tripartite jars with sharp carination and everted-rim.
16. Slack-shouldered jars with relatively short upright or hollowed necks.

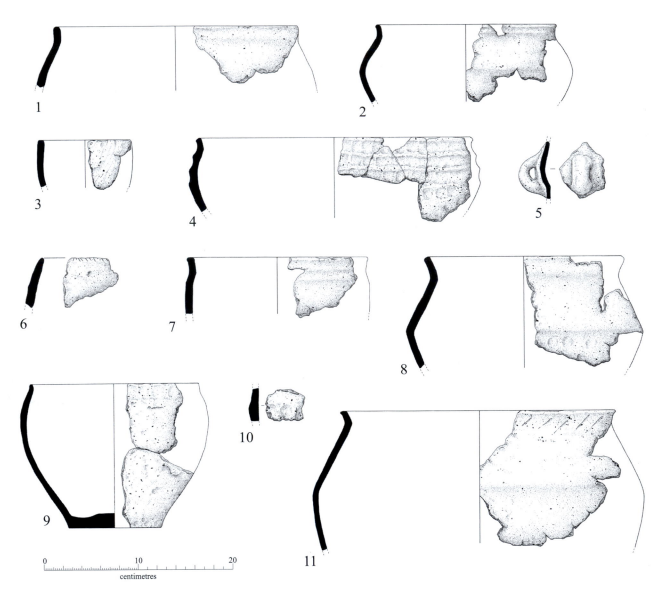

0　10　20
centimetres

Figure 2.10. *Later Bronze Age Pottery: 1) Form 11 Class I jar (F.128. Fabric F1; rim diameter 26 cm - all rim diameters are internal measurements); 2) Form 12 Class I jar (F.128. Fabric F1; rim diameter 19 cm); 3) Form 1 Class V cup (F.474. Fabric F1; rim diameter 8 cm); 4) Form 9 Class III bowl with above-shoulder corrugations/wide furrows (F.369. Fabric F1; rim diameter 29 cm; 5) Strap-handle from fineware vessel (F.369. Fabric QF2); 6) Form 13 Class I jar with rim-exterior finger-nail impressions (F.112. Fabric GF1); 7) Form 10A Class I jar (F.655. Fabric QF3; rim diameter 19 cm); 8) Form 14 Class I jar (F.714. Fabric QF3; rim diameter 21 cm); 9) Form 16 Class I jar (F.45. Fabric F1; rim diameter 18 cm); 10) Finger-tip impressed shoulder from coarseware vessel (F.45. Fabric F1); 11) Form 11 Class I jar with diagonal stab marks on neck (F.656. Fabric F1; rim diameter 29 cm).*

Assemblage characteristics

The assemblage was highly fragmented, with a MSW of just 7.8 g. 73% of all sherds were small (under 4 cm in size), with only 1% falling within the large-size class (over 8 cm in size). As expected, the MSW of the residual pottery was slightly lower than the assemblage average (6.2 g), whilst that recovered from Late Bronze Age contexts was slightly higher (8.3 g). On the whole, the residual material was more fragmented and abraded, with 83% of sherds being of small-size, compared to only 70% from non-residual contexts (Fig. 2.11).

Burnt-flint gritted sherds dominated the assemblage, notably the coarseware fabric F1 (Table 2.4). The addition of crushed burnt-flint is characteristic of Late Bronze Age PDR assemblages across southern Cambridgeshire and most of East Anglia (shell-tempered fabrics typify assemblages from fen-edge sites around Cambridgeshire). By weight, 88% of the Hutchison Site's pottery had burnt-flint inclusions, 10% displayed a combination of burnt-flint and sand, whilst the remaining 2% was shared between sherds with burnt-flint and grog and those with shell. It is possible that the small numbers of sherds with shell inclusions were of Middle Bronze Age date, given the preference for shell-tempered wares during that period. Equally, as burnt-flint was used in the production of both Neolithic and Late Bronze Age ceramics, it is plausible that some of the pottery assigned a PDR date *could* be considerably

TABLE 2.4. *Late Bronze Age Pottery: Fabric frequency, and its relationship to burnishing and vessel counts.*

Fabric	No./weight (g) sherds	% assemblage by weight (g)	No./weight (g) burnished	% fabric burnished	No. vessels	No. vessels burnished
F1	715/5782	70.9	-	-	33	-
F2	54/785	9.6	-	-	2	-
F3	38/215	2.6	13/85	39.5	4	-
F4	33/212	2.6	-	-	1	-
F5	8/17	0.2	8/17	100.0	1	1
F	84/154	1.9	4/6	3.9	4	-
QF1	21/155	1.9	11/83	53.5	3	-
QF2	23/184	2.6	17/146	79.3	2	2
QF3	61/426	5.2	-	-	6	-
GF1	2/55	0.7	-	-	1	-
GF2	1/14	0.2	-	-	-	-
GF3	2/35	0.4	-	-	-	-
S1	4/112	1.4	1/2	1.8	1	-
S2	3/10	0.1	-	-	-	-
Total	**1049/8156**		**54/339**		**58**	**3**

FIGURE 2.11. *Later Bronze Age Pottery: Percentage of small-, medium- and large-sized residual and non-residual sherds.*

TABLE 2.5. *Late Bronze Age Pottery: Frequency of forms and their relationship to fabrics.*

Form/Fabric		F1	F2	F3	QF3	GF1	Total
Cups	1	1					1
Bowls	2			1			1
	9	1					1
	10A	1	1		1		3
	11	3					3
Jars	12	2					2
	13					1	1
	14	1			1		2
	16	1					1
Total		**10**	**1**	**1**	**2**	**1**	**15**

older. Distinguishing between the Neolithic and Late Bronze Age ceramics can be problematic, particularly when presented with small, abraded, non-diagnostic body sherds.

The assemblage was composed of a range of jars and bowls typical of Late Bronze Age PDR assemblages from across Cambridgeshire and much of Eastern England (Fig. 2.10). For the purposes of this study, vessel forms have been classified using a modified version of a PDR typology developed by the author (Brudenell forthcoming); the relevant sections of which are reproduced here. In addition, vessels have been assigned to vessel class following Barrett (1980).

In general, relatively few forms were identifiable, owing to the fragmented condition of the pottery. However, based on the total number of different rims and bases, the assemblage represents a minimum of 58 vessels, with a rim Estimated Vessel Equivalent (EVE) of 1.6 (42 different rims, 17 different bases — one of which forms a complete profile). In total, 15 vessels were sufficiently intact to allow ascription to form. These included 100 sherds (1343 g), representing 10% of the assemblage by sherd count or 16% by weight (Table 2.5, Fig. 2.12). Coarseware jars (Class I) dominated, notably straight-sided 'cylindrical-shaped' jars (Form 10A) and jars with rounded-shoulders (Forms 11 & 12). Forms with 'early' affinities include the Form 13 convex-walled jar with slightly in-turned

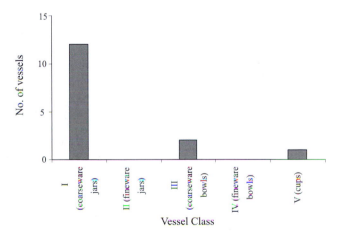

FIGURE 2.12. *Later Bronze Age Pottery: Form assigned vessels expressed as Barrett's (1980) five vessel classes.*

or 'hooked' rim (No. 6). Typologically, these vessels tend to be early in the PDR sequence, possibly dating around the eleventh–tenth century BC; the shape of the jars recalling the bucket/barrel urns of the Middle Bronze Age Deverel Rimbury tradition. In contrast, the angular-tripartite Form 14 vessel (No. 8) is more likely to be late in the PDR sequence, perhaps indicating activity at the very end of the Late Bronze Age in the latter stages of the ninth century BC or early eighth century BC. This was not an isolated example, as other sherds displaying angular shoulders were also recovered from F.45 and F.502.

No fineware jar or bowl forms (Class II and IV) were identified, though two coarseware bowls were present (Class III). The first comprised a simple bi-conical bowl with an internally-bevelled rim. The second was a large, deep round-bodied bowl with short out-turned lip, and internal rim diameter of 29 cm (No. 4). The vessel displayed an unusual form of decoration, comprising a series of three crude 'corrugations' or wide furrows above the shoulder. This decorative scheme is best paralleled by a Late Bronze Age fineware bowl from Maidscross, Suffolk, dated typologically to the tenth–eighth century BC (Needham 1995, 165). To date, no comparable examples have been found in Cambridgeshire, though round-bodied bowls are a common feature of Late Bronze Age plainware PDR assemblages. A single cup (Class V) of simple, straight-sided form with an internal rim diameter of *c.* 8 cm (No. 3) was also identified.

Burnishing (encompassing careful smoothing and polishing) was rare, with only 54 sherds (339 g) thus treated. This represents just 5.1% of the assemblage by sherd count or 4.2% by weight. On the whole, burnished fineware sherds were slightly smaller than the coarsewares, with 78% falling within the small-size range as opposed to 73% of the coarsewares. Although only a minor difference, this probably reflects how the thin walls of the fineware sherds were more susceptible to breakage than their thicker coarseware counterparts. Given this increased fragmentation, coupled with the likelihood that some sherds may have lost their original surfaces, burnished sherds are probably under-represented in the assemblage. However, even allowing for this bias, the frequency of burnishing is not uncommonly low for Late Bronze Age pottery assemblages from Cambridgeshire. Patterns emerging from the analysis of recently excavated sites suggest that burnishing frequencies below 10% are the norm in this area, suggesting that finewares formed a minor component of most assemblages.

Burnishing was restricted to just six of the 14 different fabric groups identified, principally those with the finer, better-sorted inclusions which facilitate smoothing and polishing, such as QF1, QF2 and F5. The general correlation between grit-size and burnishing implies that clays and tempers were carefully selected with this treatment in mind. Burnishing was not, therefore, an afterthought or alternative option at the end of the production process. Rather, the creation of finewares would have been planned from the primary stages of ceramic production.

As another form of surface treatment, decoration was equally rare as burnishing, with only 19 sherds (252 g) embellished (1.8%) from a maximum of 10 different vessels (Table 2.6). With the exception of a single incised fineware sherd (2 g), decoration was restricted to the coarsewares. In the absence of independent dating

TABLE 2.6. *Late Bronze Age Pottery: Type and frequency of decoration.*

Type of decoration	No. sherds	Weight (g)	MNV
Rim-top finger-tip and rim-exterior finger tip	1	4	1
Rim-exterior slashed	1	4	1
Rim-exterior finger-nail and perforated neck	1	27	1
Diagonal stabbed impression on neck	3	62	1
Corrugation/wide furrows above shoulder	8	124	1
Finger-tip on shoulder	1	15	1
Finger-tip impression	1	5	1
Incised horizontal line	1	2	1
Deep circular stab-mark/ near-perforation	1	7	1
Perforation	1	2	1
Total	**19**	**252**	**10**

evidence or clearly stratified ceramic sequences, the frequency of decoration is often used a guide to assessing the chronological position of LBA/EIA assemblages, particularly for the distinction between early 'Plainware' and later 'Decorated' Post-Deverel Rimbury pottery (Barrett 1980). Unfortunately, the frequency of decoration cannot be calculated in a straightforward manner, as ornamentation tends to be confined to restricted zones on the vessels (primarily rim, neck and shoulder). Gross counts, such as the proportion of decorated to undecorated sherds/feature sherds tend to either over- or underestimate the incidence of decoration (Needham 1996, 112).

One quantification method which appears more reliable and readily comparable is the frequency of rim decoration. Of the 42 different rims in the assemblage, only three (7%) have some form of ornamentation. Such low frequencies are characteristic of PDR plainware assemblages dating from *c.* 1100–800 BC, and can be matched by figures obtained from other Late Bronze Age pottery groups in Cambridgeshire.

Distribution and deposition

With the exception of a single sherd (3 g) from Structure 1, all the non-residual PDR pottery was recovered from three major feature groups, including pits, 'working hollows', and postholes. In all, 21 pits yielded pottery (633 sherds, 5419 g), five of which contained substantial groups over 500 g (Table 2.7). These pit-assemblages were the largest from the site, and account for 50% of the total pottery assemblage or 82% of the non-residual ceramics (both by count). Four of the five pits clustered in the southeast corner of

TABLE 2.7. *Late Bronze Age Pottery: Groups over 500 g in weight.*

Feature	No. sherds	Weight (g)	MNV	No. refits	MSW	% Small (<4 cm)	% Medium (4–8 cm)	% Large (>8 cm)
45	79	972	6	14	12.3	65	29	6
128	197	1083	8	26	5.6	84	16	<1
154	75	551	2	4	7.3	71	29	0
369	113	1142	6	22	10.1	52	47	1
474	57	659	2	4	11.7	60	39	1

the site, whilst F.45 was more centrally located. The pit deposits contained sherds from numerous different vessels in varying states of fragmentation. The assemblages were characterized by small- and medium-sized sherds mixed amongst the occasional larger piece (never more than 6%). Such mixed and varied pottery deposits appear to be composed of sherds with diverse post-breakage histories. Intriguingly, deposits of this nature seem to characterize Late Bronze Age pit-based pottery assemblages from across the region (Brudenell forthcoming; Brudenell & Cooper 2008). This type of group may derive from 'pre-pit contexts' such as surface rubbish heaps, where the mixing of ceramic material could occur prior to deposition.

Of the remaining non-residual pottery, 77 sherds (701 g) derived from five of the 'working hollows' in the northeast corner of the site. The pottery from these features was less fragmented than elsewhere, with a MSW of 9.1 g (8.7 g for pits and 5.2 g for postholes). 27 postholes yielded pottery, totalling 65 sherds (338 g). The postholes were widely distributed over the southern half of the site, with denser clustering towards the southeast corner of the excavation area. Most postholes contained between one and four sherds, though F.342 yielded 13 sherds (48 g).

To date, the assemblage of Late Bronze Age pottery from the Hutchinson Site forms one of the largest groups of Post-Deverel Rimbury ceramics recovered from Southern Cambridgeshire. The material contains at least five substantial pottery assemblages from pits, which will form key comparative groups for the local ceramic studies. The presence of shouldered-jars and round-bodied bowls, coupled with the low levels of vessel decoration, suggest that the assemblage belongs to the 'Plainware' PDR phase, dated *c.* 1100–800 BC (Barrett 1980). More precise dating within this bracket is problematic as the assemblage contains a number of formal characteristics indicative of activity at both the beginning and end of this time-frame. At present there are few large published assemblages from Cambridgeshire with which to compare this material. However, the pottery has clear parallels with the small assemblages from Fulbourn (Brown & Score 1998), and with ceramics from Stonea (Needham 1996).

Other artefacts
<088> [214] (2001 Evaluation) - Unidentified complete copper-alloy object with tapering flat surfaces at one end and rounded at the other. The sides to the mid-point are flat and have a thin lozenge cross-section. Dimensions: length 23 mm, weight <1 g. The flat surfaces appear polished or smoothed, suggesting the object may have been used as a burnishing tool, used in leather working, or even for chasing in repoussé work, inserted and fixed at the rounded end into an organic handle, or a possible awl (similar objects identified as awls, dating to the Bronze Age, were recovered during excavations at the Power Station site, Fengate, Peterborough: Coombs 2001, 267 & fig. 10.6); possibly Late Bronze Age.

<2711> *Unstratified* - Rectangular fragment of a later Middle or Late Bronze Age socketed axe with evident curvature, surviving rim and casting seam on the internal surface, surface pitting and a pale green patina. Dimensions: 30 mm × 25 mm, thickness 2 mm, weight 15 g. The ragged edges (there are no cut or chisel marks present) suggest the socket may have failed due to brittleness of the metal, although only metallurgical analysis can confirm this inference.

F.529 - Baked clay spindle whorl, bun-shaped with horizontal 'rilling' from a Late Bronze Age pit. Measures 15 mm high, 25 mm diameter on upper side and 15 mm diameter on lower side. The central perforation tapers from 10 mm at the top to 8 mm at the bottom. Hard fabric with reduced surface and no visible inclusions.

F.468 - Fragment of a worked bone point or gouge, 75 mm long from a Late Bronze Age pit. Produced from a long bone (possibly a metatarsal) of a sheep-sized animal. The bone has been split down its length so as to retain the inner curvature.

Environmental and economic evidence
Only a modest quantity of animal bone was recovered from Bronze Age contexts (see Swaysland below). One Middle Bronze Age pit, F.157, yielded small quantities, including a cattle mandible. Meanwhile, of the twelve analysed features from the Late Bronze Age, the identifiable material consisted of cattle (48%), sheep (38%) and pig (14%).

The three environmental bulk samples taken from this phase of the site's usage contained only very small amounts of plant remains, including a single cereal grain of wheat/barley (see Roberts below). One sample, from F.31, produced a relatively large amount of molluscan remains, including some indicative of damp or wet conditions, and others suggesting an open environment.

Discussion
As now found elsewhere in much of the region, evidence of Middle/later Bronze Age land allotment has been forthcoming from two other sites within the wider Addenbrooke's environs, that at the Babraham Road Park-and-Ride facility (Hinman 2001) and Fulbourn Hospital (Brown & Score 1998). Both included quite robust 'big-ditch' boundaries, by whose 'open' layout it is difficult to be certain to what degree they relate to fieldsystems as opposed to more ubiquitous modes of 'enclosure' (the settlement component at both being relatively minor). Whereas the attribution of the Babraham Road system is primarily based on radiocarbon dating, at Fulbourn Middle Bronze Age ceramics were recovered from the lower ditch fills and later Bronze Age forms occurred in the upper profiles (the relative portion of Middle to Late wares seemingly comparable to those at the Hutchison Site). Of more 'gully-like' scale, the Hutchison's possible Bronze Age ditches were much smaller than either Babraham Road or Fulbourn. While it is conceivable that they also had mid second-millennium BC origins (as do most of the period's fieldsystems in the region), given the nature of the evidence it is impossible to determine this with certainty. Equally, though it is difficult to account for the relative paucity of the site's Middle Bronze Age 'presence' (and convincingly characterize its nature), as opposed to the scale of its 'Late' usage, their relative

TABLE 2.8. *Artefacts from features dated by pottery to the Middle and Late Bronze Age respectively (does not included material occurring residually in later features).*

	MBA	LBA
Pottery	176 (1255 g)	1049 (8156 g)
Baked clay	7 (105 g)	28 (564 g)
Worked flint	-	222 (1289 g)
Burnt flint	-	30 (248 g)
Burnt stone	6 (156 g)	120 (9000 g)
Bone	82 (1503 g)	441 (3583 g)
Worked bone	-	1 (1 g)

recovery/representation would be entirely typical of most of the region's Bronze Age landscapes.

While the site's Late Bronze Age occupation was relatively substantial (Table 2.8), its extensive, unenclosed settlement swathe seems fairly typical of this period in eastern England. Such 'spreads' could be produced by occupation plots undergoing short-distance shifts over time within a given area of the landscape, a notion which may be supported by the fact that houses from other sites of the period rarely show more than one or two phases of construction.

The phase's finds assemblages from the site do not seem particularly distinguished, there being, for example, no evidence for specialized crafts such as metalworking. Beyond pottery and flint, the range of finds is limited, although craft activity is evinced by a spindle whorl and a possible bone gouge. However, the probable socketed axe fragment (unstratified metal-detector find) can be generally associated with this activity. Evidence for grain processing is elusive, as no querns were found and only a single cereal grain was recovered from the environmental samples.

Late Iron Age and Conquest Period settlement

These phases (3 & 4) represent the hub of the site's sequence, when it sees its most intense occupation and usage. It spans the later Iron Age and earlier Roman times (i.e. pre-Flavian): the Conquest Period. However, it is in the nature of this 'transition' that it is essentially impossible to adequately disentangle these two horizons. Yes, a series of curvilinear Iron Age enclosures can be distinguished as dominating the western third of the site (west of the cricket pavilion) and east of these, a grid-iron pattern of rectangular paddocks are the most apparent, with the point of their division being the westernmost main northeast-southwest boundary, F.19, F.1053 and F.1013. Yet the two enclosure systems 'inter-penetrate', making this distinction much less clear-cut. Equally, there is a

problem of finds attribution, as the intensity of these phases of occupation means that artefact residuality becomes a major factor. There is, moreover, also a considerable potential for contemporarily 'mixed' assemblages, and it is possible that Iron Age-tradition pottery continued to be made after the introduction of more distinctly Roman-type wares (see Hill, in Evans 2003a,b for further discussion). It is for these reasons that the teasing out of the interrelationship of these two phases — distinguishing what *The Conquest* meant in the local landscape — represents the crux of the site. It would simply be too arbitrary to here strictly divide these two horizons from the outset and, therefore, they are discussed (and analysed) together.

Late Iron Age (Phase 3)

The core of the Late Iron Age settlement lay in the central and western parts of the site (Fig. 2.13). It was primarily composed of a series of ditched enclosures (A–H), which can be seen to extend beyond the excavated area as cropmarks. The curvilinear nature of these enclosures contrasts with the rectilinear layouts of the subsequent systems. Nonetheless, there is a sense of a northwest–southeast/northeast–southwest landscape axis that was maintained by the Conquest Period layout. Other features datable to this phase include at least two roundhouses and a series of 'U'-shaped structures.

The following enclosures were distinguished (Fig. 2.13):

A A possible enclosure that extended beyond the western edge of the excavation, suggested by a pair of parallel ditches, F.943 and F.945, that branched off in a northwesterly direction from Enclosure B. These ditches were not visible as cropmarks, and their course is thus uncertain; however, they could form an enclosure with a roughly parallel ditch seen in aerial photographs extending from the northern point of Enclosure B (see below). F.943 was 2.20 m wide and 1.38 m deep, while F.945 measured 1.00 m across and was 0.3 5m deep.

B The largest of the Late Iron Age curvilinear enclosures; portions of its east and western sides were uncovered, with the remainder laying outside the area of excavation but clearly visible as a cropmark, measuring *c.* 60 north–south by 50 m east–west. The aerial photographs also show two further ditches extending off from the northern point of the enclosure in northwesterly and northeasterly directions respectively. As excavated, the enclosure ditch on the east side (F.855) was 1.13–1.70 m wide and 0.37–0.90 m deep, while that on the west side (F.809/942) was 1.50 m+ wide and 0.21–0.64 m deep.

C An enclosure defined on its southern and eastern sides by ditch F.832. It was open on its western side, while the postulated northern side lay beyond the limit of excavation. The area of the enclosure, as exposed, was 14 m east–west by 17 m north–south. The enclosure ditch was 1.80–2.20 m wide and 0.37–1.03 m deep.

D A sub-circular enclosure which, again, only partly fell within the excavated area, measuring 24 m northeast–southwest by 20 m+ northwest–southeast. There appeared to be an opening at least 9 m wide on the northwest side. The enclosure ditch on the south and west side (F.835) was 0.85–1.30 m wide and 0.38–0.57 m deep, while that on the north side (F.885) was 1.07

Phase 3 (Late Iron Age)

Phase 4 (Conquest Period)

FIGURE 2.13. *Late Iron Age and Conquest Period features (top) and, below, the Conquest Period system. (Reproduced by permission of Ordnance Survey on behalf of HMSO. © Crown copyright 2008. All rights reserved. Ordnance Survey licence number 100048686.)*

m+ wide and 0.19 m deep (Fig. 2.14). The ditch on the east side lay outside the excavated area.

E   A small, sub-rectangular enclosure adjacent to the northern side of Enclosure D, measuring *c.* 12 m northeast–southwest by 12 m northwest–southeast. It contained a possible roundhouse, Structure 7. The southwest side of the enclosure was formed by F.885 (Enclosure D), while the southeast side may have been obliterated by the Phase 4 Enclosure J. The enclosure ditch on the northeast side (F.628) was 0.70 m wide and 0.11 m deep, with that on the northwest side (F.891) being 0.60 m wide and 0.17 m deep.

F   A 'V'-shaped ditch setting with its apex to the south, measuring 32 m along its east/southeast side and 23 m along its southwest side. The enclosure ditch on the east/southeast side (F.55) was 0.74–0.92 m wide and 0.25–0.33 m deep, while that on the southwest side (F.1106) measured 1.00–1.70 m wide and 0.14–0.43 m deep. It is possible that F.1106 kinked before continuing for a further 25 m northwestwards as F.1085, the relationship between the two ditches being obscured by the later Enclosure J.

H   A sub-rectangular enclosure conjoining the southeast side of Enclosure I, open on the southwest side and measuring 25 m northwest–southeast by *c.* 17 m northeast–southwest (*c.* 425 m²). The enclosure ditch was 0.690–.85 m wide and 0.10–0.29 m deep, and probably effectively represented a continuation of the primary-phase ditch (F.68) of Enclosure I.

I   A small sub-rectangular enclosure measuring 16 m northwest–southeast by 14 m northeast–southwest, with a 5 m wide opening on the northwest side. The ditch forming the southwest side of the enclosure continued northwestwards (as F.280) to conjoin with Enclosure F. The enclosure ditch had been re-cut along most of its length, with the original ditch (F.68) truncated on its inner side by F.12. F.68 was *c.* 0.85 m wide and 0.18–0.32 m deep, while F.12 was larger, measuring 0.95–1.30 m wide and 0.32–0.51 m deep. The northwest side of the enclosure (F.64) differed in being formed of a single, slighter gully, 0.25–0.49 m wide and 0.17–0.19 m deep.

The northern edge of the Late Iron Age settlement is perhaps demarcated by northwest–southeast aligned ditch, F.718 (*et al.*). This was 0.35–1.45 m wide and 0.23–0.58 m deep; its line is echoed by the later Phase 4 ditch, F.720/930.

Mid–late first century AD (Phase 4)

The Phase 4 layout consisted of a rectilinear enclosure system on a northwest–southeast/northeast–southwest alignment (Fig. 2.13). This was dominated by a large sub-rectangular enclosure (J), subdivided into various smaller compounds (J1–6). The southern edge of the enclosure was demarcated by a northwest–southeast-aligned roadway with paired flanking ditches. A series of pottery kilns were found at the margins of Enclosure J, especially on its western side, although in some cases these must have been relatively late in the phase as their stokeholes were dug into the enclosure ditch after it had partially silted-up. Further ditches striking off from Enclosure J to the north and west delineated other enclosures or fields. Immediately to the east of Enclosure J, and to the north of the road, lay a small unenclosed cemetery, which was broadly contemporary with this phase. If the settlement core of this phase is

taken to be Enclosure J, then the focus of activity had shifted eastwards from the preceding period.

The roadway was demarcated by parallel ditches 13 m apart, extending right across the southern part of the site, with a length of 95 m exposed. No trace of metalling was present. The northern side (F.4, F.5, F.381–2 & F.1011) appeared to have been re-cut along most of its length, while the southern side consisted of a pair of parallel ditches (F.973–4 and F.975) that may, again, represent two phases. The individual ditches measured 0.44–1.00 m wide and 0.09–0.41 m deep. While at its western end the road was aligned northwest-southeast, there appeared to be a slight kink to an alignment more westnorthwest–eastsoutheast at the eastern end.

The main enclosure system, Enclosure J, measured 180 m northeast–southwest by 65 m northwest–southeast (*c.* 11,700 m²).

The southwest side of J was formed by the northern flanking ditch of the roadway (F.5), discussed above. The remaining three sides showed multiple re-cuts along their lengths. On the southeast side (F.8/24/194), the individual ditches measured 0.58–1.25 m wide and 0.2–1.02 m deep, while on the northwest side (F.19/1053: Fig. 2.14) they were 0.35–1.52 m wide and 0.10–0.80 m deep. The northeast side was demarcated by a more robust ditch with a probable entranceway situated roughly midway. The western length of this ditch (F.22) was *c.* 1.50 m wide and 0.95–1.44 m deep, with smaller re-cuts of around 0.30 m deep (Fig. 2.14). The eastern length (F.23) measured 0.56–1.56 m deep, the full width being unclear due to later truncation. The entranceway underwent repeated re-cutting and remodelling, but the precise form and width at any one stage was unclear due to truncation by the later ditch F.21. Branching off from F.22 and flanking the entrance on its western inner side was a further ditch, F.30: 0.80–1.20 m wide and 0.28–0.43 m deep.

The enclosure system's other components consisted of:

J1   A trapezoidal enclosure comprising the northern part of Enclosure J, measuring 75 m long on the northeast and southwest sides by 36 m on the southeast side by 53 m on the northwest side (*c.* 3375 m², or *c.* 2935 m² excluding J2). While the northwest, northeast and southeast sides were all formed by the ditches of Enclosure J (see above), the southwest side was composed of ditches F.16 and F.339/597/599. These two lengths of ditch butt-ended together at a point that may represent an entranceway. F.16 measured 1.49–1.70 m wide and 0.56–0.60 m deep, while F.339/597/599 was 0.50–1.50 wide and 0.09–0.50 m deep. J1 contained a large pond, F.770, described below.

J2   This was located in the southwest corner of J1, measuring 26 m northwest–southeast by 17 m northeast–southwest (*c.* 440 m²). The northwest side was formed by F.19 (see J) and the southwest side by F.16 (see J1). The ditches on the remaining two sides (F.18 and F.20) were 1.35–1.75 m wide and 0.42–0.64 m deep.

J3   A sub-rectangular enclosure located in the northeast corner of the southern part of Enclosure J. It measured 35 m northeast–southwest by 22 m northwest–southeast (*c.* 770 m²); the southeast side was formed by F.24 (Enclosure J) and the northeast side by F.339 (Enclosure J1). The ditches on the remaining two sides (F.13 and F.86) were 1.15–1.65 m wide and 0.46–0.76 m deep. Parallel to the west side of the enclosure, at a distance of 2.5 m, was a further ditch, F.205: 18 m long, 0.50–0.92 m wide and 0.13–0.35 m deep.

Section 231

SE   NW   NNW

F.627

F.19

Section 284

SW   NE

F.1259

F.22

Section 562

S   N

F.887

144

145

F.885

Section 520

E   W

F.1038

Section 400

W   E

F. 42

0   2

metres

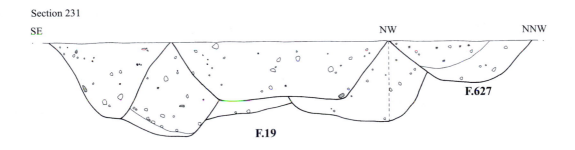
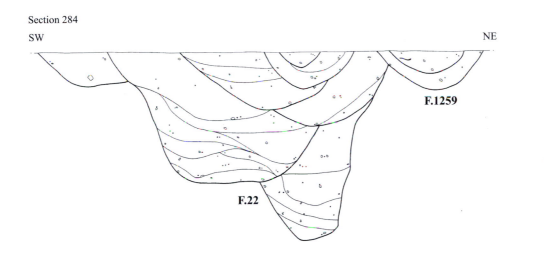
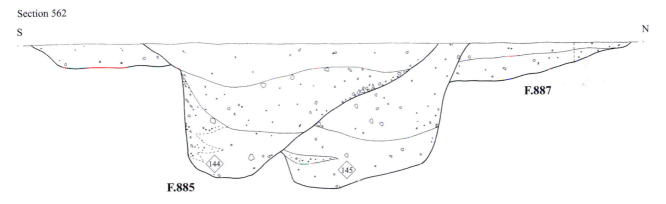
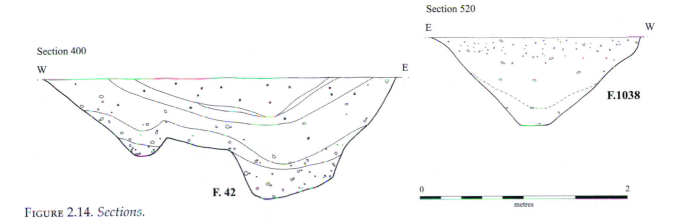

FIGURE 2.14. *Sections.*

J4   A sub-rectangular enclosure located on the western side of the southern part of Enclosure J. It measured 25 m north-east–southwest by 18 m northwest–southeast (*c.* 450 m^2), and was open on the southeast side. The northwest side of the enclosure was formed by F.1053 (Enclosure J). The enclosure ditch on the northeast side (F.36) was 0.70–0.84 m wide and 0.13–0.29 m deep. That on the southwest side (F.38) was 0.54–1.13 m wide and 0.19–.048 m deep; this extended to the southeast beyond the open southeast side of the enclosure, totalling 40 m in length. A further ditch (F.56) was located within Enclosure J4, extending from F.1053 in a southeasterly direction for 18 m; it measured 0.66 m wide and was 0.20 m deep. This subdivided Enclosure J4, the northern part forming **J4a** with the slightly smaller **J4b** to the south.

J5   A 'free-standing' enclosure located approximately at the centre of the southern part of Enclosure J. In plan, it comprised three sides of a rectangle, open on the northeast side, measuring 15 m northwest-southeast by 12 m northeast–southwest (*c.* 180 m^2). The enclosure ditch (F.1) was 0.70–1.54 m wide and 0.12–0.42 m deep.

J6   A sub-rectangular enclosure located in the southeast corner of Enclosure J, measuring 30 m northeast–southwest by 26 m northwest–southeast. The southeast side was formed by F.8 (Enclosure J) and the southwest side by the northern flanking ditch of the roadway. The remaining two sides (F.3 and F.11) were 0.95–1.50 m wide and 0.26–0.53 m deep. A further ditch, F.746, projected from F.8 for 10 m into the enclosure and may represent a sub-division.

To the north of Enclosure J were a series of ditches that followed the same alignment as, and were clearly part of, the same system as this enclosure. These demarcated two further 'enclosures', K and L, although as both continue beyond the excavated area it is unclear whether they were 'closed' units in the same way as Enclosure J. In the case of Enclosure K at least, the internal area contained only a few features, and must represent part of a fieldsystem rather than an occupied settlement area.

K   This was demarcated by ditches continuing the line of Enclosure J northeastwards, measuring 70 m along its southwest side and 95 m+ along its southeast side. The southwest side was formed by F.22 and F.23 of Enclosure J. The northwest side (F.28) was a continuation of F.19 of Enclosure J, measuring 30 m+ long, 2.00 m wide and 0.30 m deep. Meanwhile, the southeast side was an intermittent continuation of F.24 of Enclosure J, consisting of F.26 and parallel ditches F.735–738; the latter extended beyond the northern edge of the excavation. F.26 was 8.8 m long, 2.20 m wide and 0.19 m deep, while F.735–738 were slighter, ranging from 0.58–1.79 m wide and from 0.07–0.23 m deep. Further ditch fragments on the same alignment occurred within Enclosure K (F.709 and F.739) and to its east (F.25, F.619 and F.1226). F.619 was a particularly substantial, northwest–southeast aligned linear, measuring 2.67–3.20 m wide and 1.18–1.50 m deep; it lay beneath the Phase 5 fieldsystem ditch, F.21, which at that point followed a similar alignment.

L   This was demarcated on its southeast side by F.28 and on its northeast side by a frequently re-cut ditch, F.720/930, which represents the continuation of F.22 of Enclosure J. The dimensions of the enclosure were 40 m+ long on the southwest side and 30 m+ long on the southeast side. The individual ditches on the southwest side measured 0.35–2.95 m wide and 0.23–0.80 m deep.

The area bounded on the southeast by J and on the northeast by L is referred to as Enclosure M. This area contained a series of smaller enclosures, M1–5.

M1   A sub-rectangular enclosure located in the northeast corner of M, which measured 10m northeast-southwest by 10 m northwest–southeast with an entrance at the southwest corner (*c.* 100 m^2). It was bounded on the southeast side by Enclosure J (F.19) and on the northeast side by Enclosure L. The remaining two sides (F.684 & F.780) were 1.1–1.9 m wide and 0.33–0.67 m deep.

M2   A sub-rectangular enclosure on the eastern edge of M, measuring 19 m northeast–southwest by 13 m northwest–southeast (*c.* 247 m^2). It was open on the southwest side, with the southeast side formed by F.19 (see J) and the northeast side by F.684 (see M1). The ditch on the remaining side (F.34) was 0.56–1.15 m wide and 0.16–0.57 m deep.

M3   A possible sub-rectangular enclosure to the west of M2, measuring *c.* 10 m northeast–southwest by 10 m northwest–southeast. It was open to the northeast, with the remaining three sides (F.903 and F.906) measuring 0.35–1.16 m wide and 0.11–0.39 m deep.

M4   Further to the south lay a sinuous, north–south aligned boundary formed by ditches F.868, F.1038 (Fig. 2.14) and F.1076. A 4 m wide gap between F.1038 and F.1076 may have formed an entranceway. Immediately to the north of this, an irregular boundary consisting of intercutting ditch segments (F.1246–1252) ran for 10 m northwest–southeast from the butt-end of F.1076 to meet ditch F.1053 (the boundary between J and M). M4 was assigned to the area bounded by F.1246–52 to the south, F.1076 to the west and F.1053 to the east/southeast.

M5   This was a rectilinear enclosure, one corner of which was uncovered at the western edge of the excavation, measuring 20 m+ along its southeast side and 17 m+ along the northeast side. Part of the southeast side of the enclosure was demarcated by parallel ditches, 0.5 m apart. The enclosure ditches (F.810, F.811, F.1193 and F.1194) were 0.34–0.89 m wide and 0.13–0.30 m deep.

Late Iron Age and Conquest Period structures

Two probable, and two possible, roundhouses or circular buildings were represented in the northwestern part of the site by curved gullies (Fig. 2.16). One (Structure 5) had two concentric gullies marking the wall line and outer eavesgully (Fig. 2.15), while the

FIGURE 2.15. *Iron Age Structure 5 (photograph taken from north).*

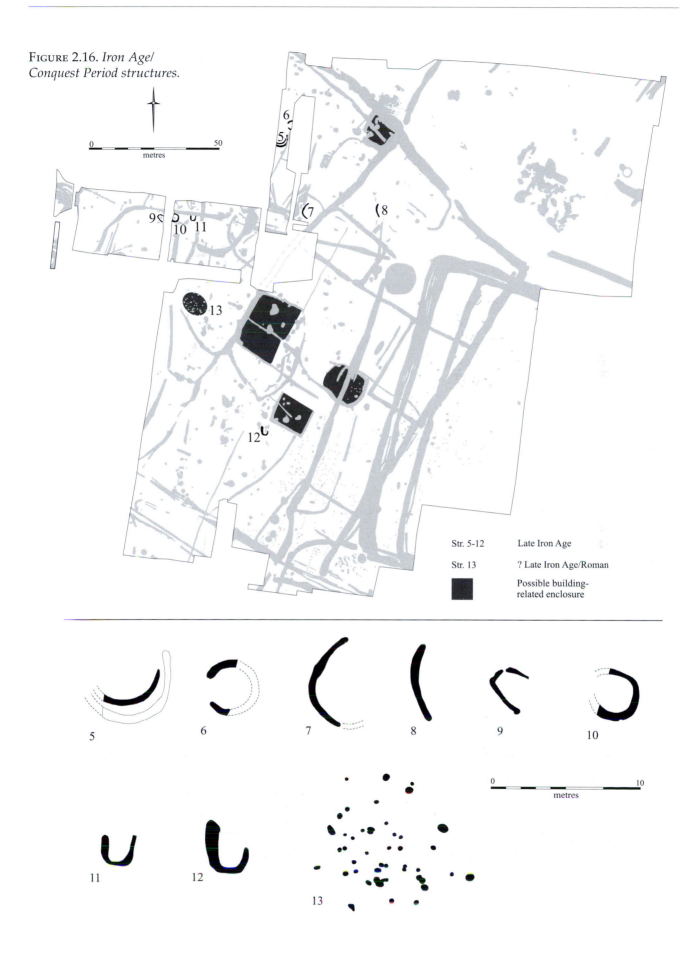

FIGURE 2.16. *Iron Age/Conquest Period structures.*

Str. 5-12   Late Iron Age

Str. 13   ? Late Iron Age/Roman

Possible building-related enclosure

other buildings were delineated by single gullies. With the possible exception of Structure 8, which may have been *c.* 10 m in diameter, the buildings were all relatively small at only 3.5–5.0 m diameter (measured from gully mid-points). The closely neighbouring Structures 5 and 6 may represent a paired unit; both contained large quantities of artefactual material (Table 2.9). The pottery from the circular structures was generally of Late Iron Age character, though a few sherds may be post-Conquest, including a tiny fragment of Samian from Structure 6.

Structure 5 (F.907/908) - Two concentric gullies forming the eastern half of a penannular structure with an opening to the north; the western half of the structure lay outside the area of excavation (Fig. 2.15). The outer ring-gully, F.907, had a diameter of *c.* 6 m. It was 0.42–0.61 m wide and 0.20–0.35 m deep, with a single silt-sand fill. F.907 appeared to be cut by gully F.906, immediately to the east. The slighter inner ring-gully, F.908, had a diameter of *c.* 4.5 m. It measured 0.30–0.38 m wide and 0.08–0.16 m deep, again, with a silt-sand fill. The two gullies are likely to be contemporary, with the inner ring representing the wall-line and the outer ring an exterior eavesgully. This is supported by the fact that the inner gully contained only a single sherd of pottery whilst the outer gully yielded much more material (Table 2.9). Two possible postholes lying within the northern entranceway were investigated (F.910 & F.911), but were thought unlikely to be real features.

Structure 6 (F.913) - Two gullies forming a penannular structure with a west-facing entrance, the eastern half of the structure falling outside the area of excavation. The gully was *c.* 3.5 m in diameter, 0.36–0.46 m wide and 0.13–0.20 m deep with a 'U'-shaped cut and a sand-silt fill. The entrance measured 1.5 m across. The large quantities of artefactual material found (Table 2.9) may indicate that the gully was an open feature, rather than a wall foundation trench. It may have been a drainage gully around a small ancillary building, granary or hayrick associated with the Structure 5 'roundhouse', lying immediately to the southwest.

Structure 7 (F.893) - A curved length of gully that might represent the western side of a circular structure, *c.* 5 m in diameter. The gully itself was 0.46–0.52 m wide and 0.10–0.33 m deep, with a silty fill. A possible posthole within it towards the northern end suggests that it may have been structural.

Structure 8 (F.635) - A curved length of gully, 5.0 m long, that might represent the western side of a circular structure, *c.* 10 m diameter. The gully measured 0.40–0.43 m wide and 0.17–0.23 m deep, and had a clay fill.

Four small structures consisting of 'U'-shaped gullies were found within the western part of the site, three of which lay close together in an east–west aligned row (Fig. 2.16). These typically enclosed an area of *c.* 5 m² and, in three cases, an oval pit was found in the centre of the structure. Postholes were found within two of the gullies themselves, suggesting that they were structural foundation trenches. Neither the gullies nor the central pits contain much artefactual material, with just a few sherds of Late Iron Age pottery and a small amount of animal bone recovered. This makes it difficult to assign them a precise function, though they are likely to have been small ancillary buildings.

Structure 9 (F.828/829) - Two gullies forming a 'U'-shaped structure with its entrance to the southeast. There was a short gap in the circuit at the northeast corner, and the northern arm of the gully continued beyond the edge of the excavated area to the east. The structure enclosed an area of *c.* 2.0 m by 2.5 m. The gully was 0.30–0.50 m wide and 0.10–0.19 m deep, with a dark sandy fill. Four postholes could be seen within the gully along the southern and western sides of the structure, including one marking the southeastern butt-end. These postholes shared the same fill as the gully itself. Approximately central within the enclosed area was an oval pit, 0.6 m diameter and 0.29 m deep, with a similar fill to the gully.

Structure 10 (F.871) - Three sides of a 'U'-shaped or sub-circular gully, the western part of which lay beyond the excavated area. As exposed, the structure enclosed an area of *c.* 2.0 m east–west by 2.5 m north–south. The gully was 0.28–0.40 m wide and 01.8–0.36 m deep, with a dark sandy silt fill. A single posthole could be discerned within the northern side of the gully, and sharing the same fill. Approximately central within the enclosed area was an oval pit, F.872, measuring 0.56 m wide and 0.19 m deep, also with a similar fill to the gully.

Structure 11 (F.867) - A 'U'-shaped gully with its entrance facing north, enclosing an area of *c.* 2.0 m north–south by *c.* 1.5 m east–west. The gully measured 0.38 m wide and 0.18 m deep, and had a loamy fill containing some charcoal.

Structure 12 (F.101) - A 'U'-shaped gully with its entrance facing north, enclosing an area of *c.* 2.0 m east–west by 2.5 m north–south. The gully measured 0.40–0.68 m wide and 0.20–0.33 m deep, with an orange-grey silt-clay fill. Approximately central within the enclosed area lay an oval pit, 0.67 × 0.39 m and 0.20 m deep, with a pale brown sandy silt fill. A further elongated pit, F.103, lay immediately to the north of the gully, and perhaps formed part of the same structure. This measured 1.70 × 1.10 × 0.25 m deep and was filled with a dark brown sandy silt.

Structure 13 is the designation of an amorphous cluster of 33 postholes on the western edge of the excavation (F.1129–37, F.1139–52, F.1155–6, F.1158–61, F.1163–66 and F.1176). These ranged in size from 0.18–0.50 m diameter and from 0.08–0.28 m deep, variously having orange, orange-brown and grey-brown sandy and silty fills. No finds were recovered, and no building plan can be discerned, even when like postholes are compared with like. An association is possible with inhumation burial F.1162 on the western edge of the posthole cluster. A date for the structure in the Late Iron Age or Early Roman period seems more likely than the later Bronze Age, due to its location within the site.

TABLE 2.9. *Artefact assemblages from circular structures.*

	Pottery	Bone	Baked clay
Structure 5, outer ring	69 (711 g)	13 (340 g)	20 (82 g)
Structure 5, inner ring	1 (19 g)	-	-
Structure 6	155 (1843 g)	13 (8 g)	-
Structure 7	19 (277 g)	6 (127 g)	11 (21 g)
Structure 8	11 (82 g)	1 (32 g)	-

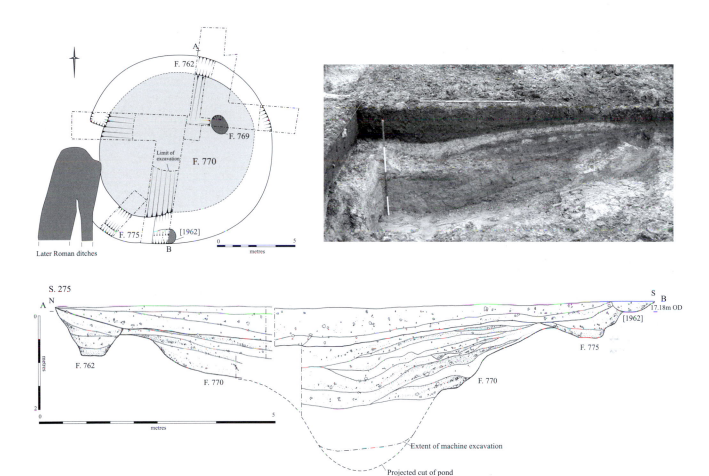

FIGURE 2.17. *The F.770 Pond-well.*

The 'Pond-well'

Lying within Enclosure J1 was a large 'pond-like' well feature (F.770: Figs. 2.13 & 2.17), approximately 10.00 m in diameter and more than 3.00 m deep (the base was not reached). This contained a complex series of deposits, with generally dark brown upper fills and a paler, more clayey lower deposit. F.770 was enclosed by a penannular ditch, F.762/775, which was later slighted by a re-cut of the pond; the ditch was 1.60–2.15 m wide and 0.68–1.02 m deep, with its entrance to the west. It is presumed that the purpose of this encircling ditch was to keep stock (and perhaps children) from falling into the well; an alternative reading of its layout would have the well's water poured into this ditch so that animals could drink from it.

The dating evidence from F.770 suggests that it was established in Phase 4 and probably continued to be maintained into Phase 5.

Burials

(NATASHA DODWELL with KATIE ANDERSON & SAM LUCY)
During the excavations a number of graves, both inhumation and cremation, were identified. The majority were clustered into a distinct cemetery containing 16 inhumation and three cremation burials, all of which are argued to date to the later first century AD. Outside that area, within the settlement enclosures were a further six inhumation burials, which are also thought to be broadly contemporary. In the text that follows, the cemetery will be discussed first, followed by the isolated burials. Reporting on the skeletal material and burial sequence is by Dodwell; Anderson reported on the pottery and Lucy contributed to the discussion.

The cemetery

A small cemetery, dating to the mid/later first century AD, was located on the southern edge of the site, tucked into an external corner of the Conquest Period system formed by the northern roadside flanking ditch and the northeast–southwest Enclosure J ditch, F.8 (Fig. 2.18). Three urned cremation burials dating to the later first century AD and sixteen inhumations, the majority of which lacked dating evidence, were identified (Fig. 2.20). A fully articulated dog was also buried alongside one of the graves (Fig. 2.19).

All of the cremation burials were urned. Grave

FIGURE 2.18. *Interment locations.*

2 contained two brooches and four complete pottery vessels, along with copper-alloy sheet fragments and iron fragments; Grave 3 was accompanied by two vessels and copper-alloy fragments.

The inhumation burials displayed a range of orientation and body positions: thirteen were supine (one with legs flexed), one was flexed and two were prone. Both sexes were represented and all of the burials were adult, except for the child in Grave 9. One skeleton (in Grave 14) appeared to have been buried without a skull (several of the skeletons had lost their skulls due to truncation, but this was relatively untruncated). Three of the inhumations contained definite or possible grave goods. A fragment of copper-alloy pin was recovered from the grave fill of the child buried in Grave 9 but it may be residual. The prone burial

in Grave 12 contained a near-complete pot placed beside the head, while the flexed burial in Grave 15 contained part of a copper-alloy bracelet and several copper-alloy rings were found behind the skull. The spherical flint nodule (*c.* 0.06 m diameter) found in the dog burial seems likely to have been deliberately placed beside its head.

One further notable feature of the cemetery was a pit (F.389; 0.90 m × .36 m and 0.12 m deep), which contained a quantity of partially articulated animal bone, of which Swaysland reports:

The bone was in poor condition, with chemical abrasion and root-etching removing surface detail. It was recovered in five distinct clusters:

1) left carpals, left metacarpal, two phalanx 1, one phalanx 2 and a phalanx 3;

2) a small quantity of rib fragments;
3) two phalanx 1, three phalanx 2, four phalanx 3;
4) a small quantity of ribs;
5) right carpals, right metacarpal, one phalanx 1, one phalanx 2, fragmentary vertebrae, proximal ulna fragment.

All the bone is consistent with having originated from an individual calf. All epiphyses were unfused, excluding proximal metacarpals that fuse before birth. However, none of the elements recovered are in the early fusing category and therefore it can only be said that the animal was less than 1.5 years at death, though it is probable that it was younger than this. The bones recovered are predominantly from the lower leg and are non-meat-bearing; these are generally considered to be waste material and of little economic value.

The location of these bones from a juvenile cow in a grave-shaped cut in a cemetery is intriguing. Whilst it is possible that they represent food debris from a ceremony relating to a burial rite, such an interpretation is brought into question by the low meat-bearing qualities of the remains (i.e. they may just relate to butchery waste, its placement within the cemetery being coincidental).

Turning to the cemetery itself, the cremation burials will be reported on first, followed by the inhumations and, then, the isolated burials from the settlement. The burials will then be discussed as a whole in the context of the site and with regard to wider themes of burial practice in Roman Britain.

Vessels containing cremated bone were lifted whole and examined in the laboratory where the contents were excavated in spits in order to identify any possible spatial organization of skeletal elements. Other deposits of cremated bone were subject to 100% recovery as whole earth samples and these were wet sieved and bone >4 mm was extracted for analysis. Animal bone and any artefacts were separated and given to relevant specialists. The methods for the identification, ageing and sexing of cremated bones are the same as those used for unburnt bone, although because of the degree of bone fragmentation and the often small quantity of bone recovered (see below), age-categories had to be extremely broad and it was not possible to attribute a sex to any of the burials. General methods used in the osteological evaluation of all the skeletal material are those of Bass (1992), Buikstra & Ubelaker (1994) and Steele & Bramblett (1988). An assessment of age was based on the stages of dental eruption (Ubelaker 1989) and epiphyseal union, on the degree of dental attrition (Brothwell 1981) and, where possible, on changes to the pubic symphysis and auricular surfaces (Brooks & Suchey 1990; Lovejoy *et al.* 1985). Metrical data was utilized where possible; the age-categories employed are:

neonate	<6 months
infant	0–4 years
juvenile	5–12 years
sub-adult	13–18 years
young adult	19–25 years
middle adult	26–44 years
mature adult	45 years+.

The stature of the individuals was calculated where possible from the combined femur and tibia lengths (Trotter & Gleser 1952). Although many of the long bones had suffered post-mortem breaks, these were recent and clean and refitting was straightforward.

The key information is presented below in tabular format; detailed recording of pathologies, dentition and the metrical data is held in the archive.

FIGURE 2.19. *The Cemetery (looking north), with Inhumation F.416 in the right foreground (and F.417 behind); left-centre is Cremation F.411 and, before it, the nodule-accompanied dog burial (F.412).*

Cremations

The cremation burials in the cemetery varied in depth from 0.10 to 0.53 m. Grave 1 was heavily truncated, whereas the other two cremation burials appeared undisturbed (Fig. 2.21). All the vessels recovered in these burials were broken and, whilst in some instances this may have been a deliberate part of the funerary ritual, it is probably the result of post-depositional activities. Unfortunately, pot-breakage meant that separating bone that had been originally contained within a vessel from any which had been placed outside it was often difficult or impossible. The cremated bone recovered from the three burials was a uniform buff-white colour, indicative of the full oxidization of the organic part of the bone. The bone fragment-size was generally small (10–30 mm) and the majority of the identifiable fragments were limb bone shafts. The small fragment-size inhibited the quality of the information that could be gleaned from the burnt bone.

Grave 1/F.391 [3331] Adult - A disturbed adult cremation with a greyware pedestal base and fragments of a beaker, lying just to the east of Grave 10. The bone (243 g) may originally have been contained in the vessel. The depth is estimated at 10 cm.

Grave 2/F.408 [3616] Sub-adult - This cremation, in an oval pit measuring 0.79 × 0.68 × 0.33 m deep, contained four vessels, with the cremated bone (356 g in total) held within two (Fig. 2.22). These were a butt beaker with cordons and rouletted decoration, and an unusual carinated pedestalled bowl. Accessory vessels consisted of a kiln-product flagon and a small necked bowl. The four vessels

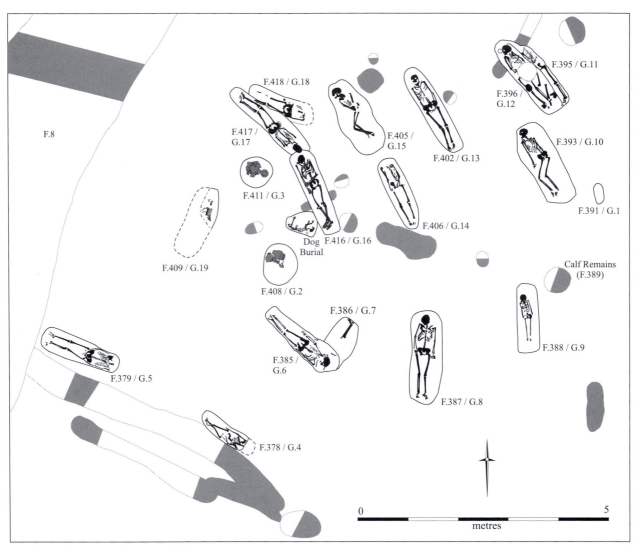

FIGURE 2.20. *Cemetery Base-plan.*

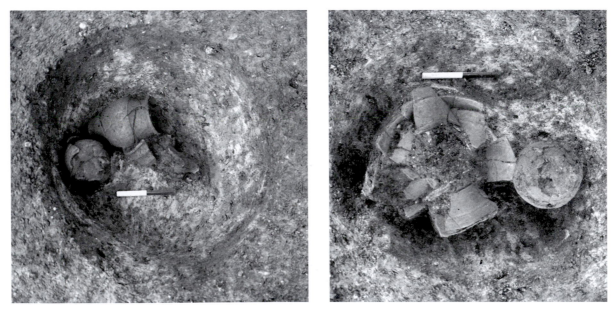

FIGURE 2.21. *The Cemetery Cremations: left, F.408; right, F.411.*

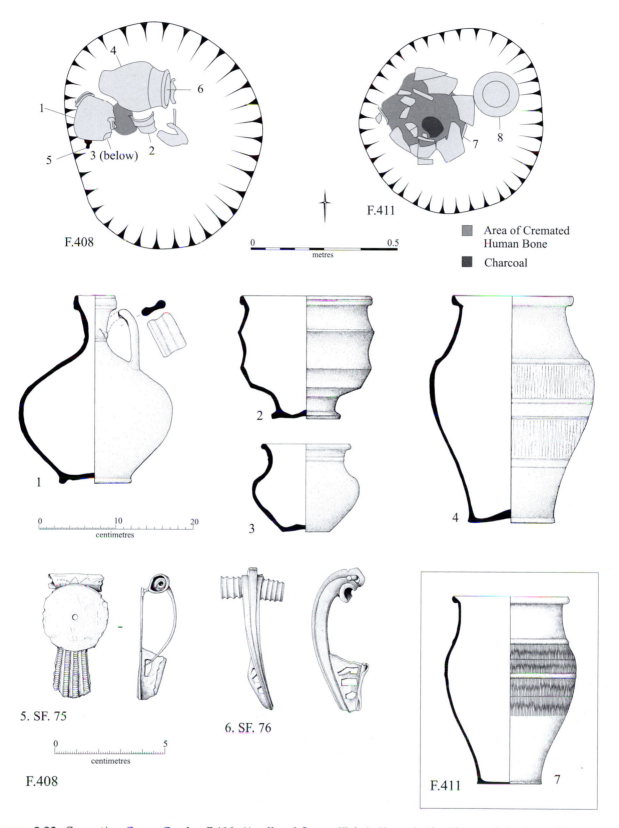

FIGURE 2.22. *Cremation Grave Goods - F.408: 1) collared flagon (Fabric K, wm); 2) wide-mouth beaker, with cordons and constrictions (Fabric Q3, wm); 3) small wide-mouth jar, cordoned (Fabric Q5, wm); 4) butt-beaker with cordons and bands of roulelling (Fabric Q3, wm); 5) rosette/thistle family brooch (SmF 75 <2525>; see Haselgrove below, no. 11); 6) Colchester Derivative brooch (SmF.101 <2788>; see Haselgrove below, no. 14); F.411; 7) butt-beaker, with two cordons and rouletted bands; AD 50–80 (F.411, [1954], Fabric FW2).*

were all complete, but broken. Part of a greyware lid was also recovered. The group as a whole can be dated *c.* AD 50–80. It would appear that the majority of the burnt bone was in a concentration outside the pots and, from its position, has been interpreted as having spilled out of the vessels. (The vessels were all lifted and excavated in the laboratory, although they were not found to contain much bone.) The majority of the bone came from a concentration of material which may or may not have originally derived from one of the larger vessels. There was burnt and unburnt animal bone (including fish) and also many unidentifiable calcined fragments. Recognizable elements include burnt fragments of pig skull, ulna and humerus, a goat's radius, four large fish vertebrae and burnt and unburnt immature small mammal remains; the character of the bone suggesting that remains had been thrown into the fire after they had been eaten.

The interment was accompanied by two copper-alloy brooches: a rosette deposited with the accessory vessels and a Colchester-derivative in the butt beaker. A fragment of copper-alloy sheet was also found associated with the cremation (see Appleby below). The dating of the metalwork is consistent with the pottery assemblage (see Haselgrove below). Hazelnut shell was found in an environmental sample from this burial.

Grave 3/F.411 [3663-5] Adult - This lay 1.00 m to the north of F.408 in an oval pit measuring 0.65 × 0.62 × 0.16 m deep. The cremated bone was contained within a complete butt beaker with cordons and rouletted decoration; there were also the fragmented remains of a second vessel with rouletted decoration, probably another butt beaker (Fig. 2.22). A total of 1315 g of bone was recovered. Some unburnt animal bone (a cow's tooth and an animal rib-end) was identified, and fragments of copper alloy were recovered (see Appleby below).

Inhumations

The summary data of the interred populace is presented in Table 2.10. Of the 16 inhumations in the cemetery, 13 were supine (one with legs flexed, 12 extended), two were prone and one was flexed on the right side. The burials seen to deviate from the more common supine, extended position were all female. The majority of the inhumation graves were aligned northwest–southeast, seven with heads in the northwest and five with their heads in the southeast; two graves were aligned southwest–northeast and, two more, north to south. There are three groups of intercutting graves and, as space would not appear to have been restricted, their placing may have been deliberate: the grave of an older middle male, Grave 11, has been cut by the grave of an older middle/mature adult female (Grave 12), who was buried prone with a small pottery vessel on the left side of her head; the unsexed adult skeleton (Grave 7) was cut by the grave of a young female (Grave 6) and, buried head-to-head on an orientation at right angles to her; Grave 17, a mature adult female, was just cut by Grave 16, a middle adult female. These individuals may have belonged to the same family, but there is no evidence for this from the osteological data.

It is interesting to note that all of the graves containing possible grave goods differ from the majority, two being prone, one crouched and one juvenile; all but one of the remaining burials were of supine adults, although of course this only accounts for grave-goods that survived the burial environment. Of the grave-goods, only the pottery vessel in Grave 12 was datable. This pedestal-base beaker dates to the later first century, indicating that this inhumation at least was contemporary with the cremation burials.

A series of furrows truncated the cemetery. The graves varied in depth from 0.06–0.40 m with most being between 0.15–0.30 m deep. In some of the shallower graves skeletal elements have been lost, disturbed or damaged by earlier ploughing and during machine-stripping (see Fig. 2.19). The degree of truncation and disturbance suggests that shallower graves may have been destroyed. There

are also several intercutting graves (6 & 7, 11 & 12 and 16 & 17) and disarticulated bone, presumably from the disturbed graves, was recovered from the later ones. Grave 12 had been cut by a later posthole, and elements were missing from its skeleton. The completeness of each skeleton was assessed during recording and assigned to one of three categories: <25% complete, 26–75% complete and >76% complete. Amongst the skeletons identified in the cemetery it was found that 12.5 % (2) were <25% complete, 31.25% (5) were 26–75% complete and 56.25% (9) were >76% complete. This data shows that the majority of the skeletons from the cemetery were largely complete.

The surviving skeletal elements are generally in good condition, although many of the bones, particularly the skulls and long bones, have suffered recent post-mortem breaks (probably the result of heavy plant-movement) and much of the cortical bone has been etched by small roots and insects. Green staining resulting from contact with copper-alloy objects buried with the body was observed on the bones of the skeleton in Grave 15.

When traits believed to be hereditary (i.e. septal aperture and metopic sutures) were recorded and plotted, there were no obvious clustering or similarities between the graves. Septal apertures were observed on skeletons Graves 6, 15 and 18, while the skeleton in Grave 8 retained its metopic suture.

Details regarding the age and sex of the interred individuals are presented in Table 2.11. All bar one of the skeletons is adult, and amongst the adults most of those which could be sexed are female. Long bones were sufficiently well preserved to calculate the stature of 11 of the 15 adults recovered from the cemetery. Where possible, calculations were made using a combined femur and tibia length, which is the most accurate method for calculating stature; if that was not possible, the femur length only was used followed by the tibia length. Using the combined femur and tibia lengths gave a female (*n* = 5) height range of 1.56–1.63 m (5'1"–5'4") with a mean of 1.59 m (5'2"), and a male range (*n* = 2) of 1.61–1.68 m (5'3"–5'6") with a mean of 1.65 m (5'5"). Using all methods, stature could be calculated for a total of eight females and three males. There is a female range of 1.45–1.63 m (4'9"–5'4") with a mean of 1.55 m (5'1") (this mean is far lower than the previous figure as it has been brought down by the tiny lady from Grave 4, only 1.45 m high) and a male range of 1.61–1.70 m (5'3"–5'7") with a mean of 1.66 m (5'5").

Pathology

The major pathological changes recorded are presented below. Detailed descriptions of all the pathologies observed are held in the archive and a note of each condition appears in the summary tables. No pathologies were observed in the cremated material.

Joint disease - Osteoarthritis (OA) is one of the most commonly seen pathologies in the archaeological record and is the result of a combination of wear and tear on the joint and of age degeneration. It was recorded according to the criteria of Rogers & Waldron (1995, 44). Unsurprisingly, the spine was by far the most commonly affected region of the skeleton, with 85.7% of the preserved adult spines (12/14) exhibiting a combination of at least three of the following: osteophytic lipping, porosity, Schmorl's nodes and eburnation (Table 2.12). Osteoarthritic changes were more often observed on the joints of the right side of the body but many were bilateral; e.g. both the left and right hands or knees of an individual were affected.

A possible case of diffuse idiopathic skeletal hyperostosis (DISH), or at least the early stages of the disease, was observed in the skeleton of the older middle adult male in Grave 11. It is a disease process of unknown aetiology, characterized by excessive bone growth on the spine and inflammation and bone growth on the insertions of ligaments and tendons, and is more commonly found in elderly men. Large (8 mm) marginal osteophytes, Schmorl's nodes and new bone were observed on the surviving lumbar and thoracic vertebrae. In addition, flowing osteophytes were recorded

TABLE 2.10. *Summary data of cemetery inhumations (OA = Osteoarthritis, AMTL = Ante-mortem tooth loss).*

Grave no.	Feature/Context no.	Age	Sex	Stature (m)	Pathology and morphological variation	Orientation (direction of head given first)	Grave dimensions (L x W x D) in metres	Body position	Grave goods	Notes
4	F.378 [3601]	Mature adult	Female	1.45	OA in spine, l. elbow, l. & r. hands, r. & l. hips, AMTL	SE–NW	1.02 × 0.32 × 0.10	Supine, extended		Truncated by machine
5	F.379 [3710]	Older middle adult	Male	1.61	OA in spine, AMTL, calculus	E–W	1.63 × 0.50 × 0.12	Supine, extended		Squashed in grave; truncated by machine
6	F.385 [3667]	Young adult	Female	1.56	Schmorl's nodes, ?TB, calculus. Septal aperture	E–W	1.67 × 0.45 × 0.15	Prone, extended		Cuts Grave 7
7	F.386 [3695]	Adult	?	1.50–1.55	None observed	SW–NE	0.57+ × 0.58 × 0.25	Supine, ?extended		Cut by Grave 6; only lower legs. No dentition
8	F.387 [3643]	Older middle adult	Male	1.7	OA in spine, AMTL, calculus. Metopism	N–S	1.85 × 0.60 × 0.30	Supine, extended		Squashed in grave
9	F.388 [3489]	Older infant	?	?	None observed	N–S	1.38 × 0.43 × 0.40	Supine, extended	Cu alloy pin in area of r. ribs	
10	F.393 [3492]	Mature adult	Female	1.58	OA in spine, ankylosis of C2 & C3, r. shoulder, AMTL	NW–SE	1.70 × 0.67 × 0.30	Supine, legs flexed to the r.		
11	F.395 [3442]	Older middle adult	Male	?	OA in spine, cribra orbitalia, calculus,	NW–SE	1.60 × 0.26 × 0.11	Supine, extended		Cut by Grave 12
12	F.396 [3445]	Older middle/mature adult	Female	?	OA in spine, r. & l. knees, in ?l. foot, AMTL, calculus	NW–SE	1.80 × 0.44 × 0.21	Prone	Pot beside head	Cut by post hole; cuts Grave 12
13	F.402 [3486]	Mature adult	Male	1.68	OA in spine, both acromio-clavicular joints & r. foot, caries & calculus	NW–SE	1.90 × 0.43	Supine, extended		
14	F.406 [3619]	Mature adult	Female	1.56	OA in spine, r. shoulder, sacro-iliac joint	NW–SE	1.50 × 0.47 × 0.30	Supine, extended		Skull missing
15	F.405 [3495]	Middle adult	Female	1.49	OA in spine, compression fracture & spondylolysis (L5), AMTL, calculus. Septal aperture	NW–SE	1.55 × 0.85 × 0.25	Flexed, lying on r. side	Cu alloy rings, bracelet frag.	
16	F.416 [3632]	Middle adult	Female	1.63	OA in spine & r. knee, calculus, AMTL, caries	NW–SE	1.78 × 0.50 × 0.21	Supine, feet crossed	A dog burial cuts the lower part of the grave.	Truncated by machine; cuts Grave 17
17	F.417 [3653]	Mature adult	Female	1.6	OA in spine, r. hip, l. foot, button osteoma, AMTL	SE–NW	1.68 × 0.38 × 0.30	Supine, forearms crossed		Cut by Grave 16
18	F.418 [3611]	Mature adult	Female	1.54	OA in spine and l. & r. hand. Septal aperture	SE–NW	1.15+ × 0.38 × 0.10	Supine, extended		No dentition; truncated by machine
19	F.409 [3614]	Adult	?	?	None observed	N–S	1.05 × 0.45 × 0.06	Supine, extended		No dentition. Very truncated

TABLE 2.11. *Cemetery inhumation-population summary table.*

	Female	?	Male	Total
mature	5	0	1	6
older mid/mature	1	0	0	1
older middle	0	0	3	3
middle	2	0	0	2
younger middle	0	0	0	0
young	1	0	0	1
adult	0	2	0	2
infant	0	1	0	1
total	9	3	4	16

TABLE 2.12. *The crude prevalence rates (CPR) of osteoarthritic changes in different areas of the body (adults only; i.e. 15 individuals).*

Joint affected	No. of adults affected	Male	Female	CPR%
Spine	12	4	8	80
Sternoclavicular	0	0	0	0
Acromio-clavicular	1	1	0	6.7
Shoulder	2	0	2	13.3
Elbow	1	0	1	6.7
Wrist	0	0	0	0
Hand	2	0	2	13.3
Sacro-iliac	1	0	1	6.7
Hip	2	0	2	13.3
Knee	2	0	2	13.3
Ankle	0	0	0	0
Foot	2	1	2	20

on the left/posterior of five of the lower thoracic vertebrae, several of which were close to fusing. Large entheses (spurs of new bone) were recorded on the pelvis (pelvic brim and the ischial tuberosity) and on the proximal left fibula. The changes are not classic DISH, as the flowing osteophytes characteristic of this disease usually form on the right side of the vertebrae and fusion of at least four contiguous vertebrae is necessary for a diagnosis (Roberts & Manchester 1995, 120). An alternative diagnosis of ankylosing spondylytis has been considered, but no extra spinal bone formation occurs in this disease process and fusion occurs at the small joints of the vertebrae.

Infectious diseases - A possible case of tuberculosis was recorded in the lower thoracic and lumbar vertebrae of skeleton of the young adult female in Grave 6. Because the disease is relatively rare in the Roman period, a detailed description of the lesions observed in the spine is presented below.

The surviving mid to lower thoracic vertebrae have Schmorl's nodes (including some linear ones) on their bodies. The inferior body of T12 and the superior body of L1 exhibit severe destructive lesions: there are multiple large, deep, scalloped erosions that cover the posterior of the vertebral bodies and penetrate over halfway into them. The margins of the bodies remain intact, although the posterior portions of the bodies have been eroded (in addition, there are two smooth-edged hollows in the posterior part of the body of T12). Although there appears to be no proliferation of new bone, the scalloped erosions are smooth and some of the trabecular bone

appears dense and cream in colour, suggesting that there may have been some remodelling of the bone. Two smooth-edged cloacae were recorded, one on the right side of the body of T12 (7.5 mm) and one on the posterior of the body of L1 (5 mm). Unfortunately, the inferior aspect of the body of L1 has been damaged post-mortem and L2 (and ?3) is missing. The two remaining lumbar vertebrae (which are probably L3 & 4 or 4 & 5) also exhibit lesions characteristic of tuberculosis: the articulating inferior/superior bodies show lobulated, destructive cavities (masked slightly by post-mortem erosion) with lumps and hollows that refit. These two vertebrae have also collapsed (wedge-like fractures). In addition, there are irregular deposits of new bone on the anterior parts of the bodies.

Alternative diagnoses of osteomyelitis and brucellosis (known as undulant fever in humans) have been considered. Whilst the cloacae observed in T12 and L1, and the new bone recorded on the posterior of the bodies of the lower lumbar vertebrae, suggest an infection of the bone such as osteomyelitis, the scalloped, destructive cavities are more suggestive of either brucellosis or tuberculosis. In brucellosis, however, the complete collapse of vertebrae and para-vertebral abscesses are rare (Ortner & Putschar 1985, 138–41). In conclusion, the scalloped erosions, their location, the wedged collapse of the vertebral bodies and the lack of involvement of the vertebral arches all suggest a diagnosis of tuberculosis. In a rural community, the infection is likely to be the less virulent bovine form contracted through the intestinal tract from infected milk or meat. During recent excavations nearby at Duxford, a young female with probable TB-related lesions in her spine, dated to the late Iron Age to Early Roman-British period was recorded (Duhig, in Roberts 2003 & Lyons in prep.). Having two individuals dating to the same period and so close by, has interesting implications and supplements the small number of recorded cases of the disease.

Metabolic diseases - Small holes and worm-like lesions, characteristic of cribra orbitalia, were recorded on the orbits of the male skeleton in Grave 17. These are indicative of iron deficiency anaemia.

Trauma - Only fractures to the vertebrae were observed. Two vertebral compression fractures were recorded: one in the spine of a middle adult female in Grave 15 in the cemetery and the other in a mature adult female in isolated Grave 20. Whilst compression or stress fractures are commonly produced by a heavy impact from above or a fall from a height, landing on the feet or buttocks, an underlying disease process may predispose an individual to this type of fracture. Although neither skeleton was diagnosed as having osteoporosis, a condition which usually occurs after the menopause, both the age and sex of the individuals suggests that they may have suffered from this condition, which reduces the bone density and might predispose an individual to a compression fracture with little or no trauma. In Grave 15, the compression fracture of L5 is associated with bilateral spondylolysis and some proliferation of bone, suggestive of soft tissue injuries. In Grave 20, the 4th lumbar vertebra is wedged and has fused to the 5th at the bodies and the articulating processes. Ankylosis of the C2 and C3 vertebrae at the left articulating facets of the skeleton in Grave 10 may have limited the movement of the neck.

Dental disease - The dentitions of 11 adults could be examined and a total of 129 teeth were observed. Five carious lesions were recorded (including three teeth with such large cavities that they survived only as roots). The number of tooth positions observed was 237 and the number of teeth lost ante mortem was 67, which gives a prevalence rate of 28.3%. This figure is considerably higher than the mean tooth-loss in the Romano-British period, which is 14.1% (Roberts & Cox 2003, 135), although other sites with similarly high rates of tooth-loss are known. The high prevalence rate is likely to be the result of the age profile of the sample. Deposits of calculus, mineralized plaque, were recorded on the dentitions of eight adults in the cemetery and enamel hypoplasias, defects in the enamel caused by nutritional deficiencies or childhood illnesses, were recorded on the canines of the skeleton in Grave 12.

Neoplasms - A button osteoma, a common form of benign tumour, was recorded on the frontal bone of the skeleton in Grave 17.

In summary, amongst the inhumation burials, both male and female adults were identified in this small burial group, with all but one skeleton being adult individuals. Mature females dominated the cemetery population by a ratio of over 2:1; there were nine females, four males and two adults who could not be sexed. This contrasts with the burials from the Late Iron Age/Roman cemetery at nearby Duxford where the sex ratio is exactly 2:1 in favour of males (Duhig, in Roberts 2003 & Lyons in prep.). Cultural reasons for the large number of females at the Hutchison Site may account for the difference in ratio observed here or it could merely be an artefact of the small sample number; this issue is further discussed in this chapter's *Concluding Discussion*.

The only young adult identified was a female and the hazards associated with pregnancy and childbirth are often proffered as the reasons for females in this age category dying. This female, however, was also identified as having TB (see above). The only immature skeleton recovered was an infant who was *c.* 4 years old at death. The paucity of immature remains is a common phenomenon in archaeological cemeteries of most periods and explanations usually focus on the fragility of the immature skeleton or on differential burial practices. The presence of the infant demonstrates that immature individuals were interred in this cemetery and indicates that, given the relatively shallow depths of the remaining graves, it is possible that further burials of immature individuals may have been truncated and thus lost. At Duxford, two sub-adults, two infants and a full-term foetus were identified in the contemporary cemetery.

Isolated burials within the settlement

Five isolated burials containing full skeletons were uncovered, three of which occurred within ditches (Fig. 2.18). A sixth individual was also identified, but in a grave that was almost entirely truncated (summary details are presented in Table 2.13). In addition, two pits contained human bone (a mandible and two baby bones respectively).

One inhumation (Grave 20) was uncovered in the butt-end of a Conquest Period ditch. The body was that of an adult female, lying supine, southeast–northwest, with the head to the southeast. Rather than a grave having been excavated, it appeared that the body had simply been placed in a partially silted ditch terminus and then covered with domestic rubbish (pot sherds and animal bone) and soil. The ditch then continued in use and was possibly re-cut, but without disturbing the skeleton. A pot found close to the skeleton may well have been buried with it.

The second ditch burial (Grave 23) occurred in Conquest Period ditch, F.1013. This lay within its own grave cut that was dug below the level of the ditch base. The body was that of a prone adult male, lying north–south, with the head to the north. Although excavation demonstrated that the grave did not cut through the ditch backfill, the grave could either

be fully contemporary with the ditch (having been deliberately dug into the ditch base and backfilled to the same level) or simply predated the ditch and was coincidentally slighted. Given the central position of the grave within the ditch cut and its relative depth, the ditch and the grave were probably contemporary.

A third isolated skeleton was identified in Grave 21; the northern end of this burial cut the Conquest Period ditch F.22. The body was that of a supine young adult male and was aligned northeast–southwest, with the head to the northeast. To the northwest of the cemetery, seemingly sealed by the cobbled surface F.314, lay another burial, Grave 22, which contained a supine adult male aligned east-west with the head to the east.

Grave 25 ([1313]) was only partially uncovered within Evaluation Trench 13 on the western side of the site. Found within a Phase 5 ditch (no cut distinguished), this was the supine burial of an older sub-adult whose head (unexposed) lay eastwards.

The remaining human skeletal material consisted of small amounts of disarticulated or truncated bone. Grave 24, on the western side of the site, was severely truncated and consisted of articulated hands and sternum and skull fragments. On a vaguely north-south alignment with the head to the north, this would have been a prone adult burial. Pit F.37 (Phase 3) contained an adult mandible and pit F.668 two neonate bones (Phase 4).

Of the six inhumations identified outside the cemetery (Graves 20 to 25; Fig. 2.18), five were adult and one was an older sub-adult; of the four where it was possible to attribute sex, three were male. With the exception of the heavily truncated/disturbed skeleton in Grave 24, which is represented only by the hands and fragments of torso and skull, the isolated burials are generally well preserved.

Details regarding the age and sex of the isolated burial populace are presented in Table 2.14 below. Stature could be calculated for four individuals. The lone female was 1.59 m (5'2") tall (calculated using only the femur). The male range (*n* = 3) using all methods was 1.70–1.74 m (5'6"–5'8") with a mean height of 1.72 m (5'7"), which is somewhat higher than the males buried in the cemetery.

Osteoarthritic changes were recorded in two of the isolated burials (the female in Grave 20 and the male in Grave 23) and, as in the cemetery, the spine was the most common area of the skeleton to be affected. When the hands were affected, the condition was recorded in both the left and the right.

Of the non-cemetery interments (*n* = 6), four dentitions could be examined and a total of 104 teeth observed. A single carious lesion was recorded. The number of tooth positions observed was 121 and the number of teeth lost ante-mortem was four, which gives a prevalence rate of 3.31%, far lower than the mean for the period (Roberts & Cox 2003) and that recorded in the cemetery.

Disarticulated human bone was recovered from three features (F.37, F.42 & F.668). The mandible of a younger middle adult (25–35 years) male was recovered from a large pit, F.37, together with slag, scored pottery and a large stone. This mandible exhibited a possible abscess, calculus and hypoplasias. An adult right tibia shaft and a fragment of parietal bone were recovered from the upper fill of a large north–south boundary ditch (F.42). It may be that the bones derive from the cemetery, which lies approximately 20 m to the

TABLE 2.13. *Summary data of isolated burials (NSPI = Non-specific periosteal infection), AMTL = Ante-mortem tooth loss).*

Grave no.	Feature/ Context no.	Age	Sex	Stature	Pathology and morphological variation	Orientation	Body position	Location
20	F.23 [1433]	Mature adult	Female	1.59	OA in spine, r. elbow, l & r. hands, compression fracture of L4, calculus	E–W	Supine, l. leg & arm flexed	Basal fill of ditch butt
21	F.687 [1915]	Young adult	Male	1.72	NSPI, Schmorl's nodes, calculus	NNE–SSW	Supine, arms & right leg flexed. Squashed into grave	Grave cuts ditch
22	F.752 [952]	Younger middle adult	Male	1.74	Incipient joint disease in spine, calculus, metopism	E–W	Supine, left leg & both arms flexed. Squashed into grave	Parallel to enclosure ditch ?below cobbles
23	F.1050 [3941]	Mature adult	Male	1.7	OA in spine, r. wrist, l. hip and knee, AMTL, caries, calculus	N–S	Prone, squashed into grave	Grave within ditch
24	F.1162 [4089]	adult	?	?	None observed	N–S	?Prone, v. truncated	4 m east of ditch
25	[1313]	?older subadult	?	?	None observed	E–W	Supine	Body in ditch; identified in Evaluation Trench 13 (not excavated)

TABLE 2.14. *Population summary for isolated burials (inhumations).*

	Female	?	Male	Total
mature	1	0	1	2
older mid/mature	0	0	0	0
older middle	0	0	0	0
middle	0	0	0	0
younger middle	0	0	1	1
young	0	0	1	1
adult	0	1	0	1
sub-adult	0	1	0	1
infant	0	0	0	0
Total	1	2	3	6

south. Two neonate bones (a right humerus and a left tibia) were recovered from a large pit, F.668. They were not identified as human on site and the feature was only half-sectioned. It is therefore not possible to determine whether these remains were actually disarticulated or only a partially excavated interment.

In addition to the F.166 later Bronze Age cremation discussed above, two other features (lying outside of the cemetery) also produced burnt bone fragments, F.344 and F.1061; the latter was definitely of Iron Age attribution. However, as they respectively only yielded 1 and 2 g of burnt material, it was impossible to positively identity whether this was human or animal.

Discussion

As detailed above, a total of 22 inhumations and three definite cremation burials were identified during the excavations; six of the inhumations were located outside the main cemetery area. The three cremation burials were well-dated to the latter part of the first century AD by their associated pottery vessels and (in the case of Grave 2) two copper-alloy brooches. The dating of the inhumations is more uncertain. While Grave 12 is clearly contemporary (dated by its associated pottery beaker), as must also be Grave 11 (it is cut by Grave 12), the others have no independent dating evidence. The common alignment of Graves 10, 13–17 and (at a slight remove) Grave 6 might also suggest that these are contemporary.

The inhumations can also be assessed for any traits of typically later Roman burial traditions, which may help to shed light on the cemetery chronology. Such traditions might include the use of wooden coffins, the inclusion of hobnailed footwear in the grave, and the deposition of personal accessories (either worn or placed with the body). All of these would typically date to the later second century AD or later (see Philpott 1991 for an overview). At the Hutchison Site's cemetery, only one definite instance of one of these traits was seen: the deposition of copper-alloy rings and a bracelet fragment with the flexed adult female in Grave 15, although the copper-alloy pin fragment with the older infant in Grave 9 may also have been a grave-good. However, while burials with bracelets or rings are more common in the fourth century than earlier, their presence is consistently seen (though in low numbers) at later Iron Age and Roman rural sites (Philpott 1991, 144). Their presence here in Grave 15 does not, therefore, offer any firm dating evidence and the objects themselves are not intrinsically dateable.

While formal prone burial (within a defined cemetery area as here) becomes more common in the fourth century (Philpott 1991, 73), its association here with a burial firmly dated to the later first century indicates that it saw sporadic earlier usage, and cannot be used to assign a later date in this instance. Moreover, there are no coffined burials (indeed, most of the burials are so tightly packed into the confines of the grave that there would have been no space for one), and there are no hobnails present. These are distinctly later traits at most other Roman rural cemeteries (Philpott 1991, 167), and their absence at the Hutchison Site may add further weight to the argument for the inhumations here being largely contemporary with the later first-century cremations.

The co-existence of inhumation and cremation burial traditions in the early Roman period is a phenomenon that has been recognized for some time in the region (Fox & Lethbridge 1925, 62). From recent excavations nearby at Hinxton and Duxford (Hill *et al.* 1999; Lyons in prep.), poorly furnished inhumation burials have been recorded, the latter having been radiocarbon-dated to the period between 100 BC and AD 200. At Wallington Road in Baldock, while cremation became the exclusive rite used by the end of the first century AD, it was preceded by a largely unfurnished inhumation tradition; like the Hutchison's burials these too had a largely northeast–southwest or southeast–northwest orientation (Pearce 1999, 67). A similar early Roman inhumation tradition has been identified in the Wiltshire/northern Somerset/Avon area (Pearce 1999, 133), and the cemeteries of London, too, have a high proportion of early inhumation burials (Pearce 1999, 139). Regional sub-traditions in burial practice must, therefore, be considered when discussing the development of Roman funerary rites.

What relationship did the cemetery, and the isolated burials, have with the settlement? The cemetery itself clearly lies outside the settlement enclosure system, but immediately adjacent to it. The dominance within this population of older females may suggest that this area was therefore reserved for burial of only a certain section of the settlement population. Until further comparative sites are published, the social significance of the general lack of grave furnishing must remain uncertain. The more elaborate furnishing of the cremations represents a more normative practice at this point in the Roman period, although it may still be interesting that the majority of the grave-goods were reserved for the youngest cremated individual in Grave 2. The placing of 'isolated' burials in or adjacent to ditches is a well documented phenomenon and it is significant that the majority of the isolated graves at the Hutchison Site are associated with boundary ditches to the settlement enclosure (Graves 20, 21, 23 & 24), with three placed close to entranceways.

Pottery kilns

A total of eleven kilns were recovered across the site (Figs. 2.23–2.26). These were mostly found at the margins of the main Conquest Period enclosure, and all probably relate to that phase. The kilns represent six distinct types (A–F), often with sub-distinctions within these groups. Two of the kilns were constructed but evidently never used. Five other features remain possible candidates as kilns, but lacked either the form or fill to confirm a definite classification. Spatially, the kiln-types showed no sign of clustering or grouping together but, with the exception of F.63, all were built along the extremities of the major rectangular Conquest Period enclosure system, and were relatively well-spaced (Fig. 2.23). Where a direct relationship existed between the kilns and the ditch system (e.g. F.340 and F.1181, both of which utilized the ditch backfill for the digging of a stokehole), it was evident that the kilns were constructed when the Phase 4 ditches were largely silted-up and only a hollow or minor re-cut still existed. Kiln F.63 lay almost in the centre of the main enclosure system, and appeared to be contemporary with some of the minor internal enclosures. The orientation of the kilns varied greatly, but favoured an opening to the east.

Type A

Two kilns fell within this category, F.63 and F.1117 (Figs. 2.24 & 2.25), and although displaying marked differences in internal structure, both were obviously products of the same tradition. Each was distinguished by a large, clay-lined central chamber with complex integral supports and a tunnel-flue at both ends leading to large stoking pits (Swan 1984, 117–20). Both lay on a broadly northwest–southeast alignment, and were backfilled with large quantities of ash, pottery and fired clay collapse from the superstructure. Individually, F.63 contained two elongated central pedestal shelves and six symmetrical pilasters. F.1117 had only one central elongated pedestal with a smaller pedestal added to the western end, and six symmetrical pilasters. In addition, F.1117 had two small entranceways excavated adjacent to the western opening, possibly representing side flues. The two kilns in Type A are identical in their basic form to kiln F.238 at Greenhouse Farm (Fig. 2.54; Gibson & Lucas 2002, 99–100). The type, otherwise, seems to be fairly unusual within a regional context (Swan 1984, map 12).

Type B

Three kilns fell within this type, F.340 (Fig. 2.24), F.786 and F.1181 (Fig. 2.25). All were, at least partially, clay-lined with a central pedestal in the main chamber, and opened towards the east *via* a narrow flue that led to an unlined stoking pit of comparable size to the main chamber. Kiln F.786 had not been used, and contained no material from a collapsed roof, suggesting that the structure was never completed. Certainly the base of the kiln had been lined with white clay, but not the sides or the tunnel-flue. The remaining two kilns had been used, and both were backfilled with large amounts

FIGURE 2.23. *Kiln Locations: 1) Hutchison Site; 2) Greenhouse Farm, Cambridge (after Gibson & Lucas 2002).*

of ash, pot and structural collapse. Worth noting is that the stoke pits of all three were excavated into the backfill of earlier ditches, probably in part utilizing the hollow still in existence, while the main chamber was excavated into predominantly virgin ground. F.340 was the most distinctive of the group, having a much wider flue and flared sides (possibly accidentally so). F.1181 had been partially re-dug after going out of use, a pit being excavated into the stokehole until the tunnel-flue was exposed, and the body of an adolescent cow being placed in the pit, with its head through the tunnel and lying in the main chamber (Fig. 2.27). This burial had seemingly taken place before the superstructure collapsed, for pieces of roof collapse were found overlying the animal's head.

Type C
Type C consisted of an individual kiln of classic dumb-bell shape, which would have been included in Type B except for the absence of a central pedestal. Kiln F.1119 (Fig. 2.26) was lined with white clay but completely unfired, with no kiln waste or debris in its backfill. No evidence of a collapsed superstructure existed, suggesting that the feature was never completed, which may also explain the absence of a pedestal. However, there were two very close parallels to this kiln at Greenhouse Farm (Group 4), both unpedestalled and of a comparable size (see also White 1964a, 14 for an example of the same from War Ditches).

Type D
Two kilns were included as Type D: F.626 (Fig. 2.24) and F.1078 (Fig. 2.26). Although their main chambers were very similar to Type B, both had an elongated flue but no surviving stoke pit. Both were, however, severely truncated and there was no reason to assume that the stoke pit was significantly higher than the main chamber.

F.1078 was clay-lined with a central pedestal, and had been dug into the top of a large, amorphous feature probably representing a tree-throw. F.626 was not clay-lined, but had a central clay pedestal. However, this pedestal ([1701]) was slightly off-centre, and a second pedestal was present ([1700]), asymmetrically placed at the rear of the north wall. Pedestal [1700] was not as well-fired as [1701], and may represent a collapsed side pedestal. Both of these kilns lay on the western edge of F.19/1053, but their flues were pointing in opposite directions, F.626 towards the east and, F.1078, westward. Significant quantities of kiln waste from F.626 had been deposited in the upper fill of F.19. It would appear that it was a kiln of this type that Lethbridge found at the War Ditches in 1939 (Lethbridge 1948, 124, pl. XII).

Type E
Kiln Type E included two adjacent kilns, F.1077 and F.1254, both sharing the same stoking area, F.1255 (Figs. 2.24 & 2.26). Neither was clay-lined, although both had a central pedestal of fired clay. A later re-cut of F.1255 had obliterated any stratigraphic sequence between the two, but a direct parallel to this double-kiln form was present at Greenhouse Farm (F.309/310; Fig. 2.54) and it seems generally comparable to the arrangement of Kilns 1–3 at Longthorpe (Dannell & Wild 1987, 35–41, fig. 8). Given their 'individuality' (only one other kiln, F.626, was not clay-lined), their use of the same stoking area, and the existence of parallels elsewhere, it is likely that the kilns were fully contemporary, rather than successive. The pottery firing process may account for the doubling of the kilns, the one being packed/built while the first cooled after firing (R. Jefferies pers. comm.). The reason for re-cutting the stoke pit/s once the kilns had gone out of use is obscure. However, a still recognizable stoke pit backfilled with kiln waste would have provided a ready and

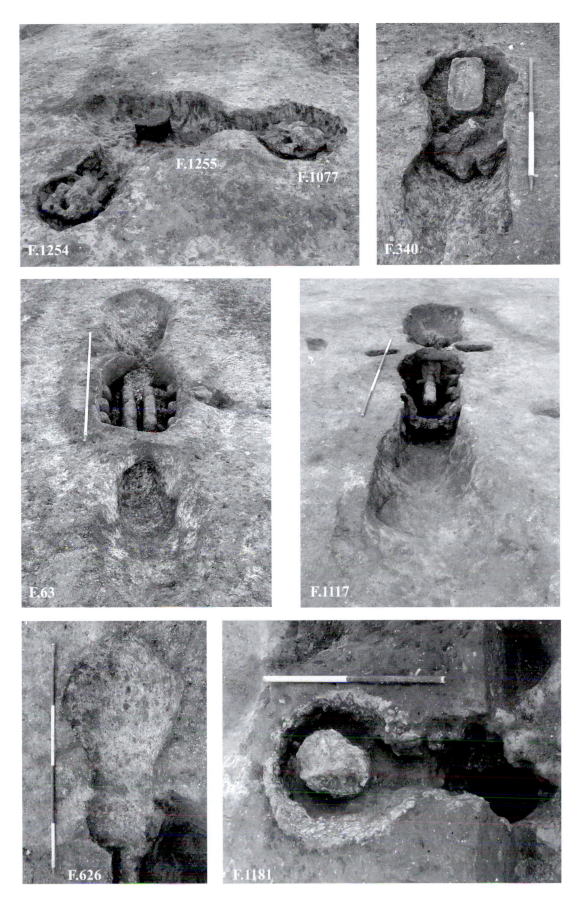

FIGURE 2.24. *Selected Pottery Kilns.*

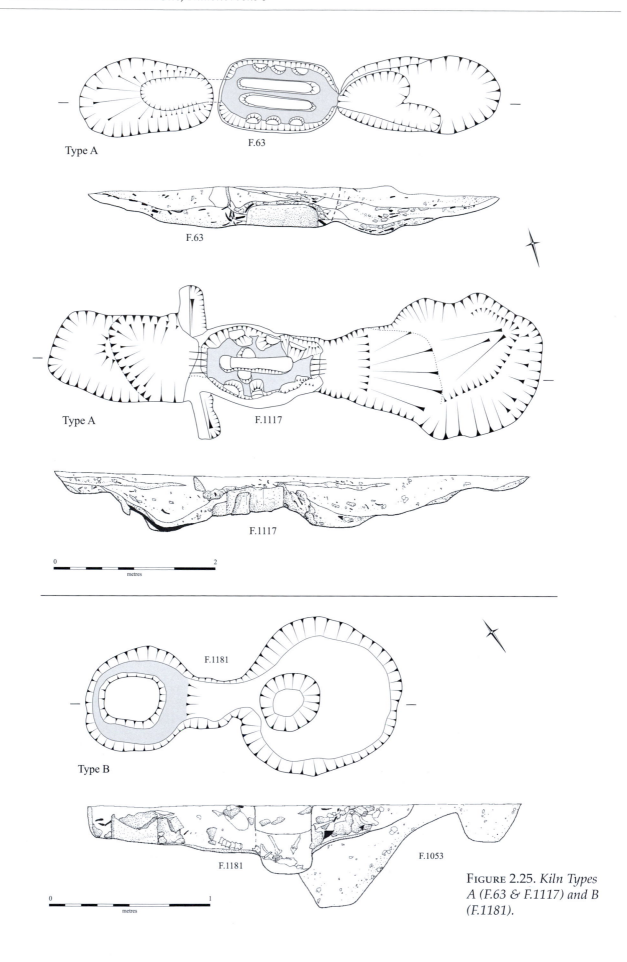

FIGURE 2.25. *Kiln Types A (F.63 & F.1117) and B (F.1181).*

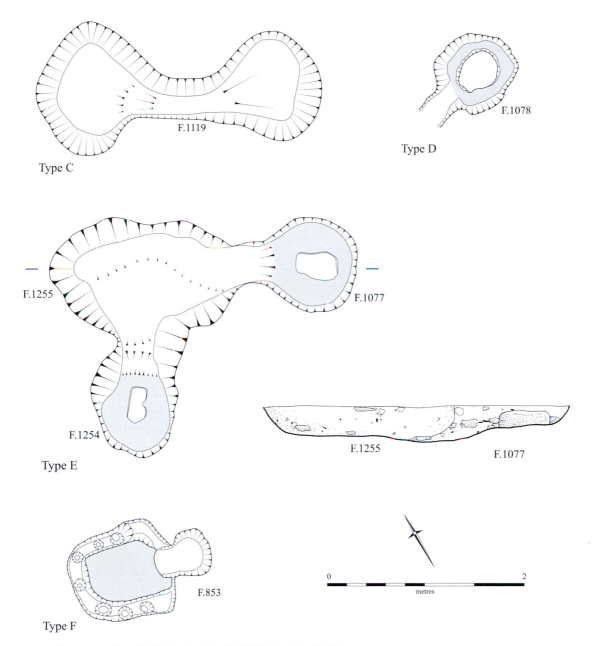

Type C

Type D

F.1119

F.1078

F.1255

F.1077

F.1254

F.1255

F.1077

Type E

Type F

F.853

0 metres 2

Figure 2.26. *Kiln Types C–F (F.1119, F.1078, F.1077/1254 & F.853).*

easily extracted supply of pottery wasters from which to produce grog for further pottery production.

Type F

The single kiln of this type, F.853, lay on the western edge of the site. It had been severely truncated during car-park construction works, and was also significantly rooted/burrowed (Fig. 2.26). Consisting of a sub-rectangular chamber with an eastward facing flue, several intercutting pits (F.854) provided a stoking area and kiln waste disposal dumps. What remained of the kiln was clay-lined, with a possible clay shelf to either side of the flue, and probable stake-holes around the sides and rear of the chamber. A shallow pit on the western end of the kiln was also seemingly related to it, but no flue linked the two, and the feature had been almost entirely truncated. The stoking and refuse pits on the eastern side were more deeply cut, and produced a large amount of pottery.

Others

Two further features can also be put forward as possible kiln candidates: F.636 and F.680, pits in the northwest area of the site, both contained a large amount of pottery and burnt material. Of particular interest was a flue-like extension at one end of F.636, but the cut was so shallow that natural disturbance could not be ruled out. Perhaps a more likely interpretation of both features is that of pits backfilled with kiln waste.

All of the above features fall broadly within the category of 'Belgic'-type early Romano-British kilns as defined by Swan (1984). The structure and orientation of the kilns is discussed here; further aspects of their use are considered below in relation to the baked clay and kiln furniture.

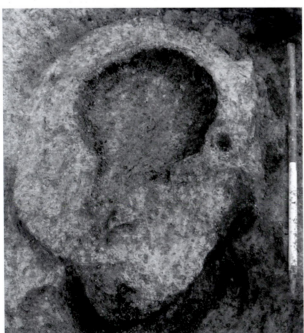

FIGURE 2.27. *Top, cow remains in kiln F.1181; bottom, oven F.783.*

The orientation of the kilns varied greatly, but generally favoured an opening to the east. This is in direct contrast to Greenhouse Farm (see Fig. 2.23), *c.* 5 km to the northeast, which produced the only directly comparable and contemporary kiln group in the region (Gibson & Lucas 2002), where a west-facing opening was dominant. It is difficult to ascribe this reversal to a difference in the prevailing winds, which at a distance of only 5 km, with no major geological features close by to channel the wind, would undoubtedly have been in the same direction. Interestingly, the two most intricately constructed kilns, F.63 and F.1117, had double-openings, and F.1117 also had small side flues, potentially enabling the potters to exploit any change in the wind direction. The double-opening was also present in the most complex of the Greenhouse Farm kilns. This raises the possibility that the smaller kilns were intended for use over only a very short period, perhaps only a matter of days, and were, therefore, built to favour the wind direction at the time of construction. This might even account for the two unused kilns having been abandoned in the face of a changing wind, and also for the striking difference in alignment represented on the two sites.

The second most notable difference between the Hutchison Site and Greenhouse Farm kiln groups is the presence in the former's kilns of a central pedestal shelf (or variation of) in all but one of the kilns (F.1119, which was unfired and therefore possibly incomplete). Other than this distinction, the main kiln types are remarkably similar, particularly F.63, which was to all intents and purposes identical to Greenhouse Farm Group 2. Although, over such a short distance, the possibility of the same individuals constructing the kilns on both sites cannot be ruled out, the distinctions are perhaps great enough to suggest that the individual settlements were creating their own variants within the same basic tradition, tailoring each group to the particular conditions and needs of the site.

The location of the kilns, at the margins of the Conquest Period ditch system with the stokeholes in some cases placed in its partially silted-up ditches, seems to be typical of the period. It can be paralleled elsewhere in Cambridgeshire at War Ditches (Lethbridge 1948), Greenhouse Farm (Gibson & Lucas 2002), Longthorpe (Dannell & Wild 1987) and Haddon (Hinman 2003).

Oven

Lying within Enclosure M1 was a small keyhole-shaped oven, F.783 (Figs. 2.23 & 2.27). This consisted of a dump of clay within a hollow which had been moulded to form a circular chamber, 0.56 m in diameter, with a short northwest-facing flue, 0.18 m long. The oven chamber survived to 0.14 m deep, and would presumably have originally been enclosed by a domed superstructure. Two soft rectangular bricks revetted the exterior of the oven wall. The interior of the chamber showed signs of firing and contained a black, burnt fill. Keyhole-shaped ovens have often been interpreted as corn-dryers, but the small example here is more likely to have been used for domestic-scale baking. The environmental sample from the oven contained only sparse plant remains that gave little clue of its function.

Pitting hollows

As indicated on Figure 2.4, a number of the site's pits yielded no direct dating evidence and cannot, therefore, be confidently assigned to any phase. There was a marked concentration of these in the northeastern corner of Enclosure J, where, in fact, the eastern length of its northern ditch truncated a large irregular 'pitting hollow' (and which just extended north into the southeastern corner of Enclosure L). Although given the intensity of their intercutting (and that the excavation constantly flooded at that point) it proved impossible to satisfactorily distinguish individual features and determine their function, it is likely that they related to either the puddling of clay and/or its extraction and, thereby, could have been associated with the site's pottery production.

Equally, in this context the ambiguity of the F.650 (*et al.*) quarry hollows should also be remembered (Fig. 2.6). While assigned to the site's later Bronze Age on the basis of the pottery recovered from them, by the intensity and scale of their cutting, and also the roughly straight alignment of their southern sides (running parallel with the Phase 4 ditch system), a Conquest Period-association still has to be suspected.

Artefact studies

Iron Age coins (ADRIAN POPESCU)

Small Find No. 1 - Uninscribed British Class II potin coin. Obverse: head left, plain border; reverse: 'bull' left, above two crescents, below pellet, plain border. Cu/Sn cast bronze II, weight 1.43 g. Second half of first century BC (cf. BMCIA 715).

Small Find No. 17 - Late Iron Age Catuvellaunian copper-alloy coin. Northern bronze, inscribed 'RVES', attributed to Tasciovanus. Obverse: bearded head right, before [...], border?; reverse: horse right with helmeted rider, before VII, pellet border. AE unit VIII, weight 1.89 g. Second half of first century BC. cf. BMCIA 1700.

Small Find No. 23 - Badly corroded copper-alloy coin, 15 mm diameter. Possibly Late Iron Age.

Small Find No. 64 - Late Iron Age silver coin. Icenian Pattern/Horse type, reverse ECE, EDN or Symbol.

Small Find No. 88 - Late Iron Age copper-alloy quarter stater. Possibly a contemporary forgery of Cunobelin, North Thames *c.* 10-40 AD (cf. *BMCIA* 1850).

Late Iron Age and Roman Pottery
(LEO WEBLEY, *with* KATIE ANDERSON)

The excavations at the Hutchison and at the adjacent Day-Care Centre Sites between them produced a very substantial assemblage of Late Iron Age and Romano-British period pottery, totalling 20,876 sherds (273.3 kg) or 163.61 EVEs. All of the material has been examined, and details of form and fabric recorded on the basis of rim EVEs. Table 2.15 shows the quantities of material for each phase, with a category for material which could not be easily defined as either Phase 4 or Phase 5.

Fabrics

A key issue for this assemblage is determining which elements of it were produced in the kilns on site. Care is needed here, as cracked or warped sherds can result from secondary burning or reflect the use of 'seconds' made off-site. For this analysis, only those wares incontrovertibly made on site have been designated as kiln fabrics. The main source of evidence is the large dumps of pottery from kilns F.63 and F.1117, which are dominated by a single fabric group and contain numerous certain wasters (cracked, spalled or fused together). The kiln wares form 37% of the total assemblage, though the proportion is much higher for Phase 4 contexts (Table 2.16). The bulk of the rest of the assemblage consists of generic sandy wares that cannot be sourced to specific production sites. These form a spectrum rather than falling into clearly distinct types, and hence they have been allocated to broad fabric *groups* for the purposes of this analysis. It is entirely possible that a significant amount of this material was also made on site, as the inclusion *types* are largely the same as for the kiln wares, although their relative proportions and the conditions of firing differ. The stated quantity of kiln wares should thus be taken as the *minimum* possible level of pottery made on-site. It is also important with this assemblage to assess how the material fits into the local area, in terms of production and consump-

TABLE 2.15. *Late Iron Age and Roman pottery by site-phase.*

Phase	No.	%	Wt (g)	%
Phase 3	3091	14.8	36,304	13.3
Phase 4	9876	47.3	163,366	59.7
Phase 5	1751	8.4	22,558	8.3
Mid–late 1st AD	6158	29.5	51,100	18.7
TOTAL	**20,876**	**100**	**273,328**	**100**

TABLE 2.16. *Late Iron Age and Roman Pottery: fabrics by phase.*

	Phase 3 LIA (%)	Phase 4 settlement/ enclosure (%)	Phase 5 settlement (%)
LIA	83.6	4.7	1.1
Romanizing	16.4	19.4	2.6
Kiln	0	31.8	5.2.1
Greywares	0	9.0	46.0
RB Coarse	0	33.4	19.1
RB Fine	0	1.7	26.0

tion. A number of Late Iron Age/Early Roman sites are known in the area, including Cherry Hinton War Ditches, a little under 5 km northeast, which have kilns dating to the Early Roman period and are, therefore, comparable with the Hutchison's.

In all, 27 fabric groups have been distinguished, listed below. The distinction between Late Iron Age and 'Romanizing' types, and between 'Romanizing' and Romano-British types, must necessarily be somewhat arbitrary, as there is no generally agreed definition of where these boundaries should be placed. Here, the term 'Romanizing' is simply used to identify a set of fabric groups that seem to occupy a transitional position *at this one particular site* between those wares clearly within an Iron Age tradition and those which clearly represent something different. Of the sourced, non-local Romano-British wares, all come from East Anglia or the southeast Midlands. There is only a tiny amount of imported material, of Gaulish and Catalan manufacture (0.1% by EVEs).

Fabric series

Fabrics marked with an asterisk are represented by body or base sherds only. It should be noted that the distinction between Late Iron Age and 'Romanizing' wares, and that between 'Romanizing' and Roman wares, is to some extent arbitrary with a good deal of overlap.

Late Iron Age types
Q1　LIA Sandy Wares
　　Moderate–common fine to medium quartz. Sparser fine–coarse chalk, ferrous or flint inclusions often present. Generally reduced and fairly hard. Handmade and wheelmade.
GR　LIA Grog-tempered Wares
　　Moderate–common medium grog, sparse fine quartz. Generally reduced and of moderate hardness, often with a soapy feel. Handmade and wheelmade.
VG　LIA Vegetable-tempered Ware
　　Moderate voids from vegetable inclusions. Oxidized, fairly soft. Handmade.
SH1　LIA Shelly Wares
　　Moderate fine–medium shell inclusions. Reduced, hard. Handmade. Probably non-local, deriving from a Jurassic clay source.

'Romanizing' types
PGW 'Proto-greywares'
　　Moderate fine to medium quartz. Chalk, iron or flint inclusions often also present. Grey fabric with buff or brown-grey surfaces, hard. Wheelmade or rarely handmade.
Q2　Romanizing Coarse Reduced Sandy Wares
　　Broad grouping of coarse wares with moderate-common medium quartz, and often sparser quantities of fine–coarse chalk, ferrous or flint inclusions. Brown-black, often with a sandwich-fired effect with the surfaces lighter than the core, and sometimes with a reddish tinge to the margins. Generally hard. Wheelmade or rarely handmade.
Q3　Romanizing Fine Reduced Ware 1
　　Moderate fine quartz, sparse fine–medium chalk. Mid brown surfaces and black core, hard. Wheelmade.
Q4　Romanizing Fine Reduced Ware 2
　　Moderate fine–medium quartz, sparse fine chalk. Orange-brown surfaces and black core, hard. Wheelmade.

Kiln wares
K　Kiln Fabric
　　Moderate medium quartz, common to very common silver mica, sparse fine–medium iron oxide, rare medium–coarse chalk. Moderate hardness, often with a powdery surface. Oxidized, bright orange to buff. Sometimes has a white

slip to the exterior (0.90 EVEs). Wheelmade or rarely handmade.

Romano-British Coarsewares
Q5　Generic Coarse Reduced Sandy Wares
　　Broad grouping of coarse wares of Romanized appearance with moderate to common fine–medium quartz, and often also sparser quantities of fine–coarse chalk and/or ferrous inclusions. Soft to hard. Often with a rough feel due to surface quartz grains. Wheelmade or rarely handmade.
Q6　Generic Coarse Oxidized Sandy Wares
　　As above, but oxidized to a buff colour. Wheelmade or rarely handmade.
GW　Greywares
　　Moderate fine–medium quartz. Fabric pale–medium grey throughout, hard with a relatively fine fracture. Wheelmade or rarely handmade.
SH2　South Midlands Shelly Ware
　　Common coarse fossil shell. Generally oxidized to a deep orange or red, hard. Probably originates in the Northamptonshire/Bedfordshire area. Exclusively associated with channel-rim jars. Handmade and wheelmade.
WAT Wattisfield Reduced Ware
　　A wheelmade, medium grey, highly micaceous ware (cf. Tomber & Dore 1998, 184).

Romano-British Finewares (all hard and wheelmade)
FW1 Generic fine reduced wares
　　Broad grouping of finewares with sparse–moderate fine quartz and occasionally sparse fine chalk.
FW2 Generic Fine Oxidized Wares
　　As above, but oxidized.
M1　Fine Reduced Micaceous Ware 1
　　Moderate fine quartz and moderate fine–medium silver mica. Pink fabric with grey surfaces.
M2　Fine Reduced Micaceous Ware 2
　　Moderate fine quartz and moderate fine silver mica. Dark grey fabric.
M3　Fine Oxidized Micaceous Ware
　　Moderate fine quartz and sparse fine silver mica. Orange fabric.
M4　Fine Micaceous Greyware
　　Moderate fine quartz, moderate silver mica, sparse medium chalk, rare medium black ferrous inclusions. Pale grey fabric, hard. Exclusively associated with 'London ware'-style bowls.
CH　Cherry Hinton Ware
　　Fine–medium quartz and chalk. Oxidized, ranging from pinkish white to orange. Exclusively associated with barbotine-decorated beakers (cf. J. Evans 1990; Lucas 1999).
PK　Pakenham Mica-dusted Ware*
　　Micaceous orange-brown ware with gold mica dusting (cf. Tomber & Dore 1998, 182–3).
WW　White Ware*
　　Unsourced white ware with moderate fine–medium quartz and sparse fine red ferrous inclusions.

Imports
SGS　South Gaulish Samian
CGS　Central Gaulish Samian
NGW North Gaulish white ware*
AM　Catalan amphora*

Forms

The identifiable rim sherds have each been assigned to one of eighteen form categories, as follows:

	Form	Hand-/Wheelmade
J	Jars/deep bowls, medium-sized (10–30 cm rim diameter)	hm & wm
J1	Necked jars/bowls, plain	hm & wm
J2	Necked jars/bowls, cordoned/rippled shoulder	hm & wm
J3	Necked jars/bowls, rilled	hm & wm
J4	Narrow-necked jars/flasks	hm & wm
J5	Ovoid neckless jars	hm & wm
J6	Channel-rimmed jars	hm & wm
J7	Handmade Middle Iron Age-type jars/bowls	hm
Jx	Jars, rim only	hm & wm
S	Large, necked storage jars (>30 cm rim diameter)	hm & wm
C	Cups/miniature jars (<10 cm rim diameter)	wm
O	Coarse open bowls/dishes	hm & wm
D	Fine open bowls/dishes	wm
Z	Pedestal bowls	wm
P	Platters	wm
B	Butt beakers	wm
K	Other beakers	wm
F	Flagons	wm
M	Mortaria	wm
L	Lids	wm

Wheel-thrown sherds account for 90% of the Late Iron Age and early Roman pottery, based on minimum number of vessels and not including sherds for which manufacturing-type was unclear. Handmade vessels account for just 10% of the identifiable wares; however, it is interesting to note that for Phase 3, handmade wares represent 41% whist 59% of vessels from this period were wheel-made (Table 2.17).

The large percentage of wheelmade vessels is closely linked with the dominance in the assemblage of the kilns' products. However it is worth noting that two handmade vessels in the kiln fabric were found in F.593 and F.806, thus highlighting the fact that the tradition of making vessels by hand had not been completely usurped by the wheel. Overall, kiln products represented 37% of the total assemblage. Table 2.18 shows the vessel forms by phase, while in Table 2.19 the relationships between form and fabric are shown.

Phase 3 (c. 50 bc–ad 50)

The 17.01 EVEs of pottery found in the Late Iron Age enclosure system and associated pits form 10% of the total assemblage. The majority of the material (59%) is wheel-thrown or wheel-finished. Sandy fabrics predominate over grog-tempered fabrics, as commonly seen elsewhere in Late Iron Age south Cambridgeshire (Thompson 1982, 17). However, the incidence of grog-tempering is much higher for handmade wares (33%) than for wheelmade wares (9%). There are some pits that stand out for their relatively high proportions of handmade, grog-tempered wares (e.g. F.1061; see Fig. 2.28:4-6), and it would be tempting to suggest that these are

Table 2.17. *Late Iron Age and Roman Pottery: Proportion of wheelmade wares.*

Phase	% Wheelmade/finished (by EVEs)
3	59.1
4	95.7
5	98.7

early in the sequence, with a shift towards wheelmade sandy wares occurring later. However, the available stratigraphic relationships cannot prove this either way.

Handmade 'slack-shouldered' bowls and jars in the Middle Iron Age tradition are uncommon in the assemblage. They are likely to be contemporary with the Late Iron Age-style material rather than representing a separate earlier phase. Two vessels carry combing or scoring, one also with a row of fingertip impressions on the shoulder. One further vessel has fingertip impressions along the rim top. No vessels with curvilinear La Tène style decoration were found to match the example from Cra'ster's (1969) excavations, although there is one burnished globular bowl decorated with incised lines and small impressed dots (F.855; Fig. 2.28:1).

Medium jars/necked bowls form the overwhelming majority of the assemblage, and burnt food residues show that these were often used for cooking. These vessels frequently have cordoned or rippled shoulders, and handmade examples often have chevrons or diagonal meshes of burnished or lightly incised lines on their lower body, a feature paralleled at Castle Hill, Cambridge (Alexander & Pullinger 2000, pl. XLIV, 137). One other medium necked jar carries irregular scoring or combing. Large necked storage jars also occur, and typically have arced or vertical combing on the body.

Although jar bases are typically flat, two base sherds show that 'pedestal urns' were also present. Other vessel forms are restricted to imitation butt beakers and a single open bowl. The butt beakers are all in 'Romanizing' fabrics and carry combed or rouletted decoration. They are typically fairly crude and in some cases resemble butt beaker/jar hybrids.

The pottery from this phase tends to be relatively fragmented and incomplete when compared to the later material. However, a few contexts stand out as different by containing deposits of substantially complete necked jars/bowls, accompanied by little or no other pottery. These are F.1053 (two vessels: Fig. 2.28:2–3), F.1061 (three vessels: Fig. 2.28:4–6), F.1200 (two vessels: Fig. 2.28:7–8) and F.1109 (one vessel: Fig. 2.28:9). Clearly, these contexts show the operation of depositional practices that differed from the norm at this site, and which can perhaps be viewed as 'structured'.

Four of these relatively complete jars, along with one further example from Phase 4, have post-firing perforations drilled through their base (F.782, F.1053, F.1061, F.1109 and F.1200). There are up to four perforations per vessel, and they measure 6–10 mm in diameter. One vessel has internal burnt food residues, and the perforations were thus perhaps made subsequent to its use in cooking. Fulford & Timby (2001) discuss drilled bases from other Late Iron Age and Romano-British sites, considering the possibility of ritual 'killings' of pots, but concluding that they probably had a functional purpose. Two points can be made about the Hutchison's examples. Firstly, drilled bases are restricted to Late Iron Age and Romanizing wares, and vessels with pre-firing perforations (e.g. colanders or cheese presses) are absent from the whole assemblage. Thus, if perforated vessels had a functional purpose, it was one that became obsolete following the Conquest. Secondly, it is notable that all five of these vessels were deposited relatively complete. A deposit of a complete perforated vessel very similar to Figure 2.28:3 also occurred in a ditch at Castle Hill, Cambridge (Alexander & Pullinger 2000, fig. 2.2.6). Such apparently selective depositional practices raise the

TABLE 2.18. *Pottery forms by Phase.*

Phase	LIA		Rom 1		Rom 1 63		Rom 1 117		Cemetery		Rom 2 enc		Rom 2 sett		Residual		Total	
Form	EVE	%	EVE	%	EVE	%	EVE	%	EVE	%	EVE	%	EVE	%	EVE	%	EVE	%
J	15.66	92.1	61.91	84.1	14.25	67.6	15.63	85.5	1.19	21.5	2.16	68.6	13.77	57.4	0.82	91.1	125.39	76.6
J1	4.69	27.6	14.66	19.9	0.40	1.9	0.39	2.1	1.00	18.1	0.40	12.7	3.70	15.4	0.00	0.0	25.24	15.4
J2	6.91	40.6	6.90	9.4	5.34	25.3	3.39	18.5	0.07	1.3	0.52	16.5	2.23	9.3	0.19	21.1	25.55	15.6
J3	0.21	1.2	11.26	15.3	2.81	13.3	3.62	19.8	0.00	0.0	0.00	0.0	1.34	5.6	0.17	18.9	19.41	11.9
J4	1.25	7.3	1.26	1.7	1.34	6.4	0.55	3.0	0.00	0.0	0.00	0.0	0.92	3.8	0.00	0.0	5.32	3.3
J5	0.55	3.2	0.52	0.7	0.00	0.0	0.00	0.0	0.00	0.0	0.06	1.9	0.00	0.0	0.00	0.0	1.13	0.7
J6	0.00	0.0	0.42	0.6	0.00	0.0	0.00	0.0	0.00	0.0	0.00	0.0	0.49	2.0	0.00	0.0	0.91	0.6
J7	0.39	2.3	0.10	0.1	0.00	0.0	0.00	0.0	0.00	0.0	0.00	0.0	0.00	0.0	0.00	0.0	0.49	0.3
Jx	1.66	9.8	26.79	36.4	4.36	20.7	7.68	42.0	0.12	2.2	1.18	37.5	5.09	21.2	0.46	51.1	47.34	28.9
S	0.42	2.5	2.75	3.7	0.97	4.6	0.27	1.5	0.00	0.0	0.43	13.7	0.14	0.6	0.00	0.0	4.98	3.0
C	0.00	0.0	1.22	1.7	0.00	0.0	0.00	0.0	0.00	0.0	0.00	0.0	1.07	4.5	0.00	0.0	2.29	1.4
O	0.07	0.4	1.13	1.5	3.14	14.9	0.20	1.1	0.00	0.0	0.05	1.6	1.54	6.4	0.05	5.6	6.18	3.8
D	0.00	0.0	0.10	0.1	0.00	0.0	0.00	0.0	0.00	0.0	0.00	0.0	3.02	12.6	0.00	0.0	3.12	1.9
Z	0.00	0.0	0.00	0.0	0.00	0.0	0.65	3.6	1.00	18.1	0.00	0.0	0.00	0.0	0.00	0.0	1.65	1.0
P	0.00	0.0	0.60	0.8	0.07	0.3	0.03	0.2	0.00	0.0	0.10	3.2	0.13	0.5	0.00	0.0	0.93	0.6
B	0.45	2.6	1.09	1.5	0.00	0.0	0.20	1.1	2.00	36.1	0.00	0.0	0.00	0.0	0.00	0.0	3.74	2.3
K	0.00	0.0	0.85	1.2	0.82	3.9	0.00	0.0	0.00	0.0	0.00	0.0	3.16	13.2	0.00	0.0	4.83	3.0
F	0.00	0.0	0.71	1.0	0.00	0.0	0.65	3.6	1.00	18.1	0.12	3.8	0.00	0.0	0.00	0.0	2.48	1.5
M	0.00	0.0	0.20	0.3	0.00	0.0	0.00	0.0	0.00	0.0	0.00	0.0	0.00	0.0	0.00	0.0	0.20	0.1
L	0.00	0.0	1.05	1.4	1.80	8.5	0.51	2.8	0.32	5.8	0.07	2.2	0.86	3.6	0.00	0.0	4.61	2.8
?	0.41	2.4	2.02	2.7	0.03	0.1	0.15	0.8	0.03	0.5	0.22	7.0	0.32	1.3	0.03	3.3	3.21	2.0
Total	17.01	10.4	73.63	45.0	21.08	12.9	18.29	11.2	5.54	3.4	3.15	1.9	24.01	14.7	0.90	0.6	163.61	100.0

TABLE 2.19. *Relationships between pottery fabric and form.*

DATE	Late Iron Age					Romanizing			Kiln			Romano-British Coarse			Romano-British Fine							Imports		TOTAL
FORM	Q1	GR	VG	SH1	PGW	Q2	Q3	Q4	K	Q5	Q6	GW	SH2	WAT	FW1	FW2	M1	M2	M3	M4	CH	SGS	CGS	TOTAL
J	13.36	3.62	0.06	0.04	5.93	11.59			50.10	19.61	9.16	15.29	0.91		0.70									130.37
J1	4.07	0.87	0.06		1.79	4.05			6.00	2.15	1.06	4.71			0.48									25.24
J2	5.26	1.11			1.16	1.00			9.39	2.79	2.76	2.08												25.55
J3	0.55	0.12			1.64	1.34			9.30	4.72	0.55	1.19												19.41
J4	0.67	0.28			0.53	0.48			1.89	0.39		1.08												5.32
J5	0.52			0.04					0.06	0.12	0.39													1.13
J6													0.91											0.91
J7	0.33	0.16																						0.49
Jx	1.56	0.76			0.81	3.15			21.93	9.24	3.48	6.19			0.22									47.34
S	0.40	0.32				1.57			1.53	0.20	0.92	0.04												4.98
C									0.10	0.30	0.56	1.33												2.29
O	0.12	0.07		0.05	0.23	0.05			3.71	0.66	0.47	0.78		0.04										6.18
D															2.05	0.10				0.75		0.05	0.17	3.12
Z							1.00	0.65																1.65
P									0.38	0.33	0.10	0.08			0.04									0.93
B	0.45	0.56				0.49	1.00			0.16	0.08					1.00								3.74
K							0.15		0.82						1.31	0.69	0.47	0.65			0.74			4.83
F									1.91		0.35								0.22					2.48
M											0.20													0.20
L									3.72	0.16	0.35	0.38												4.61
?	0.37	0.13			0.07	0.14			1.22	0.53	0.40	0.35												3.21
TOTAL	14.30	4.38	0.06	0.09	6.23	12.27	2.15	0.65	61.96	21.75	11.67	18.21	0.91	0.04	4.10	1.79	0.47	0.65	0.22	0.75	0.74	0.05	0.17	163.61

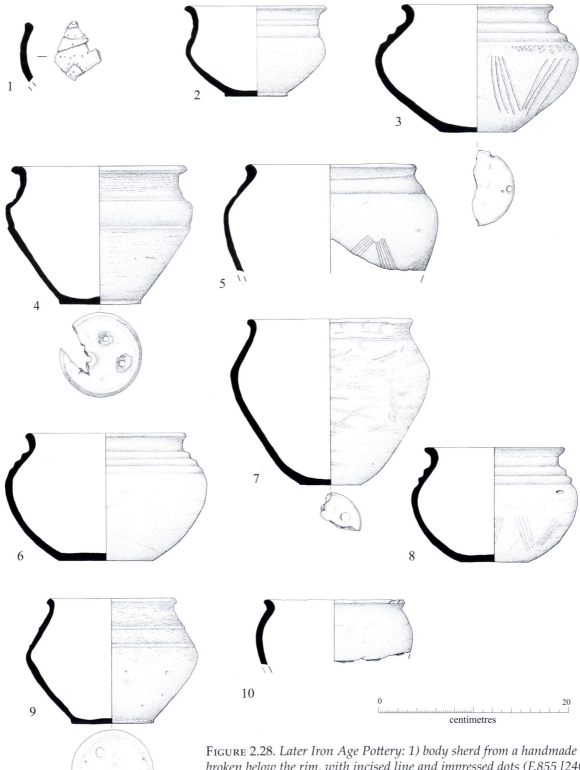

FIGURE 2.28. *Later Iron Age Pottery: 1) body sherd from a handmade bowl, broken below the rim, with incised line and impressed dots (F.855 [2401]; Form J7, Fabric Q1); 2) cordoned wheelmade bowl (F.1053 [4078]; Form J2, Fabric PGW); 3) cordoned handmade bowl with incised lines on lower body and perforated base (F.1053 [4103]; Form J2, Fabric Q1); 4) cordoned wheelmade bowl with perforated base (F.1061 [4569]; Form J2, Fabric GR); 5) cordoned handmade jar with lightly incised lines on lower body (F.1061 [4569]; Form J2, Fabric Q1); 6) cordoned handmade bowl (F.1061 [4569]; Form J2, Fabric Q1); 7) handmade jar with scored body and perforated base (F.1200 [4279]; Form J1, Fabric Q1); 8) cordoned handmade bowl with decorative burnished lines on lower body (F.1200 [4279]; Form J2, Fabric Q1); 9) cordoned wheelmade jar with perforated base (F.1109 [4371]; Form J2, Fabric Q1); 10) handmade bowl (F.715 [1665]; Form J7, Fabric GR).*

possibility that vessel perforation was not merely a functional expediency.

The extreme scarcity of vessel forms other than jars makes it difficult to precisely tie down the chronology of this phase. Many contexts, particularly those containing much handmade grog-tempered pottery, would not be out of place in the second half of the first century BC. However, the paucity of Middle Iron Age-type vessels hardly suggests a foundation date very early in the Late Iron Age, given their strong presence throughout the period at sites elsewhere in south Cambridgeshire. Those contexts containing butt beakers cannot be earlier than *c.* 15/10 BC (Fig. 2.34) and, by comparison with assemblages elsewhere in the region (Hill 2002), it is perhaps unlikely that the occupation as a whole dates to any significant extent before this. Meanwhile, the presence of 'proto-greywares' and of some 'Romanizing' rim forms suggests that the Late Iron Age enclosure system continued in use for a period beyond the Conquest.

Phase 4 - Settlement and kilns (c. AD 50–80)

The settlement and industrial features ascribed to Phase 4 account for the clear majority (69%) of the total assemblage, due in no small part to the fact that this was the main period of pottery production on the site. There is a fair degree of continuity in vessel forms and styles, but there is also a notable increase in the range of specialized forms, with flagons, platters, ovoid beakers and lids all appearing for the first time, along with a single mortarium.

Of the kiln assemblages, those from the two 'Type A' kilns, F.63 and F.1117, are outstanding in size, with 45 kg and 31 kg of pottery respectively (Table 2.20). In both cases, the material includes numerous wasters and is overwhelmingly of Fabric Group K, although that from F.1117 has a tendency to be fired to a harder finish and paler buff-orange colour than F.63. A white slip is present on a small number of jars from F.1117 (0.48 EVEs), but is not seen in F.63. The minimum number of kiln products from these two kilns were 109 vessels from F.63 and 90 vessels from F.1117. In terms of fabrics, the vessels produced at the Cherry Hinton kilns are somewhat different from those produced at the Hutchison's kilns, however, the uniform sandy fabrics are very difficult to accurately source and it should be assumed that both kiln sites were exploiting local clays.

The forms found in each case are dominated by cordoned and rilled medium-sized necked jars. Although these jars often show Romanized details, particularly in terms of rim profiles, there is no marked break in style from some of the material from Phase 3. Also abundant in F.63 are large, coarse, open bowls/dishes with a rim diameter of 24–35 cm (Fig. 2.29:10). These can have straight or concave walls, and plain, reeded or 'T'-shaped rims (see Table 2.21). Conical lids with a diameter of 28–38 cm are also common in F.63 and it seems clear that these were intended for the large bowls (Fig. 2.29:8). Other kiln products present in smaller numbers in F.63 and

F.1117 comprise beakers, flagons and large storage jars with combed bodies (Fig. 2.29:6, 7, 13 & 15). A number of the Cherry Hinton forms can be paralleled at the Hutchison's kilns, including wide-mouth and narrow-mouth cordoned jars. However, decoration did differ, Cherry Hinton ware jars being combed, while the Hutchison's jars were more commonly rilled. This is perhaps evidence of a chronological gap between the two sites as the combed decorated jars have their origins in the Late Iron Age, while rilled jars tend to be slightly later.

Of the remaining kilns, F.1181 contains a fairly substantial assemblage that includes some wasters in Fabric Group K, including a flagon, but only a minimum of three vessels. The rest contain only modest amounts of pottery, none of which can be confidently assigned as 'kiln products', and thus is characterized as miscellaneous settlement waste. It is notable that these features also contained much less baked clay and kiln furniture than F.63, F.1117 and F.1181. All of the kilns have been included in Phase 4, except for the two unfired kilns F.786 and F.1119, which contain late first–earlier second century material and have been placed in the following phase.

Some 23% of the pottery from the Phase 4 enclosure and associated settlement features consists of kiln products. The forms largely mirror those identified in F.63 and F.1117, an exception being the presence of a few collared platter sherds. Also notable is that a small proportion of the kiln products from these features appear to be handmade, including a plain, ovoid, necked jar from F.806 (Fig. 2.29:16) which in terms of form would be perfectly at home in the Late Iron Age. This emphasizes the point that the inception of the kilns did not mark a clean break in potting traditions.

The remainder of the pottery from the Phase 4 enclosure/settlement is dominated by coarsewares, consisting largely of 'Romanizing' wares (19%) and generic Romano-British wares (31%); Late Iron Age-type fabrics account for only 5%. No source can be suggested for the bulk of the non-kiln products. This situation is not helped by the paucity of maker's stamps, with only a single

TABLE 2.20. *Kiln assemblages (*= unfired kiln).*

Kiln	Kiln type	Wt (g)	EVEs
F.63	A	44,834	21.08
F.1117	A	30,974	18.29
F.340	B	1673	0.75
F.786*	B	935	0.61
F.1181	B	4879	1.18
F.1119*	C	1133	0.82
F.626	D	1798	0.85
F.1078	D	810	1.10
F.1077	E	1281	0.71
F.853	F	58	0

TABLE 2.21. *Vessels in Fabric Group K from kilns F.63 and F.1117, by EVEs.*

Form	F.63		F.1117	
J1 Plain, necked jar	0.40	2.1%	0.07	0.5%
J2 Cordoned, necked jar	4.42	23.3%	3.16	20.9%
J3 Rilled, necked jar	2.81	14.8%	3.32	22.0%
J4 Narrow-necked jar	1.34	7.1%	0.55	3.6%
Jx Jar, rim only	4.10	21.6%	6.77	44.8%
S Storage jar	0.19	1.0%	0.21	1.4%
O Coarse bowl/dish, sub-form 1	0.23	1.2%	0	0
O Coarse bowl/dish, sub-form 2	1.28	6.7%	0.07	0.5%
O Coarse bowl/dish, sub-form 3	1.63	8.6%	0	0
L Lids	1.75	9.2%	0.40	2.6%
K Beakers	0.82	4.3%	0	0
F Flagons	0	0	0.43	2.8%
Uncertain	0.03	0.2%	0.14	0.9%
TOTAL	**19.00**	**100%**	**15.12**	**100%**

Note: O sub-form 1 = Large bowl with almost straight sides, simple flat rim. Height 11.5 cm, base 21 cm, rim 30 cm (one example only). O Sub-form 2 = Large bowls with gently curved sides, and 'T'-shaped or reeded rims designed to seat a lid. Heights 12–13 cm, base diameters 23–25 cm, rim diameters 30–38 cm. O Sub-form 3 = Medium-sized bowls with curved sides and a reeded rim. Rim diameters 23–24 cm.

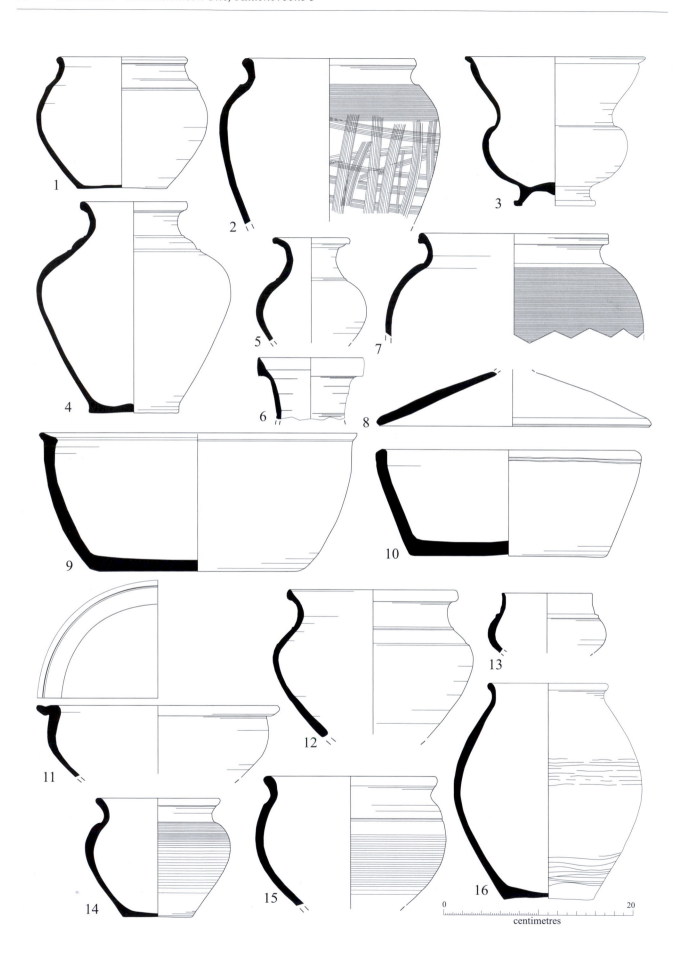

Figure 2.29 (left). *Conquest Period and Roman Pottery (1): 1) cordoned globular jar; Pre-Flavian (F.782 [2578], Fabric Q1); 2) everted rim jar with an upper band of horizontal rilling and lower combed hatching; Pre-Flavian (F.23 [1432], Fabric Q2); 3) pedestal beaker, with waist and tapering sides, imitation of Gallo-Belgic ware pedestal cup; Flavian (F.1117 [4208], Fabric Q4); 4) narrow-mouth jar, cordoned neck; Flavian (F.1117 [4206], Fabric K); 5) narrow-mouth, long-necked jar, cordon at the base of the neck; Flavian (F.1117 [4206], Fabric K); 6) collared flagon; AD 50–80 (F.1117 [4200], Fabric K); 7) rilled jar, bifid rim; Flavian (F.1117 [4206], Fabric K); 8) shallow conical lid, with a slight beaded rim; AD 50–70 (constitutes part of a set with [859], Fig. 2.24:10; F.63 [852] & [859], Fabric K); 9) large bowl, upturned, flat topped/lid seated rim; AD 50–70 (F.63 [852], Fabric K); 10) bowl, slightly convex, plain rim; AD 50–70 (part of a set with [852/859], Fig. 2.24:8; F.63 [859], Fabric K); 11) large bowl with a down-bent 'snub' rim; AD 50–70 (F.63 [859], Fabric K); 12) medium-sized jar, cordons on neck and an everted rim; AD 50–70 (F.63 [859], Fabric K); 13) small globular beaker, with a vertical rim and cordon; AD 50–70 (F.63 [857], Fabric K); 14) small rilled jar, everted rim; mid-late first century AD (F.1117 [4200], Fabric K); 15) wide-mouth rilled jar, everted rim; mid-late first century AD (F.1053 [4703], Fabric K); 16) narrow mouth jar, slightly everted, beaded rim; mid–late first century AD (F.806 [2202], Fabric K).*

Table 2.22. *Painted Wares.*

Feature	Phase	Fabric group	Form	Decoration
780	4	FW2	Beaker	Horizontal bands and a row of 'bird's feet' in red-brown paint (Fig. 2.30:8)
1117	4	FW2	?	Bands of red paint over rouletted decoration
1117	4	FW2	?	Two bands of brown paint separated by rows of stabbed decoration
832	5	FW2	Bowl	Diagonal lattice and horizontal bands in red paint (Fig. 2.30:6)
1053	5	Q3	?	Horizontal and diagonal bands in red paint
1099	5	WW	Jar?	Trees/feathers, horizontal lattice bands and diagonal lines in grey paint
1181	5	K?	?	Horizontal bands of red paint

example, an illiterate stamp on the base of a small jar in Fabric Group Q5 from F.18 (Fig. 2.30:4). The small number of finer wares includes a near-complete though fragmented pedestalled bowl of imitation 'Gallo-Belgic' type in Fabric Group Q4, dumped in kiln F.1117 (Fig. 2.29:3). There are also fragments of three vessels with painted decoration (Table 2.18). The best example is a fine beaker or bowl with a rippled profile from F.780, with horizontal bands and 'bird's feet' in red-brown paint (Fig. 2.30:8). This vessel is closely paralleled at Colchester, from a context dated to before AD 61–65 (Hawkes & Hull 1947, pl. LXXVII, 6).

Romano-British material that can be sourced includes one body sherd from F.881 with red barbotine ring-and-dot decoration, originating from the Cherry Hinton kilns, 2 km to the northeast (dated *c.* 55–90: J. Evans 1990). Meanwhile, F.19 contained one body sherd of mica-dusted ware from Pakenham, Suffolk, *c.* 50 km to the northeast. Also present are several channel-rim jars in Fabric SH2 (Fig. 2.30:3), from the Northamptonshire/Bedfordshire region (Friendship-Taylor 1999).

Imports are few in number. South Gaulish Samian was recovered from three features, including a Dr. 18/31 dish from F.25 and part of a small cup from F.885. The latter shows an attempted repair with pitch or resin along one of the broken edges, the only example of such behaviour in the assemblage. It has been noted elsewhere that Samian is more likely to be repaired than other types of pottery on Romano-British sites (Willis 1998). There is also a single body sherd from a Catalan amphora from F.770.

The cemetery (c. AD 50–80)
Only three cremations and one inhumation contained relatively complete vessels that can be regarded as grave goods. The vessels include a high proportion of imitation 'Gallo-Belgic' forms and are contemporary with the Phase 4 enclosure system. The dominance of vessels connected with serving and consuming liquids (beakers and flagons) contrasts with the settlement and kiln assemblages, a typical pattern for the region (Biddulph 2005).

Grave 1/Cremation F.391 contained a greyware pedestal base and fragments of a beaker.

Grave 2/Cremation F.408 had four complete vessels (see Figs. 2.21 & 2.22). The ashes were held within a butt beaker with cordons and rouletted decoration, and an unusual carinated pedestalled bowl. Accessory vessels consisted of a kiln-product flagon, and a small necked bowl. Part of a greyware lid was also recovered. The group, as a whole, can be dated *c.* AD 50–80.

Grave 3/Cremation F.411 contained a complete butt beaker with cordons and rouletted decoration (see Figs. 2.21 & 2.22). There were also fragmented remains of a second vessel with rouletted decoration, probably another butt beaker.

Grave 12/Inhumation F.396 included the lower part of a greyware beaker.

The remaining material from the burials consisted of individual sherds, doubtless residual; as none were burnt they are unlikely to be the remains of pyre offerings. Most were Late Iron Age and early Romano-British coarsewares, though there was one sherd of South Gaulish Samian (Dr. 33) from inhumation F.406 (Grave 14) and a North Gaulish whiteware flagon handle from inhumation F.387 (Grave 8).

Phase 5 - Enclosure system (c. AD 80+)
With only two per cent of the total assemblage, the Phase 5 ditch system contains only one tenth as much pottery as the Phase 4 enclosures. One significant deposit of 2.5 kg of pottery is present in F.21 ([1615]), largely comprising kiln wares, but most other deposits are fairly small. The pottery consists entirely of coarsewares in Late Iron Age, Romanizing and Romano-British fabrics. There are a few recognizably Flavian to early second-century types, and one Nene Valley colour-coated sherd (AD 150+). A significant proportion of sherds are abraded. Clearly, only limited settlement activity can

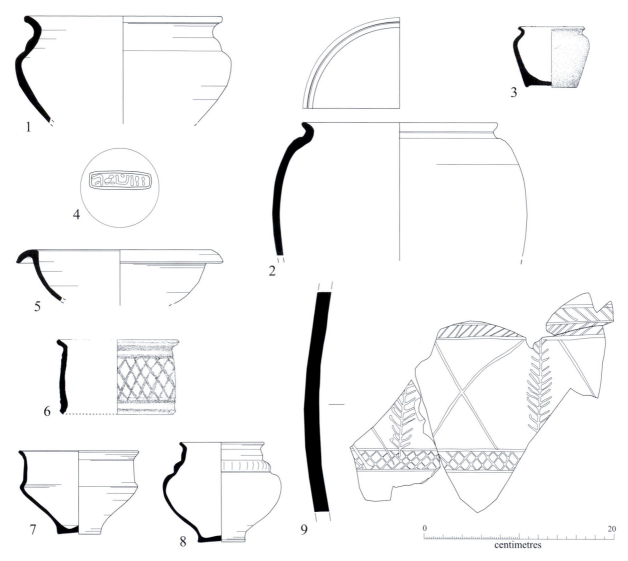

FIGURE 2.30. *Conquest Period and Roman Pottery (2): 1) cordoned, everted rim, wide-mouth jar; mid–late first century AD (F.38 [1148], Fabric K); 2) jar with flat topped/lid seated rim; mid–late first century AD (F.876 [2407], Fabric K); 3) channel rim jar; mid–late first century AD (F.577 [696], Fabric SH2); 4) stamp on base of small jar; AD 50–80 (F.18 [1808], Fabric Q5); 5) dropped flange bowl; AD 50–80 (F.832 [4612], Fabric Q6); 6) possible upper half of a girth beaker (imitation of a Gallo-Belgic form), with red painted lattice and horizontal bands of decoration; mid–late first century AD (F.832 [4571], Fabric FW2); 7) carinated bowl with everted rim; mid–late first century AD (F.1099 [4168], Fabric GW); 8) jar with out-turned rim and wide cordon, with burnished vertical lines; mid–late first century AD (F.1099 [4168], Fabric GW); 9) body sherds probably from a jar. Grey painted 'feather' decoration with an upper band of chevrons and a lower band of lattice decoration; mid–late first century AD (F.1099 [4168], Fabric WW).*

have taken place in the vicinity of these ditches, and it is likely that much of the pottery found within them is residual.

Although kiln products make up 65% of the material from the enclosure ditches, this only amounts to 2.07 EVEs. Thus, although a few of the kilns utilize the partially silted ditches of the Phase 4 enclosure — and could theoretically have been in use contemporary with the Phase 5 ditch system — there is no evidence for large-scale pottery production at this time.

Late settlement activity
The latest settlement activity on the site comes from a group of pits and other features at the eastern edge of the site, containing pottery

dating to the late first and early second century BC. These show a marked change in the character of the assemblage. Late Iron Age and Romanizing fabrics fall away to an insignificant level (1.1% and 2.5% respectively), and kiln products also fall markedly (5.1%), suggesting that production of these wares had ceased. The fabrics tend to be more classically Romano-British than before, with grey-wares rising dramatically to 45.6% of the assemblage. Finer wares (broadly defined) also increase markedly to form 25.9% of the total, and there is a wider range of fineware fabric groups represented. A caveat should be added here, that the figures could be skewed slightly because the presence of certain types of diagnostic fineware will have aided the identification of given contexts as late in date.

Nevertheless, the contrast between these late deposits and those of the preceding phase is clear enough. Despite these changes in the character of the pottery, most is still of a 'generic' character that cannot be sourced.

In terms of form, jars still form the majority of the assemblage, although their dominance is reduced. This is, in part, due to a rise in beakers and fine bowls/dishes. Jar forms do not change radically, although one new type characteristic of the late settlement features is a greyware jar with a rippled shoulder incised with chevrons. Non-local channel-rim jars in Fabric SH2 continue to occur in low quantities (Fig. 2.30:3).

Bowl/dish forms include several examples with flanged rims, in both coarse and fine fabrics. This includes one from the kilns at Wattisfield, Suffolk, *c.* 60 km to the northeast. Also characteristic of the late settlement group are a number of fine 'London Ware'-style bowls with compass-incised and combed decoration. The fabrics for these (Group M4) may suggest a source in East Anglia (perhaps West Stow), rather than the London area (cf. Rodwell 1978, 248–58).

Beaker forms include both ovoid and sharply carinated examples. Ovoid beakers from the Cherry Hinton kilns with barbotine ring or ring-and-dot decoration become more common than before, occurring in four features (F.832, F.1099, F.1115 & F.1248). One further ovoid beaker, in Fabric Group M2, is decorated with large barbotine pellets. Meanwhile, butt beakers seem to have gone out of use.

Painted decoration occurs on Romano-British sherds from four features. In three cases this consists of small fragments bearing bands or lattices of red paint, one of which *may* be a kiln product. The remaining example, from F.1099, is quite different. This consists of part of the body of a fairly large jar in a white ware fabric, painted with stylized trees or feathers, diagonal lines and horizontal lattice bands in black or grey paint (Fig. 2.30:9). The decoration is very similar to an example found in the Roman town of Cambridge at 19–37 Castle Street (Cessford in Evans & Lucas forthcoming), although there red paint was used and the fabric also differs. While the source of these painted wares is unknown, similar motifs of trees/feathers are found on products of the kilns at Weekley, Northamptonshire, which have been dated to *c.* AD 45–60 (Jackson & Dix 1987; Woods & Hastings 1984).

The only imported wares from the late settlement group consist of Samian. These occur in four features, including part of a small cup in South Gaulish Samian from F.832, and two Central Gaulish cups, from F.1099 (Dr. 27) and F.969 (Dr. 33).

The settlement is likely to have ended by around the middle of the second century AD, and there is no evidence for further activity at the site prior to the Middle Saxon period. The only Romano-British pottery from the site that is certainly later than *c.* AD 150 consists of three small body sherds of Nene Valley colour-coated ware, which may indicate no more than manuring activity.

It is fortunate that the Hutchison's assemblage can be compared with data from a number of other Late Iron Age and Roman settlements in the immediate vicinity. In this way intriguing insights can be gained into long-term changes in practice within the rural communities that lay in the hinterland of the developing town of Cambridge. There is a clear trend through time in the vessel forms used by the Hutchison's community (see Table 2.18). This can be characterized as a long-term transition from an Iron Age-type assemblage dominated by multi-functional medium-sized jars, to a much more diverse assemblage with an increased range of specialized tablewares. The more varied range of

vessel forms seen in the later phases at the Hutchison Site can be taken as an expression of 'Romanization', although the process of adopting tablewares began before the Conquest here as elsewhere in southeast England.

The declining frequency of medium-sized jars at the Hutchison Site is shown in Figure 2.31. Such vessels comprise the entirety of the assemblage at Cra'ster's (1969) Middle Iron Age site, and the large majority of the material from the Late Iron Age phase at the Hutchison site. The frequency then falls to 84.1% in the first Roman phase (AD 50–80), and more dramatically to 58.7% in the second phase (late first to early second century AD). Subsequent developments elsewhere in the local area can be followed by drawing upon data from the Vicar's Farm settlement, 1.25 km to the west of Roman Cambridge (see below; Evans & Lucas forthcoming). The first phase here is dated to AD 80–180, thus overlapping with the final phase at the Hutchison Site, and shows a comparable proportion of medium-sized jars (64%). The downward trend continues through time in the Vicar's Farm assemblage, with the proportion of medium-sized jars reaching only 47.4% in the final phase, dated mid third–fourth century AD. Data from other local sites also fits the pattern. At Greenhouse Farm a group of kiln assemblages dated to *c.* AD 45–68 shows a lower, but nonetheless comparable, level of medium jars compared to the contemporary phase at the Hutchison Site (Gibson & Lucas 2002). Meanwhile, recent evaluation trenching at a third- to fourth-century AD cropmark site at Longstanton, 7 km northwest of Cambridge (see Chapter 3 below), has produced an assemblage with a very similar level of jars to the corresponding phase at Vicar's Farm. The data thus suggests a remarkably consistent development in pottery traditions within the Cambridge hinterland.

The one site in south Cambridgeshire that does not fit the identified trend is Foxton, 11 km south of Cambridge, where the pre-Flavian (*c.* AD 45–70) deposits produced an assemblage with no more than 52.1% jars/necked bowls and a high proportion of tablewares, particularly beakers (Lucas 1997). However, this site seems to have been of a very different character to those discussed above. The remains of a masonry building were uncovered, interpreted as a possible cook-house or sauna, and certain other features of the site led to the suggestion that it was military in character (Maynard *et al.* 1997). This raises the possibility that during the period immediately following the Conquest there was a contrast in pottery types — and thus in ways of preparing, serving and consuming food and drink — between military or 'official' establishments and local rural settlements.

The evidence from the Cambridge hinterland shows that the transition from a restricted Iron Age-type pottery assemblage to a diverse 'Romanized' one, with its associated changes in cooking, eating and drinking practices, was a long and gradual process (cf. Willis 1996), although the first century or so following the Conquest is the steepest part of the curve. A schematic expression of the trend in the Cambridge hinterland, with the time axis 'to scale', is shown in Figure 2.32. It is unfortunate that comparisons are not possible with the town of Cambridge itself, as no quantified data is available for the 1956–88 Castle Hill excavations (Alexander & Pullinger 2000), while more recent investigations have produced only small pottery assemblages from secure Romano-British deposits (Cessford, in Evans & Lucas forthcoming).

The pattern seen at the Hutchison Site during the Late Iron Age differs from that in regions further south, where there was an earlier adoption of a varied range of vessel forms. Hill (2002) has shown that this diversification can be seen at settlements in Hertfordshire and Essex from the beginning of the Late Iron Age, with tablewares typically representing 10–13% of vessels in the first century BC and 25–47% in the early–mid first century AD. He contrasts this with northern East Anglia where similar changes probably did not begin until the first century AD, and even then only a few specific forms were adopted, with Middle Iron Age forms continuing alongside them even beyond the Roman Conquest. Lying between these two regions is south Cambridgeshire, where Hill argues that 'widespread adoption of the full repertoire of southern forms' into settlement assemblages 'probably took place post 10–1 BC' (2002, 157). The community at the Hutchison Site clearly did not adopt anything like this full repertoire, however, and the restricted form-range is more reminiscent of that seen at sites in northern East Anglia, though without the same continuity of Middle Iron Age-type vessels. On the other hand, the Late Iron Age assemblage from Castle Hill includes some vessel types not seen at the Hutchison Site, notably platters (Alexander & Pullinger 2000). This could perhaps reflect a special role or status for the Cambridge settlement; quantification of the Castle Hill material would be needed to thoroughly investigate this issue.

Although the assemblage from the Hutchison Site becomes more diverse and 'Romanized' following the Conquest, there are still no indications that this was anything other than a fairly unexceptional rural settlement, and overall the composition of the settlement assemblage is typical of a Late Iron Age/early Roman rural settlement, with coarsewares dominating and a small range of fineware vessels. Imports are

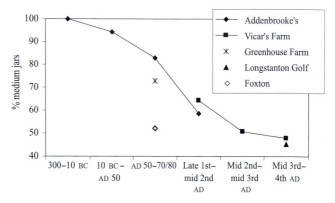

FIGURE 2.31. *Increasing diversity of pottery forms through time at rural sites in the Cambridge hinterland, expressed by the decreasing frequency of medium jars.*

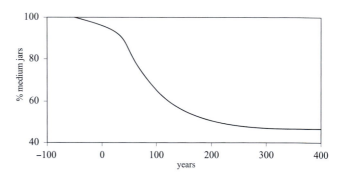

FIGURE 2.32. *Schematic graph of trend in proportion of medium jars at settlements in Cambridge hinterland, with years 'to scale'.*

scarce, as are the highest quality Romano-British finewares. Although the proportion of jars falls through time, they always formed a majority of the assemblage, which Jeremy Evans (2001) has shown to be a diagnostic attribute of 'ordinary' rural sites.

The paucity of 'prestige' pottery from both the pre- and post-Conquest phases could be interpreted in two ways: firstly that the community could not obtain these goods, due to a lack of sufficient 'wealth' or of access to circulation networks, or, secondly, that such pottery was simply not especially desired by the community, or possibly even actively rejected. These two factors are, of course, not mutually exclusive. While the issue is a complex one, the fact that attempts were made to repair one of the very few Samian vessels present on the site is a possible hint that such exotic goods *were* valued, but were not readily obtainable. The one exception to this is the Clay Farm 'rich' cremation, some 700 m to the west (Site IX; see Chapter 3 below). It is therefore the quantity of material, rather than its composition, which sets the site apart from others. While the presence of the kilns obviously has a significant effect on the number of vessels on the site (37% of total assemblage), the non-kiln products still account for 61% of the assemblage.

The discovery of the Hutchison Site kilns further emphasizes the dense distribution of pottery production sites in the landscape around Cambridge during the later first century AD, preceding the consolidation and emergence of large regional production centres that occurred later in the Roman period (Lucas 1999; Gibson & Lucas 2002). The Cherry Hinton War Ditches settlement provides the closest parallel, where two distinct kiln products were made. First, the coarseware vessels, comprising a variety of jars, primarily recovered from the 1960s excavations (see Inset; White 1964a). This material was sandy and tended towards a dark red colour. The vessels tended to have fairly thick walls and thickened rims and, although wheelmade and kiln-fired, are still clearly influenced by later Iron Age traditions.

The second products comprised the finer and more well known 'ring-and-dot' vessels; primarily fine sandy white and buff wares with painted barbotine decoration (Hughes 1904a) These vessels were finer in fabric and tended to be very thin walled and well-made. J. Evans (1991) suggests that the two Cherry Hinton industries were unrelated and represented two separate groups of potters. Given the nature of the forms and fabrics this may be true; however, it should also be considered that the difference in the two types of kiln product is above all a reflection of chronology, with the coarseware vessels being earlier than the fineware vessels.

Lucas similarly raises the possibility of more than one phase of production at Cherry Hinton (Lucas 1999), with a suggestion that the painted wares were later than the other kiln products (*c.* AD 55 for the painted wares, pre-Flavian date for many of the other wares, although some continuing after this period). The second phase of production at Cherry Hinton is less comparable with the Hutchison's kilns. There are some examples of fineware vessels, namely platters, flagons and beakers, although there is just one possible example of an Hutchison's kiln product with painted decoration (F.1181).

These findings have implications for the Hutchison's kilns in terms of the date. As discussed above, although still having much in common with Phase 3 material, the kiln products from this site are more 'Romanized' in form and fabric. It is, therefore, possible that the Hutchison's kiln wares were slightly later than the Cherry Hinton coarsewares. It is unclear whether they are earlier or contemporary with the Cherry Hinton finewares.

Interpreting the organization and socio-economic context of the kiln production at the Hutchison Site is difficult without evidence for the distribution of the kiln wares beyond the site. Further still is the seeming lack of evidence for the distribution of wares from other contemporary local kiln sites such as Greenhouse Farm, and even Cherry Hinton is only cited as a production site when the distinctive ring-and-dot decorated vessels are identified. Gibson & Lucas (2002) have argued that production at Greenhouse Farm was carried out during transient visits by potters as part of seasonal gatherings. This argument partly rested on the fact that the kilns at this site appeared to be marginal to contemporary settlement. While it is possible that the Hutchison Site kilns were similarly made and used by peripatetic craft-workers, an alternative interpretation seems more likely. This site's kilns differed from Greenhouse Farm's in that they seem to have been an integral element of a functioning settlement; this issue will be further explored in this Chapter's *Concluding Discussion*.

Some clear similarities can be observed at the Hutchison Site between the kiln products and the pottery of the pre-Conquest settlement. An example is provided by the rilled jars, handmade versions of which occurred in the Late Iron Age settlement, to be replaced by the wheelmade versions which were produced in the kilns in some quantities. The presence of some handmade kiln products, particularly the 'Late Iron Age-style' jar from F.806, also indicates a certain degree of continuity in potting traditions. It should, moreover, also be stressed that the indifferent quality of many of the kiln products means it is not necessary to envisage an alien group of highly skilled, specialist potters.

Late Iron Age and Early Roman brooches
(COLIN HASELGROVE)
Seventeen brooches were recovered. All but the last are of copper alloy.

Boss-on-bow brooch
1) *Small Finds No. 76* (Fig. 2.33:1) - Simple wire brooch, with small boss on bow (now in two pieces), broken at catchplate (surviving L. 33 mm). Internal chord, 4-coil spring. A rather small and simple version of Stead's type 2 (1976; cf. e.g. the example from Deal in Parfitt 1995, 405, no. 3).

Nauheim or related brooch
2) *Small Finds No. 45; F.591* (Fig. 2.33:2) - The flat, tapering bow relates this brooch to the Nauheim family (surviving L. 60 mm). Only the start of the spring and part of the catchplate, which could have been open or solid, survive. There is incised decoration along the edges of the bow and possibly a central incised line; there are also two or more transverse lines towards the foot end. A not dissimilar brooch, with surviving open catchplate, was found at Baldock (Stead & Rigby 1986, 109, no. 1). The continental Nauheim has a 4-coil spring and internal chord, whereas related British brooches often have a 2-coil spring and external chord.

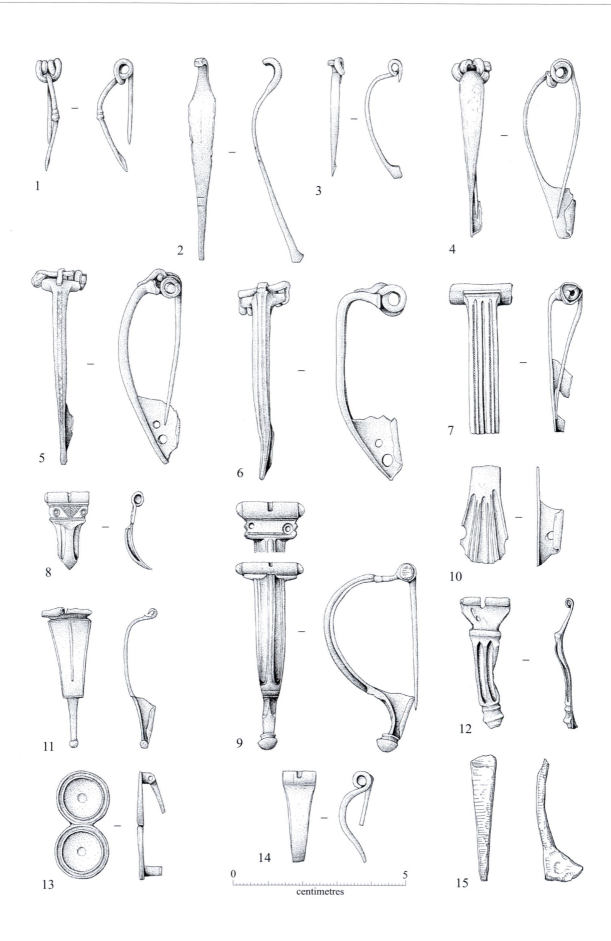

FIGURE 2.33. (left) *Late Iron Age and Romano-British Brooches: 1) boss-on-bow ([3650]); 2) Nauheim or related (SmF 45); 3–4) simple brooches with solid catchplate (F.23 & F.1113); 5–6) Colchester (SmF 40, F.111); 7) Langton Down (SmF 27); 8–9) Aucissa (SmF 37, SmF 95); 10) Rosette/Thistle family (SmF 63); 11–12) simple Hod Hill (SmF 28, SmF 38); 13) plate brooch (F.591); 14) strip-bow (F.98); 15) iron brooch (SmF 22).*

Although none of the brooches have been analysed, nos. 1 and 2 are most likely to be of bronze, as is the case with nearly all the British Late Iron Age brooches related to continental La Tène D1–D2 types that have been analysed.

Simple brooches with solid catchplate (Hawkes & Hull Type VII)
3) *Small Finds No. 60; F.23* (Fig. 2.33:3) - Bow and part of spring and catchplate (surviving L. 35 mm). The bow is flat and narrow, and the catchplate is most likely to have been solid.

4) *Small Finds No. 84; F.38* (Fig. 2.33:4) - Complete brooch with flat, tapering and curving bow and solid catchplate (L. 53 mm). Internal chord, 4-coil spring.

In Britain, these brooches are often classified as 'Nauheim-derivatives', but they are far removed from the continental Nauheim, and should be considered separately. Around 60% of the examples from elsewhere that have been analysed are of bronze, a further quarter brass, and the balance gunmetals (Bayley 1988, 54).

Colchester brooches (Hawkes & Hull Type III)
5) *Small Finds No. 40* (Fig. 2.33:5) - Brooch with rounded bow and zigzag decoration down the centre, with short plain wings, 6-coil spring and hook (L. 57 mm). The catchplate has two circular perforations. The foot and part of a very similar brooch was found at Braughing-Puckeridge (Potter & Trow 1988, no. 32).

6) *<88>* (Fig. 2.33:6) - Brooch with ribbed bow and plain wings, 6-coil spring, and hook (L. 57 mm). The catchplate has two circular perforations.

Apart from having circular perforations on the catchplate instead of the more usual rectilinear ones, both examples resemble the standard form of Colchester brooch. Over 90% of Colchester brooches are made of brass (Bayley 1988, 54).

Langton Down Brooch (Hawkes & Hull Type XII)
7) *Small Finds No. 27; F.591* (Fig. 2.33:7) - Copper-alloy brooch (L. 43 mm), with straight-sided bow of flat cross-section and a straight head, cylindrical spring-cover. The bow has two rows of beading flanking a central groove, which may have contained an inlay, possibly of silver or lead (cf. Stead & Rigby 1986, 113). The footplate is incomplete, but appears to have a single perforation.

Langton Down brooches are normally brass, or sometimes gunmetal; typically they also contain up to 2–3% tin (Bayley 1988, 54). On most Langton Down brooches, the top of the bow is rounded; the variety where the head of the bow is squared, as here, is less common, but can be paralleled locally (e.g. Baldock: Stead & Rigby 1986, nos. 93–5).

Aucissa brooches (Hawkes & Hull Type XVII)
8) *Small Finds No. 37* (Fig. 2.33:8) - Head and a small portion of the bow of a hinged brooch with an iron pin (surviving L. 23 mm). The head is decorated with transverse mouldings and the 'eyes' are formed by ring and dot ornaments. Between them is a triangular motif. The bow is plain apart from edge mouldings.

9) *Small Finds No. 95* (Fig. 2.33:9) - Complete brooch, with sharply arched bow, tapering towards the foot (L. 55 mm). Flat, with ribbed decoration; short, solid catchplate. The bow terminates in an applied moulded knob. The pin is hinged on an iron bar. The head has a transverse moulding and the 'eyes', which are typical of the Aucissa type, are represented by holes for two studs.

Aucissa brooches are almost without exception of brass (Bayley 1988, 54).

Brooches of the Rosette/Thistle family (Hawkes & Hull Types X & XI)
10) *Small Finds No. 63* (Fig. 2.33:10) - Fantail-shaped foot, from a brooch of the Rosette/Thistle family (surviving L. 28 mm). The foot is reeded (although the upper part is plain) and the catchplate is perforated by a single, circular hole.

11) *Small Finds No. 75* (Fig. 2.22:5) - The brooch consists of a flat, keyhole shaped plate, on to which an applied rosette, now missing, would have been fixed, *via* the central perforation (L. 58 mm). The fantail-shaped foot is reeded and the catchplate is pierced by a trapezoidal hole. This example has a spring, encased within a tubular cover. The brooch was found among the grave goods accompanying Cremation F.408/Grave 2.

Rosette/Thistle brooches are normally brass, but usually also contain up to 2–3% tin (Bayley 1988, 54).

Simple Hod Hill brooches (Hawkes & Hull Type XVIII)
12) *Small Finds No. 28* (Fig. 2.33:11) - Hinged brooch (in two pieces) with trapezoidal bow; tinned or silvered (L. 40 mm). The bow is defined by a slight edge moulding and there is also a central moulding. The foot has a solid catchplate and a small knob; pin missing.

13) *Small Finds No. 38* (Fig. 2.33:12) - Hinged brooch missing the foot and pin (surviving L. 33 mm). The tapering ribbed bow is separated from the foot and head by transverse mouldings.

About 70% of Hod Hill brooches are brasses; the remainder are almost equally divided between bronzes and gunmetals (Bayley 1988, 54).

Colchester-derivative brooch (Hawkes & Hull Types IV & V)
14) *Small Finds No. 101; F.408* (Fig. 2.22:6) - Found in butt beaker containing cremated bone (F.408/Grave 2). Burnt and twisted two-piece brooch with the spring and pin missing (L. 65 mm). The bow is ribbed, as are the semi-cylindrical side wings. The catchplate is pierced by three near-rectangular holes, and apparently still contains the tip of the pin. The spring is missing, but a short portion of the external chord survives, held in place by what appears to be either a lug or front-facing hook; due to the burning, it is difficult to be certain which. There is no lug below the head to retain a spring bar; the spring was presumably soldered to the underneath or end of the wing.

Mackreth (1992, 122) notes that corrosion products behind the wings on Colchester-derivatives tend to occur on the left-hand side, as on the present brooch, implying that they were soldered at that side, farthest from the pin. Most of the specimens with this kind of spring-fixing arrangement have a reversed hook, which does not seem to be the case here.

About 80% of Colchester derivatives are leaded bronzes, with a small minority of leaded gunmetals and bronzes (Bayley 1988, 54).

Plate brooch

15) *Small Finds No. 52; F.591* (Fig. 2.33:13) - Plate brooch, consisting of two adjoining discs with moulded border; tinned or silvered (L. 32 mm). Each disc will have held an enamel setting, probably with a central boss. There is a very similar brooch from Harlow Temple (France & Gobel 1985, 80, no. 75) and part of another was found in a mid first-century AD context at Skeleton Green (Partridge 1981, no. 45).

Strip-bow brooch

16) *Small Finds No. 102* (Fig. 2.33:14) - Small hinged brooch, with a plain, flat and tapering bow. Broken at the foot (surviving L. 27 mm); burnt?

Iron brooch

17) *Small Finds No. 22* (Fig. 2.33:15) - Fragment of brooch with flat bow and part of catchplate, which was probably solid (surviving L. 37 mm).

This appears to be an iron version of the simple bow brooch with solid catchplate (above, nos. 3–4) or possibly a hinged strip-bow type (cf. no. 15).

This is a small but interesting group of brooches, much as one might expect to find on any Late Iron Age–Early Roman settlement of consequence in south-east England. Two of the finds are almost certainly first-century BC types (nos. 1–2) and the same may be true of a third (no. 17). Most, however, are varieties that were current in the region from *c.* 15–10 BC and the mid first century AD, including the simple bow brooches (nos. 3–4), the Colchesters (nos. 5–6), the Langton Down (no. 7), the Aucissas (nos. 8–9), the Rosettes (nos. 10–11) and probably the strip-bow brooch (no. 16). In contrast, brooch types that only came into widespread use in the mid first century AD are less well represented; these include the two Hod Hills (nos. 12–13); the Colchester derivative (no. 14); and the plate brooch (no. 15). Two of the brooches were associated with a cremation burial dating to the late first century AD (nos. 11 & 14), the rest coming from settlement contexts.

Previous work has shown that brooch deposition on individual sites is influenced both by factors specific to the site, such as the function and chronology of the excavated areas, and more general ones, such as the regional popularity of different brooch varieties and the length of time that each of them lasted in circulation (e.g. Haselgrove 1997). To make detailed inferences from the composition of an assemblage, it is therefore necessary to look beyond the particular site. At the Hutchison Site, for instance, the scarcity of first-century BC brooches compared to types belonging to the final phase of the Iron Age should not be seen necessarily as indicating more intensive occupation in the early first century AD, since the number of personal items of all kinds deposited on Late Iron Age sites rises dramatically at this time throughout

southern Britain (Hill 1997). If anything is unusual about the assemblage, it is more the presence of two or three brooches from the earlier part of the Late Iron Age. These normally account for less than 1 in 20 of all brooch finds from sites of this period, whilst specimens closely related to the continental Nauheim type are rare in Britain. Together, these points imply that the first-century BC occupation on the site was of some significance.

Although the Hutchison Site assemblage is too small for reliable quantification, we can draw some conclusions simply by comparing the types present with the brooches from other Late Iron Age and/or Early Roman sites in East Anglia (Haselgrove 2003). Within the region, the most useful reference sites are Chatteris (Evans 2003b) and Stonea Grange (Jackson & Potter 1996) in Cambridgeshire; Fison Way (Gregory 1991) and Saham Toney (Brown 1986) in Norfolk; Harlow Temple, Essex (France & Gobel 1985); Baldock (Stead & Rigby 1986), Braughing-Puckeridge (Partridge 1981; Potter & Trow 1988); and King Harry Lane, St Albans (Stead & Rigby 1989) in Hertfordshire.

As already noted, the first point of significance is the elevated proportion of first-century BC types (nos. 1–3). In the reference group, this is paralleled only at Fison Way, which was already a site of some importance by the start of the Late Iron Age, and to a lesser extent at Skeleton Green, Puckeridge, where occupation began in the mid first century BC. Closer at hand, however, the Iron Age site at Trumpington has yielded a number of first-century BC brooch types, as well as earlier varieties (N. Crummy pers. comm.). The Trumpington finds are almost all of iron, however, which implies limited overlap between the two sites, a conclusion that the pottery also supports (J.D. Hill pers. comm.).

The Trumpington site certainly has none of the earlier first-century AD brass brooch types (nos. 5–11), which form the bulk of the Hutchison Site's assemblage. Within this group, the Rosette and Aucissa types are slightly better represented than on most sites of the period, whilst the Colchester — the commonest of all British types — appears under-represented. There is no reason, however, given the small size of the assemblage, to suppose that most of these variations are of any significance. Colchesters, for example, are also under-represented at Harlow Temple, despite intensive deposition there in the earlier first century AD, whilst present in above-average quantities at the nearby Braughing-Puckeridge complex, and at King Harry Lane. More relevant perhaps is the above-average number of Thistle/Rosette brooches in the King Harry Lane cemetery; one of the two examples from

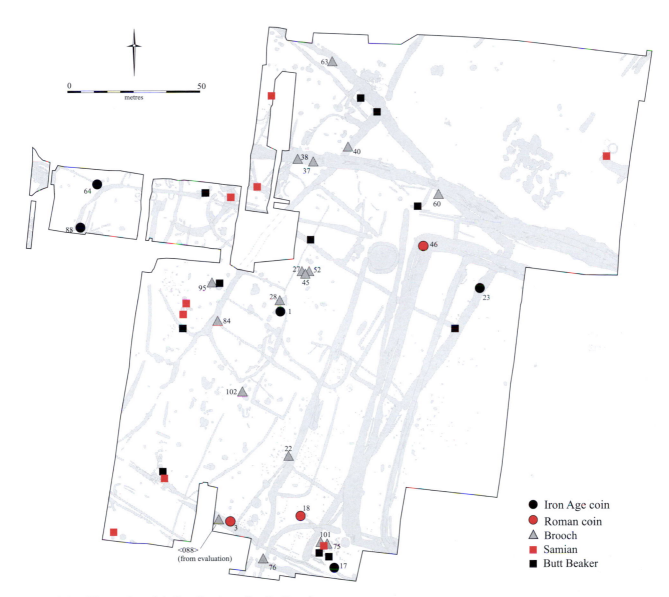

FIGURE 2.34. *Phases 3 and 4 distributions (by SmF no.).*

the Hutchison Site is also from a burial, and the series was clearly particularly well adapted to ostentatious display. All these brass types have strong Continental affinities and some may be actual imports, although not the Colchesters, which appear to be standard insular varieties.

Belonging chronologically with this group are the two bow brooches with solid catchplates (nos. 3–4) and the strip-bow brooch (no. 16). A slight under-representation of the former is echoed at several Cambridgeshire and Norfolk sites, including Chatteris, Fison Way, Saham Toney and Stonea Grange, and does appear to be a regional trend (Haselgrove 2003, 240 & fig. 2.28). The strip-bow type is also commoner elsewhere. The absence of penannular brooches at the Hutchison Site is probably down to sample size, but

if not might be chronological or functional. An iron example was found at Trumpington (N. Crummy pers. comm.) and the series is well represented at Fison Way and on several sites with Roman military phases, including Colchester, Hod Hill and Cadbury Castle (Haselgrove 1997).

The other feature of the Hutchison's group that calls for comment is the general under-representation of types that first came into widespread use in the mid first century AD (nos. 12–15), and of Colchester-derivative brooches in particular. The latter type is particularly well represented on East Anglian sites, not just those with mid first-century AD origins, but also at sites like Fison Way, Gorhambury and Harlow, with important pre-Roman phases. Even in a sample of this size, the scarcity of Colchester-derivatives is likely to be of some significance, especially as the solitary example is from a burial rather than a settlement context. In this respect, the brooches accord well with other evidence implying changes in the character and function of the site in or soon after the mid first century AD.

The brooches are well dispersed across the site (Fig. 2.34). One cluster of three brooches found together from pit F.591 could hardly have less chronological coherence, comprising the Nauheim or related type (no. 2), the Langton Down (no. 7) and the plate brooch (no. 15). Whilst the earliest examples do not obviously focus on the first Late Iron Age enclosure complex (Phase 3), most of the remainder occur within the area of the large rectilinear Enclosure J (Phase 4). This perhaps strengthens the argument for this latter arrangement having been laid out before the Roman Conquest. Both Colchester brooches were found in different sections of the Enclosure J ditch. Finds from outside the Phase 3 and Phase 4 settlement core include the early boss-on-bow brooch (no. 1) from just beyond the south-west side of Enclosure J; the two brooches found in Cremation F.408 beside its south-east corner; and an Aucissa and a Hod Hill brooch (nos. 9 & 13) found close to one another in the late first-century AD fieldsystem (Phase 5); they could well therefore have both been dislodged together from an earlier context.

To summarize, the Hutchison Site's brooch assemblage implies continuous occupation on the site from the first century BC until at least the mid first century AD. The settlement evidently began before brass brooch types became common, but probably after the mid first century BC, otherwise more iron brooches might have been expected. In the early first century AD, the assemblage seems generally to follow regional trends, but there is a noticeable deficiency of mid–late first-century AD types compared to other East Anglian sites. This is not obviously due to the small sample size and should therefore indicate a change in the character of activity on the site from this period.

Other metalwork finds (GRAHAME APPLEBY)
The cemetery assemblage
Copper alloy
Grave 9/F.388; Small Find No. 73 - Small fragment of curved/bent rod with roughly circular cross-section. Surface is pitted and friable. Dimensions: 26.5 mm, diameter 3 mm. Possible brooch pin fragment.

Grave 15/F.405 - Curving fragment of 'D'-shaped section rod, probably a bracelet (see Crummy 1983), with surviving(?) terminal slightly flattened and broadened into a rectangular shape (Fig. 2.35:1). Dimensions: length 51 mm, width 3.5–4 mm, weight 4 g. The item has been conserved. Found as a grave inclusion with <2696>, dated by pottery association to *c.* AD 50–80.

Grave 15/F.405; Small Find No. 74 - Three complete copper-alloy rings of increasing size. Each has a roughly circular to square cross-section (Fig. 2.35:2). The intermediate-sized ring is partially damaged, with an almost complete transverse break. Dimensions: 24.5 mm, 23 mm and 21 mm. The rings each weigh 2 g. The similar weight of the rings suggest the larger two were made by heating and expanding smaller-sized rings. Found as grave inclusions with <2695>, dated by pottery association to *c.* AD 50–80. The discovery of these rings is not unusual, with several examples of similar size known from sites in Britain, for example Camerton (Jackson 1990, 48), Bancroft villa (Hylton 1994, 309) and Silchester. Interestingly, at the latter of these sites, the ring is identified as a harness ring (Boon 2000, 345, fig. 159).

Cremation 3/F.411 - 12 small crumbs of copper alloy. The crumbs are friable and may have been burnt.

Grave 2/Cremation F.408 - Irregular and distorted, roughly rectangular piece of thin copper-alloy sheet. Dimensions: 31 mm × 25 mm, weight 1 g. Found in association with a Colchester derivative brooch (SmF 101; see Haselgrove, above) and several vessels dating to the pre-Flavian period. This fragment may be from a decorative plate or a thin-walled vessel.

Iron
Grave 7/F.386; Small Find No. 83 - Fragment of a Manning Type 1B nail (Manning 1985) with square cross-section and rectangular head. Dimensions: length 52 mm, weight 15 g.

Grave 2/Cremation F.408 - Eight small undiagnostic lumps; weight 4 g. Found in association with a Colchester derivative brooch (see Haselgrove above) and pottery vessels dated AD 69–96.

Other contexts
Copper alloy
Small Find No. 15; F.9 - Corroded small fragments of a copper-alloy sheet. One fragment has a corrugated appearance suggesting this may be fragments from a brooch or decorative item. Recovered from the surface of ditch F.9, close to the junction with ditch F.18. Undiagnostic; Conquest Period.

Small Find No. 86 <069> - Domed oval copper-alloy stud with central piercing (Fig. 2.35:3). The central part has a circular raised area with a sloping surface, and a vertical brake of slope. The underside is concave. The object has an 'eye'-like appearance. A similar shaped object was recovered from Stonea and interpreted as the butt-plate from a knife hilt (Jackson & Potter 1996). Possibly decorative stud. Unphased; possibly medieval or even post-medieval.

Small Find No. 12 <2522> - Fragment of a wide strip armlet or bracelet, crudely pierced at one end, with two narrow longitudinal grooves either side of a wider central longitudinal groove (Fig. 2.35:5). Numerous similar early examples have been recovered from sites in Britain dating to the mid to later first century AD (Crummy 1983; 1997). The strip may also potentially be a decorative scabbard binding or mount (see Bishop & Coulston 2006, fig. 41.3 & 41.4; Webster 2002, 117–19). Dimensions: width 13 mm, weight 5 g. The object has been conserved. Recovered from ditch F.381; Conquest Period.

Small Find No. 14; F.3 - Small bent ('S'-shaped) rectangular piece of a copper-alloy bar or bracelet recovered from the surface of a Conquest Period boundary ditch, adjacent to a large pit (F.500) attributed to the Saxon period. The ends show no obvious sign of breakage. Dimensions: 25 mm × 6.5 mm, weight 1 g. The function of this piece is unclear, but it may be a retaining clip, originally held in place by tension. Recovered from Ditch, F.3; Conquest Period.

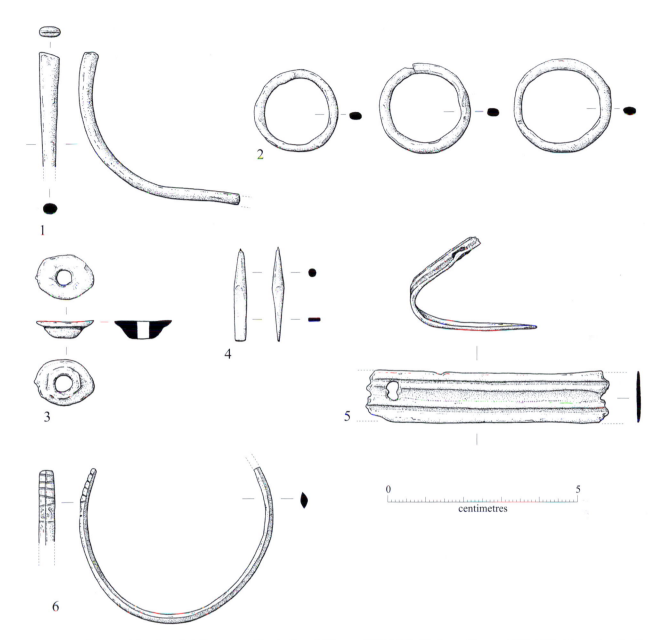

FIGURE 2.35. *Roman Metalwork (all copper alloy): 1) rod (Grave 15/F.405); 2) rings (Grave 15/F.405); 3) stud or knife 'butt-plate' (SmF 86); 4) awl ([214]); 5) armlet/bracelet fragment (F.381; SmF 12); 6) armlet (F.918).*

Small Find No. 33; F.2 - Small flat irregular fragment of copper alloy. There are no obvious cutmarks indicative of reduction for scrap/recycling. Recovered from ditch F.2. Dimensions: 9 mm × 6 mm, thickness 4 mm, weight <1 g. Undiagnostic; Conquest Period.

Small Find No. 35; F.63 - Small complete ring with circular cross-section. Dimensions: internal diameter 9 mm, weight 1 g. Similar types of rings of varying sizes are recovered from numerous Roman sites and are largely undiagnostic. Recovered from Kiln F.63; Conquest Period.

Small Find No. 47; F.40 - Irregular, roughly rectangular, fragment of copper-alloy sheet. The surface is almost completely covered in a friable pale green bloom (verdigris). Dimensions: 55 mm × 21 mm, weight 8 g. Surface find from ditch F.40; Early Roman.

Small Find No. 59 <2708> - Small, fragile triangular shaped fragment of sheet copper alloy, with a central raised ridge. The surface is degraded and corroded, covered with a powdery green bloom (verdigris). Dimensions: *c.* 10 mm × 13 mm, weight <1 g. The raised ridge suggests this fragment may be from a larger item, possibly with repoussé decoration. Unphased.

<2527>; F.918 - Slightly distorted largely complete penannular armlet, with D-shaped cross-section and central longitudinal groove on the upper surface, with six horizontal grooves at the surviving terminal (Fig. 2.35:6). Dimensions: diameter 49 mm, weight 6 g. The item has undergone conservation. Copper-alloy armlets are attested for the whole Roman period, albeit intermittently (Cool 1998, 61). Recovered from pit F.918; Late Iron Age.

<2710>; F.340 - Undiagnostic fragment of cylindrical copper-alloy rod, possibly from a hairpin, needle (Crummy 1983; Niblett 1999), or brooch, thicker in the middle, tapering to narrow broken ends. The ends have five or six flat facets where the rod has been hammered. Found during excavation of a kiln, F.340; Conquest Period.

Lead
Small Find No. 96; F.1032 - Small flat ovoid casting spill. Dimensions: 11 mm × 7 mm, weight < 1 g. Pit F.1032; possibly intrusive within prehistoric feature.

Small Find No. 97; F.1032 - Irregular triangular-shaped thin sheet fragment with a possible cut/clip mark. Dimensions: 37 mm × 11 mm, weight 4 g. Pit F.1032; possibly intrusive within prehistoric feature.

Iron
Small Find No. 11 <022> - X-rayed corroded object of unknown function (cart fitting?). Short bulbous rod, with circular ring and rounded finial at terminal with a flattened bulb on the ring. The ring appears flattened, although probably circular in cross-section. Dimensions: length *c*. 60 mm, weight 50 g.

    Recovered from the corner of a Conquest Period ditch immediately adjacent to a large Iron Age enclosure ditch (F.12), the unidentified iron object found here (<022>) presents an enigma. Clearly well made, with a rounded finial and bulbous central rod, the identification of the item as a linch pin is uncertain, but a distinct possibility (see Jackson & Potter 1996, 66, 300). Although recovered from the surface fill of a ditch phased to the Conquest Period, heavy for its size, this object may be residual, and thus possibly be even early medieval or later in date.

Small Find No. 24; F.339 - Shank/fragment of a square cross-sectioned nail. Similar to Small Find 51. Length 99 mm, weight 17 g. Recovered from ditch F.339; Conquest Period, although possibly intrusive.

Small Find No. 31; F.156 - Lozenge-shaped fragment. Dimensions: 33 mm × 8 mm × 11 mm, weight 5 g. Undiagnostic. Recovered from posthole F.156; undated.

Small Find No. 51; F.12 - Shank/fragment of a square cross-sectioned nail. Length 93 mm, weight 13 g. Recovered from ditch F.12. Late Iron Age; possibly intrusive.

Small Find No. 53; F.746 - Fragment of a Manning Type 1B nail (Manning 1985), with square cross-sectioned and rectangular head. Dimensions: length *c*. 60 mm, weight 16 g. Recovered from ditch F.746; Conquest Period.

Small Find No. 100; F.1214 - Fragment of a small Manning Type 3 nail (Manning 1985) with surviving head. Dimensions: length 24 mm, weight 3 g. From undated pit F.1214.

<062>; F.599 - Fragment of a small Manning Type 1B nail (Manning 1985) with a flat roughly rounded head and square cross-sectioned shaft. Dimensions: 21 mm, weight 3 g. Retrieved from ditch F.599; Conquest Period, although possibly intrusive.

<064>; F.19 - Fragment of handmade nail, with square cross-section shaft and roughly circular head. Dimensions: 47 mm, weight 10 g. Recovered from ditch F.19 and probably dating to the Early Roman period; though, possibly medieval or post-medieval and, thereby, intrusive.

<068>; F.881 - Fragment of a large nail or stud with a roughly rectangular head and only a small proportion of the shaft surviving. Dimensions: length 27 mm, weight 14 g. Recovered from ditch F.881; Early Roman.

Coin
<009> *Small Find No. 46* - Fragment (approximately 50%) of a small copper coin. The surfaces are corroded, with a pale green to reddish patina. Found at the corner of the late first- to mid second-century ditch, F.40/957, during the metal-detecting survey.

Dating from the Conquest or immediately post-Conquest Period, the recovery of three rings and possible bracelet and brooch pin fragments from grave F.405, in addition to brooches found during excavation of the cemetery, attest to the adoption of Roman-style metalwork, especially decorative items or jewellery. The possible burnt lumps from a cremation (F.411) may also indicate that personal items or metalwork were included in the funeral pyre; although uncertain, the copper-alloy sheet from a second cremation, F.408, may also have been included in the pyre. The lack of metalwork from the cemetery suggests that access to new forms of metalwork following the Conquest was possibly limited and reflects the relative wealth of the population. If metalwork from the graves was disturbed due to medieval and later ploughing (this part of the site was severely furrowed) the discovery of additional items in adjacent features and/or the top- or plough-soil during metal-detecting and excavation would have been expected, although the bracelet/scabbard fragment (*Small Find No. 12*) recovered from the road-side ditch on the southern edge of the site may have originated from the cemetery.

    The remaining copper-alloy, lead and iron metalwork is in itself unremarkable, largely retrieved from features dated to the Conquest and/or Early Roman periods, distributed across the site, with the exception of a bracelet fragment recovered from a pit located in the northern part of the site (<2527>). The two lead items are indicative of heat treatment and reduction (clipping), but the paucity of other lead casting spill or scrap suggest that these, as with the majority of the non-cemetery assemblage, were brought to the site as a result of manuring. In contrast, the discovery of a copper-alloy ring (*Small Find No. 35*), a probable pin fragment (<2710>) and possible fragment of decorative copper-alloy sheet (*Small Find No. 59*), argue for these potentially being lost by the operators of or visitors to the kilns, and accords with the large number of brooches found across the site.

Fired clay
A total of 7183 pieces of fired clay was recovered (192.6 kg). The assemblage differs from what would be expected from a 'normal' Late Iron Age or Roman settlement, where most finds are typically daub fragments or amorphous lumps. Here, the assemblage is dominated by fragments of flat plates, blocks or slabs that were presumably associated with the pottery kilns

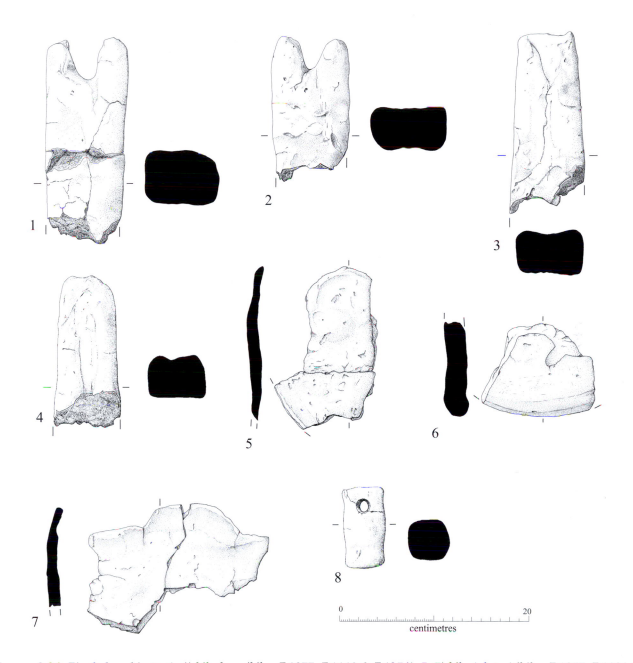

FIGURE 2.36. *Fired clay objects: 1–4) kiln bars (kilns F.1077, F.1119 & F.1254); 5–7) kiln 'plates' (kilns F.1077, F.1181 & F.1254); 8) loomweight ([1768]).*

or other industrial activities. Unfortunately, most of the material was too fragmented to reconstruct. The recognizable kiln furniture from the kiln contexts themselves is discussed first, before moving on to the remaining artefacts.

Kiln furniture

Three principal varieties of kiln furniture can be distinguished, namely kiln bars, thin 'plates' and thick marl or clunch 'slabs' (Fig. 2.36). The distributions of these may indicate differences in the methods of use

of the various kilns (Table 2.23), although it should, of course, be remembered that material dumped within a kiln need not necessarily have been functionally related to it.

Kiln bars

At least 29 fragments of kiln bars were recovered from five contexts associated with kiln F.1181, representing a minimum of ten bars. Additional *possible* fragments were recovered from kilns F.1077, F.1119 and F.1254. None can be reconstructed to completeness, the longest surviving fragment measuring 24 cm long. The bars bifurcate at one end to two rounded prongs, joined at a 'U'-shaped cusp (Fig. 2.36:1–2). The shaft is roughly rectangular in cross-section,

TABLE 2.23. *Distribution of kiln furniture (excluding unfired kilns).*

Kiln	Kiln type	Total weight fired clay/ clunch (kg)	Bars	'Plates' (Roofing?)	'Slabs' (Walling?)
F.63	A	39.11	No	No	Yes
F.1117	A	39.01	No	No	Yes
F.1181	B	35.86	Yes	Yes	Yes
F.340	B	1.28	No	No	No
F.626	D	1.93	No	No	No
F.1078	D	0	No	No	No
F.1077	E	2.10	?	Yes	No
F.1254	E	6.52	?	Yes	Yes
F.853	F	0.35	No	No	Yes

tapering along its length down to a rounded butt-end (Fig. 2.36:3–4). The bars measure 7.5–9 cm wide at the pronged end, 4.5–5.5 cm wide at the butt-end, and are 3.5–5 cm thick. The fabric is hard and oxidized with voids from plant temper. No parallel for such pronged bars is provided by the standard work on Romano-British kilns (Swan 1984). The kiln bars from other Conquest Period/Early Roman kilns in Cambridgeshire at Greenhouse Farm, Swavesey and Haddon were of the more normal 'cigar-shaped' type with two tapering ends (C. Evans 1990; J. Evans 1998; Gibson & Lucas 2002 and Hinman 2003).

'Slabs'
Many large, thick, irregular slabs of baked marl or clunch were recovered from kilns F.63, F.853, F.1117, F.1181 and F.1254. These typically measure 40–60 mm thick and, generally, show evidence for scorching on one surface only. A role as some kind of kiln-lining or covering, as opposed to free-standing kiln furniture, is thus indicated.

'Plates'
Numerous fragments of thin, roughly made, flat though slightly undulating 'plates' were recovered from kilns F.1077, F.1181 and F.1254 (Fig. 2.36:5 & 7). These are 5–15 mm thick, and often show a slight 'curl' at the edge. Due to the fragmentation of the material, the overall size and form of these items is unclear. They have a very hard oxidized fabric with abundant chaff or plant impressions.

At the Roman kiln site of Bursea House, East Yorkshire, the kiln fabric was divided into two groups: thicker pieces (30–70 mm thick) which were interpreted as the lining of the permanent walls of the kiln, and thinner, often curved pieces (10–24 mm thick) which seem to have been irregular plates used to create a temporary roof during the firing (Halkon & Millett 1999, 123). A similar interpretation is possible for the 'slabs' and 'plates' seen here.

One item from a non-kiln context ([581]) should also be noted here. This is a fragment of a circular 'platter', *c.* 30 cm diameter and 2.5 cm thick, in a hard oxidized fabric. Parts of similar objects were found at Haddon and Bursea House, At the latter site it was proposed that these were spacers between pots in a kiln during firing (Halkon & Millett 1999, 123); this

item would also compare to Hughes' Cherry Hinton 'griddles' (see Inset below).

Other fired clay artefacts
The remaining objects of fired clay that are recognizable as artefacts are:

F.30 - Fragment of large slab, 4 cm thick. Straight edge on one side, 13 cm long; survives to 24 cm long across opposing axis. Hard mottled oxidized/reduced fabric with sand and flint.

F.34 - A weight, probably a loomweight, measuring 85 mm high (Fig. 2.36:8). The cross-section is roughly square (*c.* 40 × 40 mm), with rounded corners. There is an oval perforation, 15mm below the top of the object, *c.* 18 × 16 mm in size. Hard reduced fabric with fine quartz.

F.648 - Two bricks that externally revetted oven F.783. Both originally measured *c.* 18 × 8 × 5 cm, but are now very fragmented. Fairly soft oxidized fabric with voids from plant material.

<2257>; [4213] - A complete loomweight of triangular form, perforated through each of the three corners. As is often the case, one side is slightly shorter than the other two, measuring 14 cm compared to 15 cm long. Loomweights of this form were in use from the fifth century BC into the Roman period. Hard oxidized fabric with one flint lump visible.

Worked stone (SIMON TIMBERLAKE)
A total of 11 pieces of worked stone and fragments were recovered (18.5 kg). These were largely small rotary or beehive querns used on a domestic scale for processing and grinding cereals.

<1136>; F.18 - A split pebble (possibly naturally formed) which *may* have been used as a rubbing stone with a saddle quern. Dimensions 130 × 80 × 57 mm, weight 670 g. Composed of quartzitic sandstone, possibly a redeposited Bunter (Trias) cobble, perhaps originating from a Midlands source, but then glacially transported and collected from the local drift.

<1366> F.791 - A fragment of a small East Anglian type of beehive quern (Watts's Type 9e: Watts 2002) showing a section through the inverted flask-shaped eye and basal spindle or axle-hole (between 50 and 23 mm in diameter — narrower at the base above the grinding surface). This is a small-size quern (originally this would have been no more than 250–260 mm in diameter and 110 mm high). The fragment itself was 100 mm high and 80 mm wide and weighed 1.071 kg. The lithology of the rock is distinctive, and consists of Hertfordshire Puddingstone conglomerate, identical to <1737>.

<1514>; F.832 - A fragment of a possible saddle quern composed of basalt or dolerite; 417 g, dimensions 100 × 70 mm, and 35–40 mm thick. The underside and edges have been crudely faced, but the upper surface has been ground flat through use. A dense crystalline rock with the typical lath-like matrix of a dolerite, but with altered mafic (pyroxene) phenocrysts and a slightly vesicular texture. A non-local rock, perhaps collected from the glacial drift.

<1545>; F.852 - A naturally weathered cobble of quartzitic sandstone with a slightly sand polished and frost-pitted upper surface (625 g). Probably washed out of the glacial drift and included within local gravel beds. No evidence of being worked or collected.

<1614>; F.663 - A naturally weathered cobble of quartzite (929 g), possibly derived from the Bunter (Trias) Pebble Beds or else a Carboniferous source, evidently glacially transported. There is no evidence of this having been worked or purposefully collected.

<1737>; F.885 - A fragment of the outer (basal) edge of a upper stone of an East Anglian type of beehive quern (Watts's Type 9e: Watts 2002). A small area of the lower (flat) grinding surface survives; this forms the rather distinctive bevelled edge of this type of quern. Dimensions: 100 × 40 mm and 20–60 mm thick; 296 g. Original quern size probably up to 380 mm in diameter.

The quern is composed of Hertfordshire Puddingstone conglomerate (Lower Eocene) with red-black flint pebble clasts (5–35 mm diameter) within a silica cemented sand matrix. Abington Piggotts in Hertfordshire was a well known source for these from the Iron Age through to Roman times (Wilkes & Elrington 1978) These were traded well outside the East Anglian area, but quite possibly would have been more common locally than other sorts of querns in rural communities within Cambridgeshire.

<2016>; F.1036 - A fragment of the upper stone of a small beehive rotary quern, possibly of a Yorkshire or 'Roman Legionary' type (Watts's Type 9d: Watts 2002) The form of this particular stone is quite distinctive. It also shares some similarities with the Sussex or Wessex types. Dimensions of quern fragment: 130 × 70 mm and between 70–80 mm thick; 1 kg.

The original quern mill would probably have been 220–230 mm wide and up to 140 mm tall (including both top and bottom stones). The upper stone has a carefully dressed circumference which slopes outwards (at an angle of approximately 75° to the flat–slightly concave basal grinding surface), with a bevelled lower rim and an inward sloping upper surface or hopper. The edge of the grain eye has not been preserved within this smaller fragment. The lower dressed grain grinding surface of the stone is fairly worn. The fragment appears to have been used as a part of a rubble fill following its breakage.

The lithology of the stone is quite distinctive; this is a type of medium–fine grained ganister sandstone, a fairly pure orthoquartzite, but with occasional black coaly inclusions and fossil rootlets. Almost certainly from the Upper Carboniferous (Westphalian) Coal Measure sandstones; an origin somewhere in the North of England seems likely.

<2088>; F.1013 - A weathered cobble of slightly vesicular basalt or dolerite (284 g) with a thin coat of secondary lime (calcium carbonate) concretion in places, possibly deposited from spring water. It does not appear to have been worked, although it may have been collected for some purpose. This is composed of the same dense crystalline rock as <1514>, and may be an erratic from the local drift (Boulder Clay or gravels). A glacially transported British origin is likely, either from Derbyshire, the North of England or the Hebrides.

<2157>; F.1076 - A worn fragment of an upper stone of a small beehive quern; 130 × 125 × 105 mm, with grain eye approx. 70 mm diameter (at top), 15 mm (at base) and hole for handle > 90 mm long × 15–20 mm diameter (c. 4 kg).

The form of the stone, with its flattened top and level smooth worn grinding surface, the funnel-shaped eye and narrow handle hole (that doesn't penetrate through to the hopper) are all features reminiscent of the 'Yorkshire' type of beehive quern (after Heslop 1988; Watts's Type 9d: Watts 2002). This general type, although Iron Age in basic design, was still being used by the Roman military in the first century AD (Curwen's 'Roman legionary type': Curwen 1937), and reached Scotland in advance of the Roman army (Watts 2002). The thin handle and basal termination of the axle-hole within the upper stone suggests that both handle and axle spindle may

have been made of iron. The basal grinding surface of the stone seems worn and highly polished through use.

The lithology of the stone suggests a fairly mature sandstone/grit unlike the coarse arkosic lithologies of many of the Millstone Grit beds. However, the presence of rounded grains of quartz and jasperized silica (up to 1–2 mm diameter) within a finer grained quartz sand matrix and cement, yet without any sedimentary structures or fossils, suggests that this rock might be an Upper Carboniferous sandstone, and from the Midlands or the North of England.

<594>; F.500 - A fragment of tufa limestone building stone 250 × 180 × 60 mm (c. 2 kg). Irregular-shaped broken fragment with no dressed facings. Tufa was used extensively as a building stone in Southern *Britannia* (K. Hayward, in Evans & Lucas forthcoming). It was light and easily transportable, easily worked (a freestone), and also strong and durable as a foundation.

The source of the tufa is unknown. The lithology of this example seems better cemented with the inclusion of shelly material and oolitic or peletal concretions, quite unlike the known sources which have formed along spring lines at the base of the chalk outcrops in southeast Britain. Possible sources may lie further afield, either within Northern Britain or perhaps even the Continent. A coastal source is not out of the question.

Roman tile (KATIE ANDERSON)

A small quantity of Roman tile was recovered from the excavations, just 26 pieces (1903 g). The assemblage comprised seven different *tegulae*, most of which were relatively small and abraded, although there was one with part of its flange (F.1117). There were also three *imbrex* tiles and a flue tile, which had combing on the exterior. The remaining pieces were too small to be identified by form, but were recorded as Roman because the fabrics were similar to those from the diagnostic pieces.

Overall, the quantity of the tile is too small to confirm the presence of any building on the site. Most of the pieces came from features that also contained Early Roman pottery, which implies that the tile is also of this date. However, there were also some pieces that were residual within Phase 6 Saxon contexts and others that were intrusive, thus dating the tile more specifically becomes difficult.

Environmental and economic evidence

For the Late Iron Age, the faunal assemblage showed a ratio for the major domesticated species of 53% cattle, 38% sheep, and 8.5% pig (see Swaysland below). The figures remain fairly similar for the Conquest/Early Roman period, with 55% cattle, 41% sheep and 4% pig; horse, dog and goose were also present in both phases. A Late Iron Age pit, F.69, contained a substantial deposit of 90 sheep bones, some articulated, possibly suggesting the remains of a feast or other mass-cull event. The age-data from these demonstrated that there was a culling strategy geared towards maximizing meat production; the cattle bone from these phases indicates that some animals had been used for traction.

The environmental samples from the Late Iron Age and Early Roman period show relatively small amounts of cereal grains and chaff, including wheat and barley. The exceptions to this are samples from kiln contexts, which attest to markedly raised levels of spelt and emmer chaff, suggesting the use of wheat straw as fuel. The weed seeds from these phases come from both disturbed waste ground and arable land, with some wetland plants also found. The molluscs are mostly indicative of open-ground, with a few suggesting damp conditions.

Discussion

Although not without interruptions and irregularities, Phase 4 clearly saw the establishment of a 'grid-iron-like' system of paddocks coming off (and respecting) the line of the southern road (Fig. 2.13). In many respects the key question here is the degree to which this system had its origins in the preceding Late Iron Age landscape.

As has been defined, Phase 3 involves two types of enclosure: more robustly bounded enclosures of sub-circular plan and, also, an irregular 'linear' system. In the former category, extending over some 2085 sqm the main enclosure would be B (Fig. 2.13), which registered so prominently on the site's aerial photographs. Although closely corresponding to features revealed in the course of the excavations, there has to be some doubt whether the cropmark register of its northern half/third is not somewhat 'confused' by other features/systems. (Here it warrants notice that, as shown from the air, its seemingly internal sub-divisions actually related to the position of the Phase 4 enclosure M.5.) Given its configuration and scale, Enclosure B would seem to be a 'farmstead type' compound entirely typical of the period and probably attributable to the later Iron Age. Unfortunately the stratigraphic relationship between it and the Iron Age enclosure (A) it 'overlaps' in the western, Robinson Way-side trenches was not established. However, Enclosure A — which was also robustly ditched — was probably of comparable function and date. The same, however, is not true of Enclosure C which clearly respected 'B' and, obviously post-dating it, probably represents an elaboration and expansion of the larger enclosure. (Sub-)Enclosure C was itself truncated by the western side of a much smaller, sub-circular enclosure, D. Approximately 22 m across (and also visible on aerial photographs), this probably bounded a building rather than delineating a larger compound *per se*. The layout of Enclosure D is of direct relevance as, based on the plan evidence at hand, it would not seem to have been completely discrete. In other words, it could not have been entirely (sub-)circular, but

rather came off the western side of a linear ditch. This can only have been a precursor to the western side of the main Phase 4 paddock enclosure, J. Also of Late Iron Age attribution, Enclosure F must similarly have shared a ditch on the same alignment. This would, therefore, suggest that by the time of the construction of Enclosures D and F, what was to become the Conquest system's alignment had been established. This would be further confirmed by the fact that Enclosure I (whose western boundary was truncated by Enclosure F features) was itself truncated by ditch F.68 that continued east (as F.177, F.197 & F.198) where it 'ghosted' or pre-dated the southwestern axis of the Phase 4 paddock (J; this Iron Age paddock being referred to as H). Similarly, the alignment of ditch F.929 along the northern side of the Phase 4 paddock, Enclosure M, would also suggest a Late Iron Age origin for its layout.

Ignoring for the moment any question of Iron Age precursors, there can be no doubt that the main enclosure, J, of the Phase 4 system was laid-off the axis of the southern road. The 'ropey' or interrupted quality of the road's flanking ditches would seem, at least in part, to relate to the fact that access into the paddock system was from it. Indeed, as indicated by the entrance gap in the northern paddock the main axis of movement through the enclosure paddocks would seem to have been north–south.

The relative regularity of the Enclosure J layout would seem to relate to the fact that it was the main focus of settlement at this time (the distributions of buildings and industry are discussed below). With its smaller internal paddock sub-divisions (J.2, J.3 & J.6; see below for J.4 & J.5) and the almost 'monumental scale' central well in J.1, it does seem quite formal in its arrangement. In this context, why the southwestern axes (F.2, F.1013 & F.1038/1071 in M.4) should curve northward is unknown. This would not seem to be determined by any obvious topographic factor and, rather, it can only be presumed that it pertains to 'accommodation' with the earlier, Late Iron Age layout.

The sense of a Conquest Period 'grid-iron' is again expressed across the northwestern quarter of the site and can be seen in the M.5 layout. It would also be apparent in the fact that within the cropmark plots a ditch is shown running northwest from the northern side of Enclosure A that is clearly the continuation of the ditch line dividing paddocks J.1/J.2 and J.3, even though it did not continue across the western margin of the site *per se*. Equally, that the line of ditch F.718 (*et al.*), dividing Enclosures L and M was also picked up in the 2002 Day-Care Centre investigations (Fig. 2.13; Whittaker 2002a) demonstrates the further continuance of the 'paddocks' grid'. This being said, within the site north of this line (in the area of Enclosures L & K) the ditch lines were more irregular and discontinuous (interestingly though the F.26 & F.735 boundary in K is shown on the geophysical plots as continuing southwest to join with Enclosure J). This may relate to a more major land-use distinction, for the northern Enclosure J/M boundary (F.22, F.23 & F.718 *et al.*) was extremely 'ropey' and irregularly scarred, and this may be the result of plough-turning along its line. (The Phase 5 boundary at this point also has the same 'feathery' character.) What this would suggest is that arable fields lay north of Enclosure J and M, with settlement and presumably also animal paddocks occurring within their bounds.

The southern east ditch within the area of Enclosure K (F.619) was relatively large. It can only be presumed that it continued eastward and was joined by the two complementarily-aligned ditches in the eastern end of the Access Road area: F.654 and F.1226. The latter of these was of robust proportions and would seem to have been a major boundary. In the field, it was suspected that these two parallel ditches might define a *c.* 9.00 m wide, northeast–southwest oriented track or even a roadway, but of this there was no conclusive evidence (see Fig. 2.13). It should equally be stressed that while in the geophysical survey across the unexposed southeastern portion of the playing fields there are also 'ghosted' alignments that could hint of the continuation of F.654 and F.1226, their register is too dispersed and indistinct to definitely ascribe their projection.

The site's Iron Age round buildings exclusively occur within the northwestern quarter of the site (Fig. 2.16). Defined by minor eavesdrip gullies, these are relatively small being only 3.5–10.00 m in diameter (Structures 5–8). There is much greater ambiguity concerning the attribution of the western posthole (-only) defined roundhouse, Structure 13. There is less certainty of the details of its plan and, indeed, its date (whether Phase 2 or 3). The status of the very small, 'U'-shaped structures, 9–12, is equally problematic and these have little obvious parallel. They definitely seemed 'structural' (i.e. not tree-throws, etc.) and may relate either to small sheds or 'ricks', or even some manner of industrial activity (e.g. clamps, kilns or ovens), though it should be noted that there was no direct evidence of burning. (An irregular, building-suggestive sub-circular gully was also distinguished at the 2002 Day-Care Centre site; Trench A: Whittaker 2002a.)

Within the main area of excavation there was one other possible later Iron Age structure, the I/F.64 sub-rectangular/-ovoid ditch setting (Fig. 2.13). No posthole pattern was found to confirm this interpretation and, rather, this suggestion arises from the regularity

of its gully-/ditch-'surround'. The character of Late Iron Age building techniques within southern Britain has long been a major question: were buildings round or rectangular, and to what degree were they without earth-fast foundation (i.e. sleeper beam construction)? This becomes all the more relevant given that many definite Iron Age roundhouses are themselves only defined by their eavesgullies and were clearly without substantial posthole settings (e.g. Evans 2003a).

The question of whether the I/F.64 enclosure surrounded or defined a building does itself relate to the apparent paucity of the site's Conquest Period structures; occupation *per se* obviously occurred on site, but no building plans as such were recovered. However, applying the same logic as above, might not the regularity of the more rectangular ditched 'small' paddocks (Fig. 2.37) equally relate to the fact that they surround buildings? The most obvious example would be the J.5/F.1 'U'-shaped enclosure, that might, in fact, have superseded or replaced the somewhat more irregular I/F.64 setting (Fig. 2.13). Other possible candidates for this would be the J.4 (a & b; F.36, F.38, F.56 & F.1053) ditches and also the M.1/F.684 and F.780 square in the northeastern corner of Enclosure M. This issue, and particularly its ramifications for the Late Iron Age/Conquest Period occupation at the Greenhouse Farm site, will be further discussed below (see *Concluding Discussion*).

The status and attribution of the site's southern roadway will also be discussed at length below. Here, for the sake of analytical convenience, it has been assigned to the Phase 4 occupation and as a primary Roman/Conquest Period phenomenon. However, it warrants mention that the way in which the Phase 3 pitting seemed to respect its line, and the manner in which its profile was locally 'hollowed' prior to its metalling, suggests that an Iron Age 'way' on this line may well have preceded the road as such. This would certainly complement the general situation and alignment of Cra'ster's 1967 enclosure. As shown on Figure 2.13, the 'parallel' ditches south of her compound (see also Fig. 1.4) clearly represent the continuation of the roadway east of our site.

With 16 inhumations and three cremations, the scale (and 'mix') of the site's cemetery is directly equivalent to, for example, the southern burial ground at the Vicar's Farm site in West Cambridge (see *Concluding Discussion* below). Although based on its limited dating evidence the Hutchison's is here assigned to the Phase 4 Conquest Period occupation, this does not imply that it did not continue into the subsequent Phase 5 Roman usage. Indeed, the F.178/492 (*et al.*) ditch line seemed to turn south-eastwards in respect of it. Two other points warrant emphasis as regards

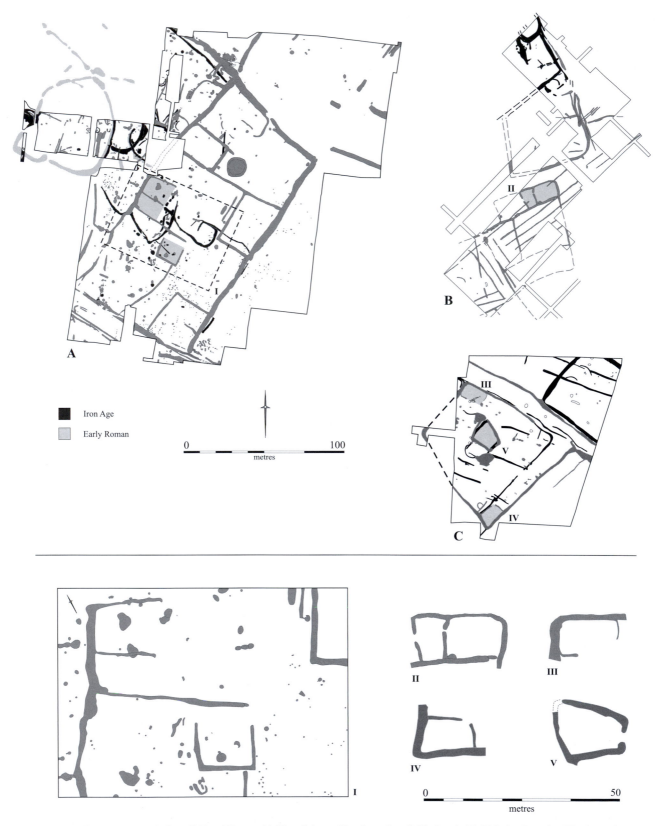

Iron Age

Early Roman

0 _____ 100
metres

FIGURE 2.37. *Conquest Period Building Plots: A) Hutchison Site (see detail I below); B) Trinity Lands, Ely (see also II below; after Evans et al. forthcoming); C) Greenhouse Farm, Cambridge (see also III–V below; after Gibson & Lucas 2002).*

the cemetery. Firstly, and again comparable to Vicar's Farm with its double horse-head setting (see below), is the evidence of animal ritual as evinced in the F.412 dog burial and also the F.398 'bone' pit. The second point relates to the apparent absence of any Iron Age interments within it, despite the fact that it also had 'Early Roman' grave good-accompanied cremation burials. Whilst this was also the case at Vicar's Farm, that site equally lacked any substantive Iron Age occupation. This is not the case at the Hutchison site, where there was direct settlement continuity during the first centuries BC and AD. This makes it somewhat surprising that its cemetery did not also span its Iron Age usage and raises the question of just where the dead were interred during this period.

For the most part, the site's significant 'type' distributions occur in such low numbers as to not be particularly meaningful. The five Iron Age coins recovered, for example, are dispersed and without any obvious concentration (Fig. 2.34). The same is basically true of the Samian, though it shows a westward propensity which could suggest that some of it may relate to pre-Conquest trade (i.e. occurring in Iron Age contexts). More meaningful, or at least convincing, seem to be the brooch distributions. These are almost entirely restricted to the Enclosure J 'block' core of the Phase 4 Conquest Period paddocks (including the cemetery: Fig. 2.34). The distribution of the site's kilns is equally insightful. Apart from two cases, they only occur along the western portion of the site, with six occurring immediately beyond the main F.19/1053 boundary (Fig. 2.23). This would equally suggest that the core of the Phase 4 Conquest Period settlement as such lay immediately east of its axis within the enclosure 'block' J core. Alternatively, as discussed by Haselgrove above, given the pre-Conquest attribution of most of the brooches this could further attest to the Late Iron Age origins of the Phase 4 system.

The group of three brooches found together in pit F.591 in the west-centre of Enclosure J here warrant some comment. As noted by Haselgrove, including a Nauheim (or relation thereof), Langton Down and a plate brooch, as a group they are not chronologically coherent and must reflect a degree of curation and, perhaps, ritual intent. Otherwise, however, the finds from this feature were not particularly distinguished (156 sherds of pre-Flavian/Conquest Period pottery and 36 animal bones; see Swaysland below), and the occurrence of these brooches need not necessarily reflect anything more than the contents of a bag/'purse'; the crucial question, of course, being whether it was dropped or so 'placed'.

Involving a comparable range of kiln types to those found at Greenhouse Farm, Cambridge (Fig. 2.54; Gibson & Lucas 2002), the site's evidence for pottery production would also essentially seem to be of pre-Flavian attribution. However, unlike at Greenhouse, here this activity directly related to contemporary settlement and not a specialist 'enclave' (i.e. a re-used later Iron Age paddock). Based on the Greenhouse Farm excavations, Gibson and Lucas postulated a model of intermittent/seasonal, strictly local production, perhaps involving itinerant specialists. The fact that the Hutchison kilns so clearly match those at Greenhouse site could be seen as supporting that interpretation, perhaps with the same 'specialists' visiting both locales. However, based on the frequency/extent of such Early Roman pottery production within Cambridge's environs now known, alternative interpretations would also be possible. One would involve a 'catch-up' or mass-production model. Rather than relating to intermittent needs (i.e. occasional/seasonal production essentially replacing broken vessels), this would be determined by an *en masse* adoption of a Roman-type ceramic repertoire and, instead of involving a regular rhythm, relate to an intense supply need (i.e. rapid 'Roman' pottery style uptake and the collapse of 'Iron Age-type' manufacture). The other interpretation would simply have the Hutchison Site as a community of 'Potter Farmers', where potting was undertaken regularly/annually on a part-time basis. Accordingly, the character of the two sites' pottery production is further explored in this Chapter's *Concluding Discussion*.

The relationship of the site's kilns to the Phase 4 paddock system warrants discussion, as in two instances (F.340 & F.1181) the kilns occurred in relationship to the system's ditches. In both cases, the kiln-derived rake-out material extended across the middle profile fills of these boundaries. From this it could be inferred that the paddocks had by then been established for some time (and they were poorly maintained) and this evidence could, thereby, also be employed to further arguments concerning the later Iron Age (pre-Conquest) origins of the system's layout.

Late first–mid second century AD (Phase 5)

A subsequent Roman fieldsystem, representing at least two distinct (sub-) phases of activity, lay on a broadly northnortheast–southsouthwest/eastnortheast–westsouthwest orientation and on quite a different alignment to the Phase 4 paddocks (Fig. 2.38). Containing very little contemporary material, the system was evidently agricultural in nature and consisted largely of droveway-related ditches. Its boundaries generally consisted of wide, shallow ditches with multiple narrow re-cuts, suggesting a considerable period of

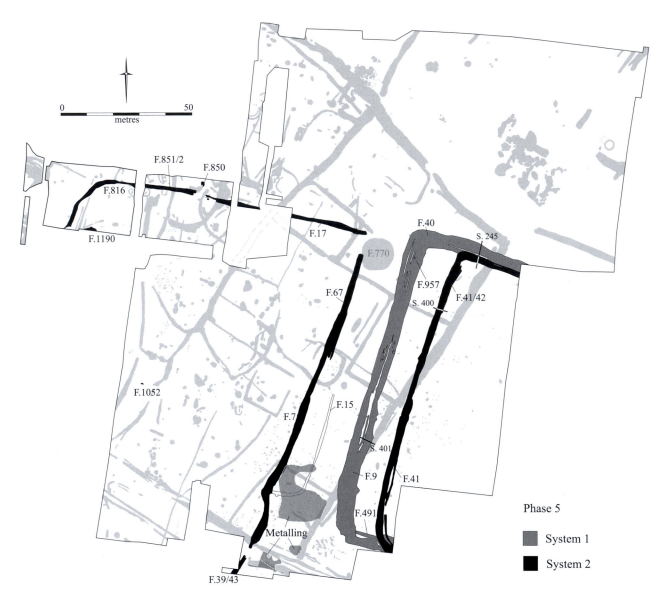

FIGURE 2.38. *Later Roman Features.*

use, and making a precise phasing difficult. We will, nevertheless, here consider each in their turn:

System 1 - F.9/957 defined three sides of a 'field block'.

System 2 - A major east–west ditch-line, with a rounded southward 'corner' at its western end, extended across the northwestern half of the site (F.17/816/851/852). With the F.17 (*et al.*) ditch obviously terminating in relationship to what would then have been the still open hollow of the large Phase 4 well (F.770), ditch F.7/67 must essentially mark the fieldsystem's southward return axis at this point. At its southern end the latter kinked/curved somewhat eastwards; it then terminated at the northern side of the Phase 4 road, but after a *c.* 7.00 m interruption continued in the line of ditch F.39/43.

Truncating the southeastern end of the System 1 ditch (F.9/957), F.41/42 also defined three sides of a 'field block' (shifted *c.* 10 m east of the System 1 line), whose western boundary ran parallel with ditch F.7/67, 30–35 m apart.

Two other components need to be added to this sequence. At the point over its southern length where the System 1 ditch F.7/67 veered eastwards, a minor tough-like 'linear' (F.15) extended east and northwards to define a 9.00 × 40.00 m 'alcove-like' paddock. Although seeming contemporary with that System 1 boundary, it was sealed by a metalled spread (F.314), which appeared laid in relationship to the F.7/67 ditch. In short, we have very little idea of the exact associations of the F.15 ditch setting. To be frank, while potentially relating to the Phase 4 layout, if it were not for its relationship to the metalling there would even be reasons to assign it to Phase 6 (see below).

The F.314 gravel spread was recorded as locally overlapping the main eastern boundary of the Phase 4 enclosure system. To the south it appeared truncated

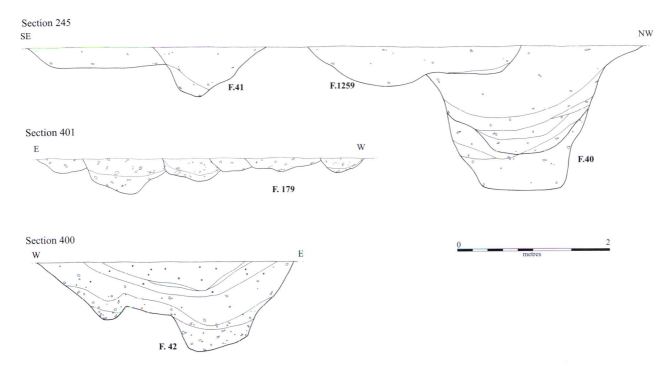

Section 245
SE   NW

F.41   F.1259

F.40

Section 401
E   W

F. 179

0   2
metres

Section 400
W   E

F. 42

FIGURE 2.39. *Ditch Sections.*

by the Phase 6/Saxon ditch-line (F.6/420), beyond which in that direction it only continued in a patchy manner. Unfortunately, given the speed at which the site had to be dug and the pressing need to clear the surface deposits, some ambiguity must exist concerning the exact extent of this horizon.

A scattering of pits can also be dated by their finds to this phase (F.850, F.1052, F.1190). Kiln F.1119 and the uppermost fill of the stokehole of F.1117 also contained material of this phase, but this seems more likely to be 'incidentally' dumped refuse than the residues of pottery production itself.

Sometime after around the middle of the second century AD, the level of activity seem to have dropped markedly. Only a few small scraps of pottery and a Barbarous radiate of the third quarter of third century AD indicate any Late Roman presence.

Pottery

New features in the ceramic assemblage from Phase 5 that indicate a late first- to mid second-century AD date include flanged bowls, 'London Ware' style pottery, possible Horningsea wares, and some new buff wares. A mere three sherds of Nene Valley colour coat pottery (mid second century AD onwards) were found. The paucity of wares common from the mid second century onwards, particularly colour coats, indicates that occupation came to an end by that time, with only manuring activity continuing.

Small finds

Small Find No. 18 <2702> - Substantially complete, corroded Barbarous Radiate dating from the third quarter of the third century AD. Retrieved during metal detecting from surface of ditch F.746, attributed to the Conquest Period.

Small Find No. 3 <2698> - *Dupondius* or *As* dating from the reign of Trajan, AD 98–117. Found during metal-detecting from ditch F.4, dated to the Conquest Period and thus probably intrusive.

<556>; F.956 - Fragment of rotary quern stone (9.2 kg; 270 × 270 × 60–110 mm). Part of a upper worn stone with outer incised rim preserved and circular rough grind ridges or grooves present on the lower surface (which slopes at approx. 5° from horizontal away from the central axle-hole), and with pitting from the original mill stone dressing surviving around the circumference and on the topside of the stone. The latter extends from the axle-hole to an undressed raised cordon up to 70 mm from the outer edge. The projected diameter of the original stone would be around 600–620 mm, with an axle diameter of 50–60 mm. The rough circular grooving on the ground face is distinctive of querns used for the initial breaking up of grain, rather than the milling of these to flour, suggesting that processing carried out here was in fact a two stage process. This contrasts with the more complex and larger dressed Roman millstones which carried out both functions together (Watts 2002). Reddening of the rough dressed side of the quern suggests that the stone had been burnt following its abandonment, perhaps to break it up for use as posthole packing or as rubble within road fill or foundations.

The quernstone lithology consists of medium–coarse arkosic grit with a fairly homogeneous grain size of 1–3 mm, with well cemented angular quartz (glassy), orthoclase (pink), and plagioclase (white) feldspar with occasional larger (<5mm) quartz or orthoclase pebbly clasts. The high incidence of orthoclase is quite distinctive of this grit horizon source. In all probability, this comes from the Millstone Grit (Upper Carboniferous), the closest outcrops of which are to be found round the southern side of the Peak District (Derbyshire). The nearest source is at Melbourne (75 miles distant), whilst the main outcrop is to be found at Duffield, just north of Derby (85 miles). A number of Roman–medieval Millstone Grit extraction sites have been identified, including Wharnecliffe Edge (SK 296795) and Hathersage (SK 232810; Peacock 1998).

In addition, three iron nails were also found: one from F.955 and two from F.956.

Environmental and economic evidence

Environmental evidence is rather sparse for this phase. The samples taken from the ditch system contained virtually no archaeological plant remains, with just a single wheat grain and a small amount of charcoal (see below).

Discussion

Dating to the later first–early second century AD, this phase marks a major change in the site's sequence. Primarily, there was a paucity of occupation *per se* within the immediate area and, instead, it was given over to fields. This interpretation is entirely consistent with the very low finds density from this time, which for the most part need not represent anything other than manuring.

While this phase, therefore, attests to a major change of land-use, unfortunately it is not possible to be absolutely certain what it implies for the potential continuance of the southern roadway. Its line was then clearly impinged upon by ditches F.39/43 and F.7/67 (and there was no evidence whatsoever of the maintenance of its flanking ditches), but it still nevertheless may have continued as a 'way'. Equally, the paucity of post-second-century pottery need not imply that this system itself was then abandoned. Indeed, representing no more than outfields (albeit on a 'big' scale), it need not have then seen any finds deposition. The recovery of a few scraps of very abraded Nene Valley wares might attest to the continuance of manuring into the third/fourth centuries.

Albeit patchy, the recovery of the metalled surface between the Systems' northnortheast–southsouthwest 'way' raises the issue whether it should be assigned the status of another road. While the lack of any roadway-specific flanking ditches makes it impossible to resolve this, it could well have been more than just a fieldsystem trackway (see *Concluding Discussion*). Whatever its entitlement, it should be noted that in the light of the difficulties of nuancing this phase's main linear components, it is quite conceivable that the western System 2 ditches may have actually overlapped with the use of System 1's boundaries; in which case, the F.7/67 and F.9/957 ditches may have defined an original 15–20 m wide version of this route.

Middle Saxon (Phase 6)

The features attributable to this phase of usage consisted of a curvilinear ditch (F.6/F.420), five wells (F.482, F.500, F.501, F.552 and F.609), a pit (F.559), and one, or possibly two, rectangular posthole buildings (Structures 14 and 15: Fig. 2.40). Most of these occurred close to the southern limit of the excavation, although a possible Saxon well occurred much further north.

Ditch F.6 was distinguished from most of the features around it due to the darkness of its fill: a rich, very dark brown clay-silt with frequent charcoal and artefacts, including Saxon pottery, fully consistent with domestic deposition (Figs. 2.40 & 2.41). The ditch narrowed as F.419 before widening out again as F.420, which itself then butt-ended. Lying just to the south of this terminus was a well, F.482, which contained Saxon pottery in its upper fills. Contained by this semi-circular enclosure was Structure 14, a post-built structure. Although containing no dating evidence, the building sits uncomfortably with the Conquest Period ditches around it, as well as the adjacent cemetery and road.

Also falling within the Saxon phase were four outlying wells, F.552, F.500, F.501 and F.609 (Figs. 2.40 & 2.41). Although only F.552 was clearly dated by Saxon pottery, the others were close enough in their form and fill to be associated with this phase of the occupation, along with a tendency for later features to contain lava quern fragments (F.609 also had a later, St Neots sherd; see below). Of the five wells included in this phase, four of them contained lava fragments, which were also found in ditch F.6/420. Excluding a piece of lava quern occurring residually in a furrow inside enclosure F.6, and another piece in Saxon pit F.559, only two other pieces occurred across the entire site (Fig. 2.40).

Buildings

Two rectangular buildings may be of Anglo-Saxon attribution, although neither yielded any datable material. Structure 15 is the most likely to be of this date, due to its location within Saxon enclosure ditch F.6, and its awkward placing in relation to nearby Late Iron Age and Roman features. The dating of Structure 14 is more uncertain, and it is very tentatively assigned to the Saxon period on the grounds of its comparable morphology and alignment to Structure 14.

Structure 14 - A rectangular structure formed of 36 postholes (F.222–43, F.245–53, F.255, F.257, F.264–5: see Fig. 2.40) distinguished by their orange-brown silty fills. The exact form of the building is uncertain, but it seems to measure approximately 11 m northnortheast–southsouthwest by 5 m eastsoutheast–westnorthwest. The west wall is formed of eight postholes (F.230–34, F.236, F.242, F.248) and

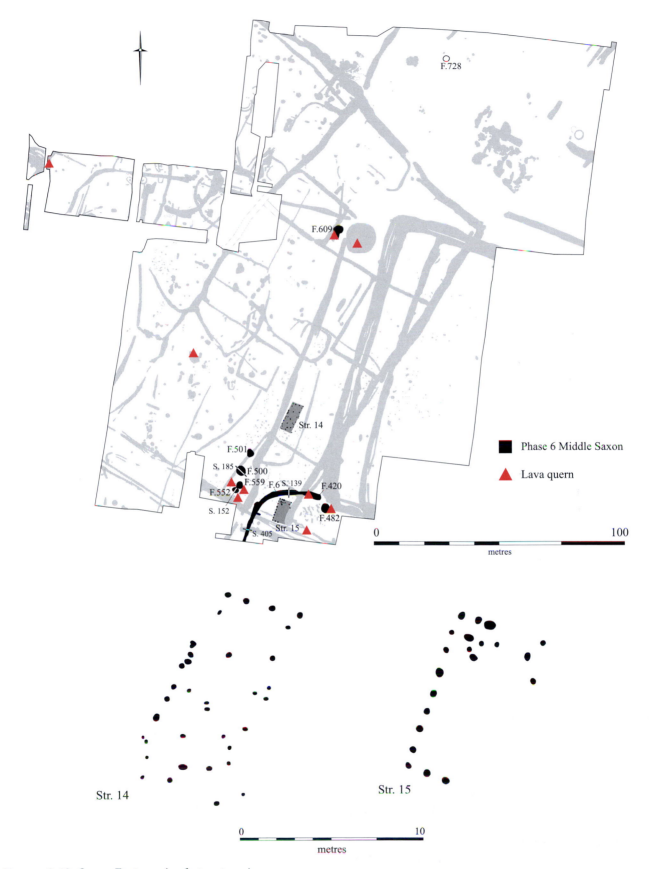

FIGURE 2.40. *Saxon Features (and structures).*

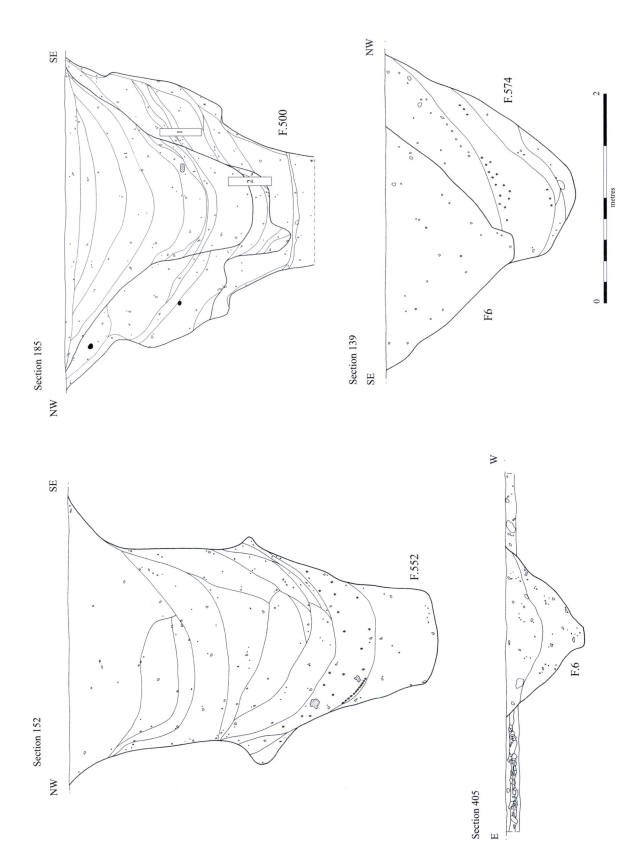

Figure 2.41. *Saxon Well and Ditch Sections.*

the north wall by four (F.222–5); the south and east walls are more difficult to trace. The postholes range from 0.17–0.47 m in diameter and 0.03–0.30 m in depth. One further posthole, F.244, is located within the area of the structure, but may not be related as it has a differing grey-brown silt-clay fill.

Structure 15 - A rectangular structure formed of 15 surviving postholes, measuring 9.25 m northnortheast–southsouthwest by 5.0m eastsoutheast–westnorthwest (see Fig. 2.40). The west side of the structure was intact, with nine postholes spaced *c.* 1 m apart (F.428, F.431, F.436, F.439, F.441–5). If corner posts are counted twice, there were four surviving postholes on the north side (F.423, F.428-30), three on the south (F.445-7) and two on the east (F.423, F.425). Further postholes on the northern and southern sides are likely to have been obliterated by a later furrow. On the east side, posthole F.425 cut ditch F.8, and further postholes were perhaps not possible to observe within the silted-up ditch, due to its similarity in colour to the posthole fills. The structural postholes ranged in size from 0.20–0.48 m diameter and from 0.03–0.32 m deep with mid brown–grey silt fills. Two small pits with dark charcoal-packed fills, F.424 and F.432, lay within the northeast and northwest corners of the building respectively, and may have been internal fixtures. F.424 measured 0.53 × 0.48 × 0.10 m, while F.432 was 0.44 m in diameter and 0.15 m deep; there was no trace of *in situ* burning. Also within the northern part of the building was a cluster of four postholes (F.433–4 and F.437–8) which had identical fills to the structural postholes. There were no finds of any kind from the structure.

Wells

Five wells have been attributed to the Anglo-Saxon period. Four of these were situated at the southern end of the site (F.482, F.500, F.501 and F.552: Figs. 2.40 & 2.41), the latter three being arranged in a closely spaced, north–south aligned row, while F.609 was located further to the north adjacent to the large Phase 4 well (F.770). The wells ranged from 2.2–4.0 m diameter, and from 2.8–3.4 m deep, with the exception of F.609 which was only excavated to 1.4 m depth (Table 2.24). All were roughly circular with vertical or near-vertical sides and fairly flat bases. The sides were presumably revetted, though no actual traces of this could be observed.

The wells typically showed a complex series of fills, with clay or silt-clay deposits predominating. Finds were generally scarce. F.552 contained 11 sherds of Ipswich Ware in secondary fill [1258], while F.482 yielded Ipswich Ware in the upper three fills. F.609 could be slightly later in date due to the presence of a sherd of St Neots-type pottery from its upper fill [1588]; this feature also contained lava quern fragments. The pottery from F.500 and F.501 consisted only of small numbers of Late Iron Age and Roman sherds, though F.500 included fragments of lava quern. In addition, a remarkable carved clunch block of uncertain date was recovered from F.501 (see below). A further well, F.728, situated at the northern edge of the site, might on morphological grounds also date to the Saxon period, although the only datable find was a single sherd of PDR pottery.

Feature	Diameter (m)	Depth (m)
F.482	3.4	3.2
F.500	4.0	3.0
F.501	3.0	3.4
F.552	2.2	2.8
F.609	3.9	>1.4

TABLE 2.24. *Anglo-Saxon wells.*

Artefact studies

Anglo-Saxon pottery (PAUL BLINKHORN)

In addition to the Ipswich ware, which constituted the bulk of the assemblage, a sherd of shelly St Neots-type ware (119 g), dating to the ninth–eleventh centuries AD, was found in F.609; this was a rim fragment with part of a bar-lug.

Ipswich Ware, dated AD 725–850 (Blinkhorn 1999) was the first pottery to be produced on an industrial scale in post-Roman England. It was made on a 'slow-wheel' or turntable, and manufactured exclusively in the eponymous Suffolk *wic*. It has the widest distribution of any native pottery type of the period, and is found all along the east coast of England from York to Kent, and penetrated westward along the major river valleys as far as Gloucestershire.

There are two main fabric types, although individual vessels which do not conform to these groups also occur:

Group 1 - Hard and slightly sandy to the touch, with visible small quartz grains and some shreds of mica. Frequent fairly well-sorted angular to sub-angular grains of quartz, generally measuring below 0.3 mm in size but with some larger grains, including a number which are polycrystalline in appearance.

Group 2 - Like the sherds in Group 1, they are hard, sandy and mostly dark grey in colour. Their most prominent feature is a scatter of large quartz grains (up to *c.* 2.5 mm) which either bulge or protrude through the surfaces of the vessel, giving rise to the term 'pimply' Ipswich ware (Hurst 1976). This characteristic makes them quite rough to the touch. However, some sherds have the same groundmass but lack the larger quartz grains which are characteristic of this group, and chemical analysis suggests that they are made from the same clay.

The Ipswich Ware assemblage comprised 20 sherds with a total weight of 1005 g. The estimated vessel equivalent (EVE), by summation of surviving rim sherd circumference was 0.62. All the sherds from this site are of Group 2 type, although it cannot be said if this is of significance, as no typological fabric or form traits have ever been identified due to a lack of suitable stratigraphic sequences. Three rim sherds were noted, two of West's Type I.C rim (Fig. 2.42:1–2) and one of his Type II.K (West 1964) All were from jars,

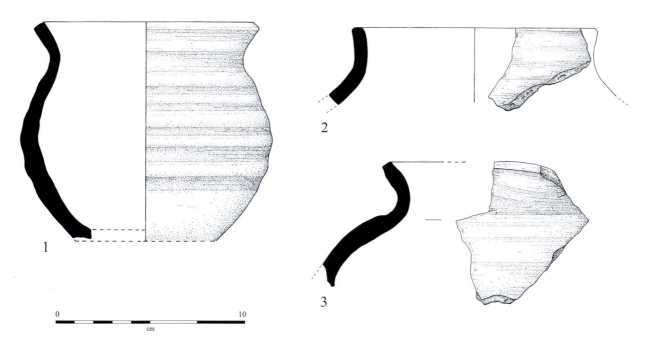

FIGURE 2.42. *Anglo-Saxon Pottery, Ipswich Ware: 1) Type I.C rim and full profile of small jar (200 mm dia; [1258], F.552); 2) Type I.C rim sherd (120 mm dia; [3514], F.482); 3) large bodysherd ([3514], F.482).*

TABLE 2.25. *Ipswich Ware.*

Sherd no.	Feature	No.	Wt (g)	Comments
1	420	1	96	Sherd from very large jar
2	420	1	31	Shoulder of small jar
3	420	1	10	Bodysherd, small jar
4	420	1	26	Large jar, joins with Sherd 5
5	420	1	54	Large jar, joins with Sherd 4
6	420	1	27	Base sherd, probably same vessel as Sherds 4 and 5
7	420	1	35	Joins Sherd 13, large jar
8	420	1	189	Bodysherd from large jar
9	420	1	62	Base from large jar
10	420	5	12	Miscellaneous fragments.
11	552	1	326	Full profile of small jar, Type I.C rim, 120 mm diameter, EVE = 48%
12	482	1	14	Rimsherd, Type II.K, 200mm diameter, 4% EVE, joins Sherd 16
13	482	1	53	Joins Sherd 7
14	482	1	17	Rimsherd, Type I.C, 120 mm diameter, 10% EVE
15	482	1	16	Bodysherd, small jar
16	482	1	37	Bodysherd, same vessel as Sherds 4,5 and 6?
	Total	20	1005	

and the body sherds revealed no evidence of any other vessel types being present. No decorated sherds were noted, although all the sherds from the upper bodies of vessels had horizontally finger-grooved surfaces, a standard technique of the industry. The number of cross-fits suggest that it is an assemblage which is more or less contemporary, and that there was not long-lived Middle Saxon activity at the site.

The pottery occurrence by number and weight of sherds per context by fabric type is shown in Table 2.25.

Querns (SIMON TIMBERLAKE)
Some 8063 g (*c.* 103 pieces) of lava querns were found, mostly small fragments 20–40 mm thick. Most of the lava querns are from Anglo-Saxon contexts, and it is likely that the majority are of this date.

F.420; [1186] - Some very small fragments of a broken lava quern, probably Niedermendig (6 g).

F.500; [1097] - Two small fragments (weathered) of lava quern, probably Niedermendig (14 g).

F.529; [261] - Some small fragments of a broken lava quern, probably Niedermendig (83 g).

<349>; F.552 - A small fragment of a broken lava quern, probably Niedermendig. Approximately 37 mm thick, possibly part of a lower stone (71 g).

<588>; F.500 - Up to 25 small fragments of a broken lava quern, prob-

ably Niedermendig. Probably part of a lower flat rotary quernstone, no more than 30 mm thick (311 g).

<920>; F.609 - At least seven fragments of the lower stone of a lava quern, three of which are adjoining, and which piece together to form a section some 110 mm in diameter (and wide) and 42 mm thick in the centre around the perforated axle- or spindle-hole (approx 20–25 mm diameter). The outer edge of this section is only 25 mm thick, thus fairly typical of a gently convex and slightly conical-shaped bottom stone of a flat-topped or collared Roman rotary lava quern. The total weight of fragments (probably all from the same stone) is *c.* 677 g and the diameter of the original stone may have been about 400 mm; composed of vesicular basaltic lava, probably Niedermendig.

<1265> F.770 - A wedge-shaped fragment of a possible saddle quern composed of lava. Dimensions 60 × 70 mm, and between 34 and 15 mm thick (224 g). The upper surface of this has been ground flat (slightly concave), the lower surface left rough. The rock is slightly vesicular, fine-grained, and possibly glassy/devitrified in places; perhaps andesitic or dacitic in composition; non-local, possibly British.

<1437> F.809 - Two small fragments (largest 60 × 50 mm) from a thin (max. 20 mm thick) lower stone of a flat rotary lava quern, probably Niedermendig (100 g).

<1863>; F.1244 - A small fragment of lava quern: 80 × 60 mm and 25–30 mm thick (225 g). Part of either an upper or lower flat rotary quernstone, with one ground and one undressed surface. Composed of basaltic vesicular lava; almost certainly a Roman import from the Eifel region (Germany), probably Niedermendig.

<1909>; F.482 - A bag of small fragments of part of a broken lava quern, probably Niedermendig (223 g). The largest fragment suggests that these came from a flat lower rotary quernstone, perhaps one which broke on account of this wearing thin (<25 mm).

<2512>; F.1066 - Fragments of a single (?) lower stone of a flat rotary lava quern (5.7 kg). The largest of the 20 or so fragments probably represents a half-section from the rounded outer circumference to the spindle-hole in the centre. The perforation for this, which penetrates *through* the lower stone, survives within just one of the fragments. The spike of the spindle or axle that passed through this may have helped to temporarily anchor these relatively light stones within the ground during the grinding process. The original stone was probably 440–460 mm in diameter, and evidently uniformly 30–35 mm thick, although there was evidence for a slight thinning in the centre. No evidence for furrow-dressing of the grinding surface can be seen; evidently this was well worn by the time it broke, or else was discarded. The stone is relatively thin and fragile, and would easily have broken if dropped. The fragments may then have been used as a rubble fill.

The lithology is fairly typical of an Eifel basaltic lava (from the Eifel region, Germany), possibly a vesicular lava from the Niedermendig quarries containing the distinct phenocrysts of felspathoid, pyroxene (augite) and some olivine. These were imported into Britain from the Rhineland from the first century AD or before, and would have made up a useful ballast cargo for boats crossing the Channel. Many of these could have travelled via *Camulodunum* (into where basaltic lava was imported and extensively used) and then along the *Via Devana* into the Cambridge area.

Small Finds No. 14; F.3 - Surface find. One large and several small fragments of lava quernstone. Probably part of the lower and very worn stone of a flat rotary quern. Largest fragment 95 × 100 mm and no more than 22 mm thick; total weight 429 g. Almost certainly of Niedermendig type basaltic vesicular lava. Roman, imported.

Carved clunch block

A rectangular clunch block with various incised markings was recovered from well F.501 ([1226]; Fig. 2.43). The piece is a well-faced 'ashlar-type' stone that could, conceivably, even have been taken from a masonry building. Parts of four finished surfaces survive, and one complete edge, the block measuring 130 mm × 120 mm+ × 65 mm+. Three of the faces have darkened surfaces, while the remaining (largest) face and the broken surfaces are noticeably cleaner. This suggests that the darkening did not occur post-deposition but while the block was in use, perhaps from exposure to smoke.

Each of the four surfaces bears markings, the clearest occurring on the three darkened surfaces. Of these, the side with the most regular ornamentation has a rectangular frame enclosing a row of double nested chevrons, fairly shallowly incised. Another side has two deeply and crudely incised incomplete motifs, and the third has a series of confused markings including one 'X' motif. The 'clean' face of the block is, meanwhile, marked with a series of fairly straight lines that may or may not be deliberate ornamentation. The differences in the character of the markings on the various surfaces suggests that they were not all necessarily carved at the same time, by the same person, for the same purpose. The markings cannot be dated stylistically, given that chevrons and crosses are common motifs through most periods of antiquity.

The 'clunch' block is composed of a hard chalk rock, probably a calcarenite horizon such as the Totternhoe Stone member of the Cenomanian Grey Chalk (Lower Chalk), which outcrops in the Addenbrooke's area, and thus was probably quarried locally. The chalk contains small amounts of fossil shell and fish bone debris.

Metalwork (ANDREW HALL)

A small group of copper-alloy and iron artefacts of Middle Saxon attribution were recovered through excavation and the metal-detecting survey (Fig. 2.44).

Copper alloy

Two artefacts were recovered from the fills of enclosure ditch F.420/F.6. These included a Middle Saxon dress pin with biconical head (unfaceted; *SmF No. 6*, <2700>: Fig. 2.44:1). The shank is decorated with three parallel incised lines 30 mm from the point. Similar examples are published from Coppergate in York (Mainman & Rogers 2000) and within West's corpus of Suffolk finds (West 1998). In addition, ditch F.420 ([450]) yielded a copper-alloy needle with the head broken off across the lumen, 115mm in length (<2688>: Fig. 2.44:2). Its robust nature and length suggests that it was used for leather working. A small fragment of cast copper alloy was recovered from well F.552 (<006>). This was undiagnostic in form and may well be residual.

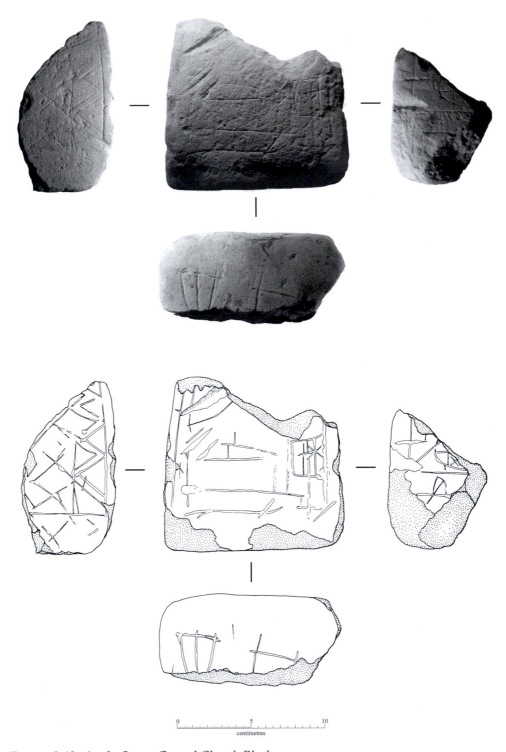

FIGURE 2.43. *Anglo-Saxon Carved Clunch Block.*

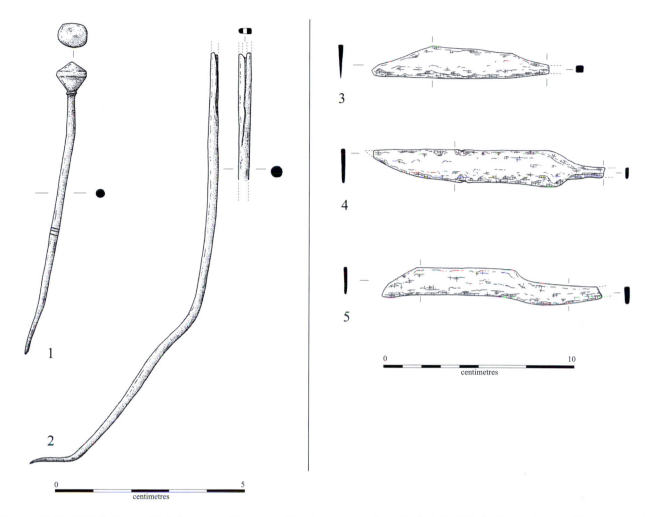

FIGURE 2.44. *Middle Saxon Metalwork: 1–2) copper-alloy dress pin and needle (F.6, F.420); 3–5) iron knives (F.42 & F.500).*

Iron

A small knife blade (*SmF No. 13*, <023>; Fig. 2.44:3) of elongated triangular form was found within the upper fill of well F.500. It measures 93 mm in length (shank snapped at shoulder), with a maximum blade width of 17 mm. Within the same feature, fill [1099] yielded two iron objects, including a 120 × 8 mm strip punctuated with three rivets (*SmF No. 49*, <035>). This is most likely a fitting or binding strip from a composite wooden object such as a bucket, similar to examples recovered from the Edix Hill cemetery at Barrington, Cambridgeshire (Malim *et al.* 1998). The other find is a round-sectioned rod fragment 90 mm long and 4 mm in diameter, with a bent over terminal (<037>; SmF 50). A further small fragment of unidentifiable iron was recovered from well F.609 ([1514]). Two knife blades, 120 mm in length, were retrieved from the upper fill of F.42 (*SmF No. 55 & 56*, <39 & 40>; Fig. 2.44:4–5). Both have close parallels with examples from the Early Anglo-Saxon settlement at Bloodmoor Hill, Suffolk (Lucy *et al.* forthcoming) and correspond to Types 2 and 4 respectively within Evison's typology (1987, 113–16).

With the exception of the final two knives, these finds were recovered from two wells and the main enclosure ditch within the core of the Middle Saxon settlement. The knives were found some 50 m to the northeast within the upper fills of a Phase 5 Roman ditch. The positioning of the main Saxon settlement features between two parallel ditches of this late Roman system, and the presence of these finds, does suggest the ditch must have still been 'open' to a certain extent and, therefore, demonstrates continuity as a functioning or relict boundary at this time.

Environmental and economic evidence

The animal bone recovered from secure Saxon contexts showed a ratio for the three major domesticated species of 54% cattle, 35% sheep and 10% pig; horse, dog, cat, goose and chicken bone was also present (see Swaysland below). The environmental samples, taken mainly from well fills, were in some cases very rich (see Roberts below). There were considerable amounts of cereals, dominated by free-threshing wheat grains, but with barley, rye and oats also represented. Celtic beans or peas may also have been grown. Of wild plants, stinking chamomile was found in large amounts, possibly indicating a change by this time to mouldboard plough cultivation of the heavy clay soils. Significant numbers of wetland plants such as rushes and sedges evinces the importation of plant materials. The molluscs include both damp and open-ground species. This evidence is supplemented by analysis of pollen from well F.482 (see Boreham below), which indicates an open tree-less environment with some evidence for arable activity and for nearby damp ground.

Discussion

With only twenty-one sherds of pottery attributable to this phase (Table 2.26), this does not seem a major occupation. Indeed, its existence was not recognized as such during the excavations and was instead only identified in the course of post-excavation study. However, by the measure of other contemporary Middle Saxon settlements within the region (see Mortimer *et al.* 2005 for overview), this must be counted as a considerable presence. This impression is furthered by the recovery of the two post-built structures of the period.

The manner in which Structure 15 was tucked into the 'alcove-like' arrangement of Roman ditches F.15 and F.7/67 would suggest that it was the earthwork survival of the Phase 5 ditches (perhaps enhanced by associated hedge-lines) that went on to influence the Saxon landscape. In other words, they made use of its remnant earthwork boundaries. In this capacity some element of doubt must exist as to whether the curvilinear ditch line F.6 actually represents a newly established feature at this time, or some manner of re-cutting of an earlier, Roman feature. Although Saxon material occurred well down within its profile, its general plan-layout does seem to mirror the arrangement of the Phase 4 ditch F.816 in the north of the site and respect — and perhaps even continue — the southern corner of the main Roman system (F.9 *et al.*).

The frequency of the wells apparently attributable to this period would also attest to the intensity of settlement-usage at this time. In this regard, the carved clunch block recovered from F.501 can only be considered an extraordinary find and one without direct parallel. It would stylistically fit either a Roman or Saxon attribution and, here, the degree of artefact residuality within the Saxon features does not particularly further its assignation.

Medieval/Post-medieval (Phase 7)

No settlement activity as such seems to have occurred on the site following the end of the Saxon

TABLE 2.26. *Summary of finds from Anglo-Saxon contexts (residual worked flint, pottery and tile excluded).*

Find	No. (weight)
Pottery	21 (1124 g)
Baked clay	101 (912 g)
Iron	3 (30 g)
Copper alloy	1 (3 g)
Lava stone	103 (7878 g)
Worked clunch	1 (1268 g)
Slag	1 (93 g)
Bone	1738 (22,192 g)

occupation. Use of the area for agriculture during the medieval and/or post-medieval periods was attested by numerous furrows, mostly on a north–south alignment (Fig. 2.45). There were, however, also a few at right-angles to that axis along the eastern side of the site and this change of alignment would suggest a field division (which actually appears to roughly co-relate with the Phase 4 ditch-line, F.9 & F.957 *et al.*). Dividing off the northern third of the area, the site was crossed by a rather serpentine/'S'-shaped 'ditch-line', F.21. Up to 8.40 m wide (and cutting over the top of Phase 4 'linears'), the 'feathery' quality of this feature was due to the fact that it consisted of a multitude of intercutting troughs and, in effect, must represent a major plough-line/field boundary. (In further proof, the furrow recorded in the site's northwestern quarter was aligned slightly more northeast-southwest and at a right-angle to the line of F.21 at that point.)

As indicated on Figure 2.45, a seam or interruption was recorded in the line of the furrows across the southern quarter of the site. Broadly corresponding to where the bulk of the Phase 5 gravel surface survived, this surely must relate to the northwestward continuation of the headland that has been plotted from aerial photographs as once crossing the area of the Hospital's grounds (and Cra'ster's 1967 site: Fig. 1.12). Its formerly upstanding ridge (*c.* 15.00 m wide) clearly interrupted the plough furrows and, thereby, locally afforded protection to the metalling below.

The Draft 1st Edition OS map of 1810 shows the area of the site as farmland, a situation that continued into the early twentieth century and the establishment of the College's playing fields.

A total of 41 ferrous and non-ferrous finds were recovered, predominantly from the lower fills of medieval/post-medieval furrows. Reported upon by Andrew Hall, of note was a silver hammered penny of Edward III, 1356–61, from the Durham mint (SmF

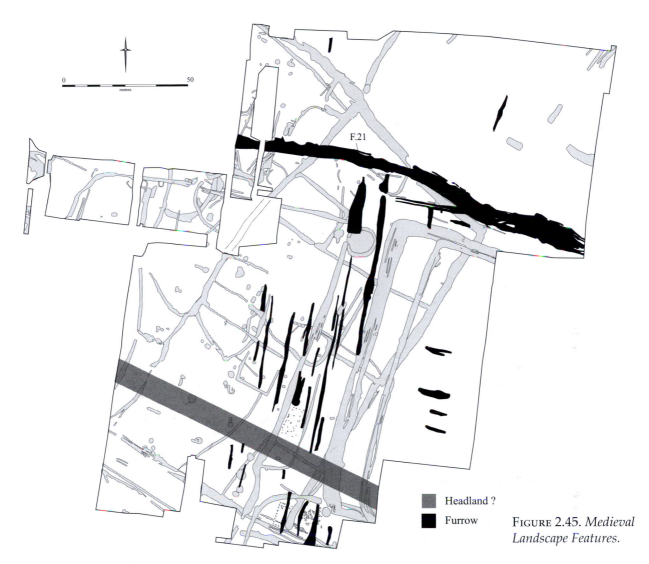

Headland ?

Furrow

FIGURE 2.45. *Medieval Landscape Features.*

no. 48), and two copper-alloy Nuremberg jettons, 1562–86 (SmF nos. 43 & 44). Other finds recovered included a lead spindle whorl of indeterminate date, a medieval iron strike-a-light, and 25 nails ranging in size from small tacks to large structural examples. A large section of an iron sickle blade and various fragments of plough-shares and other agricultural equipment complete the assemblage. These finds represent casual loses by those working the fields and material introduced through manuring.

Of this 'late' agricultural horizon, the main point to stress is that the projected line of the headland ran roughly parallel with the northwest–southeast route of the Roman road (*c.* 15.00 m north thereof) and was off the north–south alignment of the plough furrows. Potentially suggesting an early date for layout of the headland fieldsystem — and that it was strongly influenced by Roman landscape components — the full implications of this will be further explored in this Chapter's concluding discussion.

Radiocarbon dating

Four radiocarbon assays were achieved:
1) [3226]; F.474 (Beta-195160) - 2840±40 BP/1110–900 cal. BC
2) [4569]; F.1061 (Beta-195161) - 2060±40 BP/180 cal. BC–30 cal. AD
3) [887]; F.12 (Beta-195158) - 2010±40 BP/200 cal. BC–70 cal. AD
4) [3226]; F.501 (Beta-195159) - 1300±40 BP/660–790 cal. AD.

Deriving from a pit (F.474) relating to the Phase 2 settlement, the first of these directly reflects its later Bronze Age attribution. The second sample, from a possible cremation pit (F.1061) thought to be of comparable date (but without any direct dating evidence), must instead be associated with the Phase 3/4 later Iron Age/Conquest Period usage. Its register is comparable to that from F.12, a ditch of Enclosure I which, based on dating evidence and stratigraphic/ plan relationships, was from the outset assigned to that horizon. The final date, from pit F.501, was essentially submitted to double-check the assignation of the carved clunch block recovered from that feature, and proved to be Anglo-Saxon.

War Ditches — squaring (and losing) the circle

Of the earlier excavations within the area (i.e. pre-1990), it is the work at the War Ditches that is perhaps of the greatest relevance for us. Not only is this true of its great Early Iron Age ringwork, but also of the Romano-British settlement that overlay it (White 1964a,b). The key point, given that site's long and rather vexed history (see Chapter 1), is how to assemble a convincing 'picture' of its phases.

As a site, the War Ditches has never achieved its true place alongside Cambridge's other Iron Age 'forts', Wandlebury and Arbury. This is largely attributable to the fact that it had been dug in a protracted piecemeal fashion, with no full plan of its circuit having ever seemingly been recovered or, at least, published. In the course of this volume's background researches within the University Museum's Fox archives, we came across two plans of the site that had never appeared in print; one of the eastern side of the quarry that includes the enclosure's northeastern circuit and shows, indeed, that its 'circle' was complete. Excited by this, we first turned once more to White's 1964 published accounts of the University's Field Club's investigations, but where this phase of the 1949–51 work gets no direct mention. Subsequently, we trawled the Museum's archives and came across a wealth of material from the site relating to the University Field Club's excavations, which clearly were the source of this additional northeastern-area work (Fig. 2.47).

Crucially, upon computer-scanning the various plans and overlapping them to create a composite 'master', the line of the ringwork's northeastern circuit passes straight across Lethbridge's eastern 1939 trenches, where he didn't locate it and which, as outlined in Chapter One, led him to dismiss McKenny Hughes' earlier findings (Fig. 2.46:7: Lethbridge 1948). In fact, the entire tone of Lethbridge's '48 paper is rather aggressive towards Hughes and essentially questions his competence as an excavator, which is surprising as Hughes' fieldwork generally seems to have been of a high standard.

Against this background, a letter sent by Lethbridge to Cra'ster in 1963, in which he severely criticizes the quality of the Field Club's excavations ('The whole things was a masterpiece of misdirected energy'), suddenly makes sense. Here we have Lethbridge, having attacked Hughes based on the results of his own 1939 trenching, only to have a group of undergraduates start on the site and find the enclosure's northeastern circuit, proving that Hughes was right all along and that it was Lethbridge's fieldwork that was erroneous.

Having established this sequence of events, what then of the apparent omission of the northeastern quarry results (and the ringwork's complete ditch circuit) in White's 1964 publications? Look again at his 1964(a) figure 2 plan and it is clear that the detail of its southwestern corner seems inset into the area of the ringwork's northeastern sector almost to avoid showing the enclosure's line (Fig. 2.48; inset omitted). That White knew of this northeastern sector fieldwork is obvious from his account of the 1949–51 investigations, as the inner side of its circuit is clearly indicated on his general site plan (1964b, fig. 1); yet there is no basis by which to actually locate it. If being charitable, it could just be that White had little experience of technical graphics and, therefore, did not present the data in an intelligible manner. However, one cannot but think that the knowledge of the ringwork's circuit has been 'politely' suppressed to maintain Lethbridge's reputation as a 'fieldman' (i.e. pressure being brought to bear on a student; Lethbridge was, though, then in some local disrepute because of the publicity he had courted for his spurious Gog Magog chalk figures). Either

way, in all this it has been the War Ditches as a monumental ringwork that has suffered, with its plan-layout being left in doubt when the knowledge of its full circuit has been available for almost 60 years.

The results of both Hughes' and Lethbridge's initial phases of fieldwork along the western side of the ringwork proper have been outlined in Chapter One and need not be further rehearsed (Hughes 1904a; Lethbridge 1948). In the *Addendum* to his 1948 paper, Lethbridge noted that much of the remaining quarry-field had then been mechanically stripped of its topsoil (largely by bulldozer resulting in some feature-truncation) and that features were exposed; it is even mentioned in *The Journal of Roman Studies* (Wright 1950) that Lethbridge himself had undertaken some further investigations there in 1949. In his 1963 Cra'ster letter, Lethbridge outlined the circumstances of the involvement of the University Field Club. He noted that it was Grahame Clark who had asked him to provide a project for the students and that it was K.D.M. Dauncey of Birmingham University who was then first put in charge as site supervisor (aside from publishing widely on Anglo-Saxon studies, Dauncey was amongst the first to recognize the potential of soil phosphates for archaeology; e.g. 1942 & 1952, see also Smith 1997, xxii). Later, the excavations were run by C.H. Houlder, with Clark himself even being directly involved during the late 1950s, and students from the Leys school apparently also participating at weekends (White 1964a, 15, 17).

White's first 1964 paper covers the fieldwork from 1959–61 (he being in charge during 1961–62) and was concerned with the southern half of the ringwork (and its immediate exterior), including the southern side of its eastern entrance (although its plan suggests that the latter's circuit was completely excavated, it was in fact only trenched). It outlines the recovery of further skeletons within the ditch, these being deposited (i.e. 'thrown in') within the burnt rubble horizon related to the destruction of the defences. He noted the recovery of a line of six postholes running parallel with and just inside the circuit, which he considered a palisade. Otherwise, after Hughes, he attributed the ringwork to 'Iron Age A'; he considered it an unfinished fortification, arguing that it was probably destroyed in the mid second century BC, at which time its defending force was massacred (he didn't accept Fox's 1923 assertion that the site had been refortified by the Belgae: 1964a, 18–19).

Of the site's Roman usage, they excavated a series of boundary ditches, a post-built 'hut', large pits, a well and, just exterior to the ringwork on the east side, a 'dumb-bell'-shaped kiln. (The dotted lines shown on the 1961–62-phase site plan indicated the traces of a later ridge-and-furrow system, and the 'ditch-lines' indicated crossing the ringwork's circuit in the southwest corner were also thus attributed: White 1964a, 15.) The kiln was associated with first-century AD, Belgic tradition

FIGURE 2.46 (right). *War Ditches - A Miscellany: 1 & 2) Hughes's 'ring-and-dot' pottery (top) and, below, reconstructed 'fireplace' setting (1904a, pl. XX.9 & fig. 36) 3) Lethbridge's 1939 kiln (1948, pl. XII); 4 & 5) ditches sections (left, Hughes 1904a, fig. 6; right, Lethbridge 1948, fig. 4); 6 & 7) base-plans, right Hughes' (1904a, fig. 1; note that indication of a 'kiln' between Segments B & C appears to relate to recent/contemporary lime-slaking) and left, Lethbridge's (1948, 118).*

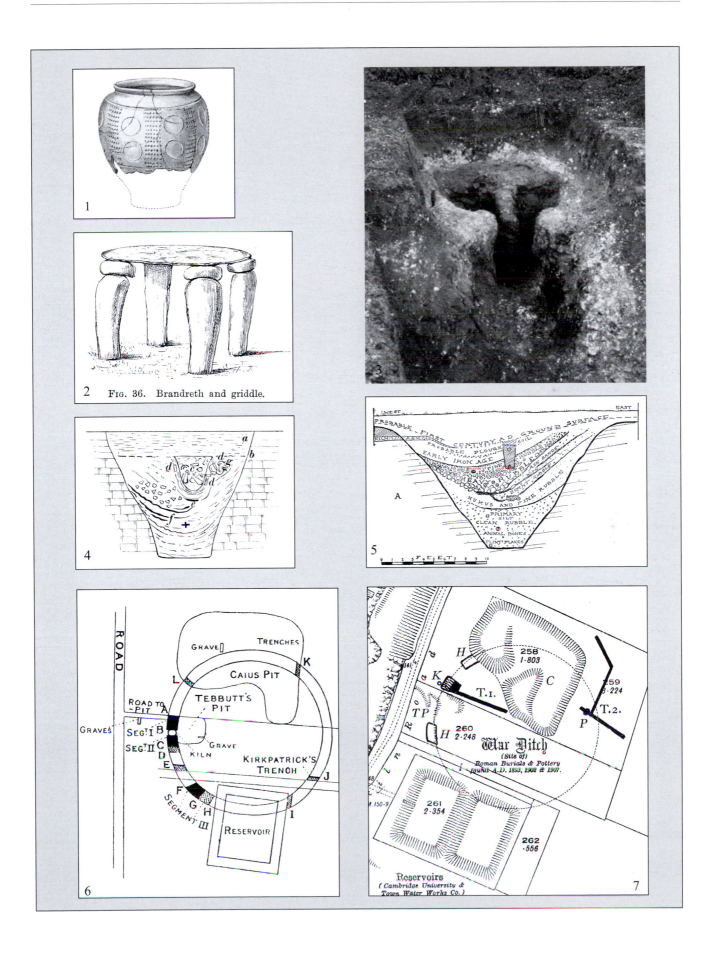

FIG. 36. Brandreth and griddle.

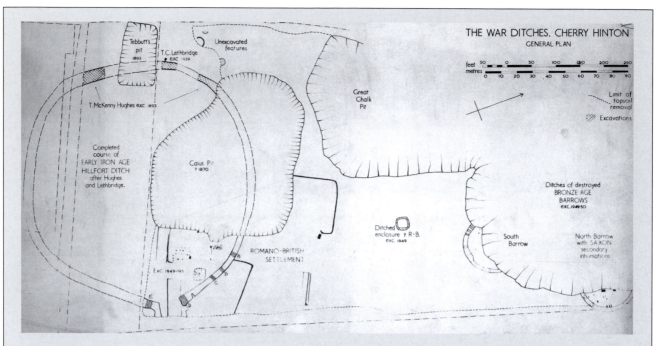

FIGURE 2.47. *War Ditches - The Plan: 1949–51 University Field Club investigations (Cambridge University Museum of Archaeology and Anthropology archives).*

wares (White 1964a, 5), with some early earlier second-century material recovered from other features.

The second of White's papers (1964b), drawing upon Dauncey and Houlder's archives, was concerned with the 1949–51 excavations within the area of the ringwork's eastern entrance and its immediate interior. Indicated as 'Hut 1' in his plan (Fig. 2.48), its main focus was a twice-rebuilt series of posthole buildings, the one ('B') being aisled (24 × 35 ft/c. 7.60 × 10.70 m) and of second-century date (White 1964b, figs. 1–3). That paper also outlined the excavation of adjacent ditches, rubbish pits, a quarry hollow, another post-built structure ('Hut 2') and a large well (3 ft/c. 0.90 m dia. and 42 ft/c. 12.80 m deep) whose disuse was dated to c. AD 140–170 (some third- to fourth-century material was apparently recovered from the latest posthole building). Although, in reference to Collingwood, White admitted the possibility that the scale of its main building could suggest 'villa aspirations', he rather concluded that it related to a farmstead (White 1964b, 37–8).

The unpublished Field Club archives covering the northeastern quarry area indicate that four cuttings were made across the ringwork's circuit on that side, and it was presumably from these that the three other skeletons (in addition to White's three) which Hughes and Denston studied, derived (White 1964a, 24–9). Just exterior to the enclosure they recorded three further, obviously Roman, ditch-lines (and a single pit). Some distance beyond, they excavated a 'sub-rectangular enclosure': a small, rounded corner 'square' (c. 8 × 8.00 m). Tentatively indicated as 'Ditched enclosure ? R–B' on the archive plan (Fig. 2.47), it might equally relate to some manner of Late Iron Age cremation setting, perhaps comparable to the Hinxton 'circles' (though no interment was recorded; Hill *et al.* 1999), or even be of earlier, prehistoric date (perhaps a small square barrow or the like). In this regard, it is relevant that White's plan of the southwestern corner-area shows a length of unattributed curvilinear ditch just inside the ringwork which does not appear associated

with the Roman settlement. Similarly, one of the 1949-phase archive plans indicates what look to possibly be roundhouse eavesgullies exterior to the ringwork on the west side near the road (Figs. 2.47 & 2.48). Unfortunately uninvestigated, these and other unattributed features could suggest an otherwise unrecognized phase of later prehistoric occupation.

The Field Club, in addition, also then investigated the two 'barrows' (probably ring-ditch monuments) in the north end of the field. Apparently both Early Bronze Age and Grooved Ware sherds were recovered from the approximate quarter of the circuit of each that were then left (excluding the centre of either), and they were duly assigned to the Bronze Age. However, nine secondary Anglo-Saxon inhumations were found inserted into the interior of the northern barrow, one being a bed burial (see Kennett 1973). Note that in 1997 excavations occurred on a tight cluster of three Early/Middle Bronze Age ring-ditches located on land just to the south of Fulbourn Road and only c. 0.5 km to the east (see Fig. 4.3; TL 491 560). Despite their intense excavation, no mortuary interments were recovered in association with these monuments (L. White 1998).

Attempting to overview at least the site's Roman occupation, the impact of the quarry's stripping and the resultant truncation of shallow sub-soil features must be taken into account. While the ditch boundaries of the period did not fall on a single alignment, they suggest a coherent network of paddocks

FIGURE 2.48 (right). *War Ditches - The Reconstructed: Top, White's plan of the ringwork's southern interior (with top-left corner detailed inset of the site's southwestern quarter omitted; 1964a, fig. 2); below, the Roman settlement as reconstructed (note that skeletons and 'fireplaces'/kilns occurring within the ringwork's grey-toned circuit have been omitted).*

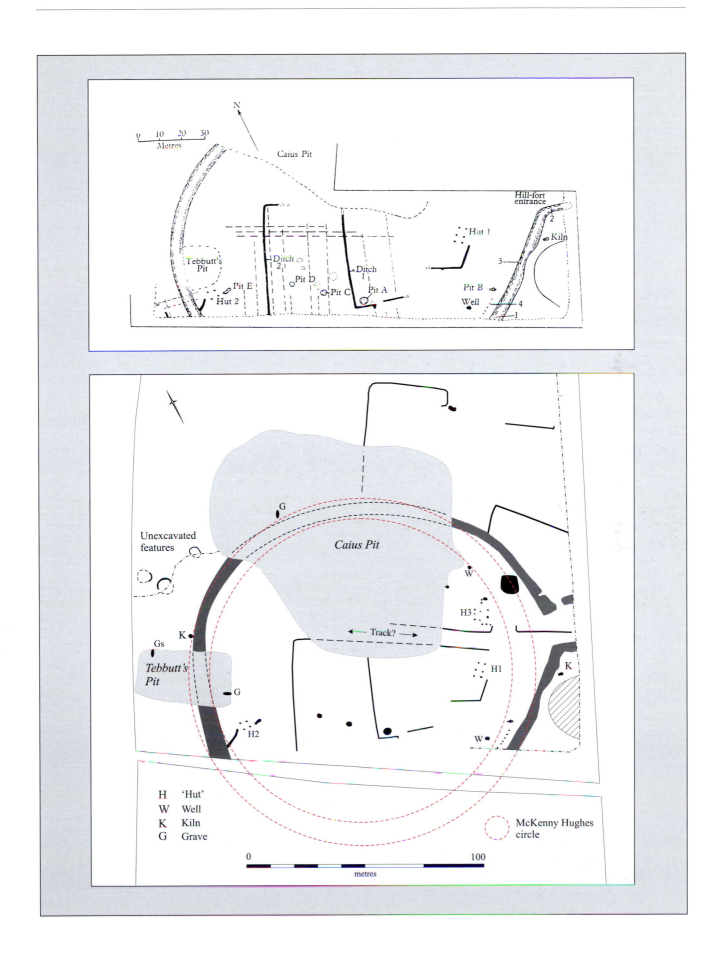

across at least 2.5 ha. In fact, combining the Field Club archives and White's plan suggests that the settlement was arranged along either side of northwest–southeast oriented trackway, and possibly even at a cross-roads as the ditch layout also hints of a return-line routeway. In total, three separate Roman building plots were distinguished. Aside from White's 'Huts 1 and 2', the Field Club evidently also investigated another sub-rectangular posthole setting (here for the sake of consistency termed 'Hut 3': Fig. 2.48), with 'Huts 1 and 3' being located astride the putative cross-roads. Primarily of first- and early second-century AD date, along with its 'Belgic tradition' kilns it would appear that this settlement was, in fact, comparable in many respects to that at the Hutchison Site.

Two facets of Hughes' work warrant note. First, is that he did recover a series of 'shallow trenches', which, despite recovering 'Roman type' pottery in association with, he evidently didn't plan (1904a, 478) and, therefore, the site's Roman ditch network must have extended further westward. The second point relates to pottery production. In the light of the kilns subsequently found by Lethbridge and White, the series

of 'fireplaces' Hughes found in the ringwork's ditch — 'constructed with brick in clay-lined cavities with brick supports' (Hughes 1904a, 465) — and which he reconstructed as cooking 'griddles' (evidently supported on pyramidal pillars/blocks: Fig. 2.46:2), were obviously the remains of kilns (see Swan 1984, 61; J. Evans 1990). Indeed, Hughes remarked that they did, in fact, consider this possibility, but dismissed it due to the quantity of domestic/cooking debris found in association (Hughes 1904a, 476). One also suspects that expectation might have here played a part. Hughes had recently worked at the 'potter's field' at Horningsea and, for example, illustrated his 1904 paper with a picture of the large Roman kiln found at Great Chesterford in 1879 (1904b, fig. 2). If anticipating all Roman kilns to be so robust, then it is little wonder that he clearly misidentified his 'fireplaces'.

Aside from providing immediate Roman settlement context for the Hutchison excavations, the intention of this section has been, in effect, to restore the full plan of the War Ditches' ringwork; clearly the unpublished portions of its archives still warrant further research and full presentation.

Environmental and economic studies

Faunal remains (CHRIS SWAYSLAND)

A total of 12,496 fragments of animal bone were hand-recovered. Excluding articulated and partially articulated remains, a *c.* 26% sample (3298 fragments) was analysed for zoological and archaeological traits. A further 2372 fragments from articulated or partially articulated specimens were also considered (40.8% total sample). Excluding the latter, the total number of fragments identified to species or broad size-category is 1345.

Material was selected that would provide a representative view of the site and would maximize the information that could be obtained from a representative sample. The sampling strategy was designed to fulfil the following criteria based loosely on O'Connor (1991):

- To represent all of the main periods of occupation;
- To include those samples particularly rich in faunal remains;
- To focus on features of particular archaeological importance.

It was decided to analyse all contexts with greater than one hundred fragments and any other contexts from the same feature. In addition, all material from Bronze Age pits, the Iron Age house-gullies and Saxon features was considered. (The assemblage from pit F.389 was also analysed, but is separately reported above in the discussion of the cemetery.) The strategy employed introduced some anomalies. Despite this, it generally succeeded: all periods and areas of the site were represented, as were the full range of feature

types. This being said, the main Conquest Period of its usage was perhaps somewhat under-represented.

The condition of the bone was variable; almost all had suffered some degree of damage caused by contact with acids in plant roots.

The material identified for analysis was individually recorded to highlight patterns in element distribution, age profiles, butchery and spatial distribution. Animal bones were identified with the aid of Schmid (1972) and the Cambridge Archaeological Unit reference collection. Bird bones were identified with the aid of Cohen and Serjeantson (1986). Where possible sheep and goat bones were distinguished following Boessneck *et al.* (1964) and Halstead & Collins (2002). Non-diagnostic elements such as ribs and vertebrae were identified to broad size category. All complete long bones were measured after von den Driesch (1976). Quantification is by number of identifiable fragments (NISP). Where it was clear that a group of fragments originated from a single bone they were grouped together and counted as a single element (i.e. 100 fragments from a broken skull were counted as one bone).

Bronze Age

The bone from 13 Bronze Age pits was studied; one was dated to the Middle Bronze Age, with the remainder attributed to the Late Bronze Age. The condition of the material from these contexts is poor. Most specimens have heavily eroded surfaces and are in fragmentary condition.

From the Middle Bronze Age pit, F.157 ([1740]), only one bone could be identified, a cow mandible. The 3rd molar was fully erupted and had wear to the front two cusps suggesting an age at death in excess of three years (Grigson 1982).

A total of 143 fragments were recovered from the Late Bronze Age pits containing animal bones (F.72, F.81, F.127, F.128, F.154, F.165, F.166, F.188, F.369, F.468, F.474 & F.498). Of these, 65 fragments (45.4%) were identified, corresponding to 26 specimens (Table 2.27).

Cattle and sheep/goat are the main species present. One humerus was identified as sheep. Pigs are of lesser importance: two right scapulae are present, one from a juvenile and another from an adult. All the bones are within the size-range for domestic species. One sheep/goat mandible indicated an age at death of 3–4 years (Payne 1973).

Late Iron Age

A range of features from the Late Iron Age was considered: four pits (F.97, F.98, F.69 & F.574), a ditch (F.64) and three house-gullies (F.898, F.907 & F.913). Cattle and sheep/goat remains dominate the assemblage from pits F.97 and F.98 (Table 2.28). A range of meat and non-meat-bearing elements were present, indicating that animals were butchered on-site. The material is characterized by fragmentary disarticulated bones, indicating domestic waste. Three goose bones were recovered; it is not known if they are from wild or domestic species.

F.69 was a shallow pit that yielded a substantial amount of articulated and non-articulated remains of sheep and cattle, as well as two non-articulated pig bones. A total of 90 sheep/goat bones were recovered, including six articulated limbs. Three left rear-legs, two left front-legs, one right front-leg and a series of vertebrae were recovered. In addition, there were two examples of complementary radius and ulna; these are bones that occur very close together in life, but are not usually fused together. All animals that could be distinguished between sheep and goat were identified as sheep. Table 2.29 shows the fusion status of the sheep epiphyses after Silver (1969). Limbs that articulate were counted once for the earliest fusing epiphysis that was in an unfused state.

Table 2.29 shows no sheep were killed below the age of 6–10 months and that relatively few (16%) were killed below the age of 13–16 months. The vast majority, however (72%), were 18–28 months or less at death, suggesting a highly selective culling strategy where most of the animals were killed between 13–16 and 18–28 months. The animals would be approaching prime size/weight for meat production and it is probable that they represent animals killed in the summer/autumn of their second year. A mandible was recovered with an age at death of 2–3 years (Payne 1973 wear stage E).

An estimation of the withers (shoulder) height can be made from the length of the long bones. The two unbroken examples were measured and their withers-heights were calculated using the factors of Teichert (undated in von den Driesch & Boessneck 1974; Table 2.30).

Harcourt (1979, in Davis 1987) gives a withers size-range of 53–64 cm for Iron Age sheep from Gussage All Saints in Dorset. Those represented within this pit, therefore, are within the smaller size-range for Iron Age sheep.

A total of 85 cow bones were also recovered from F.69, including two partially articulated lower legs; these are not meat-bearing bones. In addition, there were three complementary radii and ulnae; bones situated together in life though not fused. Two, left, cow metacarpals exhibited extended epiphyses, a trait often exhibited by animals used for traction (Bartosiewicz *et al.* 1997). Butchery marks are infrequent, though one calcaneum shows cutmarks consistent with dismemberment, and a radius had a heavy chop-mark. Analysis of the state of epiphyseal fusion (Table 2.31) indicates that 30.8% of early fusing bones were still unfused at the time of death, indicating that around a third of animals would have been killed at 1.5 years or younger, whilst 66.6% of late fusing bones remained unfused, suggesting that a further third may have lived beyond the ages of 3–4 years. The remaining third would have died between these ages. Two metacarpals showed exostoses of the distal epiphyses consistent with the use of cattle as draught animals (Bartosiewicz *et al.* 1997).

Three cattle mandibles could be aged by means of tooth eruption and wear (Grigson 1982). One had an age at death of 2.25–2.5 years; two were in excess of three years.

Iron Age pits containing articulated animal remains have provoked much debate (e.g. Hill 1995; Wilson 1992). The deposits in F.69 are not the usual fragments encountered from domestic waste. The bones have been butchered, but not very intensively, as may be seen from the ways in which cattle and sheep remains were respectively treated. The sheep were small animals; they could

TABLE 2.27. *Relative species proportions: Late Bronze Age pits.*

Species	NISP	% NISP
Cattle	10	38.5
Sheep/goat	8	30.8
Pig	3	11.5
Medium-sized mammal	3	11.5
Large-sized mammal	2	7.7

TABLE 2.28. *Relative species proportions: Late Iron Age pits F.97 and F.98.*

Species	NISP	% NISP
Cattle	25	25.8
Sheep/goat	18	18.6
Pig	4	4.1
Horse	4	4.1
Medium-sized mammal	18	18.6
Large-sized mammal	25	25.8
Bird	3	3.1

TABLE 2.29. *Sheep fusion data, pit F.69.*

Fusion category	Estimated age (months)	Percentage fused	Percentage unfused	No.
1	6–10	100	0	7
2	13–16	92.3	7.7	13
3	18–28	25	75	12
4	30–42	25	75	12

TABLE 2.30. *Estimation of sheep withers (shoulder) height, pit F.69.*

Element (L/R)	Measurement (cm)	Factor (Teichert)	Withers (cm)
Metacarpal	GL 10.9	4.89	53.3
Humerus	GL 13.0	4.28	55.6

TABLE 2.31. *Cattle fusion data, pit F.69.*

Fusion category	Estimated age (years)	Percentage fused	Percentage unfused	No.
Early	up to 1.5	69.2	30.8	13
Middle	2.5–3	62.5	37.5	8
Late	3–4	33.3	66.6	12

be processed for food with the limbs remaining articulated. The waste is, thus, deposited in an articulated state. The cattle, being that much larger, required dismemberment so that the lower legs (i.e. only the waste material), were deposited in an articulated state. Therefore, it is probable that the remains in F.69 relate to an episode of meat consumption. By the character of their deposition,

TABLE 2.32. *Pit F.53, articulated dog withers-heights after Harcourt (1974).*

Element (L/R)	Measurement GL (mm)	Factor (Harcourt 1974)	Withers-height (cm)
Radius L	111	(3.18XGL)+19.51	37.2
Radius R	111	(3.18XGL)+19.51	37.2
Ulna L	131.5	(2.73XGL)+6.21	38.1
Humerus L	119	(3.43XGL)–26.54	38.1
Humerus R	118	(3.43XGL)–26.54	37.8
Tibia L	131	(2.92XGL)+9.41	39.1
Tibia R	131	(2.92XGL)+9.41	39.1
Femur L	123	(3.14XGL)–12.96	37.3

TABLE 2.33. *Relative species proportions: ditch F.1053.*

Species	NISP	% NISP
Cattle	29	34.9
Sheep/goat	29	34.9
Pig	4	4.8
Dog	3	3.6
Medium-sized mammal	10	12.0
Large-sized mammal	8	9.6

TABLE 2.34. *Relative species proportions: pit F.10.*

Species	NISP	% NISP
Cattle	17	53.1
Sheep/goat	10	31.3
Medium-sized mammal	5	15.6

TABLE 2.35. *Relative species proportions: pit F.1046.*

Species	NISP	% NISP
Cattle	11	17.5
Sheep/goat	35	55.6
Pig	3	4.8
Horse	2	3.2
Medium-sized mammal	3	4.8
Large-sized mammal	6	9.5
Large bird	3	4.8

the bones seems to represent a single event. The quantity of meat represented by the bones in this pit would far exceed that required by a single household. Therefore, some kind of special event or feast can be envisaged. Meat-sharing in many agricultural societies is associated with major religious festivals or celebrations of life events (Grant 2002), an association Hill (1995, 102) would regard as 'ritual consumption'. This being said, the pit's assemblage seems very similar in character to pit A12 at Baldock (Chaplin & McCormick

1986), which was interpreted as possibly representing the slaughter of a breeding flock connected to the Boudican revolt.

The F.53 pit deposit is somewhat 'confused', having suffered from truncation. It contained the remains of at least three dogs, all of which were probably deposited in an articulated state. Two were 'large' and one was 'small'. The smaller dog of the three was articulated and its bones have been measured (Table 2.32). Other larger dog bones were recovered, some in articulation, but none was sufficiently complete to allow measurement. Two of the individual dogs show cutmarks consistent with skinning.

The 'smaller' of the dogs would have had a shoulder height of around 38 cm. This is at the extreme smaller size-range of Iron Age dogs (Harcourt 1974). In addition to the dogs discussed above, F.53 also yielded three fragments of cattle skull and horncore and, therefore, this pit assemblage would seem to represent the deposition of noxious waste principally after skinning activities.

A small quantity of animal bone was recovered from three house-gullies: F.898, F.907 and F.913. There were no identifiable fragments from the latter; F.898 and F.907 both contained the remains of cattle and sheep/goat. A mixture of meat- and non-meat-bearing bones of both species are represented. Overall, three cattle bones and six sheep/goat bones were recovered, one of which was distinguished as sheep. A cattle left metatarsal showed an interesting pathology. The bone had broken and re-healed in such a position that the proximal end was twisted approximately 20 degrees towards the medial side. This would have had the result that the cow's foot would have been splayed out from the normal position.

Late Iron Age/Conquest Period

The material from two ditch features, F.1013 and F.1053, was analysed. The former contained the partially articulated skull and vertebrae of a very old dog and three disarticulated cow and sheep/goat bones. Ditch F.1053 yielded cattle and sheep/goat in equal quantities (Table 2.33). All the sheep/goat that could be identified to species were sheep. A cattle metatarsal showed widening of the distal epiphysis. This suggests the use of cattle as traction animals (Bartosiewicz *et al.* 1997).

One pit, F.10, was also dated to this phase (Table 2.34). Two cattle mandibles that could be aged, from different animals, both showing an age at death of six months (Grigson 1982). Two sheep/goat mandibles from different animals were also recovered, both showing eruption and wear consistent with Payne (1973) stage D: an age at death of 1–2 years.

Conquest Period

The material from two ditches (F.18 & F.1206), two pits (F.591 & F.1046), two kilns (F.1117 & F.1181) and a 'dog burial' (F.412) were analysed.

The excavated portion of ditch F.18 contained 14 cattle bones and three sheep/goat bones. In addition to this, there were a large number of fragments from a cattle skull that may have been complete. Ditch F.1206 yielded a horse skull from a relatively young animal; incisor tooth-wear indicates an age at death of around five years (St Clair 1975). The presence of isolated skulls, particularly of horses, is recorded at other Iron Age and Romano-British sites in England. Now often ascribed a 'ritual' function (cf. Dobney 2001; Hill 1995), the deposition of primary butchery waste is the more pragmatic alternative.

The animal bone in Pit F.1046 is shown in Table 2.35. In this feature sheep/goat are the dominant species (55.6%). A sheep/goat mandible showed tooth-wear indicating an age at death of 1–2 years (Payne 1973, stage D). Three large bird bones were recovered; one was definitely identifiable as goose and another was probably of the same attribution; the other was unidentified.

All the bones from pit F.591 were severely root-etched. Seven cattle bones were identified, with a mixture of meat- and non-meat-bearing bones present. One vertebra of sheep/goat-size was recovered. In addition, a residual horse metapodial was found; this specimen was in poor condition but seems to have been worked.

Two kilns, F.1117 and F.1181, were selected for analysis on the basis of the high number of bones that were recovered from them (Table 2.36). Cattle are the dominant species in both features. A complete articulated calf was recovered from inside kiln F.1181 (Fig. 2.27). The age at death of this animal from tooth eruption and epiphyseal fusion was 12–18 months. The excavator believed that this animal was placed inside the kiln prior to the destruction of the kiln's superstructure and it may, therefore, have had a ritual intent. Alternatively, it could just attest to the convenient disposal of a diseased animal. A complete mature cattle metacarpal, with articulating 1st phalanges and one 2nd phalange, was also recovered from F.1181; these show evidence of carnivore damage. The greatest length of the metacarpal was 16.7 cm. Metacarpal length is known to be sexually dimorphic and the sex of this animal from which this bone came is unknown. Therefore, the withers-height is given as being in a range from 101 cm to 106 cm. A cattle mandible was recovered from F.1117. This had an age at death in excess of three years (Grigson 1982, wear stage 8). Sheep/goat bones also showed a mix of meat- and non-meat-bearing elements. One mandible indicated an age at death of 4–6 years (Payne 1973, wear stage G). A complete sheep metacarpal was recovered. This measured 12.07 cm, indicating a withers (shoulder)-height of around 59 cm; a sheep distal tibia showed pathology consistent with arthritis.

F.412 was located within the Roman cemetery and contained the articulated remains of a mature dog. The dog's unbroken long bones were measured and a withers (shoulder)-height was calculated using the factors of Harcourt (1974) to be around 39 cm. This is at the smaller end of the size-range for Iron Age dogs, though Romano-British dogs have a much greater range of sizes (Harcourt 1974).

Anglo-Saxon
The material from ditches F.6 and F.420, and four wells (F.482, F.500, F.501 & F.552) was analysed. The excavator considers that there may be a risk of some residual material occurring in the former ditch deposits. The species proportions in F.6 and F.420 differ (Table 2.37): F.6 had a high proportion of sheep/goat and low levels of cattle, whereas F.420 had similar proportions of cattle and sheep/goat. Both features had low levels of pig and each included one bird bone. The bird bone from F.6 was identified as domestic goose; that from F.420 was a 'bantam-sized' chicken.

The partially articulated remains of a cow were recovered from F.420 ([1186]), with the skull, atlas, axis, vertebrae, sacrum and pelvis present. All the adult maxillary teeth were present and well-worn, indicating an age at death in excess of three years (Grigson 1982). Some pathology was noted: the sacrum had fused to the 6th lumbar vertebra. The cause of this is unknown. Many bones, particularly the ribs, showed evidence of carnivore damage. A complete horse metatarsal was recovered from F.420 [1186]; a withers (shoulder)-height of 131.1 cm was calculated using the factors of Kiesewalter (1888, in von den Driesch & Boessneck 1974). The equivalent of 13 hands, by modern standards this would be considered pony-sized.

The ageing data from F.6 and F.420 is somewhat conflicting. The former contained a young pig aged 7–13 months (Silver 1969) and a cow aged 2.5–3 years (Grigson 1982). F.420 had a mature pig aged in excess of 22 months (Silver 1969), a cow aged 2.25–2.5 years and a sheep/goat aged 4–6 years (Payne 1973).

Four pit-wells were identified as Saxon (F.482, F.500, F.501 & F.552; Table 2.38). Cattle are the most frequently represented species. This material was in general quite fragmentary, although a complete metatarsal was recovered. The withers (shoulder)-height of the animal from which this bone originated was calculated using the factors of Matolcsi (1970, in von den Driesch & Boessneck 1974) and

TABLE 2.36. *Relative species proportions: kilns F.1181 and F.1117 (figures in brackets refer to an articulated calf).*

	F.1181		F.1117	
Species	NISP	% NISP	NISP	% NISP
Cattle	21 (414)	42	20	44.4
Sheep/goat	4	8	12	26.7
Pig	2	4	0	0
Horse	0	0	4	8.9
Medium-sized mammal	18	36	2	4.4
Large-sized mammal	5	10	7	15.6

TABLE 2.37. *Relative species proportions: Saxon ditches F.6/F.420 (figures in brackets refer to articulated specimens).*

Species	F.6		F.420	
	NISP	% NISP	NISP	% NISP
Cattle	6	7.3	18 (70)	24.7
Sheep/goat	23	28.0	16	21.9
Pig	6	7.3	6	8.2
Horse	0	0	4	5.5
Medium-sized mammal	34	41.5	19	26.0
Large-sized mammal	12	14.6	9	12.3
Chicken	0	0	1	0
Goose	1	1.2	0	1.4

TABLE 2.38. *Relative species proportions: Saxon wells.*

Species	NISP	% NISP
Cattle	105	42.0
Sheep/goat	45	18.0
Pig	12	4.8
Horse	22	8.8
Dog	2	0.8
Cat	3	1.2
Medium-sized mammal	15	6.0
Large-sized mammal	46	18.4

was in the range of 115–123 cm. One section of a skull from F.482 ([3827]) showed cranial perforations. It has been suggested that this is an indication of yoking (Brothwell *et al.* 1996). These traits have, however, been reported in wild bovids, thus lending support for a congenital cause for this condition (Manaseryan *et al.* 1999; Baxter 2002). Four cattle mandibles were sufficiently complete to allow an age at death to be estimated: one was from a juvenile animal aged 6–18 months and three were from mature animals aged in excess of three years (Grigson 1982).

Sheep/goat represent 18% of the assemblage. All the specimens that could be identified to individual species were identified as sheep. A small amount of tooth eruption and wear data was recovered, indicating a wide range of ages at death from six months to six years, with no one age category being predominant.

The proportion of horse bones in these features was relatively high (8.8%) and included a complete tibia. This was measured and a withers (shoulder)-height calculated of 141.7cm (Kiesewalter 1888 in von den Driesch & Boessneck 1974). This is equivalent to 13.9 hands and would, by today's standards, be considered a pony.

In all phases, all the sheep and goats that could be distinguished to species were identified as sheep. Therefore, the term 'sheep' will be used henceforth, though it should be remembered that a few goats might be included in this category. In all periods almost the entire assemblage was derived from domesticated mammals, with the vast majority coming from the three main domestic species: cattle, sheep and pig (Table 2.39). Cattle and sheep are dominant throughout. In all phases cattle proportions exceed those of sheep, though in certain features the proportions are reversed. Generally, pig is of minor importance and only in the Late Bronze Age and the Saxon periods do proportions of pig exceed 10%.

The 'blurred' transition from the Late Iron Age to the Conquest Period is the most important to us here and presents a high degree of homogeneity. Proportions of cattle and sheep remain very similar, only levels of pig alter, decreasing from 8.5% in the Late Iron Age to 3.8% in the Conquest Period. King (1991) has described a hierarchy of site-types in the Early Roman period based on meat consumption. Villas and highly Romanized sites have high levels of cattle and pig, down a gradient to non-Romanized settlements, which show a continuation of the predominant Iron Age pattern of relatively high sheep proportions. This pattern does not really fit the Hutchison Site's data as the Iron Age material does not display the high levels of sheep. However, it has been observed that not all of southern England fits the high Iron Age sheep pattern. Maltby (1981, in Dawson 2000) has shown that, in contrast to other areas in southern England, in the South Midlands the trend during the Iron Age is for cattle increasing in proportion to sheep. It is interesting that the proportion of pig is lower in the Conquest sample than in the Iron Age. Pig was considered a delicacy in the Roman world and it occurs in large amounts on highly Romanized sites (Dobney 2001). It is possible to speculate whether the Hutchison's community had been trading pigs with the Roman military, thus removing pigs from the assemblage found in the Conquest Period. Thus, it would seem that processes of acculturation or 'Romanization' from the perspective of meat consumption seem to be limited.

Age at death data is extremely limited; the only feature to have a sufficiently large sample size is F.69, dated to the Late Iron Age. This showed animals predominantly being raised until reaching prime size/weight and, thereby, demonstrating a meat economy. However, this pit seems to have served a 'special' function and it would be unwarranted to extrapolate generalized husbandry regimes from it alone.

Articulated burials are dominated by dogs; these can be interpreted in different ways. The dogs in F.53 show evidence of having been skinned and their carcasses would seem to simply represent noxious waste thrown into a pit. This is in contrast to the dog 'burial' F.412 located in the (human) cemetery and which, given its direct mortuary context, is presumed to attest to 'ritual' behaviour (the status of the F.1181 kiln-buried calf being ambiguous).

Changes in the size of cattle, due to local improvement in husbandry practices or the importation of new stock, have been observed on some Roman sites in Britain and Europe, though mainly on sites of a Late Roman date (Dobney 2001). Complete long bones were very limited in the site's assemblage: the one cow metacarpal recovered from a Conquest-phase kiln is of 'small' size and, thus, shows little sign of 'Romanization'; a Saxon cattle bone showed a withers size-increase of up to 17 cm.

A very limited amount of size-data is available for sheep. Tentatively, this suggests a small size-increase from a withers-height of 54 cm in the Late Iron Age to 59 cm in the Conquest Period. This, however, is still within the size-range for Iron Age sheep and it may, therefore, not be significant.

Overall, the assemblage shows a high degree of continuity from the Late Iron Age to the Roman period, and there is little indication of Roman influence in the Conquest Period material.

Environmental bulk samples (KATE ROBERTS)

Fifty-six samples from a variety of contexts were analysed. All were processed using an Ankara-type flotation machine (French 1972). The flot was collected using a 300 μm sieve, and the heavy residue was washed over a 1mm mesh. The flots were dried prior to their examination under a low-power binocular microscope and scanned for identifiable plant and molluscan remains. Plant remains were identified using the reference collection of the Pitt-Rivers

TABLE 2.39. *Major species relative proportions by phase (excluding articulated specimens).*

Phase	Cattle %	Sheep %	Pig %
Late Bronze Age	47.6	38.1	14.3
Late Iron Age	53.2	38.3	8.5
Conquest	55.3	40.9	3.8
Saxon	54.4	35.4	10.1

Laboratory, McDonald Institute for Archaeological Research, University of Cambridge. Plant nomenclature follows Stace (1997). The molluscan remains were identified using, and their nomenclature follows, Beedham (1972).

The contents of the flots are summarized at the end of the report in table-form; the heavy residues greater than 4 mm were examined.

Preservation was mainly by charring. This material was well-preserved and some samples were very rich. However, densities varied widely between the site's phases, ranging from 0.03 items per litre in the Roman phases to 59.17 in the Saxon. The texture of the plant remains was very well-preserved allowing a good level of identification; fragmentation was not that common.

Some samples contained uncharred plant remains; however, there were only moderate quantities of seeds. In these, it does not appear that the remains were part of a properly waterlogged assemblage as the quantities were too small. It is more likely that if these remains were waterlogged, they were remnants of formerly 'wet' assemblages.

Molluscan remains were present in large numbers in some of the samples. In the majority of cases they were well-preserved and whole, enabling identification. Only for contexts where more than fifty molluscan shells were preserved are their implications discussed below.

Charred plant remains

As can be seen below (Table 2.40; Fig. 2.49), the richest samples come from the Roman kilns and from Saxon features.

Late Bronze Age

There were three samples from this phase, within which only very small amounts of archaeological plant remains were present, including a single cereal grain of wheat/barley (*Triticum* sp./*Hordeum vulgare*) and a single indeterminate small seed; only minor quantities of charcoal were present (Table 2.41).

Late Iron Age/Conquest Period

Thirty-eight samples were taken from this phase of the site and these will be discussed as a group (Table 2.42). However, of these, the kilns (ten samples), will be considered separately below as their contents are distinctly different from the rest.

Plant remains were scarce, with cereals present in small or negligible amounts. There were small amounts of barley (*Hordeum vulgare sensu lato*), some of which was identifiable as hulled, and a single grain of which was identifiable as twisted hulled barley, suggesting the possibility of six-row barley, but there was no chaff to make this more certain. Wheat was also present, although it was only possible to identify it as *Triticum* sp. in most cases. Some grains were identified as emmer wheat (*Triticum* cf. *dicoccum*) and there were larger numbers of free-threshing wheat (*Triticum aestivum sensu lato*). There were also small or moderate amounts of indeterminate cereal grain.

Chaff was also very scarce in these samples. There were small numbers of glume bases which could have been from spelt or emmer wheat (*Triticum spelta/dicoccum* chaff), as well as a small amount which were spelt glumes (*Triticum spelta* chaff). There was also a single example of a cereal culm node.

Charred wild plant remains were even scarcer than cereal grains. Present in two samples from F.408 and F.855 were fragments of hazelnut shell. Weeds included some ruderal species such as goosefoot (*Chenopodium* sp.), curled dock (*Rumex crispus*) and dock (*Rumex* sp.) in very small numbers. There were also small quantities of arable weeds, especially indeterminate grasses (Poaceae indet.), but also occasional seeds from fescue (*Festuca* sp.), rye-grass (*Lolium* sp.), meadow-grass (*Poa* spp.) and brome (*Bromus* sp.). Other arable weeds included vetch/wild pea (*Vicia/Lathyrus* sp.), scentless mayweed (*Tripleurospermum inodorum*) and goosegrass (*Galium* sp.). There were also small amounts of plant remains from wetland plants including seeds from black bog-rush (*Schoenus nigricans*) and sedge (*Carex* sp.).

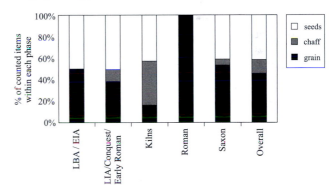

FIGURE 2.49. *Charred plant composition by percentage.*

TABLE 2.40. *Statistical summary of the charred plant remains from all phases.*

Phase	LBA/EIA 3	LIA/Conquest/ Early Roman	Kilns	Roman	Saxon	OVERALL
Total Samples	45	28	10	4	11	56
Total volume/litres		264	92.5	37	89	527.5
TOTAL CEREAL GRAIN (with oat)	1	55	213	1	2803	3073
TOTAL CEREAL CHAFF ITEMS	0	16	544	0	296	856
TOTAL NON-CEREAL SEEDS	1	72	569	0	2167	2810
TOTAL COUNT	2	143	1326	1	5266	6739
count density (items per litre)	0.04	0.54	14.34	0.03	59.17	12.78

TABLE 2.41. *Late Bronze Age environmental data: 'w' = waterlogged/uncharred; '-' = 1 or 2 items; '+' = < 10 items; '++' = 10–50 items; '+++' = >50 items.*

Sample number		<50>	<155>	<1>
Context		[1196]	[3226]	[57]
Feature number		F.31	F.474	F.166
Feature type		early slot NNE–SSW	early pit	cremation/early pit
Phase		possible LBA	LBA/EIA	LBA/EIA
Sample volume/ litres		14	10	21
Flot fraction examined		1/1	1/1	1/1
Triticum/Hordeum sp. grain	wheat/barley grain			1
small seed indet.				-
small charcoal (<2 mm)		++	++	+++
med. charcoal (2–4 mm)		+		++
large charcoal (>4 mm)		+	++	
- vitrified charcoal				
bone fragments		+	++	
burnt bone fragments				+++
pot			++	-
burnt stone			+	+
burnt flint				++
burnt clay				
intrusive roots		++	+++	+++
intrusive sesiloides	burrowing snails	+++	+++	+++
Carychium minimum/tridentatum	generally well vegetated; wet/damp	5		
Cochlicopa lubrica/lubricella	catholic	5		
Vertigo sp.	variable, generally shady	1		
Pupilla muscorum	dry, exposed places	6		
Lauria cylindracea	wood/rocks/grassland	4		
Vallonia costata	dry, open places	3		
Vallonia exentrica/pulchella	open, damp and/or dry habitats	21		
Trichia hispida/striolata	catholic	12		
Helicella itala	dry, open grassland	2		
Discus rotundatus	moist, sheltered places	5		
juvenile indet.	-	+		

TABLE 2.42. *Late Iron Age/Conquest/Early Roman environmental data: 'w' = waterlogged/uncharred; '-' = 1 or 2 items; '+' = < 10 items; '++' = 10–50 items; '+++' = >50 items.*

Sample number		<151>	<154>	<8>	<214> and <234>	<115>	<142>	<216>	<226>	<94>	<29>	<26>	<69>	<70>	<244>	<215>	<248>	<236>	<235>	<253>	<60>	<55>	<213>	<140>	<163>	<164>	<167>	<169>
Context		[3015]	[3046]	[817]	[4569] and [4609]	[2398]	[2940]	[4572]	[4494]	[2081]	[1082]	[512]	[1357]	[1360]	[4238]	[4561]	[4654]	[4010]	[3989]	[4584]	[1391]	[1355]	[4567]	[2934]	[3616]	[3616]	[3663]	[3664]	[3331]
Feature number		F.907	F.913	F.344	F.1061	F.855	F.893	F.832	F.1021	F.770	F.1	F.8	F.19		F.1038	F.1011	F.975	F.1133	F.1143	F.1007	F.636	F.638	F.1059	F.26	F.408	F.408	F.411	F.411	
Feature type		house ring gully	house ring gully	cremation	cremation	N–S ditch	ring gully but:	butt end	western pits	basal pond	rectangular enclosure	Conquest system	Conquest system	Conquest system	ditch on western edge	road ditch	road ditch	western postholes	western postholes	pit	vase contents	cremation	cremation	large sausage feature	cremation	cremation	cremation	cremation	cremation
Phase		LIA	LIA	LIA	LIA	LIA	LIA/ Conquest	LIA/ Early Roman	LIA/ Conquest	LIA/ Conquest	Conquest	Conquest	Conquest	Conquest	possible Conquest	Conquest	Conquest	possible Conquest	possibly Conquest	Conquest	Conquest	Conquest	possible Conquest	Conquest/ Early Roman	Conquest/ Early Roman	Conquest/ Early Roman	Conquest/ Early Roman	Conquest/ Early Roman	Early Roman
Sample volume/ litres		5	10	5	101/2	10	4	6	14	5	10	9	8	12	10	6	8	1	1	1	1/2	6	1	10	16	30	45	17	3
Flot fraction examined		1/1	1/1	1/1	1/1	1/1	1/1	1/1	1/1	1/1	1/1	1/1	1/1	1/1	1/1	1/1	1/1	1/1	1/1	1/1	1/1	1/1	1/1	1/1	1/1	1/1	1/1	1/1	1/1
hulled, twisted *Hordeum vulgare sensu lato* grain	6-row hulled barley grain				1																								
hulled *Hordeum vulgare sensu lato* grain	hulled barley grain														1								1					1	
Hordeum vulgare sensu lato grain	barley grain				2							1											1						
Triticum cf. *dicoccum* grain	emmer wheat grain					3																							
Triticum aestivum sensu lato grain	free-threshing wheat grain							5				1																	
Triticum sp. grain	wheat grain				2	3																1	2		1				
Triticum/Hordeum sp. grain	wheat/barley grain													3		1													
cereal grain indet.			1		16			2			-	-	-	-		1				1			1		1		1	2	
cereal frags.					+			+			-			-		-				+					-				
Triticum spelta glume base	spelt wheat chaff							1		2										2									
Triticum spelta/dicoccum glume base	spelt/emmer chaff	1	2		1			2		4																			
cereal indet. culm node	straw joint				1																								
Ranunculus cf. *flammula*	lesser spearwort									w1																			
Papaver sp.	poppy		w2																				w13						
Urtica dioica	stinging nettle		w7																										
Corylus avellana nutshell fragments	hazelnut				1																				1				
Chenopodium album	fat-hen							1															w31						
small *Chenopodium* sp.	goosefoot				3																								
Atriplex patula/prostrata	common/spear-leaved orache									w1					w1								w3						
Chenopodiaceae indet.										w1																			
Stellaria media	chickweed		w3							w3													w1						
Rumex sanguineus/conglomeratus/obtusifolius	small-seeded dock																						w11						
Rumex cf. *crispus*	curled dock				1																		w6						
small *Rumex* sp.	small-seeded dock type							1						1															
Viola sp.	violet																						w7						
small *Vicia/Lathyrus* sp. (<2 mm)	vetch/wild pea		1																										
cf. *Cornus sanguinea*	dogwood		w1																										
Aethusa cynapium	fool's parsley	w1	w1												w14	w2							w1						
Hyoscyamus niger	henbane									w30																			
Myosotis sp.	forget-me-not					1																							
Stachys sylvatica/palustris	hedge/marsh woundwort		w1																										
Ballota nigra	black horehound		w3																				w2						
Lamiaceae indet.	mint family					1																							
Plantago sp.	plantain					1																							
Euphrasia sp.	eyebright		7																										
Galium cf. *aparine*	cleavers					1																							
Sambucus nigra	elder														w1														
Carduus/Cirsium sp.	thistle									w1																			
Picris echioides	bristly oxtongue														w1										1				
Tripleurospermum inodorum	scentless mayweed							1																					
Schoenus nigricans	black bog-rush		1																										
Cladium mariscus	great fen sedge				2					w1																			
medium trilete *Carex* sp.	sedge									w3												1	w1						
Bromus spp.	brome																										1		
Festuca sp.	fescue							2						1															
Lolium sp.	rye-grass	2						3		1				1														1	
Poa spp.	meadow-grass																												
large Poaceae indet. (>4 mm)	large grass family seed				3																								
medium Poaceae indet. (c. 4 mm)	medium grass family seed	10	3		3			4		1				1		1													
small Poaceae indet. (c. 2 mm)	small grass family seed					1																1							
small seed indet.			w+		+									-					-										
large seed indet.																													
small twigs		+++	++																										
small charcoal (<2 mm)		+++	++	++	+++	++	++	+++			++			++			++	++		+++	++	+++		+++	+++	++	++	+++	++
med. charcoal (2-4 mm)		+		+	+++	+		+	+	+				+					++			+++		+	+	+	+++	++	+
large charcoal (>4 mm)			+		++	+	+	+			+			+						+++	+	-	-	++	+++	++
- vitrified charcoal					++		++	+							++														

Table 2.42. (cont.)

Sample number	<151>	<154>	<8>	<21b and 23b>	<115>	<142>	<21b>	<22b>	<9b>	<2b>	<2b>	<6b>	<7b>	<24b>	<21b>	<24b>	<23b>	<23b>	<23b>	<6b>	<55>	<213>	<14b>	<163>	<164>	<167>	<169>	<333>
Context	[3015]	[3066]	[817]	[4569] and [4669]	[2398]	[2940]	[4572]	[4494]	[20811]	[1082]	[512]	[1357]	[1360]	[4238]	[4561]	[4654]	[4010]	[3989]	[4584]	[13991]	[13551]	[4567]	[2934]	[3616]	[3616]	[3663]	[3664]	[3331]
Feature number	F.907	F.913	F.344	F.1061	F.855	F.993	F.832	F.1021	F.770	F.1	F.8	F.19		F.1038	F.1011	F.975	F.1133	F.1143	F.1007	F.636	F.638	F.1059	F.26	F.408	F.408	F.411	F.411	
Feature type	house ring gully	house ring gully	cremation	cremation	N–S ditch	ring gully butt	butt end	western pits basal pond	basal pond	rectangular enclosure	Conquest system	Conquest system	Conquest system	ditch on western edge	road ditch	road ditch	western postholes	western postholes	pit	vase contents	cremation	cremation	large sausage feature	cremation	cremation	cremation	cremation	cremation
Phase	LIA	LIA	LIA	LIA	LIA	LIA/ Conquest	LIA/ Early Roman	LIA/ Conquest	LIA/ Conquest	Conquest	Conquest	Conquest	Conquest	possible Conquest	Conquest	Conquest	possible Conquest	possibly Conquest	Conquest	Conquest	Conquest	possible Conquest	Conquest/ Early Roman	Conquest/ Early Roman	Conquest/ Early Roman	Conquest/ Early Roman	Conquest/ Early Roman	Early Roman
Sample volume/litres	5	10	5	101/2	10	4	6	14	5	10	9	8	12	10	6	8	1		1	12	6	1	10	16	30	45	17	3
Flot fraction examined	1/1	1/1	1/1	1/1	1/1	1/1	1/1	1/1	1/1	1/1	1/1	1/1	1/1	1/1	1/1	1/1	1/1		1/1	1/1	1/1	1/1	1/1	1/1	1/1	1/1	1/1	1/1
pot																												
burnt stone																												
oyster																												
flint																												
burnt flint								51																				
burnt clay																												
slag																												
mussel																												
cockle																												
indet. leaf fragments intrusive																												
intrusive roots																												
uncharred seeds, probably intrusive																												
intrusive sealoides — burrowing snails	+++		‡		‡‡	‡	‡	‡‡‡			10															‡‡		
Cochlicopa lubrica/lubricella — catholic																										1		
Vertigo sp. — variable, generally shady																										2		
Calumnella cf. edentula — catholic; usually damp places																										3		
Papilla muscorum — dry exposed places											4															10		
Lauria cylindracea — wood/rocks/grassland											32															93		
Vallonia costata — dry open places								3			39												2			23		
Vallonia excentrica/pulchella — open, damp and/or dry habitats								40			67												41			91		
Trichia hispida/striolata — catholic								42			105												28			23		
Aegopinella/Oxychilus sp. — moist & shady places																												
juvenile indet.								‡‡			‡															‡‡		
operculum								‡															1					
small eggs																							+					

Kilns

These samples were substantially richer than all of the others of this phase; they also contained proportionally more chaff (Table 2.43). While all these samples were proportionally richer, there were two samples that were particularly abundant. These were taken from F.63 and F.1117 ([4206]), and each contained over a hundred items of chaff and more than fifty counts of grain. Hulled barley (*Hordeum vulgare sensu lato*) was present in most samples, and some of this was obviously twisted or straight. However, the majority of the barley was less well-preserved and so the grain cannot be used to show definitively whether this barley was of the six-row variety. The barley chaff was not sufficiently preserved to be useful either. The wheat grain was a mixture of a small amount of spelt (*Triticum spelta*) and larger amounts of emmer (*Triticum dicoccum*), free-threshing wheat (*Triticum aestivum sensu lato*) and indeterminate wheat (*Triticum* sp.). In one sample from F.1181 a single grain of rye (*Secale cereale*) was present. There were small amounts of oats (*Avena* sp.) present in some samples; also present were large amounts of indeterminate cereal grain.

Chaff was dominated by glume bases. The majority of these were too heavily eroded to ascertain whether they were spelt or emmer wheat (*Triticum spelta/dicoccum*) but where the glumes were less poorly preserved they were all spelt wheat glumes (*Triticum spelta*). Other chaff included small amounts of barley rachis internodes (*Hordeum vulgare sensu lato*), rye (*Secale cereale*) rachis internodes, oat (*Avena* sp.) awns, indeterminate cereal culm nodes and hexaploid wheat rachis internodes (bread wheat), though these were present in only minute quantities in comparison with the glume bases.

Wild plant remains in these samples were also much more common. Ruderal species included many-seeded goosefoot (*Chenopodium polyspermum*), fat-hen (*Chenopodium album*), goosefoot (*Chenopodium* sp.), common/spear-leaved orache (*Atriplex patula/prostrata*), knotgrass (*Polygonum aviculare*), black-bindweed (*Fallopia convolvulus*), small seeded dock (*Rumex sanguineus/conglomeratus/obstutifolius*), curled dock (*Rumex crispus*) and dock (*Rumex* sp.). Arable weeds included small amounts of vetch/wild pea (*Vicia/Lathyrus* sp.), black medick (*Medicago lupulina*), clover (*Trifolium* sp.), field gromwell (*Lithospermum arvense*), cleavers (*Galium* sp.), stinking chamomile (*Anthemis cotula*), scentless mayweed (*Tripleurospermum inodorum*), fescue (*Festuca* sp.), rye-grass (*Lolium* sp.), lesser cat's tail (*Phleum bertilonii*), cat's tail (*Phleum* sp.), meadow-grass (*Poa* spp.) and indeterminate grasses (Poaceae indet.). There were also some wetland plants including seeds from great fen sedge (*Cladium mariscus*), sedge (*Carex* sp.), black bog-rush (*Schoenus nigricans*) and common spike-rush (*Eleocharis palustris*), although these were only present in very small quantities.

Roman

The four samples attributable to this phase contained virtually no archaeological plant remains: only a single wheat grain and a small amount of charcoal (Table 2.44).

Saxon

There were eleven samples taken from Saxon features, of which five were very rich (Table 2.45). These con-

TABLE 2.43. *Environmental data for the kilns: 'w' = waterlogged/uncharred; '-' = 1 or 2 items; '+' = < 10 items; '++' = 10–50 items; '+++' =>50 items.*

		<79>	<188>	<108>	<186>	<18>	<109>	<195>	<194>	<14>	<255>
Sample number		<79>	<188>	<108>	<186>	<18>	<109>	<195>	<194>	<14>	<255>
Context		[1699]	[4256]	[2350]	[4252]	[859]	[2366]	[4211]	[4206]	[978]	[4683]
Feature number		F.626	F.1254	F.783	F.1077	F.63	F.853	F.1117	F.1117	F.340	F.1181
Feature type		kiln	kiln	kiln	kiln	kiln	kiln rakeout	kiln	kiln	kiln	kiln
Phase		Conquest/Early Roman	Conquest/Early Roman	LIA/Conquest	LIA/Early Roman	Conquest/Early Roman	Conquest/Early Roman	Conquest/Early Roman	Early Roman	Early Roman	Early Roman
Sample volume/ litres		8	1/2	15	12	12	5	12	20	1	7
Flot fraction examined		1/1	1/1	1/1	1/1	1/1	1/1	1/1	1/1	1/1	1/1
hulled, twisted *Hordeum vulgare sensu lato* grain	6-row hulled barley grain			1	3				1		4
hulled, straight *Hordeum vulgare sensu lato* grain	6-row hulled barley grain								1		2
hulled *Hordeum vulgare sensu lato* grain	hulled barley grain	1				17	1	1			
Hordeum vulgare sensu lato grain	barley grain					15		6			
Triticum cf. *spelta* grain	spelt wheat grain								2		
Triticum cf *dicoccum* grain	emmer wheat grain			1	1	4			4		
Triticum aestivum sensu lato grain	free-threshing wheat grain	1				13		9	3		1
Triticum sp. grain	wheat grain			1		14	1		7		
Triticum/Hordeum sp. grain	wheat/barley grain	1		2		1	2	13	2		
Secale cereale grain	rye grain										1
cereal grain indet.				2	10	1	1		44		6
cereal frags		+	++		+	++	-	+	++		++
Hordeum vulgare sensu lato rachis internode	barley chaff							2			
Triticum spelta spikelet fork	spelt wheat chaff							1			
Triticum spelta glume base	spelt wheat chaff	11			2	36	5	30	22		2
Triticum spelta/dicoccum spikelet fork	wheat chaff					11		5	14		
Triticum spelta/dicoccum glume base	spelt/emmer chaff	21	1		6	172	1	94	100		1
Hexaploid *Triticum* sp. rachis internode	bread wheat				1						1
Secale cereale rachis internode	rye chaff			1							
Avena sp. awns	oat chaff								2		
cereal indet. culm node	straw joint						1				1
Ranunculus sp.	buttercup				1						
Chenopodium polyspermum	many-seeded goosefoot			1							
Chenopodium album	fat-hen					2					
small *Chenopodium* sp.	goosefoot					5					
Atriplex patula/prostrata	common/spear-leaved orache	8						8	12		
Polygonum aviculare	knotgrass					3		3	12		
Fallopia convolvulus	black-bindweed					1					
Rumex sanguineus/conglomeratus/obstutifolius	small-seeded dock					2					
Rumex cf. *cripus*	curled dock								1		1
Rumex sp. kernel	dock kernel					2			3		
small *Rumex* sp.	small-seeded dock type					1		1	1		
medium *Vicia/Lathyrus/Pisum* sp. (2–4 mm)	vetch/wild pea/pea						1				1
small *Vicia/Lathyrus* sp. (<2 mm)	vetch/wild pea					1					1
Medicago lupulina	black medick							1			
small *Trifolium* spp. (<1 mm)	small-seeded clover								2		
Aethusa cynapium	fool's parsley	w1		w1					w1		
Hyoscyamus niger	henbane				3						
Lithospermum arvense	field gromwell						1	3	2		2
Euphrasia sp.	eyebright				1	2	5	18	18		
Galium sp.	goosegrass										2
Anthemis cotula	stinking chamomile							1			
Tripleurospermum inodorum	scentless mayweed								5		
Eleocharis palustris	common spike-rush					1	2				
Schoenus nigricans	black bog-rush					1			1		
Cladium mariscus	great fen sedge						1	1	1		1
medium trilete *Carex* sp.	sedge								1		
Festuca sp.	fescue				1	13	4	10	103		1
Lolium sp.	rye-grass	1			2	8		7	9		1
Poa spp.	meadow-grass			1	5						
Avena sp.	wild/cultivated oat				2	2			5		3
Phleum bertolonii	lesser cat's-tail							5			
Phleum sp.	cat's tail			1							
large Poaceae indet. (> 4 mm)	large grass family seed				6		2		16		
medium Poaceae indet. (c. 4 mm)	medium grass family seed	2	6	1	20	37	2	38	120		1
small Poaceae indet. (c. 2 mm)	small grass family seed	5							1		
small seed indet.		-				+	-	-	+		+
large seed indet.					-			-			

TABLE 2.43. *(cont.)*

Sample number		<79>	<188>	<108>	<186>	<18>	<109>	<195>	<194>	<14>	<255>
Context		[1699]	[4256]	[2350]	[4252]	[859]	[2366]	[4211]	[4206]	[978]	[4683]
Feature number		F.626	F.1254	F.783	F.1077	F.63	F.853	F.1117	F.1117	F.340	F.1181
Feature type		kiln	kiln	kiln	kiln	kiln	kiln rakeout	kiln	kiln	kiln	kiln
Phase		Conquest/ Early Roman	Conquest/ Early Roman	LIA/ Conquest	LIA/ Early Roman	Conquest/ Early Roman	Conquest/ Early Roman	Conquest/ Early Roman	Early Roman	Early Roman	Early Roman
Sample volume/ litres		8	1/2	15	12	12	5	12	20	1	7
Flot fraction examined		1/1	1/1	1/1	1/1	1/1	1/1	1/1	1/1	1/1	1/1
small bone							++		++		
pot			++			++		++			
oyster								-			
flint						-					
burnt flint						+		+			
burnt clay						+++		+++			
burnt clay with straw impressions								-			
indet. leaf fragments intrusive								++			
intrusive roots		++				++				++	+++
intrusive sesiloides	burrowing snails	++			++	++	+++	+++	+++	++	
charred *Carychium minimum/ tridentatum*	generally well vegetated; wet/damp					2			1		
Cochlicopa lubrica/lubricella	catholic					1			1		
Vertigo sp.	variable, generally shady.					1			1		
charred *Vertigo* sp.	variable, generally shady.								1		
Pupilla muscorum	dry, exposed places					2			1		
Lauria cylindracea	wood/rocks/grassland					1					
Vallonia costata	dry, open places					10					
Vallonia exentrica/pulchella	open, damp and/or dry habitats					74			25		
Trichia hispida/striolata	catholic					8			24		
Aegopinella/Oxychilus sp.	moist & shady places					5			5		
juvenile indet.	-								++		
charred snail								4			

TABLE 2.44. *Roman environmental data: 'w' = waterlogged/uncharred; '-' = 1 or 2 items; '+' = < 10 items; '++' = 10–50 items; '+++' = >50 items.*

Sample number		<54>	<25>	<64>	<71>
Context		[1319]	[687]	[1407]	[1462]
Feature number		F.17	F.7	F.21	
Feature type		undated E–W ditch	later ditch system	later ditch system	ditch
Phase		Roman	Roman	Roman	Roman
Sample volume/ litres		5	12	12	8
Flot fraction examined		1/1	1/1	1/1	1/1
Triticum sp. grain	wheat grain		1		
small charcoal (<2 mm)		++	+	+	++
med. charcoal (2–4 mm)					+
large charcoal (>4 mm)		+	+		
- vitrified charcoal		-			
bone fragments		+	+	+	+
small bone		-			
pot		-	-	-	
flint		-			-
burnt flint				-	
burnt clay				-	
intrusive roots			++		++
intrusive sesiloides	burrowing snails	++	++	-	-

tained large amounts of cereal grain, but smaller amounts of chaff proportionately than the samples taken from the kilns. The cereal in these samples was dominated by large amounts of free-threshing wheat grain (*Triticum aestivum sensu lato*). There were also small amounts of emmer and spelt wheat grains (*Triticum spelta/dicoccum*). Barley (*Hordeum vulgare sensu lato*) was present in only slightly smaller numbers than the free-threshing wheat. In many cases, it was possible to tell from the keel of the grain that this was hulled barley. It was also possible in a number of instances to distinguish between twisted and straight barley, and the ratio between the two in most of the samples was roughly two to one, suggesting that these grains were definitely the remnants of a six-row hulled barley. There were also moderate to large amounts of rye (*Secale cereale*) and oat (*Avena* sp.). There was also evidence for possible cultivation of the celtic bean/pea (large Leguminaceae), although the legumes were slightly fragmentary so this is not conclusive. Finally, there were also fragments of hazelnut shell (*Corylus avellana*) in these samples.

The chaff was present in much smaller quantities, and it was also from various plants. The dominant kind was rachis internodes from barley (*Hordeum vulgare sensu lato*), and was also often from six-row barley. There were still occasional spelt/emmer wheat (*Triticum spelta/dicoccum*) glume bases. There were moderate numbers of bread wheat rachis internodes (Hexaploid wheat) and some indeterminate wheat rachis internodes. Also found was a single oat (*Avena* sp.) floret which appeared be of the wild variety, but as this was the only example it could not be used to say that all of the oats were wild. There was also a small amount of rye (*Secale cereale*) rachis internodes, as well as large numbers of culm nodes from indeterminate cereals.

Large numbers of weed seeds were also present in these samples. Arable weed seeds included corn/small-flowered buttercup (*Ranunculus arvensis/parviflorus*), corncockle (*Agrostemma githago*), field penny-cress (*Thlapsi arvense*), clover (*Trifolium* sp.), medick (*Medicago* sp.), thorow-wax (*Bupleurum rotundifolium*), scentless mayweed (*Tripleurospermum inodorum*), fescue (*Festuca* sp.), meadow-grass (*Poa* spp.), timothy (*Phleum pratense*), lesser cat's tail (*Phleum bertilonii*) and cat's tail (*Phleum* sp.), moderate numbers of field gromwell (*Lithospermum arvense*) and common knapweed (*Centaurea nigra*) and large numbers of vetch/wild pea (*Vicia/Lathyrus* sp.), stinking chamomile (*Anthemis cotula*), rye-grass (*Lolium* sp.) and indeterminate grasses (Poaceae indet.). There were also moderate amounts of eyebright (*Euphrasia* sp.) which grows on damp arable soils.

There were large numbers of wetland plants, with large numbers of seeds from black bogrush (*Schoenus nigricans*) and sedge (*Carex* sp.), as well as smaller numbers of seeds from cotton grass (*Eriophorum* sp.), common spike rush (*Elecocharis palustris*), spike rush (*Elecharis* sp.), buttercups (*Ranunculus bulbosus/acris/repens, Ranunculus flammula,*) and a large amount of sedge stem material (Cyperaceae indet. vegetal material).

Ruderal weeds included moderate or small numbers of seeds from fat-hen (*Chenopodium album*), common/spear-leaved orache (*Atriplex patula/prostrata*), knotgrass (*Polygonum aviculare*), equal-leaved knotgrass (*Polygonum arenastrum*), black-bindweed (*Fallopia convolvulus*), common sorrel (*Rumex acetosa*), sheep's sorrel (*Rumex acetosella*), curled dock (*Rumex crispus*) and dock (*Rumex* sp.). There were also very high numbers of black mustard seed (*Brassica nigra*) in one context from F.500 ([1100/1]), as well as smaller numbers from [1102/3] in that feature. Also present in the latter were seeds from charlock (*Sinapis arvensis*).

Seeds from plants that thrive in nutrient-rich soils included stinging nettle (*Urtica dioica*) and henbane (*Hyoscyamus niger*), although these were only present in very small quantities.

Waterlogged plant remains and the local environment
In most of the cases where uncharred plant remains were found they were present in very small quanti-

ties, and appeared to be remnants of waterlogged assemblages.

Late Iron Age/Conquest Period-Early Roman
One sample, from F.907, which contained uncharred plant remains, only produced a single seed from fool's parsley (*Aethusa cynapium*). This seed occurs in other samples without any other waterlogged or uncharred remains. It is possible that this is intrusive as a greater range of seeds might be expected, and so it is excluded from further discussion.

A rich sample from F.913 contained small amounts of stinging nettle (*Urtica dioica*), poppy (*Papaver* sp.), chickweed (*Stellaria media*), dogwood (*Cornus sanguinea*), hedge/marsh woundwort (*Stachys sylvestris/palustris*) and black horehound (*Ballota nigra*). This could suggest some kind of successional vegetation, due to the presence of dogwood. It also might suggest nutrient-rich soils as stinging nettles were present. The other weed seeds were all from wasteland plants. The paucity of bramble or elder seeds does imply there were no brambles or elder, as these seeds always survive longer due to their woody component. The small quantity of seeds present in this sample, and in most of the others, makes it likely that much had decomposed and means that this is an incomplete assemblage. Therefore, it is not totally indicative of the local environment and this must be borne in mind for all further local environment discussions.

A sample from the basal fill of pond F.770 contained similarly small amounts of waterlogged remains. These included minor quantities of lesser spearwort (*Ranunculus flammula*), common/spear-leaved orache (*Atriplex patula/prostrata*), chickweed (*Stellaria media*), thistle (*Carduus/Cirsium* sp.), great fen sedge (*Cladium mariscus*) and sedge (*Carex* sp.), as well as moderate amounts of henbane seeds (*Hyoscyamus niger*). These seeds indicate a nutrient-rich soil, due to the large presence of henbane seeds, but also a damp environment through the wetland plants and lesser spearwort. A wet environment is indicated by the presence of the eggs from water fleas (*Daphne* sp.) that occurred in a small quantity; these also indicate a stagnant water environment, as this is where they thrive.

F.1038, a ditch, contained negligible amounts of uncharred seeds. These included common/spear-leaved orache (*Atriplex patula/prostrata*), elder (*Sambucus nigra*) and bristly oxtongue (*Picris echrioides*). This last, however, is suspected to be intrusive, due to its good condition, and its presence in the vicinity of where the samples were themselves processed. While the elder may suggest scrub, as there was only one seed this is not a reliable indicator.

F.1059, a cremation, contained larger quantities of uncharred plant remains. These included poppy (*Papaver* sp.), fat-hen (*Chenopodium album*), common/spear-leaved orache (*Atriplex patula/prostrata*), chickweed (*Stellaria media*), small seeded dock (*Rumex sanguineus/conglomerates/obstutifolius*), curled dock (*Rumex crispus*), violet (*Viola* sp.), black horehound (*Ballota nigra*) and sedge (*Carex* sp.). Other than the sedge, these are all plants of waste/disturbed ground; the sedge could attest to a damp environment.

Saxon
These samples only included two which contained any waterlogged remains. In each case they yielded one seed only, from elder (*Sambucus nigra*); both came from the F.552 well.

Molluscan remains
As has been mentioned, while molluscan remains were generally well-preserved, there were not always enough to merit further consideration. It must also be noted that the molluscan remains were extracted from the flot and large fraction of the residue only. It is possible that mollusca that did not float could have

TABLE 2.45. *Saxon environmental data: 'w' = waterlogged/uncharred; '-' = 1 or 2 items; '+' = < 10 items; '++' = 10–50 items; '+++' = >50 items.*

		<4>	<16>	<6>	<170>	<35>	<36>	<41>	<42>/<43>	<46>	<47>	<159>
Context		[401]	[451]	[662]	[3560]	[1100/1]	[1102/3]	[1258]	[1259]	[1244]	[1245]	[3518]
Feature number		F.6	F.420	F.552	F.442	F.500	F.500	F.552	F.552	F.501	F.501	F.482
Feature type		circular cemetery enclosure	egg/cess ditch	well / grain storage pit	south post hole	Alex's well	Alex's well	well	well basal fill	well	well basal fill	well
Phase		Saxon	Saxon	Saxon	possible Saxon	possible Saxon	possible Saxon	Saxon	Saxon	possible Saxon	Saxon	Saxon
Sample volume/ litres		12	8	8	1	20	20	4	6	5	2	3
Flot fraction examined		1/1		1/1	1/1	1/1	1/1	1/1	1/1	1/1	1/1	1/1
hulled, twisted *Hordeum vulgare sensu lato* grain	6-row hulled barley grain		5	8		105	186	39		67		16
hulled, straight *Hordeum vulgare sensu lato* grain	6-row hulled barley grain		3	67		57	79	21		29		7
hulled *Hordeum vulgare s.l.* grain	hulled barley grain				1	15	45	4		5		2
Hordeum vulgare sensu lato grain	barley grain	4		89		28	25					
Triticum cf. *spelta* grain	spelt wheat grain		1	1		15						
Triticum cf. *dicoccum* grain	emmer wheat grain			20		14						
Triticum spelta/dicoccum	spelt/emmer wheat grain						7					
Triticum aestivum sensu lato grain	free-threshing wheat grain	6	2	377		63	333	51	2	10		
Triticum aestivum sensu lato tail grain	free-threshing wheat tail grain						23					
Triticum sp. tail grain	wheat tail grain			18								
Triticum sp. grain	wheat grain	4		19								5
Triticum/Hordeum sp. grain	wheat/barley grain	1	1	219		25	63	6		5		7
Secale cereale grain	rye grain		2	16		30	89	24		29		
cereal grain indet.			1	36		56	159	34		13		
cereal embryo sp.			1	1		1	3	4		5		
cereal frags		++	++	+++	-	+++	+++	+++	-	++	+	++
6-row *Hordeum vulgare sensu lato* rachis internode	6-row barley chaff					5	7	3		3		
Hordeum vulgare s.l. rachis internode	barley chaff			2		21	17	15		11		
Triticum spelta glume base	spelt wheat chaff			1								
Triticum spelta/dicoccum glume base	spelt/emmer chaff			25		1	8					
Hexaploid *Triticum* sp. rachis internode	bread wheat					10		27				1
Triticum sp. rachis internode	wheat chaff						3					
Triticum sp. awn fragment	wheat chaff						3					
Secale cereale rachis internode	rye chaff			2		2	4	3		10		
Avena sp. floret (wild?)	wild oat chaff						1					
cereal indet. rachis internode	cereal chaff					3	12					
cereal indet. culm node	straw joint	1		4		19	16	26		18		
cereal indet. culm node frags	straw joint frags						12					
Ranunculus cf. *repens*	creeping buttercup									1		
large *Ranunculus* cf. *bulbosus/acris/repens*	cf. bulbous/meadow/creeping buttercup						6			1		
Ranunculus cf. *flammula*	lesser spearwort					3						
Ranunculus arvensis/parviflorus	corn/small flowered buttercup						1					
Ranunculus sp.	buttercup						1					
Papaver somniferum	opium poppy						1	1				
Urtica dioica	stinging nettle						1					
Corylus avellana nutshell fragments	hazelnut			4			2					
Chenopodium album	fat-hen			6		10	3					
Atriplex patula/prostrata	common/spear-leaved orache			10		4	13	7				
Chenopodiaceae indet.		1		11		2	5					
Agrostemma githago	corncockle						1					
small Caryophyllaceae indet. (<1 mm)	small pink family seed			1					1			
Polygonum aviculare	knotgrass			2			2					
Polygonum arenastrum	equal-leaved knotgrass						3					
Fallopia convolvulus	black-bindweed					2						
Rumex acetosella	sheep's sorrel					2						
Rumex acetosa	common sorrel			1								
Rumex cf. *cripus*	curled dock		1			6	32			7		
small *Rumex* sp.	small-seeded dock type			2			10		2			
Brassica cf. *nigra*	black mustard					700	14					1
Sinapis cf. *arvensis*	charlock						35	1				
Brassica/Sinapis	black mustard/charlock						96					
Raphanus raphanistrum seed case	wild radish pod							2				
Thlapsi arvense	field penny-cress			1								
large legumes indet. (>4 mm)	cf. celtic bean/pea			3		6	3					
medium *Vicia/Lathyrus/Pisum* sp. (2–4 mm)	vetch/wild pea/pea		1	7		1	66	3				
small *Vicia/Lathyrus* sp. (<2 mm)	vetch/wild pea			9			8					1
Trifolium/Medicago sp.	clover/medick					2						
Medicago sp.	medicks			3						14		
small *Trifolium* spp. (<1 mm)	small-seeded clover			18								
Oxalis acetosella	wood sorrel						1					
Bupleurum rotundifolium	Thorow wax						4					
Apiaceae indet.	carrot family						1					
Hyoscyamus niger	henbane			1								
Lithospermum arvense	field gromwell					1	13					
Odontites sp.	bartsia							1				
Odontites/Euphrasia sp.	bartsia/eyebright						4					
Galium cf. *aparine*	cleavers	1								3		

TABLE 2.45. *(cont.)*

		<4>	<16>	<6>	<170>	<35>	<36>	<41>	<42>/<43>	<46>	<47>	<159>
Sample number												
Context		[401]	[451]	[662]	[3560]	[1100/1]	[1102/3]	[1258]	[1259]	[1244]	[1245]	[3518]
Feature number		F.6	F.420	F.552	F.442	F.500	F.500	F.552	F.552	F.501	F.501	F.482
Feature type		circular cemetery enclosure	egg/cess ditch	well / grain storage pit	south post hole	Alex's well	Alex's well	well	well basal fill	well	well basal fill	well
Phase		Saxon	Saxon	Saxon	possible Saxon	possible Saxon	possible Saxon	Saxon	Saxon	possible Saxon	Saxon	Saxon
Sample volume/ litres		12	8	8	1	20	20	4	6	5	2	3
Flot fraction examined		1/1		1/1	1/1	1/1	1/1	1/1	1/1	1/1	1/1	1/1
Eriphorum	cottongrass					1						
Eleocharis palustris	common spike-rush			5								
Eleocharis sp.	spike-rush					1	7	1				
Schoenus nigricans	black bog-rush			88		6	29	33				
medium trilete *Carex* sp.	sedge			7		12	94	1				
inverted trilete Cyperaceae stem frag.	sedge stem						+++	+++				
Festuca sp.	fescue			2			8	1				
Lolium sp.	rye-grass	9	2	113		3	28	2				
Poa spp.	meadow-grass			4								
Avena sp.	wild/cultivated oat			17		15	51	1		13		
Phleum pratense	timothy						1					
Phleum bertolonii	lesser cat's-tail						1					
Phleum sp.	cat's tail			2								
large Poaceae indet. (> 4 mm)	large grass family seed					3	50			19		
medium Poaceae indet. (*c.* 4 mm)	medium grass family seed	2	2	7		55	76	12		6		4
small Poaceae indet. (*c.* 2 mm)	small grass family seed		3	8		14	11					4
Poaceae rachis internode	grass chaff									3		
small seed indet.			+	++		+	+++	+		++		
large seed indet.							-					
small charcoal (<2 mm)		+++	++	+++	++	+++	+++	+++	++	+++	+	+++
med. charcoal (2–4 mm)		++	+	+++	-	+++	+++	+++		+++	-	++
large charcoal (>4 mm)		+++	++	+++		+++	+++	+++		+++		++
- vitrified charcoal		++			++							
egg shell			+++									
bone fragments		+++	++	+++		+++			+	+++	-	
pitted bone fragments							+++	+++				
small bone				+			+	++		++	+	
pot		+								-		
spherulite		-										
burnt stone		+										
oyster		+										
flint				-								
burnt flint				-	-							-
burnt clay				++								
intrusive roots		++										
intrusive sesiloides	burrowing snails	++	++		++		+					++
Lymnaea truncatula	shallow waters & flooded pastures						1					
Planorbis planorbis	hard water, ditches and ponds							1				
small Planorbidae indet.	gen. overgrown still water						1	2				
charred small Planorbidae indet.	gen. overgrown still water						1					
Carychium minimum/tridentatum	generally well vegetated; wet/damp						43	2				
Succineidae indet.	damp, waterside vegetation					2	18	13				
Cochlicopa lubrica/lubricella	catholic						40					
Vertigo sp.	variable, generally shady.					3	64	19				
charred *Vertigo* sp.	variable, generally shady.					1						
Pupilla muscorum	dry, exposed places							1				
Lauria cylindracea	wood/ rocks/ grassland					2	3	1				
Vallonia costata	dry, open places					5	10	1				
charred *Vallonia costata*	dry, open places					2						
Vallonia exentrica/pulchella	open, damp and/or dry habitats					25	65	3				
charred *Vallonia exentrica/pulchella*	open, damp and/or dry habitats						2					
Cepaea cf. *hortensis*	variable: woods, grassland, hedges						174					
Trichia hispida/striolata	catholic					21	97	7				
Aegopinella/Oxychilus sp.	moist & shady places						3	3				
Ostrea edulis	oyster						1					
juvenile indet.	-						+++	++				

been lost in the flotation process if they were smaller than 1 mm, the mesh size, or could still be in the fine fraction, which was less than 4 mm.

Late Bronze Age

One sample contained a large amount of molluscan remains. This came from F.31 and included many generic mollusca. There were some mollusca that indicate damp or wet environments; these included *Discus rotundatus* and *Carychium minimum/tridentatum*, but these were only present in small quantities. There were larger numbers of *Vallonia excentria/pulchella*, indicative of an open environment. Other mollusca present could indicate a similar environment, including *Pupilla muscorum*, *Lauria cylindracea*, *Vallonia costata* and *Helicella itala*.

Late Iron Age/Conquest Period–Early Roman

Every sample from this phase was dominated by a combination of catholic mollusca and those which live in open ground. The latter were dominated in most cases by *Vallonia excentria/pulchella*, although there were also sometimes large numbers of *Lauria cylindracea*, which is also an open-ground type. Other open-ground mollusca present in lesser quantities included *Vallonia costata* and *Pupilla muscorum*. There were also occasional mollusca that can indicate dampness, though in much smaller quantities. These included *Aegopinella/Oxychilius* sp., a charred *Carychium minimum/tridentatum* and *Columella edentula*. These last were only present in cremation F.411 and kilns F.63 and F.1117.

Saxon

The three mollusc-rich Saxon samples came from two wells. The dominant molluscan species was again *Vallonia excentria/pulchella* and it was again supported by other open-ground species, including *Vallonia costata*, *Lauria cylindracea* and *Pupilla muscorum*. There were also large numbers of the mollusc *Vertigo* sp. which attest to shade. Unsurprisingly, there were water mollusca in two of the three samples, though these were not the dominant species. They included *Planobis planorbis* and *Lymnaea truncatula*. There were also large numbers of mollusca which live on damp ground and these included *Carychium minimum/tridentatum*, Succineidae indet. and *Aegopinella/Oxychilius* sp. The Succineidae live on pond weeds and so definitely indicate the presence of water adjacent to these features.

The different phases of this site had markedly different profiles with respect to the charred remains. This is most obvious when considering the differing proportions of cereal in the Late Iron Age/Conquest Period–Early Roman and the Saxon phases (Fig. 2.50). What is also markedly different are the proportions of chaff and grain in the kiln features, as compared to the other features from the same phase.

Preservation of plant remains in the earliest samples was very poor and those from the Late Bronze Age only produced slight evidence of cereal cultivation. It was impossible to tell whether this was wheat or barley, or what the cultivation conditions may have been like. Wheat and barley are both crops that have been found before at similarly dated sites in the area (Grieg 1991).

The samples from the Late Iron Age through to Early Roman times, excluding those from the kilns, consisted of emmer, spelt and free-threshing wheat.

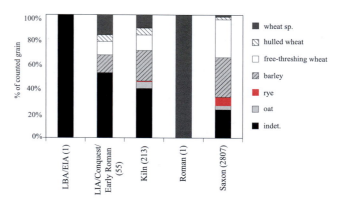

FIGURE 2.50. *Frequency of different cereal grains.*

The chaff was mainly glume bases from spelt/emmer wheat, although those that were better preserved were from spelt wheat. These samples also contained small amounts of barley, most of which was hulled. It was not sufficiently preserved to determine if it was twisted or straight and so it cannot be said if this was six-row barley. There were no oats present nor any rye. The cereals that were present agree well with similarly dated sites in Cambridgeshire, such as Vicar's Farm, West Cambridge (Ballantyne forthcoming), Greenhouse Farm, Fen Ditton (Stevens 2000), West Fen Road, Ely (Ballantyne 2005), Maxey (Green 1985), Stonea Grange (van der Veen 1996) and Wardy Hill, Coveney (Murphy 2003). Similarly to this site, Ballantyne found at West Fen Road that the chaff was dominated by spelt wheat (2005). However, chaff dominated the samples from West Fen Road, whereas this was not true of the samples from the Hutchison Site.

The weed seeds from these samples were mainly either disturbed wasteland types or arable weeds. The only seeds which did not fit with this were those from wetland contexts, although they were present in small numbers. Again, the species found amongst the wild crops resemble closely those found at Vicar's Farm (Ballantyne forthcoming) and West Fen Road (Ballantyne 2005). The main difference was the lack of stinking chamomile, which was relatively common at these sites. This may be due to the early date of these samples. Stinking chamomile only becomes common when cultivation of heavy soils becomes the norm, during the Roman period. It may be that at this site these soils were not yet being cultivated (i.e. the lower *Clay* Farm ground to the west).

The kilns are discussed separately because of their relative richness compared to all of the other samples from that phase. The kilns' profile is similar to that in the other samples, the most important difference being the increased importance of chaff. This was almost all hulled wheat glume bases and was, when identifiable, from spelt wheat, although the majority of the glume bases were too eroded to allow certainty. The chaff in these samples was present at a ratio of approximately 2:1:2 chaff : grain : seeds. According to the Hillman model (1981), glumes and small seeds should be removed at the second fine-sieving, after the grain had been pounded to remove it from the glumes. The majority of the weed seeds in these samples were either from arable contexts or from disturbed ground. There were small amounts of wetland plant seeds, but they were in the minority. Most of these seeds were small and present in small quantities. The only exception to this were the large numbers of fescue seeds, which, although small, were present in large quantities. There were also large numbers of medium-sized grass seeds, but these were still smaller than most of the grain. Also present were small numbers of field gromwell which is of a similar size to the grain, though these were only present in small numbers. This plant thrives on calcareous soils, so it is likely that the crop grew locally. The glume to grain ratio in an intact ear is 1:1. Therefore as it is, in this case 2:1, it is likely as suggested above that this assemblage is the result of fine-sieving. No other profiles of different cereal processing stages (Hillman 1981) have been found within this phase of the site, making it likely that this is the only one which found its way into the archaeological record by charring.

The presence of spelt and spelt/emmer chaff specifically in the kiln features suggests that it may have been collected deliberately for fuel. This is supported by van der Veen (1999), who suggests that chaff may have been a commercial commodity and cites examples of chaff being used as fuel in kilns both in Britain and in other countries. While it is impossible to prove here whether these remains were sold for this purpose, as a commodity, it is obvious that they were deliberately used here. Van der Veen (1999) also points to the predominance of hulled wheat over barley chaff, and states that few uses of barley chaff can be found. She suggests that this may be due to barley being used as animal fodder (including straw and chaff), as well as for human consumption, and so not coming into contact with fire as often. Barley chaff is mainly absent here too. The possible use of spelt wheat chaff as a fuel is something that has also been found at other sites where Roman kilns were excavated. Ballantyne at King's Dyke West, Whittlesey (2002) found glume wheat chaff in kiln samples; Murphy (1989) similarly found mainly spelt glume bases in a sample from a stokehole of a kiln at Stowmarket, Suffolk.

The samples from the Saxon phase are the richest of any from the site. Apart from their abundance, the main difference is the presence of rye grain, and the large amounts of free-threshing wheat. Some examples of hexaploid wheat rachis internodes were also present, meaning that the wheat could have been bread wheat. Barley, which appeared to be of the six-row variety (based on the ratio of twisted to straight grains, and on some of the chaff), was also present, along with oats; in one case there was a floret which appeared to be from a wild oat, suggesting that some of the oats may have been a wild variety rather than the cultivated variety. Grieg (1991) suggests that the common cereals at this time were free-threshing wheat, barley, rye and oats, and notes that this is in marked comparison to the dominance of hulled wheats previously. A comparison with other similarly dated sites in the area such as Cottenham (Stevens 1998) and West Fen Road (Ballantyne 2005) gives a similar impression, with free-threshing wheat dominating with barley, oats and rye also present. Interestingly, there were large numbers of vetch/wild pea/pea (*Vicia/Lathyrus/Pisum* sp.) present in these samples and a small number of possible celtic bean/pea (large leguminaceae), which may also have been a crop; these are also found at West Fen Road (Ballantyne 2005).

The wild plant remains in the Saxon phase of this site were dominated by stinking chamomile. Since this was the first time this was present in large quantities, it may be that this was due to changing land-use practices. Stinking chamomile is commonly found on heavy clay soils, and is commonly found once the change in arable technology from the ard to the mouldboard plough enables cultivation of such soils. Importantly, these were found on some occasions as charred fragments of seed heads, suggesting that at least some of the seeds had survived removal by sieving earlier by being a similar size to the grain, which would have been sieved as part of processing it for use. Also common were seeds of fat-hen and oraches (which suggest nutrient-rich soil conditions), curled dock, dock, clover, medick, common knapweed and numerous grasses, in particular rye-grass, fescue and meadow grass. Moderate quantities of eyebright were also present, suggesting damp soil. These are all fairly typical weed seeds, and are broadly similar to those found at Church End, Cherry Hinton in Saxon quarry pit contexts (Roberts 2004a). Interestingly, they are also very similar to the weed seeds found in the Saxon phases at the County Folk Museum, Cambridge (Roberts 2004b).

Wetland plants were also present in these samples to a greater extent. These included large numbers of black bog-rush and carex. There were also lesser quantities of common spike-rush and lesser spearwort, and large numbers of sedge stem fragments. Together these could indicate interaction with the wetland. It is possible that they could all have been crop weeds as damp soils were being farmed, as indicated by the presence of eyebright. It is equally possible that they indicate the use of wetland resources.

One sample, <35>, from well F.700, yielded a considerable amount of black mustard type seeds (*Brassica* cf. *nigra*). This was present in the other sample from this well (<36>), which also yielded a moderate amount of charlock seeds. Black mustard is indicative of damp ground, and was found in a well. It is also cultivated as a seasoning, however.

In terms of what they tell of the local environment, the molluscan remains from the Late Bronze Age mainly contained species indicating open-ground, although there were some that indicated damp conditions (all the phase's molluscan remains derived from F.31).

The waterlogged remains from the Iron Age/Conquest phases of the site mainly varied between successional vegetation, scrub and wasteland plants and others that indicate a wetland environment. This last was particularly indicated by the presence of sedge and great fen sedge seeds. A large amount of scrub was not indicated by the waterlogged plant remains from these samples, and as most of the seeds which come from scrub, such as bramble and elder, survive better than others in de-watered conditions due to their woody nature; it is likely that this area was relatively scrub-free. The sample from the F.770 pond indicates stagnant water, and this is supported by the presence of water flea eggs. The presence of stinging nettle, henbane and the occasional elder seed also suggest that some of the features may have been surrounded by disturbed nitrogen rich/manured soils. However, as has been observed, the poor preservation of these remains means that large parts of the local environment will remain unknown. The mollusca from this phase of the site, including the kilns, indicate an open landscape, with some indications of dampness.

The only local environmental evidence in the Saxon samples comes from the molluscan remains. Like all the earlier molluscan assemblages, these were mainly dominated by open-ground taxa. Equally, there were also small numbers of water mollusca, and some of damp ground and slum types (meaning that they can cope with the seasonal drying-out of features). These samples were all taken from wells and so it is unsurprising that they may have contained water mollusca.

Pollen analysis (STEVE BOREHAM)

Three sediment monoliths were considered. Monolith <90> ([1975]–[1977]) was 50 cm long and comprised

homogeneous light grey silty clay from which pollen samples were taken at 5–6 cm, 25–26 cm and 43–44 cm. Sediments from this monolith were attributed to deposition in the lower profile of the F.770, Conquest Period well. Monolith <89> ([1966]–[1968]), from the upper fills of the same feature (F.770) was 50 cm long and comprised homogeneous dark grey silty clay from which pollen samples were taken at 5–6 cm, 25–26 cm and 42–43 cm.

Monolith <180> ([3828]–[3829]), from Saxon well F.482, was 30 cm long. It comprised a basal grey silt unit (0–9 cm) from which a pollen sample was taken at 6–7 cm, an orange, brown and grey mottled silty sand unit (9–23 cm), and an upper light grey and white marly silt unit (23–30 cm) from which a pollen sample was taken at 25–26 cm.

Eight samples of sediment from the three monoliths were prepared using the standard hydrofluoric acid technique, and counted for pollen using a high-power stereo microscope.

Conquest Period well F.770 (Monoliths <89> & <90>)
Lower fills (Monolith <90>; [1975]–[1977])
Three sediment samples (5–6 cm, 25–26 cm & 43–44 cm) were analysed from this monolith. Pollen concentrations were moderate at between 28,665 & 30,286 grains per ml. The preservation of palynomorphs was quite good with only a few grains showing signs of oxidation and corrosion. The basal sample (5–6 cm) yielded 346 grains, whilst 25–26 cm gave 260 grains and the upper sample (43–44 cm) produced 204 grains.

All the samples were dominated by grass (33–53%), but there was a clear trend up the sequence with more trees and shrubs at the base (11.5%, 10 taxa) and fewer towards the top (3.9%, three taxa). The percentage of undifferentiated Asteraceae (Lactuceae) pollen was reassuringly low (<11%), suggesting that post-depositional oxidation processes had only modified the pollen signal slightly. Arboreal (tree & shrub) pollen was largely represented by hazel (*Corylus*), oak (*Quercus*), ash (*Fraxinus*) and willow (*Salix*). Cereal pollen was present throughout, reaching 10.8% in the upper sample. Elevated amounts of strap-wort plantain (*Plantago lanceolata*) (c. 7–12%) are particularly notable within the herbs. There is little in the pollen signal to indicate a pond environment, although sedges (Cyperaceae), ferns (Pteropsida) & bur-reed (*Sparganium*) certainly indicate damp ground nearby.

Upper Fills (Monolith <89>; [1966] – [1968])
Three sediment samples (5–6 cm, 25–26 cm & 42–43 cm) were analysed. Pollen concentrations were rather low at between 2074 and 5808 grains per ml. The preservation of palynomorphs was generally quite poor with many grains showing signs of oxidation and corrosion. The 'basal' upper fill sample (5–6 cm) yielded 111 grains, the middle sample (25–26 cm) gave only 60 grains and the upper sample (42–43 cm) produced 124 grains. All of these counts are far below the statistically desirable minimum of 300 pollen grains and, therefore, the results should be treated with caution.

The difficulty with the basal sample (5–6 cm) is that it was dominated by undifferentiated Asteraceae (Lactuceae) pollen (54.1%), indicating that soil processes have seriously altered the pollen signal. The remaining spectrum from this sample is dominated by grass, with herbs, very few trees and shrubs, and 8.1% cereal pollen. The middle and upper samples also have elevated levels of Asteraceae (Lactuceae) pollen (22–30%) indicating that oxidation of pollen may have affected the signal. Both samples were dominated by grass (45–48%), with a few herbs, and very few trees and shrubs; cereal pollen was apparently absent from these.

Saxon well F.482 (Monolith <180>; [3828] – [3829])
Two samples of sediment (6–7 cm & 25–26 cm) were analysed. Pollen concentrations were quite low at 8053 and 13,280 grains per ml respectively, and preservation of the palynomorphs was quite poor with many grains showing signs of oxidation and corrosion. As a consequence, only 138 pollen grains were counted from Sample 6–7 cm, although 291 were counted from Sample 25–26 cm, which approaches the statistically desirable minimum of 300 pollen grains.

The samples analysed produced a relatively consistent pollen assemblage dominated by grass (*c.* 50%), with various herbs and very few trees and shrubs. The percentage of undifferentiated Asteraceae (Lactuceae) pollen was rather high (>20%), indicating that soil processes had begun to alter the pollen assemblage through oxidation. This could explain the paucity of arboreal (tree & shrub) pollen, represented only by small amounts of hazel (*Corylus*) and pine (*Pinus*). Cereal pollen was present in the upper sample (25–26 cm), and nettle (*Urtica*) pollen was found in both. Damp ground taxa present included sedges (Cyperaceae), marestail (*Equisetum*), ferns (Pteropsida) & bur-reed (*Sparganium*). There appears to be no significant variation or trend between the two samples.

Monolith <90> ([1975]–[1977]) - The pollen signal from this monolith was apparently almost unchanged by soil processes, and showed a grass-dominated environment with ruderal weeds and tall-herbs. There is strong evidence for arable activity, and the presence of *Plantago lanceolata* indicates that this was occurring close to the site. The sample from the bottom of the sequence has the unmistakable signal of mixed-oak woodland, probably growing some distance from the site. However, by the top of the sequence, this signal has all but disappeared. There is little evidence for a pond at this site, although there is evidence for damp ground nearby.

Monolith <89> ([1966]–[1968]) - In many ways this is the most difficult monolith to interpret, since the amount of post-depositional modification of the pollen signal appears to be substantial. It is clear that sedimentation took place in a grass-dominated environment with tall herbs and ruderals. The basal sample shows clear evidence of arable activity nearby, although this appears to be absent further up the sequence. The presence of *Urtica* at the top of the sequence may indicate local enrichment of soils through human activity, although there is no evidence of soil disturbance. There is scant evidence for damp conditions near the site, and further interpretation is almost impossible.

Monolith <180> ([3828]–[3829]) - Although the pollen signal from the two samples from this monolith showed some sign of post-depositional modification, it is clear that this sediment was deposited in an ostensibly tree-less environment dominated by grass and tall-herbs. There is some evidence for arable activity, but the absence of the disturbed ground indicator *Plantago lanceolata* suggests that this was some distance from the site. However, the presence of *Urtica* may indicate local enrichment of soils by human activity or animal dung. There is reasonable evidence for the presence of damp ground nearby, but not for bodies of standing water.

Concluding discussion

The Hutchison Site is remarkable for the intensity and duration of its sequence. As will become apparent in the light of the subsequent environs fieldwork (see Chapter 3), aside from lacking a substantive Early/Middle Iron Age component, the site saw occupation during all the main phases of the broader landscape's usage — spanning the later Bronze Age through to Saxon times (Fig. 2.51). Fortunately, insights into its 'missing' Iron Age are, in effect, provided by Cra'ster's 1967 New Addenbrooke's Site, located only 150 m to the east (see Chapter 1), although, somewhat conversely, the Hutchison's seven-phase complexity itself suggests just what must have been overlooked during Cra'ster's excavations due to their extreme rescue conditions; it can only be suspected that less robust phases of usage must have gone unnoticed amidst the machine-churning. In other words, however convincing a 'picture' of later prehistoric occupation the New Addenbrooke's Site offered in its day, today its very simplicity would have to be considered atypical, certainly of the immediate Addenbrooke's landscape (cf. Figs. 1.4 & 2.51).

Part of what makes the Hutchison's sequence seem 'busy' and potentially confusing is that, aside from in the Neolithic (see below) — and, again, very much in contrast with Cra'ster's site — the excavation did not frame discrete settlements. In all of its main phases, the archaeology extended beyond the site's limits so that nothing was exposed in its totality. This, of course, is a common problem in developer-funded fieldwork; the area is not chosen by us and, accordingly, 'something will always lead outwards' (see Evans & Hodder 2006b). It nevertheless makes it incumbent on us to try to situate where the site lay within the larger settlement areas at anyone time: variously their core or margins.

As is clear from Figure 2.52, the focus of the site's sequence — and accordingly its 'story' — essentially lies in its later Iron Age and Early Roman phases. Its preceding prehistoric (Neolithic and Bronze Age) and subsequent later Roman and Middle Saxon usage are, of course, significant in the locale's sequence and generally tell of the long-term attraction of the

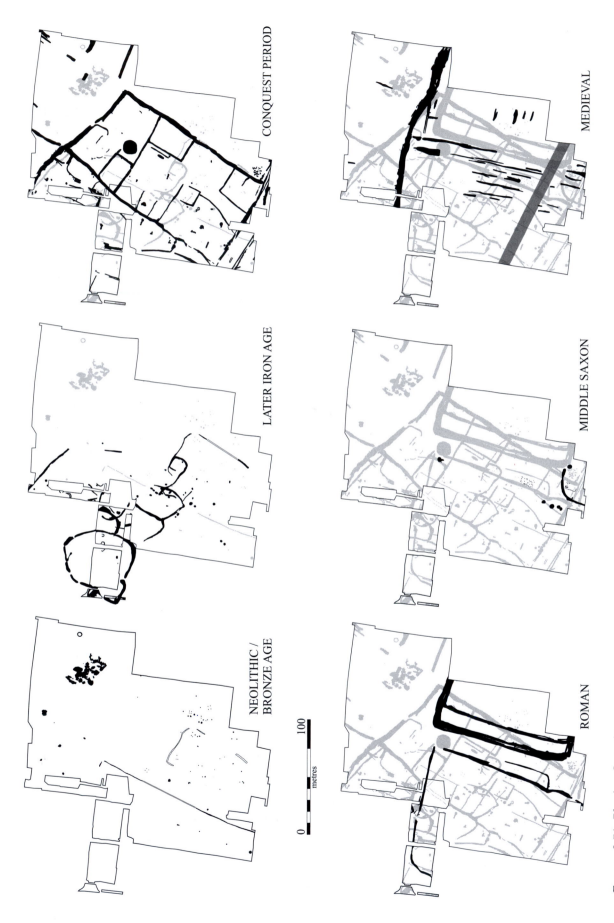

CONQUEST PERIOD

MEDIEVAL

LATER IRON AGE

MIDDLE SAXON

NEOLITHIC /
BRONZE AGE

ROMAN

100

metres

0

FIGURE 2.51. *Phasing Overview.*

Addenbrooke's landscape. Otherwise, these phases can only really be considered as 'incidental'. Therefore, in order to maintain a sense of research emphasis, those phases that bracketed the site's Conquest Period will first be discussed, before proceeding to consider its Conquest Period dynamics.

The pre-mid second-millennium BC usage would generally have to be seen as only representing 'taskscape-like' activities (e.g. Edmonds *et al.* 1999) and probably attested to no more than a series of 'short-stay' episodes. It is noteworthy that no later Neolithic/Early Bronze Age pottery whatsoever was recovered (e.g. Grooved Ware, Beaker and Collared Urn). In contrast, however, at least eight separate Early Neolithic vessels were attested to from the 120 sherds of that date. Yielding 90% of this material (108 sherds from six vessels) and 121 flints (c. 20% of the site's total flint assemblage), pit F.468 may well represent 'tidying-up' following a more intense occupation visit. Nevertheless, as shown on Figure 2.52, from the spread of its residually derived material, all of the site's Early Neolithic finds could probably have come from only one or two such stays (occurring against a background of more dispersed incidental use).

Whereas at 1049 sherds and representing at least 58 different vessels, the site's later Bronze Age pottery assemblage is clearly considerable, the Middle Bronze Age pottery is much less evident (176 sherds/seven vessels only). This being said, as shown on Figure 2.6, Middle Bronze Age material occurred throughout the area of the southeastern 'core' where most of the later Bronze Age settlement features were and, in fact, the three Middle Bronze Age features there account for 85% of the total Deverel-Rimbury assemblage (150 sherds). Therefore, although they did not mix by feature-context (i.e. forming discrete assemblages), there would be every reason to see these two wares as deriving from a related usage and not necessarily from 'interrupted' occupations. Note that the radiocarbon assay achieved from one of the later Bronze Age pits, 1110–900 cal. BC (Beta-195160), closely matches Brudenell's 1100–800 BC assignation of its pottery.

Essentially, the site then saw 'open-type' settlement. While no post-built roundhouses were identified, the pit- and post-cluster 'grammar' of the site's settlement architecture — especially the four-posters — would be entirely typical of the later Bronze Age. Otherwise, aside from reiterating that the northwestern quarry-hollow cluster might have related to the extraction of potting clays, and that Structure 4's circle could have had a 'marker' function, all that really need concern us at this point is the period's potential fieldsystem boundaries. Although they could not be firmly dated, and the fieldsystem's predominant

northnortheast/southsouthwest axis was close to that of the Phase 4 Conquest Period system, it was definitely truncated by the Roman road and continued uninterrupted beneath its line (no relationship could be established between this main 'early' fieldsystem boundary and the Phase 3 Iron Age layout). Therefore, there is every reason to associate these boundaries with the site's Bronze Age and see them as part of a much more extensive fieldsystem. As mentioned above, while its ditches would have been much more minor than those at either the broadly contemporary Fulbourn Hospital or Babraham Road Park-and-Ride Sites (see Chapter 1) — and, moreover, it would be off the latter's east-west orientation — its alignment and relatively minor proportions would be completely typical of many fieldsystems of the period within the region. However, the ramifications of this will only be more fully appreciated when set in the wider context of the environs fieldwork in Chapter Three below.

There is unavoidable ambiguity over whether portions of the later Roman boundary system should actually be assigned to the Middle Saxon occupation, or if the obvious impact of Phase 5/System 2 upon it was solely due to the lingering influence of its ditches as earthworks. The favouring of the latter interpretation here is in part due to the fact that, whereas the definite evidence of Saxon settlement was almost entirely localized within the south-central portion of the site (and obviously continued southward beyond its edge of excavation), the boundary system was clearly much more extensive.

The determination of the Middle Saxon settlement's layout was not furthered by the marked paucity of its material culture, and only 21 sherds of Middle Saxon pottery were recovered. While taken at face-value this seems remarkably low (it is, for instance, only equivalent to approximately a sixth of the site's Early Neolithic assemblage), it can be argued that such low pottery frequency is typical of the period and that, with its two post-built house structures, the Hutchison Site is broadly comparable to the Middle Saxon phase of the West Fen Road Site at Ely, with its 109 sherds of Ipswich Ware and four contemporary structures (one re-built; Mortimer *et al.* 2005). Equally, it could further be said that, given the quantity of animal bone recovered from the Hutchison Site's Saxon features (c. 1740 pieces), its low pottery numbers are not directly reflective of its usage. However, there really is no way of knowing what percentage of this bone was actually residual and derived from the site's earlier occupation. Finally, the crucial point is that Middle Saxon pottery only occurred in three pit-features and therefore does not provide a real basis by which to further the analysis of the site's occupation in this phase. Given its scale and limited finds numbers, either this must only represent a very short-lived small hamlet or, alternatively, the northern margin of a more extensive settlement whose bulk lies south of the Hutchison Site. (As discussed in Chapters 3 and 4 below, evidence of further Saxon settlement — including a distinctly 'Early' component — has since been found in the field immediately to the southwest.)

The radiocarbon date from the pit from which the extraordinary carved clunch block derived — 660–790 cal. AD (F.500; Beta-195159) — would fully accord with its Middle Saxon assignation.

If pushing inference to its limits, based on the distribution of Saxon material it could be argued that there was a relationship between the core of the settlement and the proposed line of the bank of the headland that must have crossed the site (and interrupted its pattern of plough furrows). Although we would think of this as unlikely, the divergent relationship between the furrows and the headland — and the latter's sympathetic alignment with the main Roman landscape 'grid' — would, nevertheless, point to the relatively early establishment of the headland agricultural system, whose scale across the area can be readily appreciated from the cropmark plot (Figs. 1.12 & 2.45; see e.g. Oosthuizen 2003).

Matters of economy and environment

The amassed evidence of the site's quernstone and bulk-environmental assemblages, and also its pollen cores, should leave little doubt that during, at least, Late Iron Age, Roman and Saxon times the site's economy was based on *mixed farming*, and that arable agriculture was undertaken within the vicinity. The degraded state of formerly 'wet' plant assemblages demonstrates the water-retentive capacity of the site's deeper features (and the locally 'heavy' qualities of its geology). However, based on the plant assemblages, particularly their weeds (see Roberts above), it would seem that it may have been only in Saxon times that agriculture extended onto the lower, more clayish lands west of the site proper (the eastern Clay Farm 'trough'; see Chapter 3).

Of the site's plant remains, it warrants emphasis that, in the same manner in which the presence of stinking chamomile in the Saxon samples attests to 'heavy-land' cultivation, the presence of field gromwell in the Conquest Period kiln assemblages indicates the local origin of the crops, as it is a plant that thrives on calcareous soils. Equally, other evidence points to changes in agricultural practice between later Iron Age/Early Roman and Saxon times. While the former saw the use of emmer, spelt and free-threshing wheat (and, to a lesser degree, barley) — with spelt wheat chaff extensively used as kiln-fuel or, rather, starting tinder — the Saxon samples (in which cereals were far more abundant) were marked by quantities of free-threshing wheat, rye, barley and oats, and there was possible evidence of the cultivation of the celtic bean/pea. As detailed by Roberts above, these crops are typical of other site assemblages of their respective periods.

Generally the pattern of animal husbandry on the site appears to have been very stable. Leaving aside the later Bronze Age data, in the Iron Age to Saxon assemblages cattle were dominant at 53–55%, followed by sheep at 35–41%; pig made up 4–10% of the assemblage, being highest in Saxon times (though, in truth, they had 14% representation in the later Bronze Age). These were clearly domestic economies, with 'the wild' essentially playing no role.

Based on the evidence of those contemporary sites that have been excavated within the area — Greenhouse Farm, Cambridge with 18% cattle and 75% sheep (Gibson & Lucas 2002), and Edix Hill, Barrington with 29% cattle and 55% sheep (Malim *et al.* 1998) — it could be argued that the low level of sheep in the Iron Age at the Hutchison Site was somewhat unusual. However, as shown in Higbee's recent overview, a low percentage of sheep is, in fact, common to a number of sites of the period within the wider region (in Evans, Knight & Webley 2007, 62–5, table 7). On the whole, based on the Hutchison's data, one would have to concur with Swaysland's observation that there is very little sense of a distinctly Roman economy or direct evidence of stock improvement at that time, and this surely reflects upon the status of the settlement (see also Hodder 1982a concerning an example of Iron Age to Roman economic change). Yet a note of caution is warranted in this respect; the risk of cross-period residuality of this material must be taken into account, as processes of redeposition will 'even-off' assemblages in such intense multi-period occupations and, inevitably, enhance apparent economic continuities.

As outlined by Roberts above, the molluscan and waterlogged plant assemblages both suggest that throughout its main periods the site was an open-ground environment with successional vegetation and wasteland taxa and only limited scrub-cover. Yet this picture is somewhat contradicted by the evidence of the pollen from the F.770 Conquest Period pond-well. In its lower profile there was up to *c.* 11% arboreal pollen, with hazel, oak, ash and willow all present. Equally important, though, is that the upper profile of that feature documents a marked decline of woodland over time. While perhaps attesting to a local expansion of settlement and its attendant fieldsystems, more

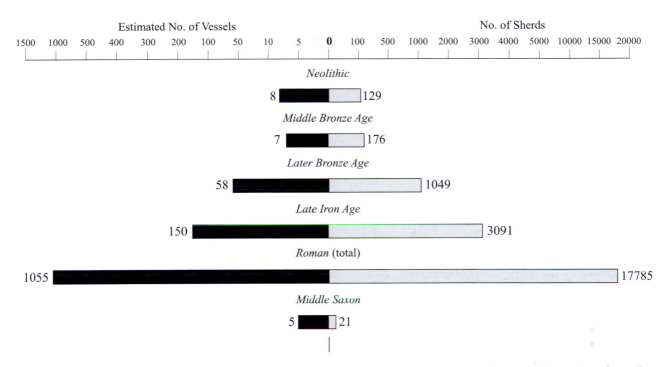

FIGURE 2.52. *Depositional 'Weight': pottery frequency per period by number of sherds and estimated number of vessels.*

likely this marks the direct environmental impact of the site's pottery industry and the provision of its requisite fuel (see Walker 2007 and Lyne & Jefferies 1979, 12–13 on kiln-fuel needs).

Potter farmers? - Pottery production and supply

As a facet of the site's economy, the Conquest Period kilns warrant discussion in their own right. So closely matching those at Greenhouse Farm (and falling hard on the heels of that excavation; Gibson & Lucas 2002), at the time their recovery seemed quite remarkable. Together with the earlier evidence of comparable production at the Cherry Hinton War Ditches (see Inset above), this certainly seems a high incidence of kiln sites and it could be interpreted as reflecting quite intense, immediately post-Conquest manufacture. Perhaps this is also symptomatic of the Aylesford-Swarling 'phenomenon' (see below), as major Early Roman kiln complexes have not, as yet, been found along the southern fen-edge or on the Isle of Ely (though see Popescu forthcoming concerning the Swavesey kilns). It might be the case that amongst more Romanized Late Iron Age communities within the 'core zone', Iron Age pottery traditions and trading networks collapsed wholesale with the Conquest proper. Alternatively, an opposite continuity-based interpretation could be postulated; it being those areas where Late Iron Age wheelmade production flourished (i.e. Cambridge and south) that subsequently saw widespread Conquest Period pot-

tery manufacture. What seems to be the Cambridge-focussed distribution of these kiln complexes might also be relevant and, if so, it raises the issue of whether they attest to town-related production. Unfortunately, the evidence is ambiguous. Over the last few years evidence of Cambridge's later first-century AD settlement has finally been found on the lower eastern Castle Hill-slope immediately above the river crossing (e.g. see Cessford in Evans & Lucas forthcoming; cf. Alexander & Pullinger 2000). Yet this could not have been an extensive settlement, one needing to draw its pottery from upwards of 4km away. Equally, until a series of Conquest Period rural settlements are excavated on a sufficient scale in the south of the County, we will not be able to resolve to what degree this scale of pottery production was regional- (i.e. within the Aylesford-Swarling 'core') or Cambridge-specific.

Gibson & Lucas's 2002 *Britannia* paper thoroughly overviewed the region's Early Roman pottery industries and related kiln technology issues. Accordingly, these will not be rehearsed here and, instead, we will largely restrict ourselves to matters of pottery supply. With its 11 kilns, how is the scale of the Hutchison's Early Roman pottery production to be gauged? To what degree was it a matter of immediate household production as opposed a specialist trade? A relative site-specific measure is provided by comparison with its preceding Phase 3 Iron Age settlement. If seeing the estimated 150 vessels generated by its *c.* 75–100 years span as 'typical' of domestic needs/consumption (at least as recovered through the 'filter' of the site's excavation-sample; see below), then the more than a thousand vessels from its ensuing Roman phase must represent something altogether different, as their duration is broadly comparable (Fig. 2.52). (This is a matter of the *estimated* number of vessels and not any formal 'minimum number of vessels'-criteria.)

The most expedient means by which to appreciate the site's production is to consider other contemporary settlements. In recent years there have been large-scale excavations of later first-century settlements at, for example, Vicar's Farm, West Cambridge and Colne Fen, Earith, neither of which yielded evidence of on-site pottery manufacture. Therefore, given that not all of the settlements of the time produced their own pottery, then *de facto* it must be presumed that it was a specialist activity, with pottery being traded. This need not, of course, have been of a major 'industrial' level and, based on the Hutchison's figures, one production site may have supplied other settlements only within the immediate vicinity. Albeit at a low level, this would nevertheless amount to *specialist production*. Equally, from the paucity of contemporary coinage both at this site and Greenhouse Farm (Lucas & Gibson 2002), its trade was probably conducted through barter and not within a cash economy (presuming that the exchange occurred on-site and that the resultant pots were not carted off to local markets). This, however, probably indicates no more than that the settlement was not involved in military supply, as the army would potentially have been the only major body to pay for goods in coinage (see Reece, in Evans 2003b).

One way to assess the site's production is by estimating the output of its kilns. If, for example, it is assumed that each of the nine that were used saw 3–4 firings, and if 50–100 vessels were fired at each time, this would then imply that some 1350–3600 vessels were produced on-site (the F.63 and F.1117 kiln assemblages were, respectively, estimated to include 109 and 90 kiln-product vessels; see Webley above). They could have potentially generated nearly 3–8 times the estimated number of kiln-produced vessels recovered (469), of which the majority must, anyway, be counted as 'waste' of some kind.

In order to provide a further measure of contemporary occupation and pottery use, the Hutchison's Phase 4 pottery could be compared to other first-century AD phase settlements within the region: Vicar's Farm with some 1750 sherds (see below), and Langdale Hale, Earith with *c.* 1500 sherds of the period (Evans with Appleby, Lucy and Regan forthcoming). As excavated, both are roughly equivalent to the Hutchison Site (though the Vicar's Farm occupation was somewhat more limited),

and a comparable excavation-sample of their linear features was implemented (10%). The latter point is particularly crucial; at first glance the Langdale Hale and Vicar's Farm assemblages would seem relatively minor compared with the *c.* 4500 sherds of kiln wares from the Hutchison Site (*c.* 95 kg). Yet, when these other assemblages are duly factored (by ten-fold) to account for their sample excavation, then the scale of the kiln-associated material is put into further perspective. (Of course, the Hutchison's assemblage would then, theoretically, also require such calculation, but given that its kilns were 100% excavated, the percentage of kiln products would decline relative to pottery from off-site sources.) Therefore, when so factored, and if providing a measure to compensate for 'missing' surface-deposit finds, these sites might have had total first-century assemblages in the order of 20,000–25,000 sherds. Unfortunately, in the case of the Vicar's Farm and Langdale Hale settlements, no estimation (aside from EVEs) was made of the number of vessels. Nevertheless, if it is assumed that each vessel would be represented by *c.* 25–75 sherds, then taking 50 as an average we would be dealing with sites having some 400–500 vessels. By this admittedly rough benchmark, the Hutchison's 1350–3600 vessel-production would equate with almost three to nine 'site's-worth' of pottery. If acknowledging the 'consumption' of their own wares by the Hutchison community (see below), it is probably reasonable to envisage them supplying three to five other settlements with pottery. It must be stressed here that these figures are not offered as any kind of absolute gauge of pottery production/consumption. Rather, in the spirit that 'numbers are good to think with (too)' (Bloch 1998), they simply indicate that the Hutchison's kilns are likely to have produced more pottery than required for the immediate needs of its community. Even this statement, though, must be tempered by the fact that the overall size of the Hutchison/Addenbrooke's Conquest Period settlement is currently unknown. Certainly appearing to extend further to the west, it could well have also continued south of the road-line. Obviously, the larger the immediate settlement its kilns were supplying, the less pottery would have been available for extra-site trade/exchange.

Given that of the site's estimated 897 Phase 4 vessels just over half derived from off-site sources, that more than 6000 animal bones are attributable to its Roman phases and that the site had its own cemetery, there is every reason to think the Phase 4 settlement was permanently occupied and that its potters were in residence. The question then becomes whether the site should be thought of as a distinct industrial quarter seeing full-time pottery production (in which case some of its potential building plots could have variously served

FIGURE 2.53. *'Core-Zone' Distributions: Top, Neolithic and Bronze Age; below, Iron Age and Roman (major deposits of pottery by context).*

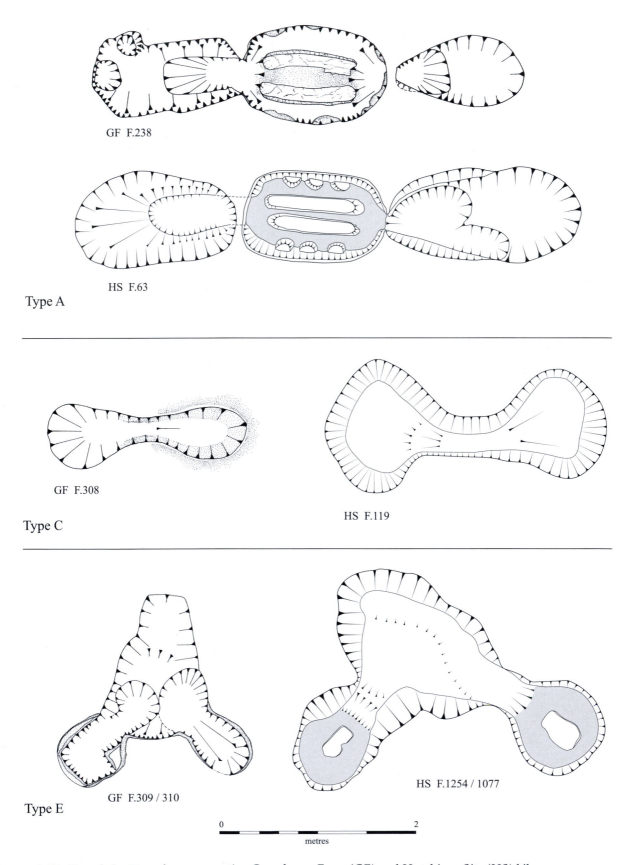

GF F.238

HS F.63

Type A

GF F.308

HS F.119

Type C

GF F.309 / 310

HS F.1254 / 1077

Type E

0   2

metres

FIGURE 2.54. *Knowledge Transfer: comparative Greenhouse Farm (GF) and Hutchison Site (HS) kilns.*

as workshops and/or drying sheds) or if its manufacture was only a part-time/seasonal activity. Here, the latter is considered the most plausible interpretation and the level of production is probably best characterized as of a *'household industry'-scale* (with some of its buildings temporarily serving as drying sheds, etc.).

The term, household industry, is from Tyers (1996, table 10) and which he took from Peacock's study of Roman pottery production that was informed by enthnoarchaeological research (1982). Oddly enough, there is almost something reassuringly 'domestic' about assigning the Hutchison's production to such a category and it has a ring of familiarity about it. Yet, in this context, it is necessary that the site's remaining *c.* 13,285 non-kiln-derived Roman sherds should not be lost sight of. The *c.* 5375 of these sherds definitely associated with its Phase 4 contexts still represent approximately three times the number generated from Vicar's Farm's and Langdale Hale's first-century AD occupation (despite their shared excavation-technique/-sample). This both attests to the density of the Hutchison's early settlement and perhaps also reflects upon its status. Almost belying the evidence of its feature traces alone, it suggests some degree of affluence, at least as reflected in the quantity of its pottery (although not its quality, it only having 0.1% imported wares by EVEs), and this itself may tell of the rewards of pottery production.

Having 'scaled' the Hutchison's production, the issue to address is whether the inhabitants should be thought of as 'Farmer Potters' or 'Potter Farmers' — which activity augmented the other? More than just a matter of semantics, what this primarily reflects upon is the interrelationship of the two pursuits; the dovetailing of pottery production and the agricultural cycle as evinced in the provision of chaff-tinder and, presumably, coppiced timbers for kiln firing. Such potting would be a seasonal activity, probably occurring after the harvest, in September or October, when there was available time, fuel and sunlight/heat to dry the vessels (R. Jefferies pers. comm.). Given the skill-level involved and the scale of Hutchison's production, the latter, *Potter Farmers* appellation is considered the more appropriate.

This interpretation of the Hutchison Site's pottery production would contrast with Gibson and Lucas' arising from the nearby Greenhouse Farm excavations (2002), and it is difficult to mesh the two. Having the same basic chronology and site layout (sub-rectangular Conquest Period enclosures with small sub-rectangular building plots: Fig. 2.23) and what was essentially a matching series of kilns (see below), they have been interpreted in opposed manners: whereas the Hutchison's production is considered to have been a component of its resident farming community, the Greenhouse Site was seemingly without permanent settlement and instead subject to the visits of itinerant potters, who may have 'camped out' within its enclosure and effectively utilized a pre-existing 'market' location (Gibson & Lucas 2002, 110–15; see also Young concerning 'migrant potters' in the context of the Obelisk Kilns in Pullinger & Young 1982, 8–9).

The two sites' kilns are compared in Figure 2.54 and, superficially, their forms/types appear to directly match. Potentially they could even be thought of as akin to 'fingerprints' and as reflecting the hand of the same makers. Yet, while certainly similar, there are crucial differences: the greater size of Hutchison's Type C and E kilns, and the fact that a number of its kilns had central pedestal supports which those at Greenhouse lacked. What, therefore, seems more important is that both sites saw the same basic variability of kiln forms/types. Indicating that they were subject to the same 'influences' (but not necessarily the same makers), the key question then becomes one of *knowledge transfer*. As further discussed in the volume's final chapter, whether or not itinerant specialists were necessarily agents of information-dispersal inherently relates to the density of contemporary settlement and just how far knowledge-skills had to spread.

The hinge point of the site's divergent interpretations is the quantity of pottery respectively assigned as kiln products; at Hutchison this amounts to only 53% (by weight; 40.5% by number), while virtually all the Conquest Period pottery at Greenhouse (*c.* 15,000 sherds) was held to be made on-site. Though very similar in their overall assemblages, whereas 12 different vessel forms in two fabrics are thought to have been forthcoming from the Hutchison's kilns, at Greenhouse the kilns were accredited as producing 28 forms in seven fabrics. It is hard to reconcile these differences given that the sites' kilns essentially share the same forms (and number) and, therefore, it is reasonable to presume that production should have been broadly comparable. In the end, a degree of compromise is probably in order. It could be the case that too little of the Hutchison material has been assigned as kiln-products, but, equally, too much at Greenhouse may have been ascribed to its kilns. In this context, the much smaller size of the Greenhouse Farm Site also needs to be borne in mind. While its excavated portions may not themselves have seen permanent settlement on the same scale as at the Hutchison, contemporary settlement could well have lain nearby within the same system, with pottery production being marginal to it. If so, then the absence of local settlement *per se* need no longer itself propel an itinerant potters model.

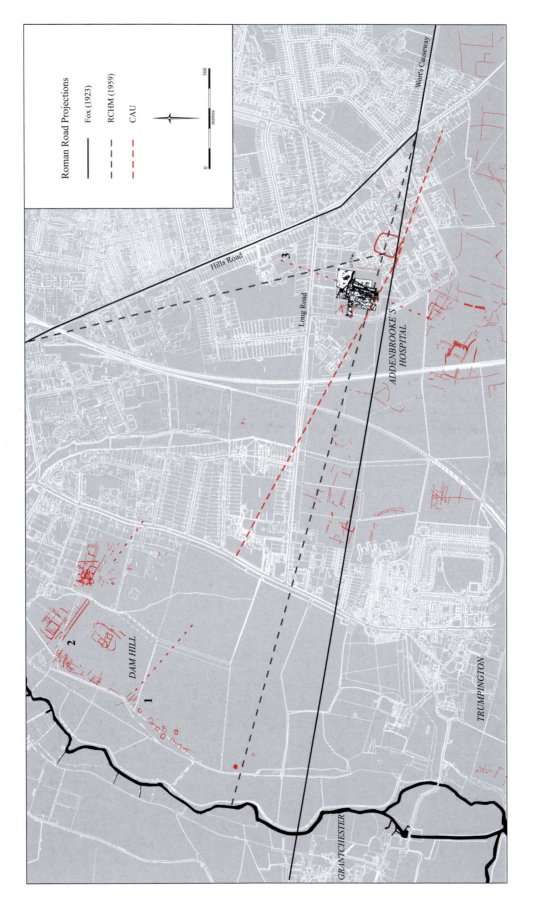

FIGURE 2.55. *The Addenbrooke's Environs Roman Roads. (Reproduced by permission of Ordnance Survey on behalf of HMSO. © Crown copyright 2008. All rights reserved. Ordnance Survey licence number 100048686.)*

Finally, although pottery could obviously be made at all of the three main Early Roman kiln sites near Cambridge — War Ditches/Cherry Hinton, Greenhouse Farm and the Hutchison Site — none of their locations seems particularly recommended by resource-access and, rather, their situation seems largely determined by their accompanying settlements. It was only the later take-off of (quasi-) industrial-level pottery production at Horningsea (J. Evans 1992; Walker 1904b; see also Frend 1998), with its more direct access to water and clay sources (and possibly fen-edge wood stands), that resource proximity — coupled together with direct canal transportation-links — came to the fore. This being said, aside from having river-transport access, the location of Late Roman Obelisk Kilns at Harston does not seem to have been obviously resource-determined (Pullinger & Young 1982). Similarly, that each of the three above-listed first-century AD kiln sites had, if not a road, then at least trackway access (Figs. 2.13 & 2.48) suggests that transportation was still then a factor in their location. Of course, the degree to which this was significant ultimately depends on the frequency-interval of such routes; the evidence thus far would indicate that Roman countryside was extensively crossed (and widely linked) by such 'ways'. Equally, we should perhaps also be wary of over-emphasizing the role played by the Horningsea kilns in Cambridge's later Roman pottery assemblages (and of models of resource-focused mass production). Aside from the Obelisk Kilns, post-first-century AD, 'other industry' wasters have been recovered from both the Jesus Lane area (Hartley 1960 and Alexander *et al.* 2004) and also, on the west side of the town, at New Hall (see Going in Evans & Lucas forthcoming).

Conquest Period dynamics

The recovery of the east–west Roman road along the southern side of the site would generally match its suggested route as postulated by the RCHM[E] and others. This being said, its alignment is not exactly as has been proposed, as it actually runs further north-over-west. From this, it would correlate with the series of Roman boundaries recorded along the southern side of Cra'ster's 1967 enclosure (Fig. 2.13) and, east thereof, the road would run some 200 m south of its putative Wort's Causeway line. Though having to involve a slight alteration in its alignment, it would rather seem to continue along the marked headland that lies south of that historical thoroughfare, and in field survey this headland has been recorded as being a 'metalled' bank (Kemp 1993). Given its definition across the width of the site, if projecting this roadway west it would cross the Cam between Grantchester and

Newnham (*c.* 400 m south of the latter), and considerably further north than either the Royal Commission (1959) or Fox (1923) would have it. As shown on Figure 2.55, on this projected line the Hutchison's road would have continued west towards the Dam Hill riverside cropmarks. While the small sub-square/circular compounds visible across the southern extent of this cropmark group are probably generally of Iron Age attribution, those in its northern half are more rectilinear and must include a substantial Roman component (see Chapter 3 below concerning Roman burials in that area). Although on the direct projection of its line there is no obvious indication of the road's route within the immediate area, just to the north a paired ditch setting could well indicate its river crossing/ford-point (Fig. 2.55:1); to meet it the road would only have to kink slightly further northwestward along its length. (A much more obvious road-to-riverside setting is visible some 400 m still north of this point, but this would require a major deviation of the Hutchison's road and must indicate still another 'way': Fig. 2.55:2.)

Aside from this positive recovery, the site also provided negative evidence of the area's Roman road system, as no trace of the postulated northward length of the *Via Devana* was observed (i.e. the 'Perse School Road'). As projected, it should have crossed through the eastern margins of the site, probably within the eastern Access Road trench, but no evidence was found of it and the possible routeway there was on a very different alignment (Figs. 2.3, 2.13 & 2.55). The only other possible candidate for a north–south roadway anywhere close to this route was the central 'seam' within the Phase 5 Roman fieldsystem, along which metalling locally survived towards the south of the site. Whilst possible, this was not entirely convincing as a Roman road and its alignment would certainly not correlate with either the Perse School or Hills Road routes (a road in this position would have had to go over the huge Phase 4 pond-well in Paddock J.1 and there was certainly no evidence of any metalling subsiding down into its fills). Yet the crucial point might be the status of the larger Addenbrooke's Early Roman settlement. The 'story' of the area's Roman road network has primarily been written from the Cambridge perspective, with it being 'the place' to reach from the south. As further discussed in Chapter Four below, if the greater Addenbrooke's settlement was some manner of minor centre in its own right, then it might itself have been the determinant of the cross-roads system; the road north to Cambridge perhaps determined more by Addenbrooke's immediate axes than the regional-scale road system.

It should not come as a surprise that there is some ambiguity concerning the duration of the site's

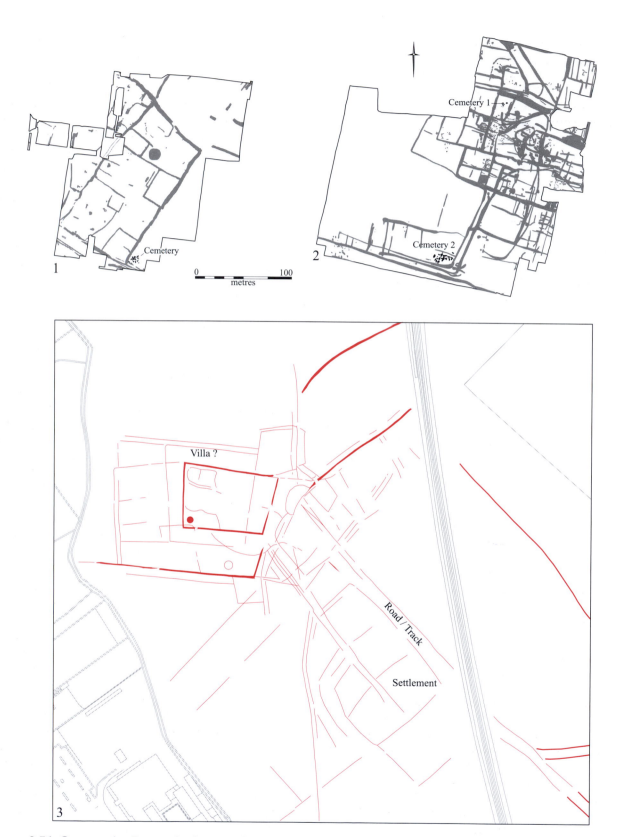

FIGURE 2.56. *Comparative Roman Settlement Plans: 1) Hutchison Site; 2) Vicar's Farm, West Cambridge (Evans & Lucas forthcoming); 3) cropmark plot of the possible Shelford Villa (Scheduled Ancient Monument, CAM 57). (Reproduced by permission of Ordnance Survey on behalf of HMSO. © Crown copyright 2008. All rights reserved. Ordnance Survey licence number 100048686.)*

southern Roman road, the crux of the matter being the question of whether its usage survived what, at the very least, was its constriction by the Phase 5 ditches (Figs. 2.38 & 2.51). On the one hand, there is no evidence of the maintenance of its flanking ditches into the second century AD, nor in the course of the broader environs fieldwork was any substantive Late Roman settlement presence found within the wider area (see Chapter 3) that, otherwise, could tell of the 'late' maintenance of the local road network. Yet, on the other hand — and here once again having to allude to Chapter Three's results — it is only within the area of the Hutchison Site (and extending into the field immediately to the southwest) that any direct evidence of Saxon occupation was recovered; it can only be suspected that the lingering influence of the roadway might have been a contributing factor.

The evidence of the site's pottery and brooch assemblages, and its two relevant radiocarbon dates (Beta-195158 & -105161: 200 cal. BC–70 cal. AD & 180 cal. AD–30 cal. AD respectively) would all indicate that the site's Phase 3 Iron Age occupation was of '*later* Late-period' attribution and dates to the second half of the first century BC, if not its last quarter. More contentious is at what date the Phase 4 paddock system was established and whether, indeed, it had its origins prior to the Conquest and the mid first century AD. Assigning it to pre-Conquest times would accord with what seems to have been the 'fluid' relationship between the Phase 4 and 5 enclosure systems, with the former including rectilinear components directly ancestral to the Phase 4 paddocks. It is quite implausible that with the Roman Conquest there came any manner of rectilinear 'worldview sea-change', and certainly the origins of the Phase 4 system (and its alignment) lay in the Late Iron Age landscape. This would also be true of the Greenhouse Farm Site, where a rectilinear system of paddocks, fields and trackways was of Late Iron Age date (Fig. 2.37: C; Gibson & Lucas 2002). Backdating the Conquest system to the second quarter of the first century AD would complement the Hutchison's distribution of Late Iron Age brooches (see Haselgrove above) and accord with the evidence that in two instances the Early Roman kilns (dated AD 50–80) had been inserted into the partially silted-up profiles of Phase 4 ditches. Yet, as remarked by Webley above, against this would be the fact that relatively little Late Iron Age pottery *per se* occurred within Phase 4 contexts (Fig. 2.53). Only representing *c.* 5% of its assemblage, this figure, though, may be somewhat misleading given the degree to which the kiln-derived pottery 'bulks-out' and contributes to the overall quantity of the Phase 4 assemblage.

Of course, ultimately, the hinge issue of the Phase 4 dating is its implications for the southern 'Roman' road. Aside from vague arguments relating to alignment, there are no direct stratigraphic grounds to point to its pre-Conquest date (this whole question would have been readily resolved had the site's roadside cemetery included any Iron Age cremations). Yet, at the same time, the area's Late Iron Age landscape would surely have included major trackways (and river fords), so that it is not inconceivable that the site's Roman road represents only the 'regularization' of an Iron Age route. Unfortunately, weighing the evidence as whole, this issue must remain somewhat ambiguous. While it cannot be absolutely proven that the Phase 4 system pre-dated (if only by one or two decades) the Conquest as such, one nevertheless suspects this to be the case.

The northeast–southwest alignment of the site's Phase 4 paddock/enclosure system and the roadway is the general or 'default' alignment throughout the region in Roman times (Fig. 2.56), and to this could now also be added the layout of the War Ditches settlement (see Inset above and Fig. 2.48). A recent study has shown, for example, that it is common to all the Roman settlements excavated on the Isle of Ely (Evans *et al.* 2007). In at least one instance there, its origins clearly lay in the later Iron Age orientation (Hurst Lane: Evans *et al.* 2007). This is also the orientation of the Late Iron Age fieldsystem at Greenhouse Farm (Gibson & Lucas 2002) — and, for that matter (and as discussed in Chapter 4 below), most Bronze Age fieldsystems within the region — and this would, therefore, further support the later Iron Age attribution of the Hutchison Site's and Addenbrooke's fieldsystem, and the road.

As shown on Figure 2.56, the cropmark plan of the possible Shelford villa site, presents something a compromise or junction of alignments. Its basic layout, though, seems easily read: the cardinal-oriented 'rectangle' of its main core (*c.* 150 × 175 m), that must either have enclosed a villa proper or other public building complex, conjoined by a northwest-southeast oriented road or track in the south, and with the ditched paddocks of the complex's attendant settlement extending along the western side of that route. (In her Cambridge volume Taylor shows this Roman road running southeast to Great Chesterford and continuing northwest through Trumpington to meet with the Hutchison road at its river crossing [1999, fig. 8]. However, as discussed in Chapter 3, the wider environs fieldwork gave no indication whatsoever of the latter's projection.) The south-eastward diagonal of the complex's southern approach route is complemented by the major fieldsystem boundaries that extend northeast from the villa's 'rectangle'. While

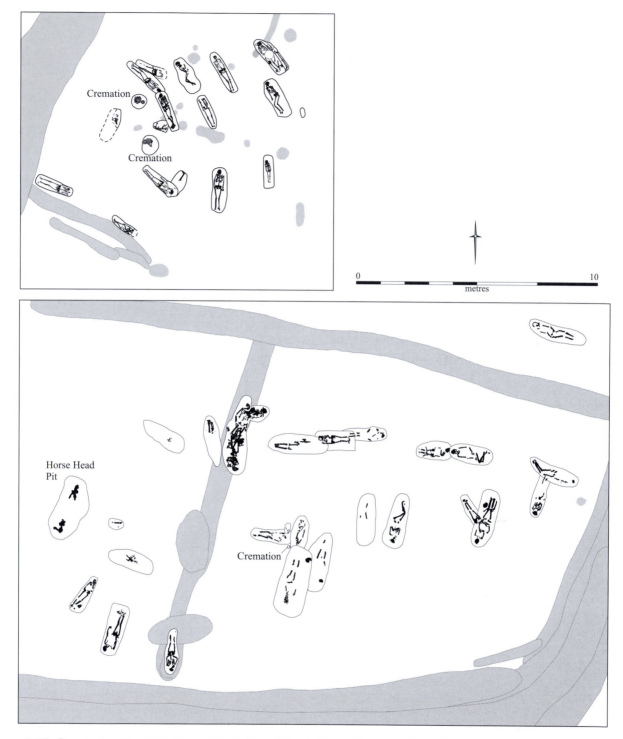

FIGURE 2.57. *Cemeteries: Top, Hutchison Site; bottom, Vicar's Farm (Cemetery 2; see Fig. 2.56 for location).*

certainly seeing a meshing of alignments, what is extraordinary in this case is the 'off-alignment' of the villa complex. Almost as if it were dropped into the landscape without any reference to what went before, it has the hallmarks of outside prestige/power. Yet its orientation also needs to be understood in relationship to the area's topography (see Fig. 1.11). It was sited at the northwestern foot of the White Hill Down, on the chalk 'plain-lands' just east of the Clay Farm 'trough' and its stream channel (see Chapter 3). Its south-eastward roadway access (and settlement) follows the low ground and hugs the flank of the Down; its northeastern axial-return skirts the Down's northern end, and its boundaries probably continued in that

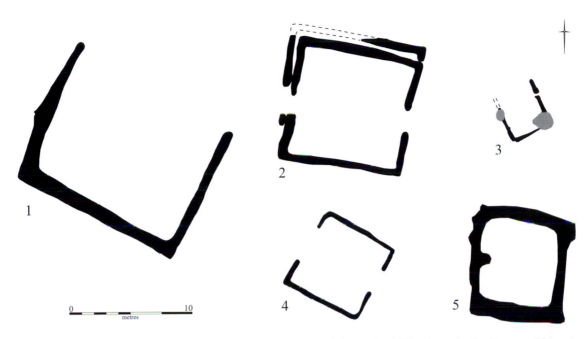

FIGURE 2.58. *Square Structures: 1) Hutchison Site, Enclosure J.5 (Phase 4); 2) Wendens Ambo, Roman Phase 2, Enclosure 3 ('barn'; after Hodder 1982a, fig. 13); 3) Late Iron Age/Conquest Period shrine, Duxford (after Lyons in prep.); 4) Conquest Period-phase shrine, The Camp Ground, Earith (Evans et al. forthcoming); 5) Stansted Airport Catering Site, Late Iron Age shrine (Structure 667; after Havis & Brooks 2004, fig. 74). There is a certain irony in Hodder's interpretation of Wendens Ambo's square structure as a 'barn', as based on its plan it most probably was, in fact, a shrine, this being all the more pertinent given that the site was published in 1982 — the same year that he published the volume that effectively announced the post-Processualist agenda: Symbolic and Structural Archaeology. The crucial factor is the obvious delay incurred in the appearance of Wendens Ambo, as, in its mode of interpretation, it is one of the very few explicitly 'New Archaeological' site reports ever issued in Britain (see Evans et al. 2006 further to this theme).*

direction (perhaps masked by the line of later plough headlands: Fig. 1.12) and presumably conjoined with the main Addenbrooke's 'plain' system.

The Hutchison Site's cemetery, with two cremations and 17 inhumations, can only be considered fairly minor (Fig. 2.57). The fact that of the 13 inhumations that could be sexed, nine were females (and only four males) is certainly intriguing. Given its Conquest Period context, this 2:1 ratio in favour of women could encourage speculation: perhaps, for example, a portion of the males were drafted into military service and died away from home or even, perhaps, this is somehow reflective of the role of female potters. Unfortunately, though, due to the variability of small-group dynamics, it would be impossible to advance such arguments further with any confidence. Regardless, given that the cemetery only reflects 50–75 years of use, then taking its numbers 'raw' this could suggest a community of, perhaps, 2–4 'households'. Based on the grave goods, with four vessels and two brooches, only Grave 2/cremation F.408 would indicate an individual of elevated status; it is also interesting that the burnt remains included a range

of animal bones, suggesting that group-feasting may have accompanied its interment.

As has been discussed above, the occurrence of inhumation burials within Early Roman cemeteries (as opposed to more typical cremations) has been noted as a regional trait (Pearce 1999). Recognized by Fox and Lethbridge at Guilden Morden (1925; see also Hill *et al.* 1999), this has also recently been found in the Duxford Site (Lyons, in prep.; Roberts 2003). Yet by no means was this a rule and it may, in fact, eventually be shown to be a measure of just how Romanized these communities were. At Vicar's Farm in West Cambridge — a major first- to fourth-century farm complex and possibly a villa (without an immediate Iron Age precursor), probably occasionally hosting a market (and certainly having a number of shrine structures; Evans & Lucas forthcoming) — two associated cemeteries were excavated. The earlier of the two, dated AD 80/90–180, remarkably lay within the northern bounds of the settlement proper and held eight cremation burials and two neonate inhumations. The main cemetery (2; Fig. 2.57), dating to the later second to the mid–later fourth century AD,

TABLE 2.46. *Relative frequency of coin and brooch recovery on selected sites.*

Site	Iron Age coins	LIA/Conquest Period brooches
Cambs. Fenland		
Stonea Grange (Jackson & Potter 1996)	61	48
Langwood Farm (Evans 2003b)	17	12
Camp Ground, Colne Fen (Evans, with Appleby, Lucy and Regan forthcoming)	2	13
Plant Site, Colne Fen (Evans, with Appleby, Lucy and Regan forthcoming)	2	6
Peterborough Fen-edge		
Cats Water, Fengate (Pryor 1984)	-	13
Werrington (Mackreth 1988)	-	5
Maxey (Pryor & French 1985)	-	8
Isle of Ely		
Hurst Lane Reservoir (Evans *et al.* 2007)	1	1
Trinity Lands (Evans *et al.* 2007)	-	-
Prickwillow Road (Atkins & Mudd 2003)	-	2
Wardy Hill, Coveney (Evans 2003a)	-	-
South Cambs.		
Castle Hill, Cambridge (Alexander & Pullinger 2000)	8	33
HUTCHISON, ADDENBROOKE'S	5	17
Edix Hill, Barrington (Malim *et al.* 1998)	4	2
Greenhouse Farm (Gibson & Lucas 2002)	-	4
North Essex/Herts.		
Stansted (Havis & Brooks 2004)	57	35
Great Chesterford (Medlycott forthcoming)	50	50
Baldock (Stead & Rigby 1986)	50	44
Skeleton Green (Partridge 1981)	40	38
Puckeridge-Braughing (Potter & Trow 1988)	28	94
Stansted (Cooke *et al.* 2008)	2	4

involved 30 inhumations and only one cremation (of the 17 adults that could be sexed, females were again dominant, with 10 being present; there were only six males). Interestingly, harking back to the Hutchison cemetery's dog burial and also telling of comparable animal-related rites, this cemetery at Vicar's Farm included an elongated pit with horses' heads set at either end and arranged to face each other.

As raised in the Phase 3/4 Discussion, the notion that the smaller 'tightly' square/rectangular gully settings might reflect the location of Conquest Period buildings is intriguing. Given its tight-corner rectilinear plan, there is little doubt over the structural attribution of Enclosure J.5's setting (Fig. 2.58:1). In fact, in different circumstances such a 'square' might be considered a potential shrine and could be compared, for example to Structure 667 at the Stansted Airport Catering Site (Fig. 2.28:5; Havis & Brooks 2004). Though considerably smaller than the J.5 rectangle, even more comparable would be the open-sided 'square' (*c.* 2.75 × 3.75 m) associated with the Late Iron Age/Early Roman cemetery at Duxford (Fig. 2.58:3; Lyons in prep.; Roberts 2003). Yet there are no real grounds to sustain such a ritual interpretation at the Hutchison Site. As shown on Figure 2.34, the J.5 setting was evidently not a focus of metalwork finds nor any other mode of 'extraordinary' deposition. Aside from the cemetery's dog burial, the only contemporary candidate for unusual deposition on the site — presuming that most, if not all, of its other animal deposits (e.g. the F.1181 cow burial) represent the disposal of the carcasses of sick/diseased stock — were the three brooches recovered from pit F.591. However, there would be no basis to advocate their direct association with J.5 as F.591 lay 45 m north of the structure and, even then, these items may represent no more than the contents of a dropped bag/'purse'. Accepting that J.5 was essentially 'domestic', then, as argued above, a number of the period's other small (sub-)rectilinear ditch/gully settings on the site also probably defined buildings (Fig. 2.16). Such structures are paralleled at the Trinity Lands Site, Ely (Evans *et al.* 2007) and in the Late Iron Age paddock system at Greenhouse Farm (Gibson & Lucas 2002), and could also be compared to the Skeleton Green buildings (Partridge 1981). This suggestion would evoke the 'classic' round *vs* rectangular Late Iron Age houses issue in Britain. It would certainly help to explain the 'missing' structures for many Aylesford-Swarling sites of the period, and Early Roman settlements in general have a marked paucity of houses. Buildings at this time could not, obviously, have been entirely restricted to either roundhouses or major *aisled* halls/barns.

This facet of the site's settlement 'architecture', along with its probable Late Iron Age fieldsystem, would demonstrate the Aylesford-Swarling affiliations of the Hutchison's community; this is in addition to its frequency of wheelmade pottery, Iron Age coin-use and brooches. (It can only be presumed that they also practised a cremation burial rite during this period, though the Iron Age settlement's cemetery was not exposed; see Chapters 3 & 4 below and Hill *et al.* 1999 for general discussion). Table 2.46 shows the recovery-frequency of Iron Age coinage and Iron Age/Conquest Period brooches on a series of sites in East England. Of course, its entries are entirely contingent on the size of their respective areas of investigation and on the intensity of excavation/metal-detecting. Nevertheless, they express a general trend. If omitting the Late Iron Age Fenland 'centres' at Stonea and Langwood Farm, Chatteris (Jackson & Potter 1996 and Evans 2003b respectively), these 'marker' categories occur in relatively limited numbers north of Cambridge and along the fen-edge, with Ely being particularly low in such finds (Peterborough having moderate brooch densities, but negligible coinage). In contrast, they occur generally on the South Cambridgeshire sites (Cambridge included). While admittedly not at the kind of levels widely encountered in the Essex and Hertfordshire Aylesford-Swarling 'core lands', they are nevertheless found at higher frequencies and with far greater regularity than to the north of Cambridge.

This same south–north trend is also apparent in the frequency of wheelmade pottery in Late Iron Age assemblages. A recent overview of the Fenland data shows that the highest recorded levels there only achieved 23.5% (at Wardy Hill: Evans 2003a) and, otherwise they only see 15% or less (Evans *et al.* 2007, table 8), whereas at the Hutchison Site 59% of the Phase 3 pottery was wheelmade. The 2006 excavations at Castle Street in the upper town heart of Roman Cambridge proper equally revealed very high levels of Iron Age wheelmade wares, with virtually all of the assemblage being so-made (Ten Harkel 2006; Evans & Lucas forthcoming). Unfortunately, the recording of assemblages south of the 'Cambridge zone' is otherwise such that comparable statistical data is not available and, therefore, no equivalent to Table 2.46's

coin/brooch listing can be assembled. Nevertheless, there can be no doubting the general propensity for higher wheelmade pottery-use in the Cambridge area and south thereof. (Some qualification of these observations is now, however, called for, as since the 2007 Hurst Lane, Ely/Fenland overview, work on the Colne Fen, Earith, Iron Age assemblages has shown that occasionally other sites north of Cambridge achieved higher wheelmade levels: in two instances out of seven, 32 and 83% [by EVE] when compared to 0–6% otherwise. These, though, seem to have been 'new foundation' settlements of the first century BC — respectively the Camp Ground and Plant Sites — and, indeed, might suggest a distinct Late Iron Age incursion into the area; see Evans with Appleby, Lucy and Regan forthcoming.)

The early uptake of such 'Roman' practices on the part of the area's Late Iron Age communities — variously through 'core-area' trade, influence and contact with Gaul and the Continent — would only be one facet of the site's Romanization. Against this, the fact that it saw settlement continuity until the later decades of the first century AD is entirely typical and is also found, for example, on the Isle of Ely settlements (Evans 2003a; Evans *et al.* 2007). The real brunt of Romanization only came thereafter, probably in the earlier second century, and was marked by the advent of the Phase 5 fieldsystem at the Hutchison Site. Evidently seeing the area turned over to agricultural land with the apparent displacement of its resident population, this attests to a major change of land use. Yet there are no apparently compelling environmental factors to account for this. Instead, a socio-political impetus might be presumed, possibly the local adoption of a villa-based economy (either that at the Perse School site or the CAM SAM 57 cropmark complex) and with it the possible 'enlistment' of the site's inhabitants as indentured labourers.

Finally, it should be stressed that the degree to which this site has been able to further understanding of the local dynamics of the Roman Conquest and the subsequent Romanization of its communities is largely due to the scale of the excavations; 'big issues' such as these require an equivalent-scale response. However, in order to more appropriately 'frame' this discussion and appreciate a greater scope of landscape patterning, it is necessary that we now progress to the results of the broader Addenbrooke's environs surveys and other comparable projects, which are duly presented in the following chapter.

Chapter 3

Environs Fieldwork and Distributional Case-studies

Christopher Evans

Having dealt with the specifics of the Hutchison Site's sequence, it is at this point that we must expand this volume's landscape coverage and progress to a broader interpretive 'frame'. The first half of this chapter duly overviews the archaeology of the broader Addenbrooke's/Trumpington Meadows landscape (including, in detail, a rich Conquest Period burial), with the second section given to a trio of comparative distributional case-studies.

Environs surveys (with Alison Dickens)

The greater Addenbrooke's/Trumpington Meadows evaluation surveys were undertaken between 2002 and 2008 over 195 ha anticipating hospital-related and housing allocation development (Fig. 3.1). From the outset it should be emphasized that these were separately implemented projects, but which shared a common methodology (the Trumpington Meadows fieldwork being independent of the rest). First, then, let us establish their methodological base-lines: the general solution struck upon was a 2.5% trial trenching sample augmented by geophysical survey and/or fieldwalking. The latter employed 20 m transect collection within 20 m long 'boxes'. Assuming a 2.00 m wide transect pick-up, this represents a 10% area sample; where appropriate, more intensive, 100%, collection then occurred with 10 × 10 m squares (see Fig. 3.4 for metal-detecting programme). The geophysical surveys that were implemented by Oxford Archaeotechnics involved 100% magnetic susceptibility scanning of the designated areas, which were subsequently sub-sampled for magnetometry survey on the basis of the magnetic susceptibility results.

With so much data to have to consider and extending over such a wide area, to facilitate systematic reference the individual fields across these survey lands have duly been lettered (some being broadly grouped together for the sake of convenience: Fig. 3.1); in addition, and for the same reason, extra-evaluation area sites/features have been also numbered (following in sequence from Fig. 1.12).

Guided Busway - It was with this programme that work commenced in the broader environs landscape in 2003 (Cessford & MacKay 2004). This involved the *c.* 100 m wide Busway corridor where the route was to pass through both the 2020 Lands and the eastern Clay Farm fields (i.e. the 'green corridor' zone; see below). In the latter's western fields, this also included four separate small excavation areas, variously covering the proposed location of balancing ponds and work depots; in total, *c.* 1000 m of trial trench was excavated (1896 sqm).

2020 Lands and the Bell School Paddocks (Fields A–C) - Undertaken between November 2004 and January of the following year, work across the hospital's 2020 Lands involved a 27 ha berm extending along the southern side of the hospital's grounds and west to the railway line. Carrying upwards of 2.00 m of dumped soil-cover (see Chapter 1 above), no ready surface-survey techniques could be pragmatically applied to the northernmost field (C); geophysical survey was undertaken across the western side of the field south thereof (Field B), with only its eastern half seeing fieldwalking. Thereafter, a 2725 m length of trial trench was excavated (5450 sqm).

In 2004, the Bell School investigations were undertaken over 7.5 ha across the paddocks bordering the southeastern side of the hospital's grounds (Field A). Its programme was considered separate from the main housing allocation sites and its methodology differed somewhat as, grass-covered, fieldwalking was not possible and nor was geophysical survey implemented (Brudenell 2004). It, instead, relied upon a 3% trial trenching sample (*c.* 1470 m length; 2717 sqm), with the location of the trenches restricted by overhead cables and, in the northeast corner, a school playing field.

Clay/Glebe Farms and the Southern Relief Road Corridor (Fields D–Q) - The main, 112.5 ha area extended from the railway line west to the back of the properties along the east side of Trumpington (*Clay Farm* area) and, in addition, continued around the southern of the village (there *Glebe Farm*; Anderson & Evans 2005; Evans *et al.* 2006). We were able to undertake fieldwalking across most of the Clay Farm fields. Though no surface collection was possible throughout the western Glebe Farm area (Fields O–Q), it was subject to geophysical survey, as were also two areas at Clay Farm (*c.* 30 ha in total).

From the outset it was known that the eastern Clay Farm fields (D–G), a *c.* 400 m wide swathe, were to be preserved as a 'green corridor' in the forthcoming development and accordingly in the initial programme no 'in-depth' investigation was to occur there (i.e. fieldwalking only). Instead, trial trenching was restricted to the western Clay Farm lands and throughout the Glebe Farm area (60 ha), and where eventually *c.* 8500 m length of trench, or *c.* 18,565 sqm, were cut. These figures also include the line of the Southern Relief Road Corridor, which extended along the southern side of the Glebe and Clay Farms fields and entailed trenching where its route would pass through the 'green corridor' and then continue northwestward (beyond the railway) to join the south side of the 2020 Lands.

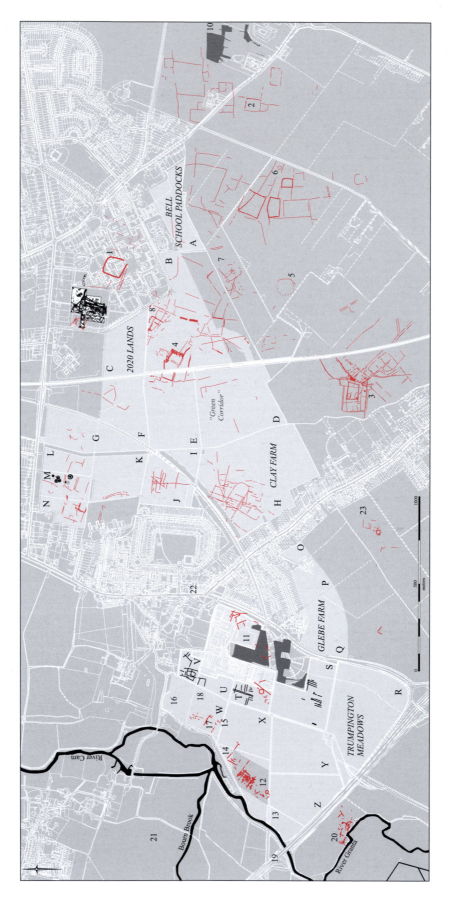

FIGURE 3.1. *Addenbrooke's/Trumpington Meadows Environs - cropmark plot (indicated in red line, with geophysical features in black). (Reproduced by permission of Ordnance Survey on behalf of HMSO. © Crown copyright 2008. All rights reserved. Ordnance Survey licence number 100048686.)*

A final trench-evaluation phase was implemented in early 2008 (Slater & Dickens 2008). This, however, was targeted to specific development-design features (e.g. balancing ponds and intensive railway-side landscaping) within the area of Clay Farm's 'green corridor', and it entailed the excavation of a further 2780 m length of trial trenching.

Trumpington Meadows (Fields R–Z) – In 2005/06 evaluation fieldwork occurred across the fields west of Trumpington (where they effectively bracketed the County Council's Park-and-Ride Site: Fig. 3.1:11; see Chapter 1 above) and bordering the riverside (Dickens 2005; Brudenell & Dickens 2007). There, the investigations focused on a *c.* 48 ha swathe proposed for intense development; fieldwalked throughout, geophysical surveys were conducted across 5 ha and, eventually, 4010 m length of trenching was excavated (7860 sqm).

Of the geology and topography across the central western environs area (the 2020 Lands being already described in Chapter 1 above), the village of Trumpington sits relatively high on Third Terrace gravels at between 17 and 18.00 m OD. Falling to 15.00 m OD along its eastern fringe, from there to the railway line — the Clay Farm fields — along its eastern 'green corridor' strip (Fields D–G) the ground lies low at *c.* 12–13.00 m OD and, as its naming suggests, is poorly drained and there is quite a pronounced trough ('officially' its geology is Second Terrace gravels, but it includes extensive clay and marl beds). There is, in fact, a distinct downslope along the southeast side of this area beside the railway line from the higher 2020 Lands opposite.

West of the village, the Trumpington Meadows area sees the Third Terrace gravels rung by lower chalk, with Second Terrace gravels generally occurring by the river itself. Down to the riverside the groundslope is quite marked, with height varying from 16–17.00 m OD to 9–11.00 m OD over a distance of only 300–500 m.

Prior to the start of fieldwork, Rog Palmer plotted the cropmarks across each area (those within the 2020 Lands having been described in Chapter 1 above). Within the northern Clay Farm fields, the rings of the WWII anti-aircraft battery were readily apparent (Fig. 1.8; Field M) and a co-axial fieldsystem also extended east-west throughout this swathe. Also noteworthy, along the western side of the field immediately south (K), aerial photographs showed a double-ditch-line slightly arcing over its north-south length (Fig. 3.1), which was suggestive of either a trackway or the perimeter of a major enclosure.

Arguably the most significant cropmark grouping in this area lies across the western half of Field H. Continuing over 5.5 ha and clearly indicating a major settlement, from the outset this was thought probably to be of Roman date. Although involving a slight twisting of their axes, components of this same complex appear to continue north within the central swathe of Field J (the western third of that field being lost to quarrying).

Aside from registering plough headlands and further quarrying pits, no archaeological cropmarks were visible in the Glebe Farm fields.

The Trumpington Meadows area not only bracketed the County Council's Trumpington Park-and-Ride Site (Fig. 3.1:11; see Chapter 1), but similarly surrounded the multi-period Scheduled Ancient Monument Cambs. 74 riverside site ('The Plant Breeding Institute Site'/PBI: Fig. 3.1:12). Its large cropmark circle was trial trenched in 1969 (Davidson & Curtis 1973). Aside from recovering worked flint, this showed evidence of three phases of ditched-enclosure development, dating from the Middle Iron Age to Roman times (Fig. 3.2). While Davidson and Curtis assigned the 'circle' itself to the Iron Age, in total only two sherds of pottery were recovered (one from their Phase 3 being certainly Roman). Some ambiguity must therefore linger over the attribution of this feature, in particular whether it was actually a Bronze Age ring-ditch. In the riverside field immediately to the north (W), a series of rectilinear cropmarks probably relate to the same complex.

Otherwise, the main cropmarks distinguished within the evaluation area itself occur within the southern end of Field T and, in addition to two linears, these show two or three circular enclosures (Fig. 3.1). Across the northern end of Field T, and also in Field S to the south, the geophysical survey revealed traces of ridge-and-furrow and other 'agricultural landscape' features of probable Medieval or later date. However, in the north-westernmost field (V) this technique demonstrated the occurrence of a series of more 'archaeological'-/early settlement-related ditched compounds.

In addition to standard evaluation sources/techniques, the Trumpington Meadow lands have also been regularly metal-detected by an individual over the last two decades. While the precise attribution of his material must include the same degree of ambiguity as all such collections, for our purposes here it has been plotted as precisely as possible. Shown on Figure 3.1, a Colchester-type brooch was apparently found south of the SAM 74/PBI settlement (no. 13) and just north thereof was a group of Early Roman brooches and Iceni silver coins (no. 14), and, separately, some 50–60 third-century AD coins (no. 15). In the northeasternmost field he has recovered Roman bracelets and earrings (no. 16), and, in Field W, both a Bronze Age chisel and awl (respectively, nos. 17 & 18). Apparently, part of a socketed bronze axe and fragments of other tools and weapons of the period have also been recovered from this field, and they may

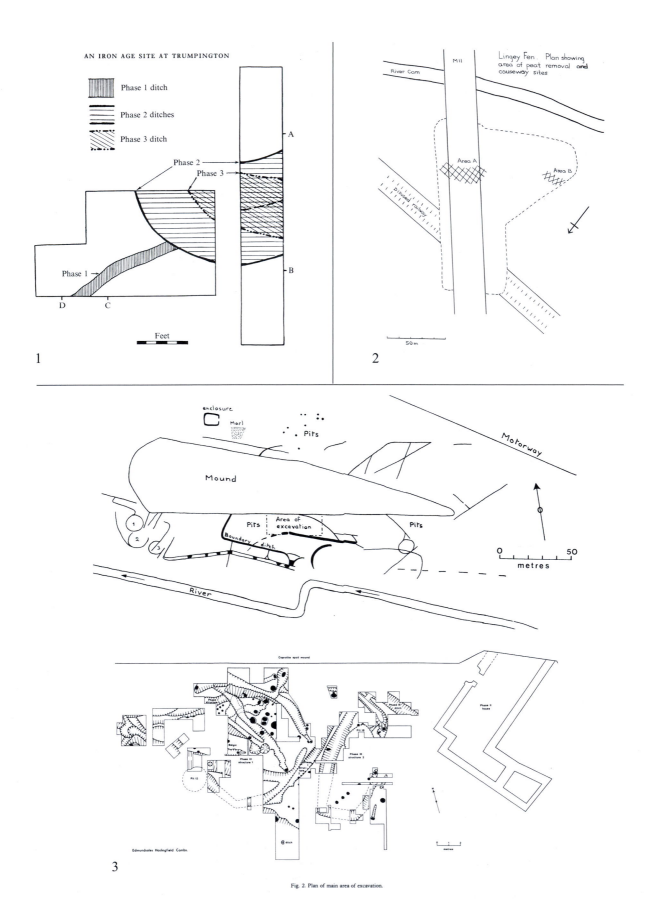

Fig. 2. Plan of main area of excavation.

FIGURE 3.2 (left). *Earlier Riverside Fieldwork: 1) Plant Breeding Institute (Davidson & Curtis 1973, fig. 1); 2) Lingey Fen (Pullinger et al. 1982, fig. 2); 3) Edmundsoles; top, area base-plan with main area of excavation below (Miller & Miller 1982, figs. 1 & 2).*

represent the remains of a dispersed founder's hoard (three seventh- to eighth-century AD strap-ends are also reported from the same general area). Though the recovery of the Late Iron Age/Roman material would essentially appear to relate to riverside settlements of that date, the Bronze Age items are less obviously explicable and, in order, to appreciate their possible context, we need now to consider other findings beyond the immediate confines of the evaluation area. Most significantly in this case is the fact that the same metal-detector has, over the years, recovered an important series of Middle and later Bronze Age weapons and tools alongside the river just south of the M11 opposite Field Z (Fig. 3.1:20; the same general area as the Edmundsoles Site, see below). Though the publication of this material is awaited (Hinman forthcoming), it apparently includes socketed axes, palstaves and chisels, plus a miniature spearhead and a complete rapier; the latter is deliberately bent and, along with the miniature spearhead, could suggest that these objects are related to 'watery' votive deposition.

It is at this juncture that the results of M11 Western Bypass excavations, undertaken in the late 1970s by members of the Cambridge Antiquarian Society Archaeological Research Group, must be introduced. Of most immediate relevance is the work at Lingey Fen and Edmundsoles, Haslingfield (respectively Pullinger *et al.* 1982 and Miller & Miller 1982; see also Haigh 1975), with Alexander and Legge's Rectory Farm, Shelford investigations (see below) and the Late Roman 'Obelisk' Kilns at Harston (Pullinger & Young 1982) occurring that much further south of the immediate evaluation area. This amounts to an intriguing body of fieldwork, and arguably represents the first co-ordinated campaign of excavations to a major rescue threat within the south of the county. However, due to a lack of funding and experience of open-area techniques, the response was clearly far too limited given the actual scale of destruction involved.

Sealed beneath *c.* 4.00 m of peat and silt, at Lingey Fen two lengths of timber causeway were identified and were thought to run between buried gravel terraces (Fig. 3.1:19; Pullinger *et al.* 1982). One, in Pullinger's Area A, consisted of upright posts with horizontal timbers and brushwood set between them; the other (Area B) involved large horizontal timbers

laid on brushwood and staked into place through notches at their ends (Fig. 3.2). Assigned to the Late Bronze Age, 1000–900 BC, three radiocarbon assays were achieved:

1) BM-1709 - 2050±50 BP/192 cal. BC–55 cal. AD
2) BM-1711A - 2620±40 BP/896–669 cal. BC
3) BM-1711B - 2560±45 BP/813–539 cal. BC.

The first sample was from an *Equus* tibia in the upper peats sealing the timbers; the latter two, from the same piece of red deer antler, were from its 'black clay peat' level.

Both large-size cattle and *Bos Primigenius* bone was recovered from the deep cuttings in the area and the dates from these attest to an earlier, 'pre-peat' Mesolithic and Neolithic presence (Legge, in Pullinger *et al.* 1982):

4) BM-1717 - 4630±50 BP/ 3629–3127 cal. BC
5) BM-1708 - 6370±70 BP/ 5475–5221 cal. BC.

Human bone fragments were also found in association with the timber settings and suggest that they also involved a degree of ritual activity, perhaps comparable to Flag Fen's Power Station alignment (Pryor 2001). Further to this, two red deer antler bridle cheekpieces, of later Bronze/Early Iron Age type, were also recovered in the motorway-derived spoil nearby (Miller & Miller 1982, fig. 15).

The Edmundsoles Site, lying just south of our environs area and beside the river (Fig. 3.1:20), was extensively fieldwalked between 1971 and '75 and then excavated over the next three years (the latter only being possible when two large mounds of spoil derived from coprolite quarrying had been removed: Miller & Miller 1982). While some 800 flints were recovered through surface collection (including two Tranchet axes), no pre-Iron Age features subsequently were. The site's sequence saw both Middle and Late Iron Age occupation, followed by three phases of second- to fourth-century Roman settlement (Fig. 3.2). Although only a fairly incomplete 'picture' of the settlement as a whole was achieved, it did include a substantial Roman building, thought to be of 'winged corridor-type' (Miller & Miller 1982, fig. 6).

On the riverside immediately opposite the Trumpington Meadows lands, the Lingey Fen causeway bordered SAM Cambs. 75, that was so designated based on its network of rectangular enclosure cropmarks; although undated as such, this settlement is presumably also of Iron Age to Roman attribution. Just north thereof, there is evidence that a major Roman site, including both timber and stone buildings (with worked stone, painted plaster, roof tiles and *opus signinum*), was destroyed through coprolite quarrying in the second decade of the last century (Fig 3.1:21; see Porter & Porter 1921).

Again largely known through quarrying, other major riverside sites are known just beyond Figure 3.1's 'frame'. Immediately to the south, and correlating with a ford-point, is Hauxton Mill where an extraordinary wealth of material has been recovered, including Bronze Age metalwork, evidence of Iron Age occupation and Late Iron Age, Roman and Anglo-Saxon cemeteries (Hughes 1891; Fox 1923, 111; Salzman 1938, 267). The Field Officer's Report within *The Proceedings of the Cambridge Antiquarian Society* for 1981 (7–12) indicates that an excavation had recently occurred within this area (TL 435524), with four phases of Roman occupation distinguished. This, the Hollicks Site, was apparently investigated in conjunction with Alexander and Legge's work at Rectory Farm, Shelford (see Inset below). To the north is Dam Hill on the river's east bank, which has been discussed in Chapter Two above, and, on the west side, Grantchester, where there have been extensive Roman findings, which Fox speculated might relate to a villa (1923, 185; Porter & Porter 1921).

Within the area of Trumpington proper, evidence of both Early Iron Age and, unsurprisingly, Saxon and Medieval settlement has been recovered (Fig. 3.1:22; Fox 1923, 111–12). Further afield, and south of the Glebe Farm lands, the cropmark plot shows fragments of a 'linear system', the main grouping there being a sub-rectangular paddock setting conjoining what appears to be a ring-ditch in its southwestern corner (Fig. 3.1:23).

Recovery rates and site gazetteer

Extending across a swathe of 1.5 × 3.3 km, the amassed environs survey coverage amounted to *c*. 20.5 km of trenching (across 195 ha) and, including many thousands of features, there clearly is little scope here to present its results in any detail. The attribution of sites will, accordingly, have to be taken at face-value, without any problematization of their definition; instead, in the section that follows there is only the scope to offer 'vignettes' illuminating critical aspects of the sequence.

Before progressing to this, the results of the fieldwalking programme should be considered. Here, a declaration must be made. Had the full scale of the Agricultural Show, which took place across much of the Clay Farm fields up to the 1960s, been known from the outset (see Chapter 1; Fig. 1.7), it is unlikely that fieldwalking would have been sanctioned there. Yet, while the topsoil there was clearly disturbed and probably truncated through Show-preparatory/-closing

'grooming', the artefact distributions still displayed some basic integrity. This is most apparent within the area of the Field H cropmark complex (Fig. 3.1). While the values were not particularly high, Roman pottery did occur there — as opposed to the northern fields (K–N), where, with the exception of a single sherd, it didn't — at comparable levels to Field B on the 2020 Lands and in the Trumpington Meadows fields (Fig. 3.3). This being said, only four sherds of Roman pottery were retrieved from its 2.1 ha 100% collection area (though flint values were relatively high). It is, therefore, possible that severe, if not near-complete, ploughsoil truncation had at least locally occurred. A second point to raise is that deeper soil-masking did not seem to be a significant factor across the lower 'green corridor' fields within that sector, and the ploughsoil cover lies no thicker throughout its 'trough'. It has to be admitted that the fieldwalking collection did not yield particularly dramatic results. This does not seem to be conditional upon specific collection factors; rather, as demonstrated through the subsequent trial trenching, the sites in question were simply not very rich and generally only yielded low densities. (As has been alluded to above, it should be mentioned here that following the Hutchison Site excavations we did attempt some 'casual' surface collection, targeting a number of discrete enclosures within the 2020 Lands [e.g. the triple-circuit compound] and also some of those lying south thereof [e.g. the No. 5 'ring']. However, the result was entirely negative and no real dating evidence was recovered from any.)

Although the densities are really too low and inconsistent to distinguish any definite patterning, there seems a general trend for higher values of worked flint to occur across the western half of the survey area, towards Trumpington and the river (Fig. 3.3). In the one 2020 Lands field fieldwalked (east half 'B'), the average values were approximately four flints per hectare, and in the eastern 'green corridor' area of Clay Farm they were two or less. Against this, the average values in both the western Clay Farm fields and across portions of the Trumpington Meadows lands range from *c*. 7–8 per ha.

Using admittedly informal criteria, at most only five scatter sites could be distinguished across the entire area (Fig. 3.3). At Clay Farm this included the higher values along the eastern side of Field E, the Field H total collection area, the south-central sector of Field M and the southern apex of Field G; at Trumpington Meadows it involved the western side of Field R. With so little material recovered and having both Neolithic and Bronze Age pieces occurring throughout the landscape generally, it is difficult to attribute any of these scatters with any confidence; all

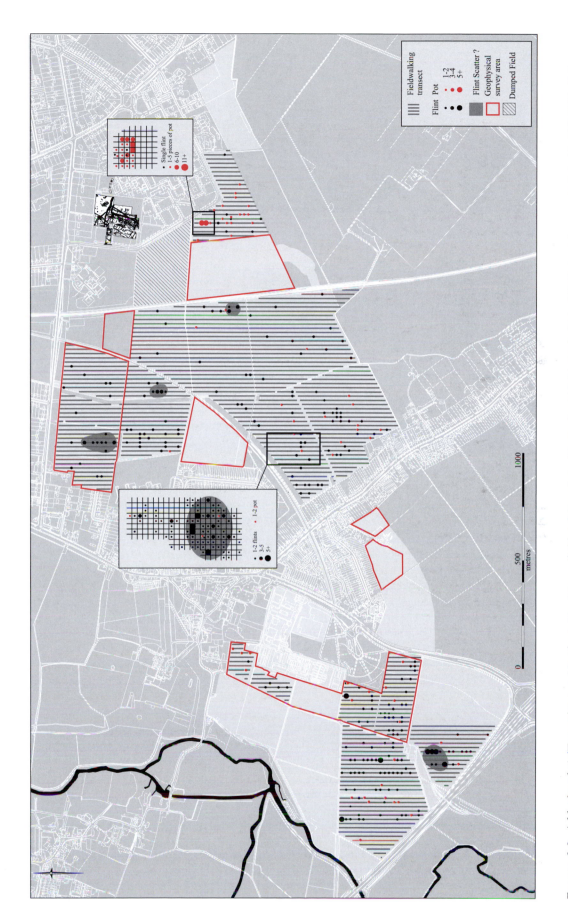

Figure 3.3. *Addenbrooke's/Trumpington Meadows Environs – fieldwalking plots. (Reproduced by permission of Ordnance Survey on behalf of HMSO. © Crown copyright 2008. All rights reserved. Ordnance Survey licence number 100048686.)*

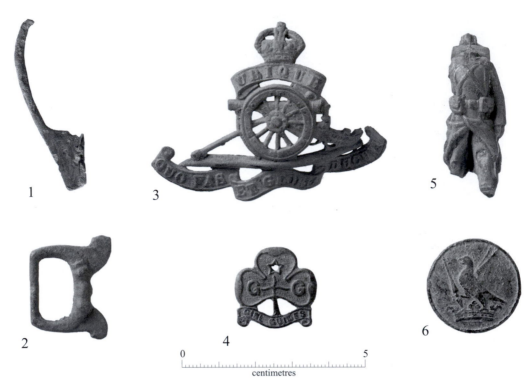

FIGURE 3.4. *Stray Finds and Stories - Metal-detecting (Andrew Hall) Over the course of the Addenbrooke's/Trumpington Meadows environs fieldwork, metal-detecting was employed in tandem with the fieldwalking, and a substantial assemblage of metal small finds were recovered from the ploughsoil. Spanning the Early Roman period to modern times, a total of 131 items were retrieved from an average 5% area-transect sample of the 53 ha surveyed. A conventional catalogue with descriptions, weights and measurements of such objects (recovered from what is often considered the 'over-burden') can fall short of an understanding of how objects related to people. Within this collection there are certain objects that stand out, not because of some intrinsic value, rarity or age, but because of another kind of appraisal: their ability to speak of past events and, more importantly, of individuals and place. Perhaps it is because within their own time these items were so personal (often presents) or chosen — often worn and displayed — symbols of identity, valued beyond any strict monetary measure. Unlike family heirlooms, there are no family tales, no memories or provenance attached to these things; that link has been cut. What is left is an unscientific empathy, an understanding and appreciation of what these objects meant that transcends time. Thus, these small finds effectively invoke an imagined series of 'shapshot-like' stories:*

A first-century fibula brooch (1) which snapped at the bow and fell to the ground, worn to demonstrate the owner was of a certain status and a follower of fashion in an age of great social and political change.

A copper-alloy belt buckle (2), probably lost by someone working these fields in the fourteenth century and likely an annoying inconvenience.

A nineteenth-century livery button (6), worn by someone in service at a local estate; a badge of ownership, this simple object that speaks of a time of great social and class divide.

A girl guide's badge from the 1920s (4), lost in the fields adjacent to her house at Clay Farm; a rare indication of childhood, otherwise so often invisible within the archaeological landscape outside of children's treatment in death.

The mid twentieth-century lead soldier (5) also invokes childhood and play. It was found adjacent to the WWII anti-aircraft battery off Long Road (Fig. 1.8), surely a tempting playground where to re-enact battles after the real war had ceased. Also found by the battery site, the Royal Artillery cap badge (6) more directly attests to that worldwide conflict and its mark on both the individuals and landscape of the area.

It could be argued that these 'stray finds' found 'out of context' are of little consequence. Ephemera, they are 'small things forgotten' (Deetz 1977), but it is through such small things that archaeologists can relate to personal stories otherwise lost to history. In turn, these often have the potential to provide insight into the major events of the time. Landscape archaeologists often tend to concentrate at a much larger scale, variously focusing on settlements, 'centres', territories and regional trends; in other words, the 'bigger picture', but perhaps, when appropriate, these small-scale 'biographies' should also be drawn into focus.

that can be noted is that those in Fields E and H did include a definite earlier Neolithic component.

Similarly, little can, nor need, be said of the Roman fieldwalking pottery. Generally the densities were low and, aside from the western half of Field B, of a level that might normally be accredited to manuring activity (Fig. 3.3). As mentioned, the Field H cropmark complex yielded very little material and it was only in the total collection area across the cropmark paddocks in the northeast corner of Field B that any really enhanced values were encountered. With the highest 10m unit value being 22 sherds (185 g), most of the pottery dated from later first to third centuries AD. Otherwise, the only noteworthy aspect concerning the distribution of Roman pottery is its almost complete absence from across the northern Clay Farm fields; this has ramifications for the dating of the 'early' fieldsystem there (see below).

Prior to outlining the discovered *sites*, the criteria of their distinction should be noted. With fieldsystems extending across much of the survey area, these do not here rank as 'sites' *per se* and, rather, that term is reserved for *settlement foci* (Fig. 3.5). Yet, inevitably, this itself is a relative measure: generally, the settlements are not enclosed/bounded and, instead, it is a matter of trying to gauge a spectrum of intensity that does not easily permit 'hard-edge' distinction. Equally, due to their ambiguous register (arising from low fieldwalking-recovery densities), none of the worked flint scatters are afforded the title of *sites*. Finally, it should go without saying that, given the site's finds densities, often a precise chronological attribution is not possible. This is especially true with regard to the distinction of later Bronze/Early Iron Age ceramic-phases. In a number of cases the occupations were 'mixed' (i.e. multiple-period usage). Therefore, to allow us to explore the relationships between sites (and also their immediate landscape setting), the following summary will be structured according to area/zone, rather than any broad cross-area chronological ordering. (Reflective of this volume's themes, no post-Saxon sites have here been distinguished; e.g. the 'rings' of the WWII battery in Field M or the cluster of medieval pits in Trumpington Meadows lands.)

2020 Lands and Bell School Paddocks

Site I - This designation refers to a large, triple-circuit sub-rectangular enclosure that extends west from Field B into Clay Farm Field E. Further discussed below, this would appear to be of later Bronze Age attribution; however, some Iron Age pottery was recovered from features immediately to the north.

Site II - Situated in the southern half of Field K, this somewhat amorphous later Iron Age and Early Roman settlement cluster (*c.* 2.1 ha) lacked a distinct cropmark 'signature'. Of note was the discovery of two dog skeletons (one articulated) and a large quantity of mid

to late first-century AD pottery from one ditch. Several roundhouse eavesgullies, ditches, postholes and pits are also present, producing largely first-century BC to mid-first-century AD grog-tempered pottery. In addition, substantial quantities of Early Roman pottery, dating from the mid-first century AD (with some possible imitation of Dorset Black Burnished wares) continuing to the early second century AD, were also forthcoming.

Note that what appears to be a ditch-flanked trackway extends southward from this site.

Site III - Field A saw a localized Late Bronze/Early Iron Age 'open' settlement superseded by much more extensive Middle/later Iron Age occupation. It included a remarkable series of fence- to successive ditch-line recutting, whose long-term implications are further discussed below (i.e. boundary fossilization).

A 'lazy-bed' horticultural system was present amid the second- to fourth-century paddock/fieldsystem extending throughout the Bell School Paddocks. In addition, possible evidence was locally recovered of what appears to be some manner of small-scale contemporary workshop/'shed-like' activity and, also, a quarried swathe in the extreme northeast corner that might relate to adjacent Roman road construction.

Site IV - Previously investigated as part of the evaluation programme for the Guided Busway scheme and during the earlier Addenbrooke's Elective Care facility evaluation, Site IV's features are most probably contiguous with Site V's. The northern extent of Site IV is without aerial photographic cover due to the depth of overburden in Field C.

Ditches, gullies, pits and possible postholes were investigated in several trenches. Although no direct evidence for structural remains was found, the nature of the fills, the quantity and type of finds, and the scale of the ditches suggest that these related to settlement *per se*. No Iron Age pottery was recovered from the site's features; in total, some 450 sherds of Roman pottery were recovered from the trenching, with a date range between the first and fourth centuries AD (predominantly second–third centuries).

Site V - This was situated in the extreme northeastern end of Field B. Largely yielding Early Roman pottery (with a couple of sherds of Late Iron Age wares), the cluster of settlement features found here did not themselves register on the aerial photographic survey. While designated as a separate site, Site V may be continuous with Site IV (and the Roman activity at Site III).

Site VI - Unusually, a low density of both later Iron Age and Middle Saxon pottery was recovered from the dispersed ditch/gully features in the northwest quarter of Field C. Subsequent service-related investigations within this area have also demonstrated Early Saxon occupation (see Inset, Chapter 4; Timberlake 2007).

Clay/Glebe Farm

All of the sites identified within the Clay Farm lands lay along its higher western fields, and none were found within the low ground of its 'green corridor'.

Site VII - Quantities of Late Bronze/Early Iron Age pottery were associated with the deeply cut 'settlement compound-type' ditches that extend over some 1.8 ha in the southeast of Field N (and just into M: Fig. 4.1). Having the same orientation as the fieldsystem throughout the northernmost fields in this area, this raises the question of whether that system as a whole is actually of later prehistoric — as opposed to Roman — origin (see below). Note that a much more minor Late Iron Age presence also occurred within this area.

Site VIII - This extensive 'early' complex (*c.* 2 ha) was identified in the centre-west side of Field H, where it correlated with the southern third of the plotted cropmark group. While including some later Iron Age material, this site is largely of Late Bronze/Early Iron Age date and its pottery assemblage is clearly significant. In some instances, the material appeared to relate to ditch features, though some is arguably of residual status, occurring in later, Roman features. Whereas some of its linear features could well prove to be large pits/hollows, in other cases the material is more probably ditch-associated. Note that fragments of human skull were found in one (and possibly two) of these features. Based on precedent, this is potentially a large 'open-settlement' of Late Bronze/Early Iron Age date, though it may not necessarily be continuous and could include multiple settlement foci.

Site IX - This is an important later Iron Age site located along the western edge of Field K (and, in part, overlapping with the area of Site X and possibly continuing north to Site VII: Fig. 4.1). A Late Iron Age/Conquest Period cremation cemetery was located immediately east of the southeastern perimeter of a later Iron Age double-ditch boundary. One grave in the cemetery cluster was excavated in the course of the fieldwork, and it was found to contain a rich assemblage of grave goods (see below). It is estimated that the cemetery might, in total, include upwards of 10–15 such cremations.

The quantity of later Iron Age pottery recovered from the double-ditch boundary both dates that system and suggests the occurrence of adjacent settlement. Yet, rather than being settlement-related *per se*, this more likely marks the line of a major north–south trackway/road, which may well have continued southward into the area of Site E as the main headland-parallel boundary (having been truncated by late quarrying across most of the intervening area of Field J). If this trackway/road interpretation is valid, then the cremation cemetery would have had a roadside location, as would also the Site X Romano-British settlement (presuming a degree of Iron Age/Roman continuity).

Site X - A relatively dense spread of Romano-British settlement features was located in the north-central sector of Field J (where it correlated with cropmark enclosures plotted there) and extended into the southwest corner of Field K (the southwestern side of this swathe being truncated by post-Medieval quarries within Field J: Fig. 4.1). The 'cardinal' north-south/east-west alignment of this settlement (as opposed to the orientation of Site XI) may reflect its roadside situation in relationship to the line of the Site IX ditch-flanked trackway.

Site XI - The Site XI Roman settlement swathe may well be semi-continuous with Site X; overlapping with the area of Site VIII, it extends over some 7.5 ha along the west-centre side of Fields H. This was, unquestionably, the most major site investigated within the Clay Farm area. Of first- to third-century, early/mid to later Roman, date, it essentially consists of an interlinked series of rectilinear enclosures that must variously represent in-field plots and stock paddocks. This being said, although the quantities of associated finds from excavated features were not particularly high, at two points the density of features (and finds) would certainly attest to settlement as such.

Note that while undertaking fieldwork in this immediate area, a local resident showed us two Roman copper-alloy bracelets which had been found in her back garden (145 Shelford Road), which may indicate the location of a settlement-associated cemetery.

Site XII - This was the only site identified within the Glebe Farm fields to the west. Although perhaps associated with the minor linear boundaries occurring there, this essentially seems to be a quite localized/minor 'open' Early Iron Age settlement, whose focus was a large watering hole. In addition to other associated, more minor, discrete features was a crouched inhumation.

Trumpington Meadows

Site XIII - Located upon a slight gravel promontory in the central-eastern side of the area, this was a 27 m diameter ring-ditch/barrow. Its surrounding ditch (3.50 m wide and 1.05 m deep) encircled a central inhumation; once identified as human, the latter was left *in situ*. Although no direct dating evidence was recovered, this is presumed to be of earlier Bronze Age attribution.

Site XIV - In Field W, near the riverside, was found a localized cluster of intercutting Late Bronze Age pits.

Site XV - This obviously represents the eastward continuation of the County's Park-and-Ride Iron Age complex and would mean that, in total, it extended over more than 7 ha. Essentially, as exposed here, it consisted of tight, almost 'arranged', clusters of large, typically cylindrical-profiled pits (up to 1.40 m deep) of Early-Middle Iron Age date associated with a few ditches and gullies. Interestingly, within the vicinity of Site XIII, the western side of the Site XV complex was bounded by a large 'V'-shaped ditch (1.70–3.20 m wide and 1.05–1.44 m deep) and its pits only occurred on one side of it; this very large and important site is further discussed below.

Site XVI - Possibly an outlier/continuation of Site XV, a few dispersed Early Iron Age pits and postholes were recovered across the southern side of Field S. Although seeming quite dispersed, substantial quantities of pottery (and animal bone) were recovered from the pits; one also yielded a fragment of human bone.

Site XVII - The southeastern corner and western side of a Middle/later Iron Age enclosure was excavated in Field U (and was found to be truncated by a large pit). Dated by pottery, the alignment of the enclosure essentially matches that of the Park-and-Ride Site's compounds and this site may, therefore, be continuous with that settlement.

Site XVIII - This correlated with a sub-circular enclosure detected by the geophysical survey in the northeastern-most field (V), which proved to be of Middle/later Iron Age date. Although possibly encircling a roundhouse (unexposed), very few finds were forthcoming and only one possibly associated pit was identified.

Site XIX - Dating to the second–fourth centuries and extending over *c.* 1 ha, this Roman settlement lies beside the river in the northern fields. Having a very high feature density, quantities of pottery and bone were present. Moreover, the occurrence of both roof and floor tiles in some numbers would suggest that this site includes a building of quality, and this would be further confirmed by the metalwork recovered: a later Roman copper-alloy buckle and a probable *Phalera* disc, as well as seven fourth-century coins (and nails and lead scrap). Locally, where there is deeper colluvium cover, associated occupation strata still survive. One point to stress is that, unlike other major riverside settlements (Site XX and Edmundsoles), no Iron Age occupation was found to precede this site's Roman settlement.

Site XX - The designation is assigned to the SAM Cambs. 74/PBI riverside settlement (see above).

Not sharing the same alignment, five ditches were recovered in the fields in the southwest corner of the evaluation area. While these probably, at least in part, represent field boundary 'outliers' from either the Site XX or the Edmundsoles settlements, aside from a single worked flint, none produced any dating evidence. This makes it conceivable that some of the ditches could be of later prehistoric attribution.

Comparable field boundary-type ditches were also exposed in the riverside fields between Sites XIX and XX (and also in Field X east of the latter). Again, only one yielded dating evidence (both a flint and a fragment of tile). Falling on a northwest/southeast axis

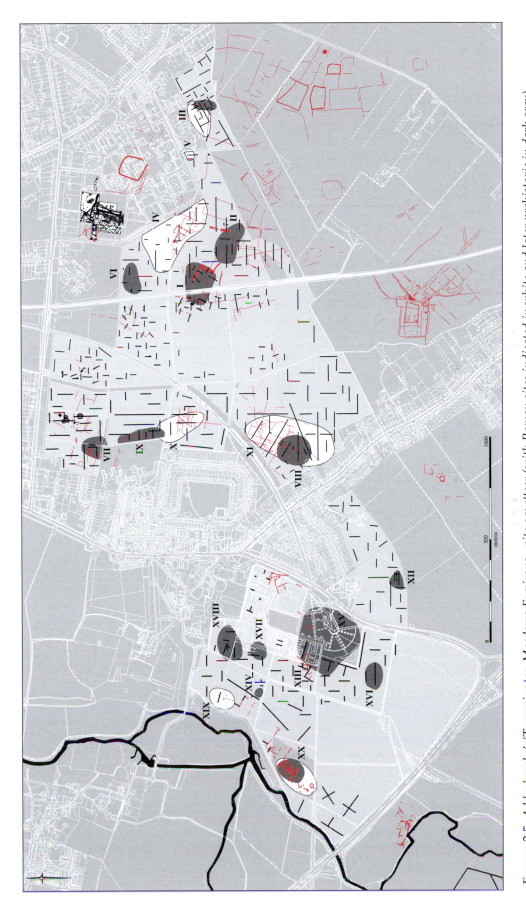

FIGURE 3.5. *Addenbrooke's/Trumpington Meadows Environs – site gazetteer (with Roman sites indicated in white and later prehistoric in dark grey). (Reproduced by permission of Ordnance Survey on behalf of HMSO. © Crown copyright 2008. All rights reserved. Ordnance Survey licence number 100048686.)*

date, perhaps being elaborated in Roman times. Its plan layout seemed very formal and, accordingly, the possibility that it might even have been some manner of shrine complex was also posited. Given these possibilities, our first surprise arose upon receiving Oxford Archaeotechnics' geophysical plot and finding that few, if any, obvious settlement-/building-related features registered across its interior (Fig. 3.7). Subsequently, the trenching revealed that there was no firm basis by which to assign it either a later Iron Age or Roman date.

The combined evidence of the cropmark and geophysical plots indicate that the enclosure had triple circuits on its northern and eastern sides (Figs. 3.6 & 3.7). It was double-ditched along its southern aspect, as was also the division though its interior; the interval between its circuits varied from 4–5.00 m. (Only one western circuit was visible on aerial photographs; subsequent trenching there, though, demonstrated that it was also triple on that side.) Where excavated in 2004, its ditch circuits proved impressive. Having 'V'-shaped profiles, they were 2.10–3.00 m wide and 1.15–1.30 m deep, though the innermost ditch-line on the eastern side was somewhat smaller (1.50 m across and 0.45 m deep). At one point, a burnt horizon bedded midway down the profile of the inner circuit; also noteworthy is that two inhumations (an adult and adolescent) were found in the upper profile of the southern terminal of the middle circuit.

Only six sherds of pottery were recovered from the enclosure's ditch proper, these being shell-tempered (with quartz-tempering present in the 20 sherds from a gully; F.223). The attribution of this material was ambiguous. While certainly including some pieces of Iron Age date, some could equally have been of later Bronze/Early Iron Age attribution. Given the importance of this enclosure, in an effort to resolve this question, three samples were submitted for radiocarbon dating (all charred material):

1) [457]; F.189 (Beta-240347) - 3230±40 BP/1610–1420 cal. BC
2) [474]; F.193 (Beta-240348) - 3980±40 BP/1430–1260 cal. BC
3) [535]; F.223 (Beta-240349) - 3260±40 BP/1620–1440 cal. BC.

These leave little doubt of the enclosure's Middle Bronze Age origins, and final confirmation of its assignation was received in early 2008 when the trenching took place on the other side of the railway along the enclosure's western aspect, where some 30 sherds of Deverel-Rimbury pottery were recovered (Knight, in Slater & Dickens 2008). This attribution does not, though, preclude the idea that the enclosure may have seen some degree of later elaboration (the geophysical survey indicating off-line recutting along

FIGURE 3.6. *2020 Lands - Site I: Top, looking southeast across triple-circuit of the enclosures (eastern aspect); bottom, Ditch F.193.*

(and its return), it is possible that these ditches could also be of both Roman and prehistoric date.

There is only scope here to further consider a few key 'site highlights' and not to discuss the results on a site-by-site basis. Among the greatest upsets of the evaluation programme was the attribution of the triple-circuit Site I sub-rectangular enclosure bisected by the railway along the western-centre of the 2020 Lands (Fig. 3.5). Based on its morphology and vague similarities to the Orsett Cock enclosure (Toller 1980; Carter 1998), it was anticipated to be of later Iron Age

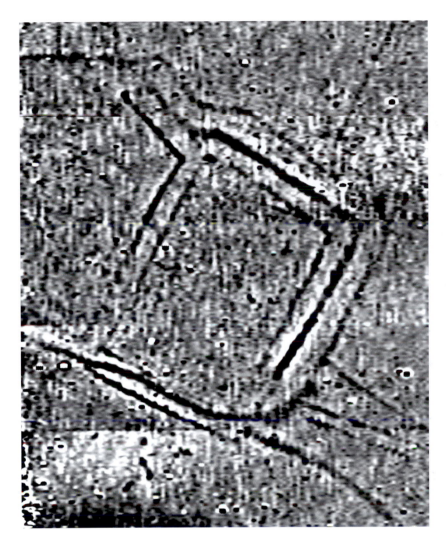

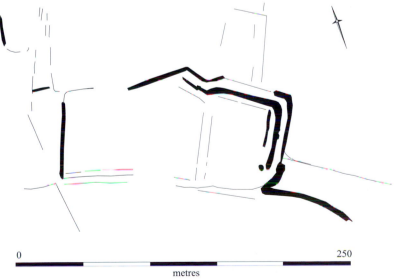

0   250

metres

FIGURE 3.7. *2020 Lands - Site I: Top, magnetometry plot (Oxford Archaeotechnics); below, enclosure plan.*

its south side). In fact, as revealed by the geophysics, the arrangement of the main circuit ditches in relationship to the enclosure's interior division would suggest that its eastern sub-square 'cell' was a later addition to the main western 'rectangle', though whether the latter was itself internally divided into two, roughly equal, squares is currently unknown.

Having established this dating, where would we have to look for any kind of parallel? As discussed at length in the Cambridge Archaeological Unit's *Fengate Revisited* volume (Evans with Beadsmoore, Brudenell & Lucas forthcoming), aside from having an additional circuit, it would have marked similarities with Pryor's Newark Road compounds (Pryor 1980). As opposed to its excavator's 'great stockyard interpretation' (Pryor 1996), the multiple ditching of their circuits surely related to embankment and, as such, they may well attest to some manner of defended farmstead. This being said, the compounds that made-up the Addenbrooke's enclosure were almost twice the size of Fengate's and, when directly compared, they seem of almost a 'monumental' scale (Fig. 4.2).

The northwest–southeast orientation of the Bronze Age enclosure essentially matches the alignment of the wider fieldsystem 'grid' throughout the northern 2020 Lands, including that of the Hutchison Site compounds and Cra'ster's enclosure (and, also, the Roman road there: Fig. 3.1:1). While, as discussed in relationship to the Bell School Paddocks below, such long-term Bronze Age-to-Roman continuities can potentially be explained — and that orientation would seem to be the preferred 'prime axis' of most Bronze Age and Roman boundary systems in the region (e.g. Evans *et al.* 2007) — this coincidence has been the source of considerable ambiguity as regards the cropmark fieldsystem that extends across the northernmost Clay Farm fields. Given that a later Bronze/Early Iron Age settlement was identified there (Site VII) and that 'background' flint occurred throughout the area, the recovery of residual prehistoric material from its ditches would not be unexpected; nevertheless, no Roman finds whatsoever were forthcoming from the excavated segments of its axes. Moreover, the double-ditching of some of the fieldsystem's boundaries apparent there (variously for hedge-lines and droves) is characteristic of Bronze Age fieldsystems, and the ditches associated with the Site VII settlement of that date also fell on the same orientation. Therefore, while certainty is not possible at this time, in all likelihood the fieldsystem in that area is probably of prehistoric date. Further credence to this argument could be drawn from what seems be to the kinking of the Hutchison Site Roman road (Fig. 2.55). If, indeed, shifting more north/northwest-ward

(together with any contemporary/attendant ditch systems/compounds), then there would be still less reason to expect the continuation of a Roman system northwest into the Clay Farm area opposite.

The Roman boundary system did, however, extend throughout the western half of the Bell School area (it having little cropmark register there due to pasture-cover) and across its northern sector the parallel ditches characteristic of a 'lazy-bed' horticultural system were present (Site III: Fig. 3.5). The most significant findings on this site, though, were of later prehistoric date and reflect upon the issue of the long-term 'fossilization' of boundaries. This occurred throughout the paddocks' central swathe and at a point where the main Roman northwest-southeast field boundary returned northeastward (Fig. 3.8). There, amid a cluster of later Bronze/Early Iron Age pits and postholes, were two roughly parallel lines of close-set posts of the same date, one of which ran straight for more than 80 m. Their lines were repeated in the alignment of a re-cut Middle/later Iron Age ditch which, while not exactly matching the later, Roman, boundary was close to it. (The series of probable Iron Age features extending throughout the south of this immediate area indicates another settlement of that date.)

The scale of this site's post-lines is reminiscent of the fence-like settings excavated at Barleycroft Farm on the lower reaches of the River Great Ouse, which are also of later Bronze Age attribution (Evans & Knight 2001). What is crucial concerning the extraordinary build-up of linear features at this point is that they suggest a mechanism whereby boundary-continuity may have actually been maintained over a span of 800–1500 years. Later Bronze/Early Iron Age post-lines were followed by re-cut Middle/later Iron Age ditches that were subsequently respected by a major Roman field boundary (see Inset below concerning the pit alignment at Rectory Farm, Shelford)

Perhaps the most extraordinary finding within the Trumpington Meadows lands is the interrelationship of the earlier Bronze Age ring-ditch/barrow (Site XIII) and the Site XV Early–Middle Iron Age pit complex (Fig. 3.5). Separated by a major northeast-southwest oriented boundary, the demarcation of the settlement swathe from the monument seems very formal, as does also the apparent 'arrangement' of the pits immediately east of that boundary (in Trench 22: Fig. 3.9); the most obvious parallel for the latter would be a sub-triangular array of Iron Age pits 'targeted' on the southern aspect of a barrow excavated at Broom, Bedfordshire (Cooper & Edmonds 2007; see also Moss-Eccardt 1988, figs. 29 & 25). The Site XV pit complex obviously represents the western side of the Park-and-Ride site (Sites XVI &

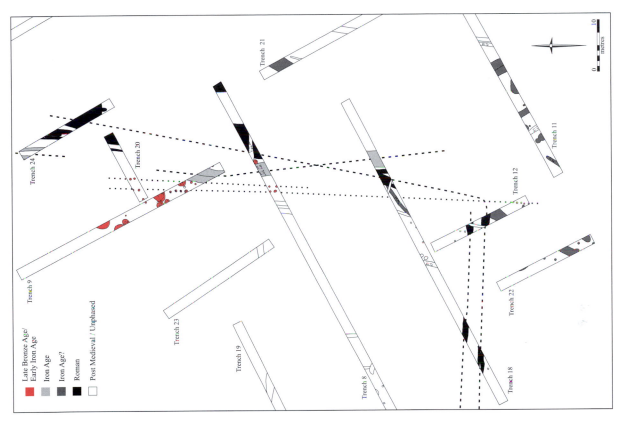

Late Bronze Age/
Early Iron Age

Iron Age

Iron Age?

Roman

Post Medieval / Unphased

Trench 24

Trench 9

Trench 20

Trench 23

Trench 19

Trench 8

Trench 21

Trench 12

Trench 11

Trench 22

Trench 18

metres

FIGURE 3.8. *Bell School Paddocks: Left, photograph of posthole alignment (Trench 9, looking south); right, base-plan showing successive alignments.*

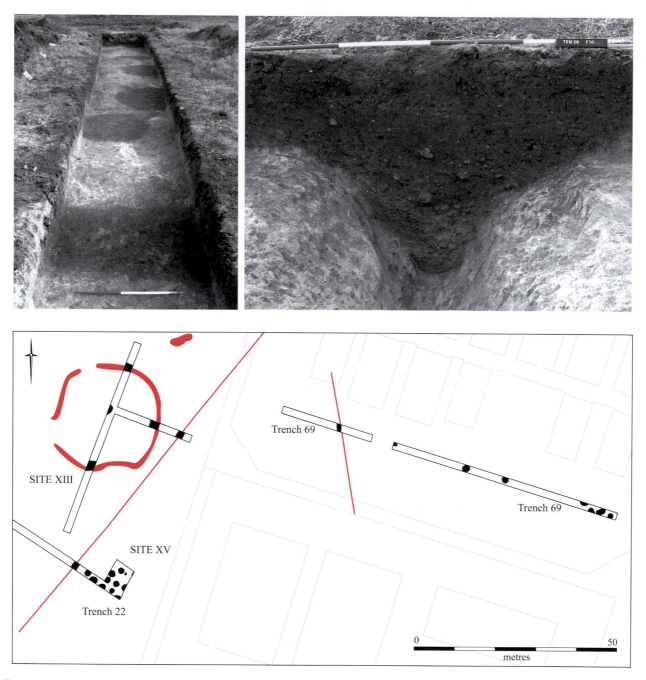

FIGURE 3.9. *Trumpington Meadows - Sites XIII & XV: Top, left looking southeast along the line of Trench 22, with Ditch F.10 in foreground and 'arranged' pits behind; top right, Ditch F.10; bottom, site plan. (Reproduced by permission of Ordnance Survey on behalf of HMSO. © Crown copyright 2008. All rights reserved. Ordnance Survey licence number 100048686.)*

XVII may similarly be part of its margins). This would mean that its core area extends over at least 7 ha and makes this an extraordinarily large site of the period; regionally, it would only be comparable to the pre-hillfort settlement at Wandlebury (French 2004). Due to the frequency of human remains and other 'placed' finds within its cut features, when the main site was excavated it was interpreted as some manner of mortu-ary-ritual centre (Hinman 2004). We, however, would rather stress the quantities of domestic material within its pits (pottery, bone, quernstones and loomweights) and argue that it relates to occupation, and possibly centralized/mass grain storage; ritual activities are thus simply a significant component of the period's major settlements (the above-cited Broom pits also included a series of markedly 'placed' deposits).

TABLE 3.1. *Site recovery rates (* indicates addition of lithic scatters).*

Period	Site no.		Site density (Min. no./per sqkm)
	Min.	Max.	
EBA	1 (+3/4*)	1 (+3/4*)	0.5
LBA/EIA	6	9	3.1
MIA/LIA	7	9	3.6
Roman	5	8	2.6
Saxon	1	1	0.5
Total	**20**	**28**	**10.3**

The environs surveys' site recovery rates are indicated in Table 3.1. The considerable discrepancy between minimum and maximum site numbers is caused by different interpretations of the degree to which individually designated entries should be grouped together as larger single complexes. Examples include whether the neighbouring (but 'axially twisting') Roman settlement Sites X and XI were actually contiguous; Sites III–V would be a more obvious case from the same period, and the Iron Age components of Sites I and II could also be cited. What is evident is that, based on the number of sites alone, the three main periods are broadly comparable: later Bronze/Early Iron Age (6 min./9 max.), Middle–later Iron Age (7/9) and Roman (5/8). Regardless of whether it is the minimum or maximum figures used, this itself could suggest considerable population stability over these periods.

The scale and situation of the Roman settlements warrants further comment. Extending over *c.* 1–3 ha, the riverside Sites XIX and XX, together with Edmundsoles to the south (and perhaps also those sites known on the other side of the Cam), can be considered typical large-scale farmsteads of the period (Taylor 2007), although their evidence could suggest a degree of 'villa-type' architectural aspiration. While if not contiguous with Site XI, Site X might be considered an equivalent to those (though lacking evidence of any building 'grandeur'), otherwise the 'inland'/off-river sites seem to represent quite different types of settlement. If Sites III–V along the southern and western margins of the Addenbrooke's grounds represent a continuous settlement, then, extending over at least some 300 × 900 m, it would be enormous. In fact, it may well even have been larger still as it could well have continued north to the line of the Hutchison's road; its potential status will be further discussed below.

Extending over some 7.5 ha, even if not conjoining Site X, Site XI at Clay Farm is also very large, though it, too, was without any evidence of high(er) status settlement. Considered together with Site X, its

situation and elongated plan could, in fact, suggest that they were road-/track-side settlements, laid-out on the eastern side of the potential double-ditched 'way' identified at Site IX immediately to the north.

The recovery of only one Middle Saxon site is not particularly surprising and such settlements are, indeed, rarely found if not associated with the margins of historical villages (more noteworthy perhaps is that no further Saxon remains were found at the 'meadow lands', adjacent to Trumpington proper).

Finally, even if including the surface-collection lithic sites, the paucity of earlier, Neolithic to Early Bronze Age, sites is somewhat more surprising. This is especially true of the riverside area by Trumpington, as the lack of immediate/ready water supply-sources elsewhere probably accounts for the absence of early 'inland' sites. Given this largely negative recovery, it would have to be admitted that the fieldwalking methodology may not have been particularly appropriate (i.e. sufficiently sensitive) to detect lithic scatters in low density landscapes.

A Conquest Period burial

Arguably the most important single feature excavated in the course of the environs-evaluation fieldwork was a rich cremation burial (F.566) within the northwest Clay Farm fields (Site IX: Figs. 3.5, 3.10 & 4.1), and, as such, it warrants more detailed reportage. Its sub-square flat-based grave-pit (*c.* 1.50 × 1.60 m) had truncated the western edge of a similar, but larger, feature (2.4 m across), and appeared to cut a northeast–southwest linear segment. For the purposes of excavation, F.566 was divided into four quadrants (I–IV), with each dug separately and all artefacts plotted on a 1:10 plan (Fig. 3.11). It had undergone severe plough-truncation and only survived to a depth of 0.15 m.

Within the northeastern quadrant (I) an amphora (SmF 26; Figs. 3.10 & 3.12:5) was found in the corner (these have been found resting upright in the corners of burials such as the 'Doctor's Grave' at Stanway, Essex: Crummy *et al.* 2007). To the west were a selection of food vessels: a Samian dish (SmF 27: Fig. 3.12:4), two Terra nigra dishes (SmFs 28 & 29: Fig. 3.12:1–2) and a Terra nigra cup (SmF 30: Fig. 3.12:3). Placed on top of the latter was a flagon (SmF 31: Fig. 3.12:6) which, at some point after deposition, had collapsed in on itself. Within the northwestern quadrant (IV) was the lower jaw of a pig (SmF 25: Fig. 3.10), which rested on a heavily corroded iron blade, possibly a triangular knife (SmF 33: Fig. 3.13:6–7). Just southwest of this was an iron rod of unknown function (SmF 32: Fig. 3.11), and two bone rectangular gaming counters (SmFs 20 & 21: Figs. 3.13:8–9); a concentration of

FIGURE 3.10. *Clay Farm - The F. 566 Cremation: Top, photograph of burial showing grave goods, with detail of pottery group below; bottom the ram's head patera handle terminal (SmF 15).*

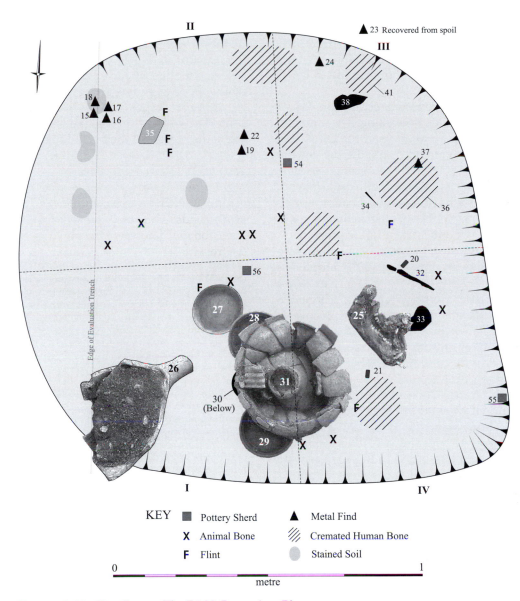

FIGURE 3.11. *Clay Farm - The F.566 Cremation: Plan.*

burnt bone was also identified within this quadrant. The southwest quadrant (III) yielded the majority of the burnt bone, with five distinct deposits identified (SmF 36 denoting the highest concentration). Three metal artefacts were there recovered: a thin fragment of copper-alloy sheet (SmF 37), a fragment of an iron sheet (SmF 38), and a small silver plaque (SmF 24). The plaque was one of three found (SmF 23 was recovered from spoil and SmF 22 from Quadrant II) and these were most likely decorative box/casket attachments or leather fastenings (Fig. 3.13:10). A small bone pin fragment (SmF 34) was also recovered from this quadrant. A total of six pieces of metalwork were recovered from the southeast quadrant (II). Found in close proximity to the SmF 22 plaque was a cast copper-alloy appliqué decorated with the image of a

crouching or curled up animal (SmF 19: Fig. 3.13:5), which could have been a rim-fastening for a hanging cauldron or similar vessel. Towards the southeast corner of the grave a set of four metal artefacts was recovered in close association (SmFs 15, 16, 17 & 18). They comprised a copper-alloy ram's head terminus from a patera handle (SmF 15: Fig. 3.13:1) and three copper-alloy pelta-shaped patera feet (Fig. 3.13:2–4; SmF 16–18). These items would probably have been found on a metal saucepan-like vessel, with the ram's head at the end of the handle and the feet arranged in a circle around the base (the SmF 19 appliqué possibly deriving from the same vessel). That only these items survive and not the rest of the vessel could suggest that they were deliberately chosen and deposited without the rest of the patera; alternatively, the vessel may simply have not survived. Such patera vessels are commonly associated with libations to the dead in the Greek and Roman world, a practice incorporated into some of the funerary practices of pre-Conquest Period Southeast England.

The entire assemblage recovered appears to have a common theme — dining or feasting. The amphora, flagon, plates and cup were all used for the storage and consumption of food and drink; the pig jaw and other animal bone fragments are representative of the food. The metal artefacts associated with cauldrons and patera mark other forms of food and libation vessels; the gaming pieces may represent other activities undertaken at a feast and/or anticipate afterlife pursuits.

As reported upon by Natasha Dodwell, the cremated human bone remains were 100% sampled on site for later wet-sieving, with bone >4 mm extracted for examination and the finer residues scanned. A total of 198 g of cremated human bone was recovered from six discrete areas in the feature. It is uncertain that any of the concentrations of bone, even that containing the largest quantity (132 g), were *in situ* as there is evidence of animal activity throughout the feature. The bones derive from a single adult individual, and all were a buff white colour indicative of efficient burning on the pyre. Whilst it is clear that the quantity of bone examined (198 g total) does not represent a complete individual, because of the shallowness the feature and the degree of animal disturbance it is uncertain whether this represents all of the bone that was originally interred. In the largest concentration (SmF 36: Fig. 3.11) the majority of identifiable fragments were limb shafts, specifically fragments of femur. Several cervical vertebrae were also identified; there were no skull fragments. The largest fragment was 69mm and almost 80% of the fragments were recovered from the 10mm fraction. Similarly, in SmF-spot 41, where a total of 55 g of bone was recovered, the majority of fragments (65%) were >10 mm and most identifiable fragments were from the femur. Very small quantities, 4 g, 5 g and two times 1 g respectively, of cremated human bone mixed with fragments of unburnt animal bone were also identified in four other discrete deposits (SmF 53, 57–9); their occurrence was probably the result of animal activity.

The 20 bulk samples processed from this feature yielded very few archaeobotantical remains (and, also little charcoal) and plants — at least any charred — were not part of the burial rite (see A. de Vareilles in Evans, Mackay & Patten 2006). One sample did, however, include 25–30 small hardened lumps of iron-encrusted soil, which suggest the near-complete decay of at least one iron object.

Once the nature of F.566 was apparent, it was determined that any similar burial features would be left unexcavated. The potential for night-time metal detectorists had already been evidenced during the fieldwork programme, and it was thought prudent not to expose any other features to those risks. (To better protect any other burials, the area was seeded with metal discs prior to the backfilling of the trenches.)

The Pottery (KATIE ANDERSON)
Eight different vessels were represented in the grave assemblage. Five were complete and were obviously grave goods, while three were only partially complete and probably not part of the grave assemblage as such (i.e. residual).

Forty-nine sherds were recovered from a Dressel 7-11 amphora (SmF 26: Fig. 3.12:5), including a very large base sherd. The upper half of the vessel is missing and it is likely to have been ploughed away, since it was leaning upright in the feature and therefore would have extended high into the ploughsoil. The vessel is Spanish in origin, most likely to have been produced in the Cádiz region, with some form of fish sauce contents. This class of amphora was produced between 30 BC and AD 75 and, given the nature of the rest of the cremation pottery assemblage, a post-Conquest date seems appropriate.

Three complete Terra nigra vessels were recovered: a small cup (Camulodunum Type 56C; SmF 30: Fig. 3.12:3), and two Camulodunum Type 8 plates (SmFs 28 & 29: Fig. 3.12:1–2). The two plates were stamped, reading 'VNDILOF' (SmF 28) and 'EDATO' (SmF 29). The date range for all three vessels is AD 20–65 (V. Rigby pers. comm.); these were produced in Northern Gaul and regularly form part of the 'Gallo-Belgic' type assemblages.

A complete South Gaulish Dragendorff 18 (SmF 27: Fig. 3.12:4), a medium-sized plate, was also recovered. This had a complete stamp on the base, although the heavy abrasion on the inside of the vessel means two of the letters were unidentifiable. Those which could be identified read 'OF IC_ _CO'. The plate was of mid first-century AD date, more specifically pre-Flavian (AD 43–68).

The final complete vessel in this group was a large collared flagon (SmF 31: Fig. 3.12:6), which had collapsed under the weight of the soil. The fabric was a soft, sandy oxidized ware with a reduced core, with evidence of a greyish slip. The fabric contained common mica and occasional red iron-ore inclusions. The exact source of this vessel is unclear as it is unlike any of the Early Roman kiln products from the local area, such as Cherry Hinton or Greenhouse Farm and the Hutchison Site's kilns (see Chapter 2 above). It is also seemingly not from any of the major production sites such as Verulamium. There is, therefore, a possibility that this vessel was also an import. In support of this view, both the fabric and vessel form have parallels with some of the Gaulish imported wares found at the King Harry Lane site (Stead & Rigby 1989). Interestingly, the fabric most similar is the Central Gaulish Standard Fabric (Stead & Rigby 1989, 119), while the forms that are most comparable to the vessel are from Northern Gaul and Lower Germany (Stead & Rigby 1989, 142, fig. 57). That the vessel is imported is uncertain; however, given the nature of the rest of the assemblage, it seems probable.

The three other vessels, not associated with the cremation, included a Samian vessel found just to the north of the main group. The latter comprised six large sherds from a South Gaulish Dragendorff 29 (SmFs 35 & 54), a decorated carinated bowl with scrolled leaf decoration, which has been identified as being the work of Salvetus, dating AD 30–35 (Geoff Dannell pers. comm.). The vessel was not complete and was found away from the main group of vessels, suggesting that this was not part of the cremation group;

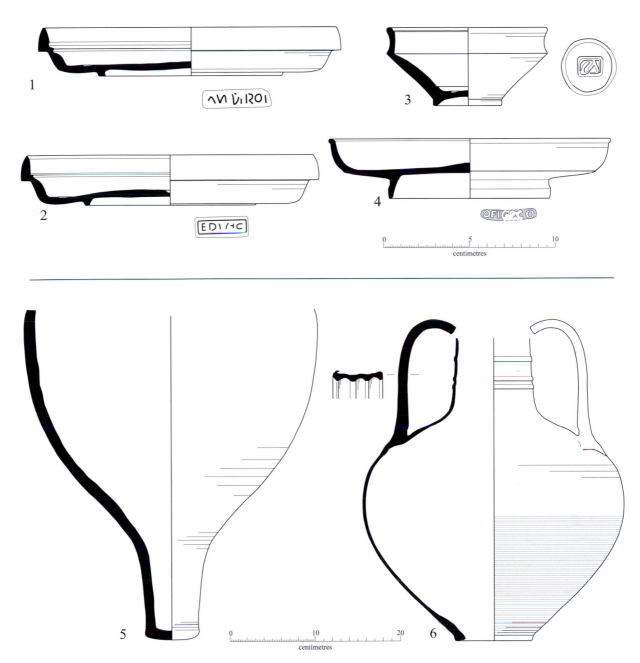

FIGURE 3.12. *Clay Farm - The F.566 Cremation Grave Goods (Pottery):1 & 2) Terra Nigra plates (SmFs 28 & 29);
3) Terra Nigra cup (SmF 30); 4) Samian plate (SmF 27); 5) amphora (SmF 26); 6) flagon (SmF 31).*

this could be supported by the discrepancy in date between the vessel and those from the main group. As well as being incomplete, the vessel was also more heavily abraded than the others, which suggests that it may have been redeposited within the backfill of this feature and possibly derives from another grave. The pre-Conquest date is of particular interest as there is no ceramic evidence from the adjacent settlement sites to suggest such early access to imported wares and, rather, it probably derives from another grave context. The two remaining vessels comprised a sandy greyware sherd from a small beaker/jar, and further Southern Gaulish Samian sherd; both were recovered from the spoil-heap and are mid–late first century AD in date.

The grave assemblage consisted almost entirely of imported, fineware vessels, broadly dating AD 30–60; the Dragendorff 29 Samian, which is certainly pre-Conquest in date, suggestive of earlier activity on the site. Comparable Late Iron Age and Early Roman cremation deposits have been found at King Harry Lane (Stead & Rigby 1989), Baldock (Stead & Rigby 1986) and Skeleton Green (Partridge 1981), which all have examples of assemblages consisting of imported wares and local wares from the pre- and post-Conquest Periods.

A date of AD 40–50s seems appropriate for the group of pottery, with the earlier end of the spectrum being perhaps more likely, as this combination of vessels have more in common with Late Iron Age burial traditions. The assemblage, therefore, presents an intriguing dilemma as to whether it should be classed as pre- or post-Conquest, which is not helped by the lack of datable metalwork (in particular brooches) that could otherwise tighten the chronological bracket. All of the pottery had a currency which spanned the period between the Late Iron Age and earliest Roman period, with only the Dr29 — that was not part of the cremation group — being confidently assigned to the pre-Conquest phase.

In fact, in this case the use of 'pre-' or 'post-Conquest' as a date is almost irrelevant, as evidence from this area suggests that the Roman Conquest had little immediate impact on pottery traditions until at least a decade after the invasion (Anderson forthcoming). Instead, the process of 'Romanizing' ceramics was probably more piecemeal and protracted than previously thought. What is significant is that during the period when the material is likely to have been deposited, pottery in the Iron Age tradition was still being made and used alongside Romanizing material (Anderson forthcoming; see also Hill, in Evans 2003a and Webley in Evans *et al.* 2007).

As discussed above, the extensive recent archaeological work within the immediate area has revealed several Late Iron Age and Early Roman sites, particularly the Hutchison Site itself (see Chapter 2). These have produced assemblages of Late Iron Age and Early Roman pottery which appear to be more typical for Cambridgeshire, comprising a combination of Late Iron Age and Romanizing vessels, with little or no evidence of such early imported wares.

Although there are as yet no examples of sites in Cambridgeshire with a directly comparable assemblage, obviously there are a number of cemeteries and single burials with similar burial practices (see Fig. 4.4). The Late Iron Age cremations from Hinxton were of first-century BC date and had graves with multiple wheelmade pots, all of which are likely to have been made locally (Hill *et al.* 1999). Including pedestal urns, these would, for example, be broadly contemporary with the Barnwell cremation (Fox 1923) and date from 89/75–25/10 BC. More comparable in date is the burial from Snailwell, Suffolk (Lethbridge 1953). Apart from weapons, this cremation contained a minimum of 15 vessels, which included both imported and local wares. Dating to the second quarter of the first century AD (the AD 30s–50s) and generally of Conquest Period attribution, the vessel forms present included three complete amphorae, a Terra rubra plate

FIGURE 3.13 (right). *Clay Farm - The F.566 Cremation Grave Goods (Metalwork and other Small Finds): 1) copper-alloy ram's head patera handle terminal (SmF 15); 2–4) copper-alloy pelta-shaped patera feet (SmF 16–18); 5) decorated copper-alloy appliqué (SmF 19); 6) iron, probable triangular knife (note wood adhering; SmF 33); 7) X-ray of 6; 8) worked bone cubic die (SmF 20); 9) worked bone cubic die (SmF 21); 10) silver plaques (SmF 22–4).*

and cup, a Terra nigra cup and bowl, five flagons, two butt beakers and a tazza. In addition, there have been a number of 'stray' Late Iron Age cremations in the Cambridge/Chesterton area associated with butt beakers, which also date to after 20/10 BC (with other single-finds of complete butt beakers also probably having been cremation-derived: Hill *et al.* 1999).

Finally, the Clay Farm assemblage is important in highlighting the different ways in which pottery was used and deposited in the Late Iron Age and Early Roman period in this area. Specifically, there is a pattern that the 'newest' vessel forms were generally restricted to deposition in grave contexts from the introduction of wheelmade vessels to the earliest imported wares, with examples from Hinxton (Hill *et al.* 1999) and Babraham (Anderson, in Armour 2006). Very few imported vessels from the first half of the first century AD are found on settlement sites in South Cambridgeshire, the Wardy Hill Ringwork proving an exception (Hill, in Evans 2003a). Instead, it is generally only within burial deposits that this type of material is recovered. The processes required to procure material of this nature, at this time, should not be overlooked, as clearly these imported vessels were not widely available.

Worked Bone (CHRIS SWAYSLAND)
Three bone artefacts were recovered from the grave: two rod-dice/gaming pieces (SmFs 20 & 21: Fig. 3.13:8–9) and a bone point (SmF 34). The dice are similar to conventional dice but rectangular in shape. In Southern Britain, their use appears to be restricted to the Late Iron Age and Early Romano-British periods. These forms of die remain uncertain and Clarke (1970) reports that, as at Clay Farm, such items are frequently found in sets of two or three. More recently, research on similar forms of dice has been reported from the Roman fort at Birdoswald (Riddler 1998) and Meare Village East (Coles 1987). The values on the dice found at Clay Farm are unusual in that the opposing faces do not add up to the conventional value of seven (see Riddler 1998, 297), and the possibility thus exists that these are a form of dice used as a 'multiplier' to adjust the value or score of other dice. Alternatively, the

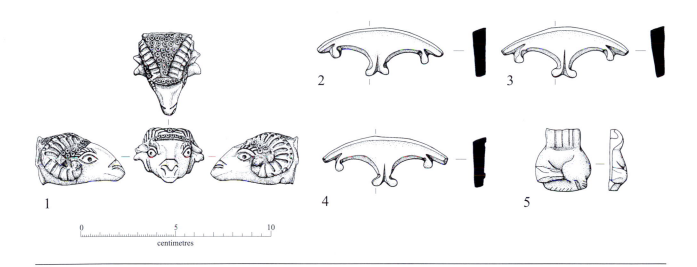

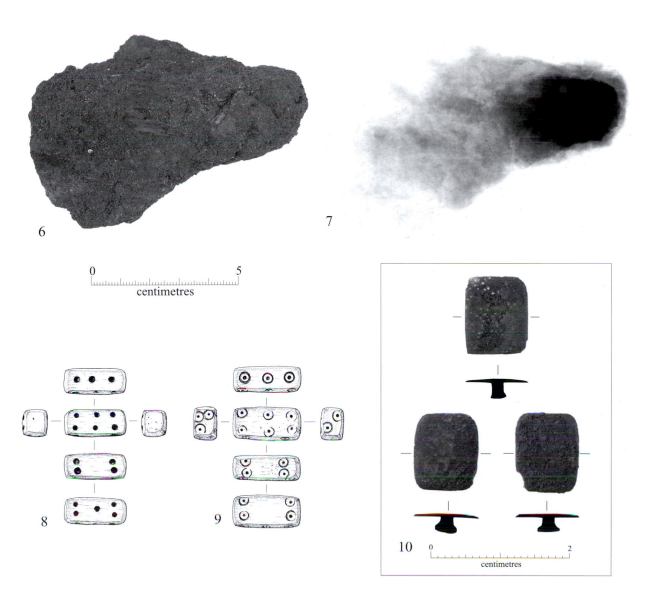

dice from Clay Farm may represent a local variation of conventional forms based on a verbal description rather than on direct knowledge of such objects (cf. Hermsen 2000).

Rectangular cubic die (SmF 20; Fig. 3.13:8) - Measuring 21.7 mm × 9.0 mm × 8.3 mm, with smooth surface and well-rounded edges. Small holes measuring between 1.7 and 2.0 mm in diameter have been drilled into the four larger faces to denote the number of the face. The holes were of varying size, drilled at irregular intervals and relatively deep. Two opposing long faces add up to 11, with five and six holes in each; the other two opposing long sides add up to seven, with three and four holes on each face. The two end faces are blank.

Rectangular cubic die (SmF 21; Fig. 3.13:9) - Measuring 23.6 mm × 10.6 mm × 8.2 mm, with smooth surface and well-rounded edges. Four ring-and-dot markings are present on two of the adjacent faces, with the other two long faces provided with three and six ring-and-dot markings. One end-face has three ring-and-dot markings arranged around the edge of the die in an 'L'-shaped configuration. The opposing face has two conventionally arranged ring-and-dot markings. Superficially similar to the other die described above, the spacing of the holes on this piece is much more regular.

Point (SmF 34) - Two refitting pieces of worked tip, measuring 33.8 mm in length and with a diameter of 3.8 mm at the larger end. The internal structure of the bone strongly indicates that the artefact has been fashioned from a horse vestigial metapodial; this is a bone that is naturally pointed and, therefore, requires little work to produce such an artefact.

Metalwork finds (DAVE WEBB)

In total, 13 metallic artefacts were recovered from the grave: three of silver, six of copper alloy and four of iron (see also Webb 2007).

Silver plaques (SmFs 22, 23 & 24; Fig. 3.13:10) - Three undecorated silver rectangular plaques complete with rivets were recovered from the grave fill. The plaques were 21 mm × 18 mm in diameter, each weighing less than 1 g. They have plain surfaces and slightly rounded corners, except Small Find 24, which has a single sharp corner. On the reverse, the rivets are centrally positioned, 3 mm in depth. The plaques were most likely decorative attachments or fastenings for leather or other organic material. No direct parallels of similar date have been found, although small rivets attached to irregular-shaped plaques have been recovered in association with hobnails in a cremation burial at Skeleton Green, leading to the suggestion that they functioned as fastenings for leather sandals (Partridge 1981). At Wardy Hill, Ely, copper-alloy plaques where found decorating a wooden stave in a chequerboard arrangement (Evans 2003a); however they were fastened in a manner similar to staples rather than being riveted. An alternative, though far less likely, interpretation is that the plaques were for repairs. Thin strips of metal with rivets were sometimes used to repair ceramic vessels. However, these are usually longer strips with at least two rivets to bind either side of the join. As repair plugs for ceramic vessels, the depth of rivet on these plaques is shallow, and could only have been used with very thin-walled pots. The depth of the rivets would, though, be suitable for metal vessels. Given that the plaques were silver and flat, with no curvature as would be expected if they were used on the side of a vessel, this interpretation is unlikely.

Ram's head patera handle terminus, copper-alloy appliqué, pelta-shaped feet and copper-alloy sheet (SmFs 15–19 & 34) - Several copper-alloy fragments were scattered in a linear manner across the eastern half of the grave. In the northeast corner was a ram's head terminus (SmF 15) and a group of three pelta-shaped feet (SmFs 16–18); from the centre of the eastern half of the grave was a suspension ring-mount, and from the southwest end a fragment of sheet bronze was also recovered (SmF 34). The grave was shallow and the distribution of the copper-alloy fragments suggests a vessel may have suffered plough damage (i.e. 'pull'). The fragments were distinctive enough to suggest that the damaged vessel had been a Patera or Trulleum. The surviving fragments were also sufficiently characteristic to be assigned to established typologies and they exhibit characteristics of Eggers' Type 154 (Eggers 1951) and Nubers' Type D ('Hagenow'; Nuber 1972).

The ram's head terminus is 40 mm long, and 35 mm from ear to ear, with a neck diameter of 24 mm. With a socket in its back, it weighs 123 g. The terminus had been hollow-cast with incised detailing. The ram's head has deeply knurled horns curled around the ears, with the tips turning outwards; the details of the eyes, nostrils and mouth are incised in a simplistic style. The fleece is represented by an irregular raised circle-and-dot pattern across the top of the head between the horns; in addition, a band decorated with circle-and-dots is modelled across the ram's brow and a series of short incised lines above the eyes gives the impression of eyebrows.

The casting of terminus and shaft as separate components to be soldered together to form the handle is a characteristic of Nubers' Type D, whilst later types were often cast as a single component. The separate casting frequently results in the terminus becoming detached, as is the case with the Clay Farm piece. Examples of the Type D handle with missing terminus come from Pleshey (May 1918), Heybridge (Eggers 1966), Hagenow (Voss *et al.* 1998), Lago di Nemi (Ucelli 1950) and Prag Bubeneč (Novotný 1955). There are also numerous examples of unattached ram's heads including several from Pompeii (Tassinari 1993) and others from Dobrichov (Sakař 1970), Monte Lato (Isler 2005), and a recent metal-detected find from Gillingham, Norfolk (UKDFD 2007a).

The combination of circle-and-dot patterning and incised décor include examples from a recent find from Gillingham (UKDFD 2007a), Biggleswade (pers. obs.), Antran (Pautreau 1999), and from Italy, at Monte Lato (Isler 2005). The use of incised decoration to model details can often be seen on patera found in the Roman provinces, in particular parts of Eastern Europe, and Ratković (2005) suggested that incised decoration is characteristic of provincial workshops and moulded decoration characteristic of Italian workshops. Although the majority of the Type D Patera are given as being of Italian manufacture (Nuber 1972), the style of incised decoration and form of the ram's head suggests a possible provincial workshop origin, most likely Gaul, for the Clay Farm artefact.

Small Finds 16, 17 and 18 comprise a 'set' of near identical cast copper-alloy pelta-shaped feet (Fig. 3.13:2–4), which range from 65 mm to 67 mm in length, 5 mm in depth (36–9 g). The three detached, flat crescent- or pelta-shaped feet have almost identical profiles. The outer concave edge and inner convex edges are slightly bevelled. At the point of each curve the foot divides into two small lobes separated by a short incised notch. The upper side that would have been attached to the base of a vessel has traces of solder. The form of attachment of the feet is demonstrated by another Cambridgeshire find, that from Snailwell, where the bowl had a single surviving pelta-shaped foot adhering to it (Lethbridge 1953). At Heybridge a detached pelta-shaped foot was found in the same vicinity as a finely fluted handle and the decorated base of a flat bowl (Eggers 1966). A more complete parallel comes from a cremation at Antran (Pautreau 1999), whose patera had three feet *in situ* evenly distributed around the base of the bowl. Other vessels with full sets of similar pelta-shaped feet come from Boscerale (Oettel 1991) and Prag-Bubeneč (Novotný 1955). Detached feet have also been found without other vessel fragments, and recently two pelta-shaped feet (identical to the Clay Farm set) have been recovered from Bedfordshire (UKDFD

2006) and Lincolnshire (UKDFD 2007b), with a further find from Thetford, Norfolk (Gregory 1991). Pelta-shaped feet only appear on Nubers' Type D bowls and they alone were supported on such footrings.

Small Find 19 was a cast copper-alloy pendant-shaped appliqué (Fig. 3.13:5), measuring 28 × 32 mm (32 g). The incised detailing is somewhat obscured by corrosive elements but appears to be either a crouching or curled up animal, possibly a hound or deer. The upper horizontal slightly cylindrical element of the pendant has five irregular incised vertical lines decorating it, and the upper segment has indentations where a suspension ring could have been attached. No patera with a suspension ring has been found in Britain; however, there are continental examples: a patera from Prag Bubeneč (Novotný 1955) has a single suspension ring attached to the bowl on its exterior wall beneath the rim opposite the handle (the bowl also rests on three pelta-shaped feet), and the bowl of the Antran Patera (Pautreau 1999) also had traces of solder opposite the handle, with an open ring found in the vicinity which suggests that a suspension ring had been attached to the vessel. The use of suspension rings is most frequent on the early, Type D forms.

Recovered from the southwest corner quadrant was an irregular, thin fragment of sheet copper alloy, 32 × 12 mm (3 g). Whilst the fragment could not be positively identified, the thickness of the sheet is similar to that of patera bowl-forms (along with numerous other types of vessel); it is, therefore, not impossible that this is a surviving fragment of the bowl after the vessel had been plough-struck.

Nuber (1972) dated the production phase of the Type D Patera to the Augustan Period, continuing until the Claudian Period with production diminishing around AD 50. The distribution of patera within Britain is largely confined to Southeast England, although examples are known outside this zone. This includes examples from as far afield as Welshpool (Boon 1961) and Annandale, Dumfrieshire (Curle 1932), but these non-southeastern feet are of later, Nubers' Types E–G forms. More immediately, within a few kilometres of Clay Farm, a later, Type G Patera was recovered during the 18th century from Dam Hill (see Chapter 2 above), 'where great numbers of human bones have been found, and many urns, pateras, and other Roman antiquities'(Farrand & Webber 1776, 20; a patera from that locale is in the Fitzwilliam Museum). The earlier, Type D form, with its characteristic pelta-shaped feet and finely fluted handles, is confined to the southeast, with examples being found at Heybridge, Essex (Eggers 1966), Pleshey, Essex (May 1918), Snailwell, Cambridgeshire (Lethbridge 1953), and Gillingham, Norfolk (Gregory 1991), with a possible example from London (Drury 1988). Although a Conquest Period date is attributed to most of the Type D finds, only the Snailwell example comes from an excavated context (Lethbridge 1953).

This form of vessel has previously been associated with the pouring of libations at altars, with more recent research suggesting that the vessel along with a jug and other vessels was used in the processes of bathing and cleansing (Nenova-Merdjanova 2000). Roman sculptures and coins also depict the use of paterae in the washing of hands at rituals and feasts (Nuber 1972). Whilst the more elaborate types are more likely to have been reserved for rituals, Hutchinson (1986) suggests that the signs of wear on some vessels may suggest more multi-functional domestic use. In burials, paterae are commonly accompanied by copper-alloy jugs, ewers or oinochoë (Nuber 1972). The pairing of these vessels can be seen in the assemblages from Shefford, Bedfordshire (Kennet 1970) and the Bartlow Hills, Essex (Powell 1963), to name but a few. The practice of including paterae and jugs can be seen in the late pre-Conquest burials at Snailwell through to the later second century at Welshpool (Boon 1961); however, the Type D form appears to be confined to the southeast and the late pre-Conquest to Conquest Period.

Iron rod (SmF 32) - Two fragments of a tapering iron rod, 154 mm in length and with a total weight of 46 g (Fig. 3.11). At the point, the artefact was broken. A 5 × 5 mm square cross-section could be observed beneath the corrosion. At the thinnest end of the rod the square cross-section measured 2 × 2 mm; the function of this artefact is unknown.

Iron triangular knife/razor (SmF 33) - A 'sub-'triangular iron blade, probably a triangular knife, 92 mm in length, 65 mm in width, and weighing 100 g, was recovered from the northwest quadrant of the grave (Fig. 3.13:6–7). It is estimated to be 80% intact, with one broken corner. Several smaller fragments were recovered adjacent to the main body of the knife, suggesting it was intact when buried. The lower edge of the blade appeared to be slightly curved. However, since the artefact has not been conserved, the corrosion prevents a definitive description of its shape; X-ray has failed to elucidate any further detail other than that the top of the knife is thicker than the main part of the blade (Fig. 3.13:7).

During metal-detecting, a copper-alloy signal was detected from the artefact. This may suggest the presence of a copper-alloy handle, perhaps akin to other knives such as the one from Welwyn Garden City, Herts. (Stead 1967). Triangular iron knives similar to the one at Clay Farm have been recovered from Late Iron Age and Early Roman burials at King Harry Lane (Stead & Rigby 1989), Snailwell (Lethbridge 1953), Welwyn Garden City (Stead 1967), Westhampnett (Fitzpatrick 1997), Strood Hall, Essex (Timby et al. 2007) and Walmer, Kent (Stead 1967).

The function of these knives is not clear and suggestions include razors, saddlers' or furriers' knives, or use in food production (Hussen 1983). The majority of artefacts in graves can be associated with feasting and an association with food processing may also be appropriate in this case, but is not certain. Where the sex of the burial could be determined, the knives have only been found associated with male graves (Boon 1991). Boon suggests that the design of these knives would make them unsuitable for the application of any force or leverage on the blade and argues for their use as razors (Boon 1991). However, this would not rule out their use in the treatment of skins or for some type of food processing. Based on size, Hussen suggests the larger Snailwell knife was not a razor, but that the Welwyn Garden one was. As the Clay Farm blade is smaller than all the other blades its description as a razor may be more appropriate. Traces of wood grain can be seen on the surface of one side of the blade and this may be the remains of a scabbard, as has been suggested for the knives from King Harry Lane (Grave KHL 316) and Walmer. This being said, it is the occurrence of the wood on the blade, combined with the other metal piece adhering to its one end (i.e. the 'handle'), that raises the possibility that this might have been some other manner of composite object other than a triangular knife; further determination must await its full conservation.

Unidentified iron fragments (SmF 38) - Flat sub-rectangular-shaped iron artefact measuring 95 × 44 mm, with a weight of 49 g. The object had two slightly upturned edges, and was recovered in five fragments, all with fresh breaks.

Iron fragment (<2726>) - An irregular-shaped iron object, 14 × 10 mm, weighing 1 g.

Only five of the artefacts can be reasonably dated: the triangular knife, the ram's head patera handle terminus and the three pelta feet. Triangular knives appear in several burials, including Welwyn Garden City, King Harry Lane and Snailwell, with dates ranging between 25 BC and AD 60 (Lethbridge 1953; Stead 1967; Stead & Rigby 1989). Equally, the artefacts associated with a patera, or other such metallic vessels, appear in the pre-Conquest Period and remain in circulation until at least the second century AD.

Overall, the metal finds in the grave represent high status items associated with eating and drinking in a 'Romanized' style. While it certainly cannot be classed as so 'grand' a burial, in general its copper-alloy items have parallels with objects from other high status burials, including Welwyn Garden City, Stanway, and Folly Lane, Verulamium (Stead 1967; Niblett 1999; Crummy *et al.* 2007). Intriguingly, most of the metalwork in F.566 is fragmentary. This may be due to disturbance by agricultural activity (plough-

ing), resulting in the heavy truncation of this feature. Certain items within the grave may therefore have been broken, displaced from their original position, or removed entirely. The fragments described are most likely from one vessel, a patera. However, it is not impossible that the copper-alloy sheet and appliqué are from another vessel, and the latter could be the base of a jug handle or a cauldron suspension ring. Conceivably, rather than complete vessels having been deposited, the fragmentary artefacts could have acted as 'token' deposits (i.e. symbolizing the complete vessel).

Rectory Farm, Great Shelford and enclosure morphology
(with JOHN ALEXANDER & TONY LEGGE)

Arising from the threat of M11 development, between 1975 and 1980 excavations occurred immediately north of the River Granta west of Shelford (TL 445 525: Fig. 1.2). Interest in the area, and indeed the reason for its scheduling as an Ancient Monument, arose from aerial photographs taken of this complex and published by St Joseph in *Antiquity* in 1965 (Fig. 3.14). The fieldwork was directed by John Alexander, David Trump and Tony Legge (and later Morag Woudhuysen), and the following summary is based on their site archives and interim reports (Trump *et al.* 1975; 1977; Woudhuysen *et al.* 1981). While for our purposes Rog Palmer has re-plotted its aerial photographs, no further analysis has been conducted of the material.

As outlined below, in total eight 'site areas' were designated (I–VIII), but with only six areas investigated as the Sites III and IV entitlements were eventually replaced by 'V' and 'VI' respectively (Fig. 3.14). (Note that an Enclosure-designation system was then also instigated, with Site V's rectangle entitled 'Enclosure I' and Site VI's circle referred to as '... II'. Here, to avoid the confusion of having two Roman-numerated series, these have been respectively altered to Enclosures A & B and this lettered listing has been extended to the terrace's other discrete enclosures: see Fig. 3.15.)

Site I - A ditch, 2.5 m wide and 0.8 m deep, that had not been seen on the aerial photograph, was exposed during excavation. Two sherds of pottery were recovered from its fill, a fragment of comb-stamped Beaker and a sherd of Food Vessel, and a number of worked flints were also found. Romano-British pottery (*c.* 100 sherds, including Samian and a mortarium sherd) was recovered from a series of pits, ditches and postholes, excavated following the surface stripping of *c.* 0.13 ha. The pottery was primarily of first- to third-century date; a quantity of building material was also recovered, including roof and floor tiles. In addition, an east–west oriented drainage ditch with a line of fence-related postholes along its inner edge was investigated, from which mid to Late Roman pottery sherds were recovered (14 in total). The ditch, *c.* 2 m wide and 1m deep, was traced for 30 m; first- to second-century pottery was recovered from its fills. The fence-line ran parallel to the drainage ditch, and consisted of a shallow (0.3 m deep), vertically-sided trough with a maximum width of *c.* 0.4 m; it had postholes set at an interval of *c.* 1.5 m.

Ten metres west of the fence, two pits were excavated, the larger being *c.* 3 m across and 0.4 m deep, from which a large quantity of second-century pottery was recovered; a third pit (4.5 m wide) was excavated 10 m east of the fence-line, from which Romano-British pottery sherds were also retrieved. Otherwise, finds from Site I included a number of quern fragments, a coin of Constantine, three unidentified coins, several iron objects and nails, a bronze pin, and a possible iron lynch-pin

Site II - An initial 4 m × 2 m trench was sited to investigate a concentration of storage pits visible from St Joseph's cropmark plan (Fig. 3.14); all the exposed pits were sampled and, eventually, 18 were fully excavated, with Early Iron Age pottery, carbonized seeds and animal bone recovered; a barbed-and-tanged arrowhead was also forthcoming and other worked flint was recovered. In some pits, horizontal and vertical banding was thought to be impressions from a wicker-lining, with lumps of clay recovered from some pits showing wicker impressions. An undated, extended inhumation burial was also found (aligned parallel to the present track); in addition, a small quantity of Romano-British pottery was retrieved from excavated features, some being sourced from the Obelisk Kilns found nearby at Harston (Pullinger & Young 1982). Other finds from the site included a square-cut piece of bone and a bronze buckle of unknown date.

Site V - Lying 200 m northeast of Site II, this consisted of a large single-ditched enclosure of sub-rectangular plan (Enclosure A; Fig. 3.16). In 1975, an initial 4 m × 2 m trench was excavated across the ditch and an area of *c.* 49 m × 38 m (1862 m^2) of its interior was investigated. The ditch proved to be 'V'-shaped, *c.* 3 m across and *c.* 1.5 m deep. Early Iron Age pottery was recovered from its fills (with over 145 sherds retrieved), in addition to a quantity of worked flint and animal bone, with concentrations of finds from the butt-ends at the entrance. In 1977 the southern side of the enclosure and its entrance (5 m wide) was completely stripped. A low bank was observed along the inner edge of the ditch in the southwest corner of the enclosure. Within the interior at that point was a very large roundhouse, *c.* 20 m in diameter, with its entrance oriented northwestward. Excavation of its eavesdrip gulley resulted in the recovery of a considerable quantity of pre-Roman Iron Age pottery ('non-Belgic'), quern fragments, charcoal, animal bone and plant remains. A large cooking hearth was inferred from the presence of two successive oval pits containing burnt stones.

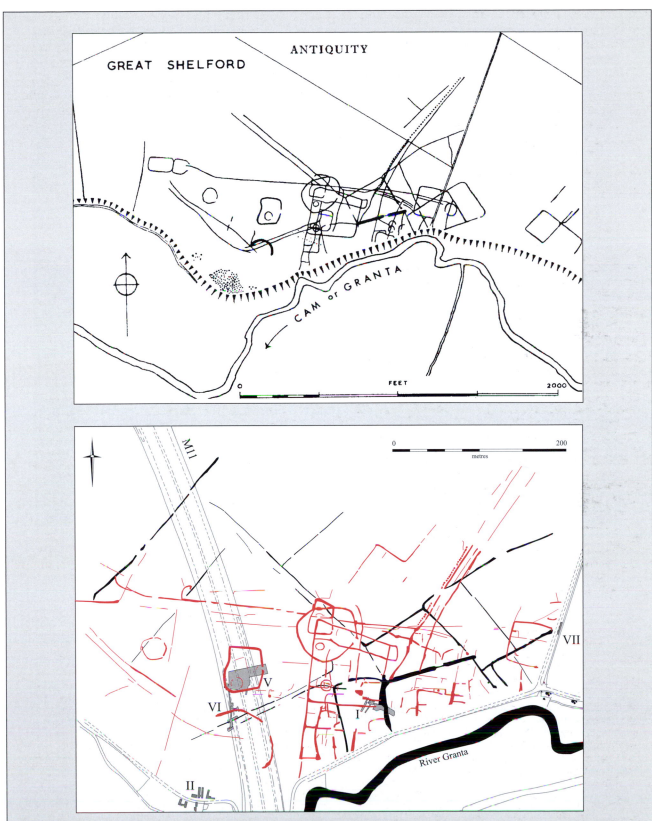

FIGURE 3.14. *Rectory Farm, Shelford - Cropmark Plots: Top, St Joseph's 1965 mapping; bottom, Palmer's 2008 rectified plan with 1975–80 sites indicated (note the 'aftermath' line of the M11). (© Crown copyright and/or data base right. All rights reserved. Licence number 100048686.)*

FIGURE 3.15. *Rectory Farm, Shelford: Aerial photograph (looking northeast) with A–F indicating individual enclosures and 'Tr.' trackways: note pit alignment running alongside the trackway in the upper right side of image, with inset detail of the same left.*

During the course of excavation, over 45 sherds of Romano-British pottery were also recovered, including both grey and Nene Valley wares, and also a piece of Samian.

Site VI - Two sections were excavated across the curvilinear ditch of Enclosure B where it intersected with two parallel droveway ditches observed on the aerial photograph of the area (Fig. 3.16). The ditch was stratigraphically earlier than the droveway ditches and attributed to the earlier Iron Age ('Period IIA') and contemporary with the Site V enclosure ditch. Despite excavation of a 10 m length of the ditch and *c.* 45 m² of its interior, no finds were recovered and the fill of the ditch was completely sterile. A later ditch was assigned to the Romano-British period in addition to the parallel droveway ditches, although these may be medieval as scraps of tile from this, or a later, date were recovered during their excavation.

Site VII - In 1977 a field boundary ditch, *c.* 3 m wide and 1.5 m deep, was sectioned and found to contain a few sherds of Romano-British pottery.

Site VIII - A trench cut in order to locate and sample the pit alignment failed to locate its features.

Following the 1975 excavation (later excavated material has yet to be analysed), some 420 pieces of animal bone were studied. Recovered from Iron Age and Romano-British features, the proportions for each phase were similar and the assemblage was dominated by cattle (55%) and sheep (28%); smaller quantities of pig (7%), horse (6%) and dog (3%) were

FIGURE 3.16 (right). *Rectory Farm, Shelford: top left, base-plan of Sites V and VI; upper right, base-plan of Site V roundhouse; below, Iron Age Enclosures: 1) Enclosure D; 2) Enclosure A; 3) Enclosure F; 4) Stone Hill Enclosure (TL 454 530); 5) the Addenbrooke's Environs 'square' (TL 464 544); 6) Cra'ster's New Addenbrooke's enclosure.*

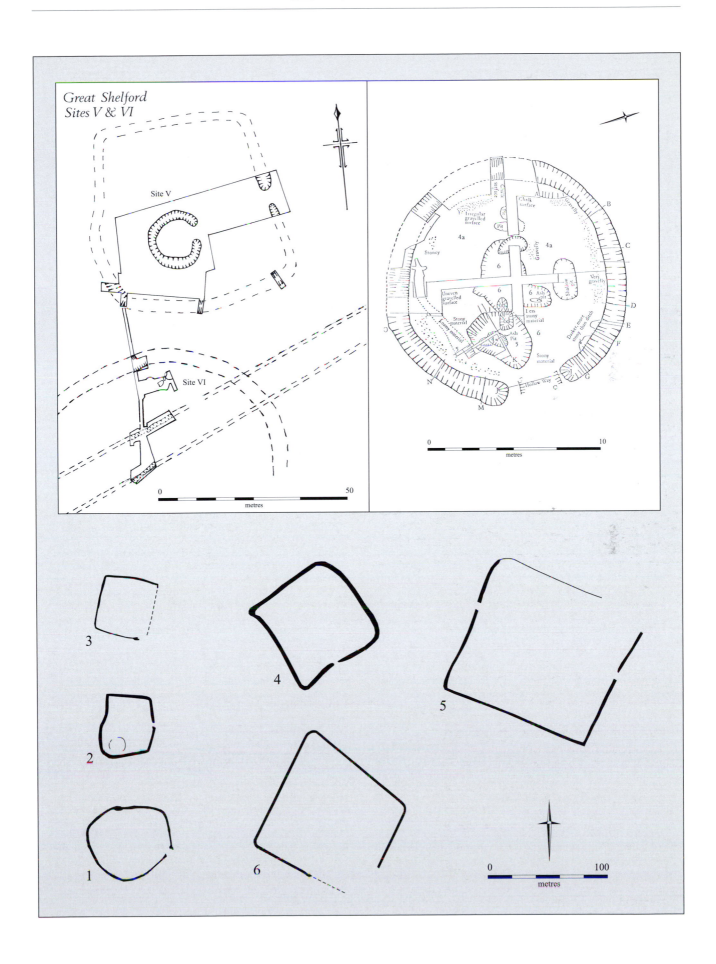

*Great Shelford
Sites V & VI*

Site V

Site VI

0   50
metres

Chalk surface

Chalk surface

Gravelly

B

Irregular gravelled surface

Pit

C

Stoney

4a

Gravelly

4a

6

Very gravelly

D

Uneven gravelled surface

6

6   Ash Pit

Shallow Pit

E

Less stony material

Darker more stony than ditch

F

O

Stony material

Stony material

6

5

Ash Pit

K

Stony material

G

N

Hollow Way

Q

M

0   10
metres

3

2

1

4

6

5

0   100
metres

also identified. Flotation of environmental samples revealed a paucity of any large grain remains, although one sample from a Romano-British hearth contained a number of carbonized grains. Similar charcoal-rich samples from the Iron Age house (Site V), excavated in 1976, produced relatively higher quantities of grain from the other samples, but carbonized plant material is sparse and scattered in most occupation debris. One pit (excavated in 1975), dated to the earliest phase of occupation, contained waterlogged seeds of several species not present in the flotation samples. Cereal and food-crops identified from the analysis of the 1975–76 samples include wheat and barley, and occasionally field pea.

Pottery recovered from Rectory Farm included a number of Beaker sherds (Sites I & II), and a small quantity of Post-Deverel Rimbury wares (Site II). A large quantity of Early Iron Age pottery was recovered from Site II and Site V's enclosure ditch (over 145 sherds). From the eavesdrip gulley of the Iron Age roundhouse at Site V, a large quantity of later Iron Age/pre-Conquest pottery was also retrieved. At Site I, *c.* 100 Romano-British pottery sherds were retrieved, including sherds of Samian and amphora and dated to the first to third centuries AD. Similarly, a quantity of Romano-British pottery was found at Site II, probably produced at the Obelisk Kilns at Harston. Recovered vessel-forms comprised grey and black coarse ware jars, platters, bowls, 'dog' dishes and flanged bowls; decoration included rilling, cording, burnishing and cross-hatching. Horningsea-type storage jars and Nene Valley wares were also found during the excavations

The site's Roman pottery was studied by the late Joyce Pullinger. Unfortunately, in its archive summary text, the material was considered together with that from the Lower Hollicks investigations, located *c.* 800 m to the east and on the north side of the river opposite Hauxton (TL 436 525; Woudhuysen 1981). Amounting to over 14,000 sherds, more than 90% must derive from the later Roman Hollicks Site, and apparently almost 8000 sherds derived from the general surface spread sealing its features. What is particularly important concerning its assemblage are the quantities of kiln-broken sherds and wasters. This was attributed to clearance from the Obelisk Kilns complex, and its vessels were also identified amongst the Rectory Farm assemblage. Yet, given that the Obelisk kilns lay some 1.7 km south of the river (Pullinger & Young 1982), it seems unlikely that the Hollicks Site would have had kiln-waste dumped there from such a distance. Instead, the local Late Roman pottery industry was probably not restricted to that one site alone and its manufacture may have been shared by a number of settlements in the immediate area (note that Obelisk kiln-produced vessels were recovered from the New Hall excavations in Cambridge; see Going in Evans & Lucas forthcoming).

Obviously the Rectory Farm cropmark plot represents a palimpsest of multi-period land-use. Based on the fact that the trackway test-excavated in Site VI apparently produced a piece of tile of Medieval or later date, the components of the sympathetically 'diagonal' paddock/fieldsystem have been attributed to post-Roman times (though it is conceivable that portions could be of later Roman date) and these are shown in black in Figure 3.14. Doing this, the cropmarks' layout is suddenly simplified and pattern is apparent. At the southern end of the large, northeast–southwest oriented trackway (with its bordering pit alignment) are the rectilinear paddocks of the Roman settlement (190+ × 190 m) and its outlying ditch boundaries. In the 'background' are a series of smaller discrete sub-circular and -rectangular ditched compounds (A–F), which essentially seem to be of Iron Age attribution (though the dating of Enclosure C's *c.* 30 m diameter circle is unknown; it maybe a small Iron Age house compound or, even, an earlier ring-ditch).

Given the size of the cropmark complex as a whole and its many component parts, the inadequacy of Alexander *et al.*'s small-scale trench investigations is, today, obvious. In truth, such exercises usually offer little more than dating evidence to elucidate the cropmark plan (e.g. artefact distribution and/or settlement space analyses are not possible). However, in this case, this itself is sufficient to provide insights into enclosure-type morphology; moreover, with associated surface deposits surviving (Fig. 3.16), the plan that was achieved of the Site V/Enclosure A roundhouse was detailed and is certainly significant in its own right. Other findings are also important. Perhaps foremost would be the scale of the area's Early Iron Age activity. Not only would this extend to the dating of the Site VI/Enclosure B's circular enclosure (and, by extension, probably also Enclosure D's), but also the dense array of storage pits recovered at the riverside at Site II, which may well resonate with the Trumpington Park-and-Ride Site. Furthermore, the pit alignment running immediately beside the main trackway in the northeast would have obvious parallels with the Bell School Paddocks post(hole) alignment (Fig. 3.8). Pit alignments *per se* are usually also attributed to the Early Iron Age (e.g. Pollard 1996a) and, in this case, this would presumably also date the layout of the trackway. Yet, the fact that a cropmark ditch boundary runs (dog-legged) parallel with this route and the pit alignment could, together perhaps with some of the other ditch-lines on this same approximate axis (Fig. 3.14), suggest the possibility of there being a later Bronze Age fieldsystem and, therefore, it is also conceivable that the pit alignment was itself of somewhat earlier date.

As opposed to Enclosures B and D's Early Iron Age circular compounds (respectively *c.* 60 & 80 m in diameter), Enclosure A's rectangle would seem to have been of later, probably Middle Iron Age attribution (its interior roundhouse providing its true dating evidence, with the earlier material in its main ditch circuit being residual); again, by extension, Enclosure F's 'square' would also probably be of that date. (Given the manner in which Enclosures E's two-celled 'rectangle' straddles what seems to be a Roman ditch boundary, it is probably of Early Roman or Late Iron Age date; note the affinities of its northern trapezoidal-shaped 'cell' to that at Greenhouse Farm; see Fig. 2.37 and Gibson & Lucas 2002).

The approximately 50 m-across square/rectangles of Enclosures A and D would be a widespread household compound-'type' of the Middle Iron Age in Eastern England (see e.g. Evans & Hodder 2006b). In the wider area, comparable enclosures can be identified on the cropmark plots and, too, a number of larger 'squares'. As shown on Figure 3.16, the latter would include a *c.* 80 × 80 m compound located 800 m northeast of Rectory Farm at Stone Hill, Great Shelford (TL 454 530) and, also, a *c.* 100 m-across setting just south of Addenbrooke's Hospital (see Fig. 1.12; TL 464 544); both would be comparable to Cra'ster's New Addenbrooke's enclosures (Fig. 1.4; see Chapter 1). As outlined in the section that follows (see the Barrington and Longstanton survey results), these type of simple, large (75 m+) square, later Iron Age settlement compounds have yet to be found in the area to the north of Cambridge. There, aside from the smaller square-type enclosures, the settlement compounds tend to be of a more irregular 'organic' layout.

Downlands and Claylands - three case-studies

Although there is not the scope here to consider their results in any depth, there are several comparative evaluation programmes that warrant précis. The first was undertaken by the CAU, anticipating golf course construction, in 2002 across 52ha at Granham's Farm, Shelford (Whittaker *et al.* 2002). It extended right the way across the top of Clarke's Hill and saw contour variation of between 19 and 46 m OD. Not only is it of significance as one of only two systematic evaluation-surveys conducted across the County's high downlands (see below), but it fell just along the southern side of the Figure 3.1's 'frame' and, therefore, is of direct relevance to the Addenbrooke's fieldwork. It should be noted that three years previously the County Council Unit had conducted a much less intense evaluation survey here (Hinman 1999a). While also including our later area, theirs included a much wider swathe at the southwestern foot of the Down

around Granham's Farm itself and, in total, extended across some 100 ha; we will, accordingly, draw upon their results.

In the course of our programme, transect-field-walking could only be undertaken across 39 ha and not all the fields were suitable for surface collection. While worked flint occurred in low densities throughout, the five lithic clusters that were tentatively distinguished all lay off the crown of the Down proper and below *c.* 30 m OD (Fig. 3.17:A–E). The diagnostic pieces indicate earlier Neolithic and Beaker/Early Bronze Age activity, with the presence of cores, hammerstones and core-rejuvenation flakes attesting to the fact that flintworking itself was undertaken at the locales.

In addition, two large natural hollows, which seasonally may well have held standing water, were found to have been utilized, if only at low intensity. Both these and the lithic clusters essentially appear to reflect Beaker/Early Bronze Age activity (one cluster — 'E' — may, though, be earlier, as it also included

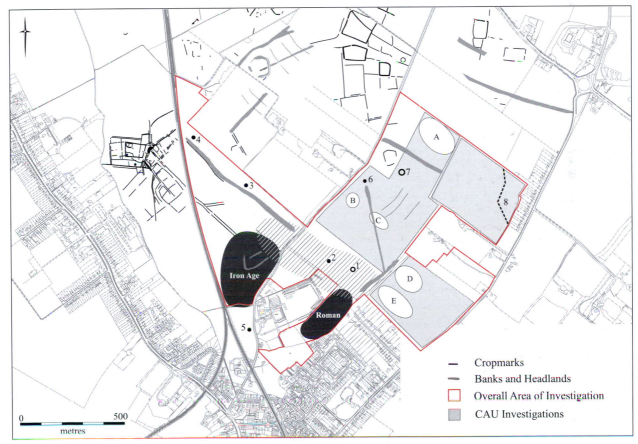

FIGURE 3.17. *Granham's Farm, Shelford - 1999 & 2002 Evaluation Results: A–E CAU lithic scatters (with diagonal hatching indicating County Council designated 'lithic concentration' swathe)' 1) ring-ditch; 2) pit-'shaft'; 3 & 4) roundhouses; 5) Late Iron Age cremation; 6) Bronze Age roundhouse (see Fig. 3.18); 7) ring-ditch; 8) WWII anti-tank ditch (see Fig. 1.9); note the County Council's period-distinction of high feature density areas on either side of Granham's Farm proper (after Hinman 1999a and Whittaker* et al. *2002). (Reproduced by permission of Ordnance Survey on behalf of HMSO. © Crown copyright 2008. All rights reserved. Ordnance Survey licence number 100048686.)*

FIGURE 3.18. *Granham's Farm, Shelford - 2002: Middle Bronze Age roundhouse, looking northwest (see Fig. 3.17:6 for location).*

Neolithic material). As has now been commonly found elsewhere (see Edmonds *et al.* 1999), aside from the hollows, flints would seem to have essentially been deposited on the surface and, when the area was trenched, no features were recovered in association with them.

Although relatively little archaeology was found up on the Down's slopes proper, the arcing length of a substantial ditch was located on its crown, which might either indicate a ploughed-out ring-ditch or barrow (Fig. 3.17:7). Otherwise, a definite Middle Bronze Age roundhouse was exposed on the south-western side (at *c.* 30 m OD: Fig. 3.18) and, elsewhere, scatterings of postholes indicate some manner of later Bronze/Early Iron Age occupation; no contemporary fieldsystem was present. Interestingly, only one Late Iron Age/Early Roman feature was recovered and, similarly, only a single sherd of definite Roman attribution.

These results are in some contrast to the County Unit's work in the fields down by the farm. There, aside from a few Neolithic pits and Bronze Age-attributed postholes, they found evidence of both Iron Age and Late Roman settlements (Fig. 3.17; Hinman

1999a). Significantly in relationship to the Clay Farm investigations, they also recovered a rich Late Iron Age cremation. Dated to AD 10–40, this included four complete pottery vessels (a central Gaulish Micaceous ware flagon, a *Terra nigra* platter, a pedastalled urn and a small bowl), with an *Aucissa*-type brooch and the head of a copper-alloy pin being found in one (Fig. 3.17:5; Hinman 1999a, 26).

Based on the Granham's Farm findings it could have been postulated that, during Iron Age and Roman times, the higher 'ridge-ground' was avoided. However, the 2005/06 investigations at CEMEX UK's Barrington Quarry certainly showed this not to be the case (of course, Wandlebury's sequence — situated high on the chalk at 70 m OD — would itself inform us of this beforehand, but then it was a 'monument'/fort). Bordering the northern side of the Cam/Rhee's river valley (and lying 9 km southwest of Addenbrooke's), the evaluation programme involved the excavation of some 12.6 km of trenching (augmented by 42 ha magnetometry survey, with 177 ha subject to magnetic susceptibility scanning) and took place over 172 ha across the crown of Barrington Down/Ridge at 65–70 m OD (Dickens 1998; Dickens *et al.* 2006). The geology divides along the top of this east–west ridge ('The Greensand Ridge': Sheail 2000), with Boulder Clay extending northward and chalk to the south, and was found to be dissected by a series of north–south oriented 'finger-like' dry valleys, which were filled with colluvium up to a depth of *c.* 4.00 m.

Lying beyond the investigation area, among the most important neighbouring sites are the six barrows located on the Money Hill rise at the eastern promontory-end of the ridge and the Iron Age cemetery and settlement excavated at Edix Hill Barrington (Malim 1997). Dug in the early 1990s, in addition to a Bronze Age ring-ditch, that site is best known for its Anglo-Saxon cemetery (Malim *et al.* 1998); another such cemetery was excavated nearby at Hooper's Field during the later nineteenth century (Foster 1881). Noteworthy also is that a series of important Late Iron Age stray finds are known from the Barrington area, including gold coins, a currency bar and an imported Arretine vessel (Salzman 1967, 229).

As indicated on Figure 3.19, eight sites were identified within the investigation area proper, of which four can only be considered major. Amongst the latter are Site I, an Early/Middle Bronze Age rectangular enclosure with an adjacent contemporary pit cluster and a large ring-ditch and Site II, denoting the finding of a second ring-ditch of the period. Otherwise, the evidence of pre-Iron Age usage was limited and only extended to two minor later Neolithic/Early Bronze Age pit clusters (Sites III & IV) and a 2.30 m deep

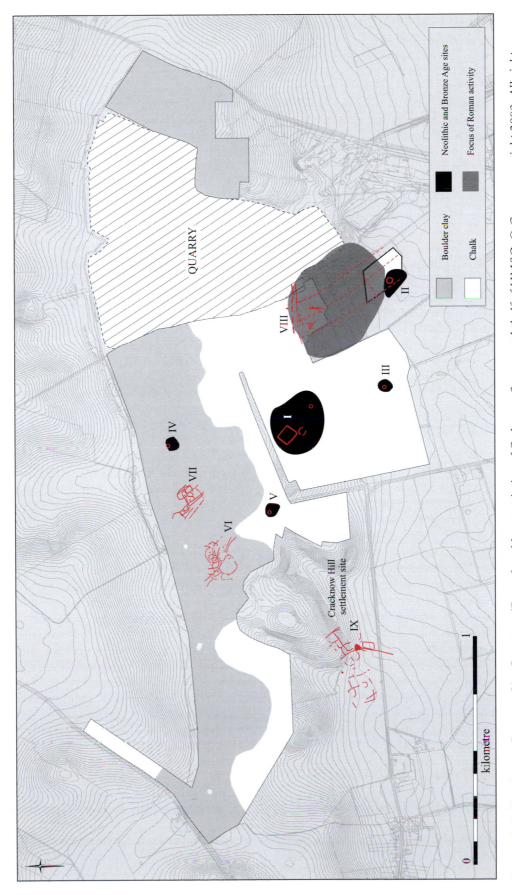

FIGURE 3.19. *Barrington Quarry - Site Gazetteer. (Reproduced by permission of Ordnance Survey on behalf of HMSO. © Crown copyright 2008. All rights reserved. Ordnance Survey licence number 100048686.)*

shaft-like pit (2.5 m dia.; Site V), also thought to be of probable Bronze Age date. Such features as the latter have been referred to as 'ritual shafts' and *de facto* assigned to the Neolithic (see Hinman 2001). In this case, however, it lay in the base of one of the 'finger' valleys and was sealed by colluvium. With this hollow possibly acting as a 'winterbourne' seasonally wet channel, it is conceivable that the shaft was intended to retain water.

The reduced line of the valley in which the pit-shaft lay was later marked by *The Whole Way*, a post-medieval track. In the north-centre of the evaluation area, major Late Iron Age settlements were discovered straddling either side of this 'hollow-way' (Site VI & VII). These seemed 'paired' with each other, with both established in the mid first century BC and only continuing into the first decades after the Roman Conquest (*c.* AD 70).

Of predominately second- to third century AD date, a large Roman settlement was found to extend across the ridge's lower slopes in the centre-southwest of the area (Site VIII). In the course of the fieldwork another settlement was identified and detailed through geophysical survey (Site IX). However, falling outside of the subsequently revised application area, it was not trench-investigated. Yet, also lying on the lower flanks of the ridge and of a rectilinear/'ladder-like' paddock layout (i.e. comparable to Site VIII), this is also probably of Romano-British attribution.

Aside from firmly disproving any claim that Iron Age and Roman settlement did not occur on the higher downlands (though the Roman sites, VIII & IX, both lay on the lower southern slopes and not the crown), among the most important outcomes of this programme are its insights into *the geological determination of settlement* (by period). Whereas, apart from the very minor Site IV pit cluster, all of the pre-Iron Age sites were situated on the chalk, the two Iron Age settlements are both located on clay. Of the latter, two final points deserve further notice. First is their sense of pairing: they essentially seem to match each other in date and their 'organic-type' enclosure layout. That they were located only 130 m apart, straddling the line of the later *Whole Way* (when no other sites of the period were present in the area), could, in fact, suggest *a historical specificity*: they are sited as if to control access in or out of an area/territory. The second point concerns their compounded 'organic' layout. This is not typical of the South Cambridgeshire area, where settlement of the period tends to be either of fairly unelaborated rectangular or sub-circular form. Instead, enclosure complexes of this form are the common type found across the region's claylands, to the west and north of Cambridge. It is in order to

better appreciate this distinction that we must turn to the final case-study, drawn from those lands and from out of South Cambridge proper.

Undertaken by the CAU between 2004 and 2006, the Longstanton evaluation surveys occurred over some 650 ha in the vicinity of the village (and throughout Oakington Airfield) and extended along new roadway corridors southeast of the line of the A14 (continuing alongside that route between its Longstanton/Bar Hill and Oakington junctions: Fig. 3.20). Any presentation of results from such a truly vast project must, of necessity, be extremely summary and there is neither the scope to detail the project's various stages, methodologies nor sites (its amassed grey literature already amounts to more than 700 pages: e.g. Evans & Dickens 2002; Evans & Mackay 2004; Evans *et al.* 2006; 2007). However, to appreciate its findings a firm sense of setting must be established. Generally lying between 10 and 20 m OD, the area falls within the clay plain north of Cambridge (6 km northwest). Essentially comprising heavy Kimmeridge and Ampthill Clays, it is bisected by the course of the Oakington Brook, whose narrow valley-corridor is marked by a 400 m wide band of lighter Greensands. Longstanton itself is located on a 700–1200 m-wide ridge of Third and Fourth Terrace gravels that continues northwest-ward towards Willingham. Crucial to its understanding is this area's 'inland' locale, as it lies distant from the region's main arterial waterways: the River Great Ouse, 5 km, and the Cam, 7 km.

These 'heavy lands' of the north-of-Cambridge plain were without any antiquarian tradition. Unlike the south of the county, the area — sometimes referred to as the 'fen hinterland' — really received no early archaeological notice. Nothing whatsoever was shown there on Fox's 1923 maps (Fig. 3.25) and it was only with the advent of serious aerial photographic reconnaissance during the 1970s and 1980s that any significant sites were detected (with only three being known prior to *c.* 1990). With expectations therefore relatively low, the programme's site-recovery rate was all the more extraordinary.

Given varying field conditions and the pressures of timetabling, the evaluation's methodologies had to be flexible (Fig. 3.20). Due to the heaviness of the topsoil cover, fieldwalking generally failed to distinguish sites, though surface collection (and also metal-detecting) across known sites did provide insights concerning their sequences and densities. It goes without saying that an enormous length of machine-trenching was deployed, more than 27.5 km. Again, where fieldwalking was not possible (and in other instances), this was augmented by Oxford Archaeotechnics' geophysical surveys. These initially

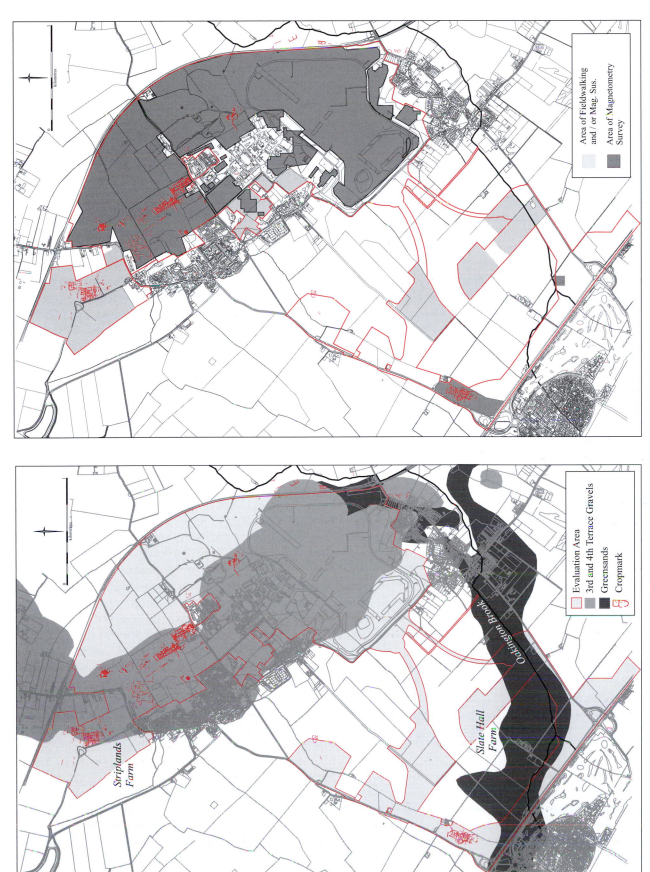

FIGURE 3.20. *Longstanton: Left, geology and relief; right, methodology (note fieldwalking and magnetic susceptibility scanning areas not indicated when they coincide with magnetometry plots). (Reproduced by permission of Ordnance Survey on behalf of HMSO. © Crown copyright 2008. All rights reserved. Ordnance Survey licence number 100048686.)*

took the standard two-tier approach: 'mass-area' magnetic susceptibility prospection followed by targeted magnetometry sub-sampling. However, the scope of this changed drastically with the discovery of 'serious' unexploded military ordnance within the airfield. Aware of this possibility from the outset, the trenching there was undertaken in conjunction with ordnance-scanning teams. As a result of finding a number of 500 and 1000 lb bombs (detonated *in situ*, resulting in the mass evacuation of the neighbouring villages), the degree of trenching across the airfield was thereafter severely curtailed (a condition also extending to the still 'active' golf course bordering Longstanton's northwestern side, though that area had seen some trial trenching prior to its construction in the early 1990s; Evans 1991). In compensation, magnetometry surveys were eventually conducted continuously over *c.* 310ha (with an additional *c.* 44ha of such coverage elsewhere). Making this the largest such survey ever undertaken, it provides an unparalleled map-record and, in effect, documents a 'three-landscape' palimpsest. Not only did it successfully recover a wide range of Iron Age/Roman settlements and an incredibly detailed plan of a WWII airfield (in which of all of the run-way phases and services are visible), but 'sandwiched' between the two are traces of the Medieval ridge-and-furrow landscape (Fig. 3.22). The latter provides a nuanced picture of its agricultural workings, including plough turning-circles and even gives insights into what upstanding components of the earlier, Roman settlements were then respected (i.e. embankments); in other words, it reveals the dynamics of a former 'earthworked' landscape.

Fortunately, there was some scope for further trench investigation of sites that were discovered through the geophysical surveys. We are, of course, fully aware of the risk of recovery-bias in this, as such survey techniques will generally only detect sites of a certain character (i.e. robustly ditched). Yet this necessary change in the evaluation only came mid-way through the fieldwork programme, by which time, a firm sense of the range of site-types that occurred on the area's heavy lands had been established (i.e. a paucity of pre-Iron Age usage and 'non-ditched' settlement).

Having laid out the project's logistical background, what then of its results? With 36 sites identified (with three more distinguished just beyond the evaluation area's 'frame': Fig. 3.21), there is only scope to discuss their broad characteristics and, for our purposes here, non-settlement-related discoveries (e.g. fieldystems alone) will not be mentioned. As above, it will be most convenient if we first chronologically bracket the extremes of the sequence before progress-

ing to outline the findings of its main periods (Iron Age and Romano-British).

Located along the northern side of the Greensand valley of Oakington Brook, a Mesolithic flint scatter was recovered in the south of the area, near the Oakington Road (Site 28). This correlates with another scatter of the same date discovered through earlier evaluation fieldwork undertaken by the Cotswold Archaeological Trust across the southwestern A14-side fields, where fieldwalking alone was implemented (Gerrard 1989). While their site (1) lay just beyond the borders of current development/survey area, together with Site 28 it suggests a propensity for early, Mesolithic use/traverse into this then-wooded landscape along the corridor of the brook. Otherwise, only very little pre-later Bronze Age material was recovered. The very low densities of flintwork suggest only an occasional Neolithic/earlier Bronze Age presence and what probably amounted to no more than woodland-resource 'tasking' (see Evans 2002a for comparative usage on the Isle of Ely's clays).

At the other end of the dating spectrum, evidence of Early medieval/Saxo-Norman settlement was confined to the extreme ends of the village proper (Sites 22 & 35), with some manner of presumably related activity identified in that portion of its core that was subject to geophysical survey alone (i.e. not trenched; Site 24). Located at some remove, and north of Longstanton itself, evidence of earlier Saxon occupation was only found at Sites 23 and 21; see Ellis & Ratkai 2001 for the Birmingham Unit's investigations along the northwest side of the village).

At least locally, the area's main occupation sequence would seem to have commenced during the later Bronze Age. In the course of the evaluation, occasional pits were found yielding burnt flint-tempered pottery characteristic of the later Bronze/Early Iron Ages. Usually occurring as seemingly isolated features, at Site 5 at Striplands Farm in the north of the area (situated at the western interface between the ridge-gravels and clays), a more extensive later Bronze Age settlement was discovered. Fortunately, this is the one area where excavation has since commenced (Patten & Evans 2005). A fairly typical settlement of the period was found, with a few dispersed linear ditches (not really sufficient to pronounce them a 'fieldsystem' *per se*), post-built roundhouses, four-posters and a series of deep pit-well watering holes. It is the latter features that are of the greatest importance in this case. Due to the area's heavy geological matrix (i.e. the water-retentive qualities of the clay), not only were these wonderfully waterlogged and produced a wealth of worked wood and superb environmental data (the pollen indicating arable production), but they

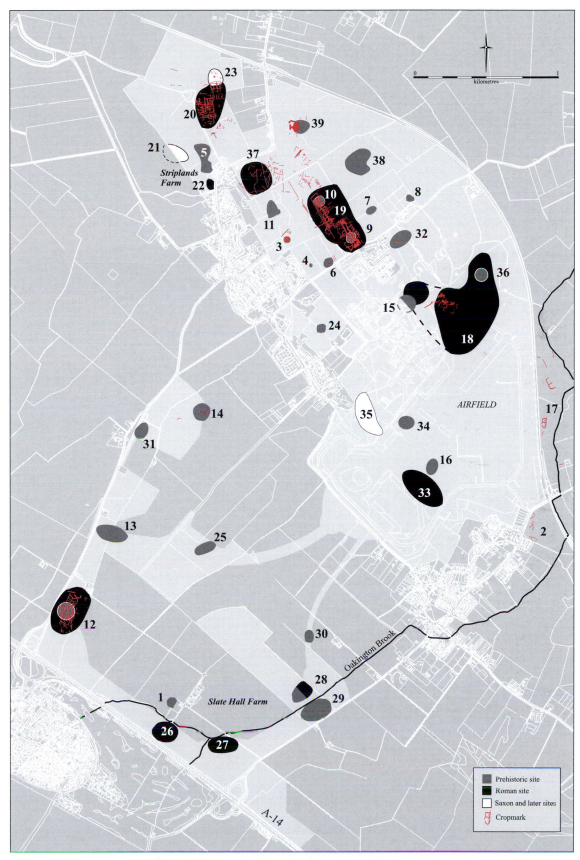

FIGURE 3.21. *Longstanton: Site Gazetteer. (Reproduced by permission of Ordnance Survey on behalf of HMSO. © Crown copyright 2008. All rights reserved. Ordnance Survey licence number 100048686.)*

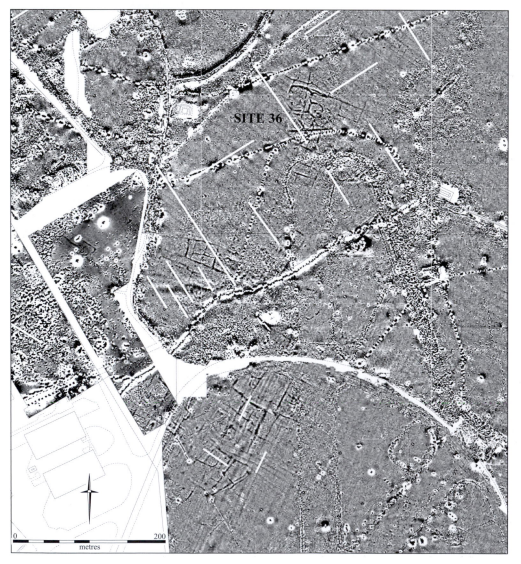

SITE 36

FIGURE 3.22.
*Longstanton -
Geophysical plots: Top,
Site 19 (including also
9 & 10); below, Site
18 (with the Site 36
Iron Age compound
occurring within
it). (Reproduced
by permission of
Ordnance Survey
on behalf of HMSO.
© Crown copyright
2008. All rights
reserved. Ordnance
Survey licence number
100048686.)*

serve as a hallmark of the area's occupation. Without such deep wells — which seem an 'invention' of the second millennium BC — unless reliant on spring-lines, permanent settlement within this 'inland' landscape would essentially have been impossible.

The most frequent site-type recovered throughout the programme were Middle/later Iron Age settlement enclosures and, with 15 identified, these appear to represent the main *colonization horizon* within this landscape. Generally these are relatively small (*c.* 0.2–0.5 ha) and consist of 'organic' combinations of interlinked sub-rectangular/-circular ditch compounds (Fig. 3.23:5–6). Although their distribution is not uniform across the area, they appear to lie *c.* 250–500 m apart, their distance-interval being somewhat closer on the gravels as opposed to the clays. Rather than see the form of these enclosures as some manner of group-specific 'blueprint' (i.e. square *vs* organic layouts), it has been suggested that their plans may in fact relate to the degree to which landscape was variously forested and cleared (J. Taylor pers. comm.). In other words, organic-type enclosures might themselves be reflective of colonization with relatively extensive wooded landscapes, whereas square(-ish) forms could have been a product of settlement within more open lands with a longer term history of allotment. If valid in the case of the Longstanton environs, then this could indicate that the later Bronze Age inroads evinced at Striplands Farm may well have been localized. Obviously, these are questions that will only be addressed through large-scale excavation and programmes of palaeo-environmental study.

Two of Longstanton's Iron Age settlements certainly appear 'distinguished'. Site 12, in the extreme southwestern corner, consisted of a sub-circular bivallate enclosure, with a diameter of *c.* 100 m (Fig. 3.23:3). Though apparently associated with other 'sub-compound' settings on its western side and, thereby, part of a more extensive complex (it is also next to a dense Roman settlement; see below), its main double circuit 'circle' is vaguely reminiscent of the Wardy Hill Ringwork (Site 15 might also have a comparable layout). Located on the ridge-flanking clays north of the village, Site 38 appears a differently 'complicated' Iron Age settlement (only found through geophysical survey and lying within the area of the golf course, it has not been trench-tested: Fig. 3.23:4). Its plan, which extends over *c.* 2.3 ha, seems to include two small 'banjo-like' settings. These, and the organic form of the period's compounds as a whole, would be comparable to the type of enclosures that have recently been found across the county's western claylands and which continue west into Bedfordshire (Mills 2007; see also Abrams & Ingham 2008 and Deegan 2007).

The principles of their layout appear to differ from the sub-square Middle/later Iron Age compounds that are frequently found along the western fen-edge (e.g. Haddenham and Colne Fen, Earith; see Evans & Hodder 2006b), though whether chronology contributed to this has yet to be fully resolved.

With the area's Romano-British sites, there is, again, some problem of ascertaining their scale and to what degree separate portions should be grouped together as one, this being the case for Sites 20/23, 22/37 and 15/18 (Fig. 3.21). Here, the decision has been made that these respective 'pairings' should each be amalgamated. Even if not doing so, the (fewer) Roman sites were clearly considerably larger than the proceeding Iron Age settlements. Moreover, rather than being distributed throughout the landscape, they concentrate in two areas: a dense series along the spine of the gravel ridge and three along the southwestern margin of the area (excluded from this count, Site 28 in that general area also included a paddock-/fieldsystem of the period). Lying close to the line of the A14, the distribution of the latter group is thought to relate to the route of the Roman Cambridge-Godmanchester Road, which must run somewhere in the vicinity. (As shown on Figures 3.23:3, the only obvious candidate for its line is a major ditch-flanked east–west trackway passing through Site 12, in which case Sites 26 and 27 would have lain south of it).

What is particularly noteworthy, given the marked quasi-linear clustering of the settlements of this period along the gravel ridge, is that they maintained a *c.* 250–400 m distance-interval (there, generally comparable to the preceding Iron Age landscape: Fig. 3.21). This is despite their much greater size and, if directly reflective of their resident populations, this implies that their accompanying 'agricultural-support lands' must have extended out onto the adjacent clays.

Of the Roman sites, three would have to be assigned to the general category of 'major farmsteads': Sites 20/23, 22/37 and 12. Only the last of these is known to have seen earlier, Iron Age occupation (Fig. 3.23:3) — the double-circuit 'circle' (one cannot, though, be certain of this in the case of Site 38 as, falling in the area of the golf course, it was not trench investigated). By no measure can the other three main sites of the period be considered typical. Trenching and subsequent geophysical survey at Site 27 revealed the plan of a major building complex, including a probable bathhouse range and a winged-corridor building (Fig. 3.23:1). Its apparent status is confirmed not only by the building materials recovered (*tegula*, box-flue and *pedilis* tiles), but also by the quality of its metalwork: a probable stylus, two first-century AD

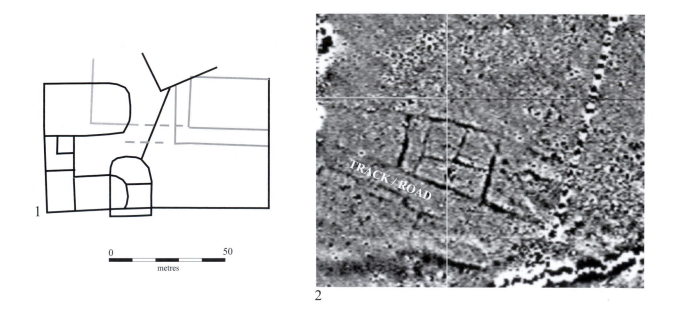

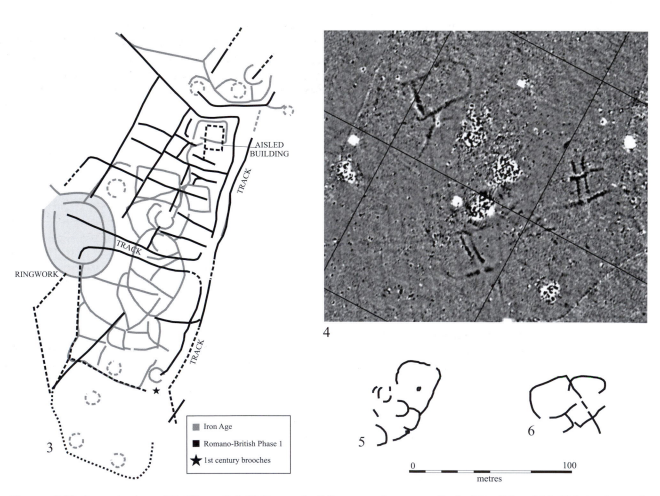

FIGURE 3.23. *Longstanton - Site Plans: 1 & 2) Roman building complex, respectively Sites 27 and 18; 3) Iron Age and Roman phases, Site 12 (with later Roman paddock system omitted); 4–6) Iron Age enclosures, respectively Sites 38, 7 and 14.*

brooches, bracelets, a decorated mount-fitting (possibly a horse harness: Fig. 3.24:2) and, remarkably, a complete hipposandal (Fig. 3.24:1; in additional to 16 third- to fourth-century AD coins and 1160 sherds of second- to fourth-century pottery). Taken as a whole, the evidence suggests that this was either a villa or, perhaps more likely, some manner of 'official complex' (e.g. *mansio* or posting station).

Two equally (though differently) distinct settlements occur side-by-side on the central gravel ridge area. Extending over 8.4 ha, Site 19 is marked by a dense series of interconnecting paddocks that were apparently arranged along either side of a major northwest–southeast oriented trackway (?road: Figs. 3.22 & 3.23). Remarkably, its southern and western sides seem variously defined by straight/parallel double- and triple-ditch circuits, which must indicate some manner of bounded enclosure, probably embanked. While this settlement complex was clearly very dense, and may have had relatively high population levels, it has not thus far produced any indicators of particularly high status. Essentially it was probably a quasi-nucleated farming 'village', but also surely included both industrial and ritual activity (the location of a possible small shrine in its southern end being suggested by metal-detector finds: Fig. 3.24:3).

Quite extraordinarily, the Site 15/18 complex, which extends over more than 24 ha (i.e. more than three times the size of Roman Cambridge), lies only 500 m southwest of Site 19 (Fig. 3.21) and, also dated to the second–fourth centuries AD, would have been fully contemporary. Again consisting of a series of interlinked rectilinear paddocks with dense multiple-settlement foci, it appears to have been situated at a crossroads where a north/northeast–south/southwest route probably met the southeastern projection of the Site 19 'track' (Fig. 3.22). Just west of their crossing, the geophysical surveys indicate a large stone-footed building (perhaps another *mansio* or the like: Fig. 3.23:2), and confirmation of this was forthcoming from the complete tiles and stone column fragment recovered from a deep cut feature nearby (Fig. 3.24:4–5).

There are unfortunately many facets of Longstanton's survey data that there simply is not the scope to further explore here; for example, the discovery of permanent 'inland' later Bronze Age occupation, the density and apparent regularity of its Iron Age settlement distributions, and also the latter's suggested social/settlement hierarchy (the 'distinction' of Sites 12 and 38). Instead, observations will have to be confined to stressing two points. First is the degree of reorganization of settlement that seems to have occurred in Roman times: as well as its series of major farmsteads, the evidence of its 'official' buildings and complexes attests to a much more complex (or at least varied) landscape/settlement structure. Second, given the density of their Iron Age and Roman settlement (and especially the scale of the latter), these north-of-Cambridge claylands should by no means be characterized as merely the 'fen hinterland'. Their heavy soils were obviously enormously fertile and supported considerable populations, and the area — despite the relatively late discovery of its full archaeological potential — clearly deserves to be considered a distinct 'landscape zone' in its own right.

Patterning and landscape densities

At this juncture, the results of our various evaluation programmes warrant comparison. As shown in Table 3.2, for our purposes here we will only draw upon the Iron Age and Roman distributions from the three main projects. In both categories, it is the Addenbrooke's/Trumpington environs that have the highest densities, with Longstanton's Iron Age densities being identical to those at Addenbrooke's/Trumpington in the Roman period.

Averaging the three projects' site densities gives figures of 2.8 sites per sqkm for the Iron Age and 1.9 for the Roman. Interestingly, these seem broadly comparable to Mills' figures from two areas in north Bedfordshire (2007), both of which include both river valley gravel terraces and claylands. In her first study area of 90 sqkm at the confluence of the rivers Great Ouse and the Ivel, there were 301 cropmark sites, giving a density of 3.3 sites per sqkm (Mills 2007, 137, figs. 61 & 62). Mills's other study area, 72 sqkm across the valley of the River Great Ouse north of Bedford (Mills 2007, 140, fig. 62), had 112 cropmark sites and an

TABLE 3.2. *Comparative evaluation survey site densities.*

	Addenbrooke's/Trumpington (1.95 sqkm)		Barrington (1.7 sqkm)		Longstanton (6.5 sqkm)	
	No.	Density (per sqkm)	No.	Density (per sqkm)	No.	Density (per sqkm)
Iron Age	9	4.6	2	1.2	17	2.6
Roman	5	2.6	3	1.8	9	1.4

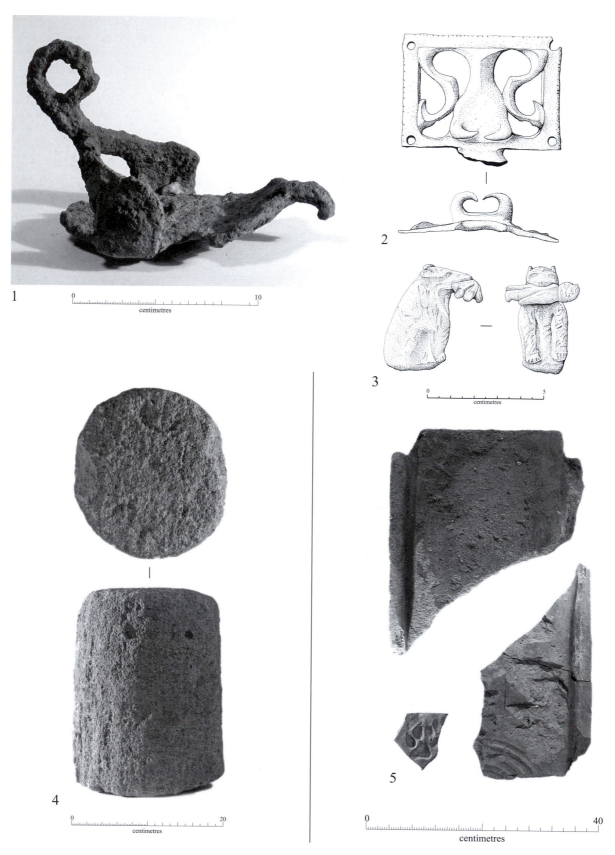

FIGURE 3.24. *Longstanton - Selected Finds: 1) iron hipposandal (Site 27); 2) copper-alloy decorated mount-fitting (Site 27); 3) copper-alloy statue (animal, possibly bear or wolf, carrying figure, possibly baby; Site 19); 4) stone column (Site 18); 5) roof tiles (Site 18).*

TABLE 3.3. *Comparative site mapping densities.*

	Fox 1923		Atlas 2000		Evaluation projects
	No.	Density (per sqkm)	No.	Density (per sqkm)	Ave. Density (per sqkm)
Iron Age	4	0.001	69	0.15	2.8
Roman	21	0.05	76	0.2	1.9

additional 12 'separate' (i.e. non-cropmark-associated) surface scatters (the area having been fieldwalked by David Hall; Hall 1991; Hall & Hutchings 1972). This gives a combined density of 1.7 sites per sqkm. All of Hall's fieldwalking scatter sites (including the 19 associated with cropmarks) were either of Iron Age or Roman date. Of course, as Mills' Bedfordshire density-figures reflect the combination of both Iron Age- and Roman-period settlements, they are not directly comparable to our evaluation single-period figures. This being said, though, they are certainly suggestive of high site densities and, as is the case with a number of Hall's surface sites, many are likely to have been of mixed/both period usage. (The Iron Age/Romano-British dating of these cropmark sites receives further support from the results of the A428 fieldwork on Cambridgeshire's western claylands from Bourn to Hardwick [Abrams & Ingham 2008]. Various degrees of Romano-British 'activity'/usage' was found on all ten of the sites located along the A428's 7.6 km route, with three large farmsteads of the period excavated; two of the sites also saw Middle/later Iron Age settlements and another included Bronze Age pits. Note that Niblett [2001, 29] also records that more than 20 first-century AD settlements are now known within a 10sqkm area of Verulamium's claylands; i.e. a density of two sites per sqkm.)

The high Cambridge project site densities have major ramifications for understanding later prehistoric and Roman settlement/social structure within not just the region, but southern England generally. Their implications will be best appreciated within a histori-cal-recovery perspective, with Fox's 1923 distributions being the appropriate starting point. As shown on Figure 3.25, of our evaluation areas, it was only within the immediate Addenbrooke's/Trumpington environs that any findings whatsoever had been made and nothing had registered within the immediate Barrington and Longstanton areas. In fact, 85 years ago, within that figure's *c.* 459 sqkm 'study frame' (centred on Cambridge), leaving aside the evidence of cemeteries and 'hillforts', only four Early Iron Age 'Living Floor or other evidence of settlement' sites were known. These were all located in the south of the county and no Early Iron Age material had then

been recorded within the designated area north of Cambridge and west of the Cam Valley.

Turning to Fox's Roman distributions, material was already known throughout the 'frame', although no settlements as such had been recorded in the Cambridge-north/Cambridge-west swathe. This being said, the number of Roman settlements and/or house/'foundation' sites identified within this area as a whole — 21 — was significantly greater than for the preceding Iron Age period.

Taken from maps in *An Atlas of Cambridgeshire and Huntingdonshire History* (Kirby & Oosthuizen 2000), Figure 3.26 allows us appraise what sites had come to light 75 years after Fox (the volume having prepared its map-data by 1998; see also Davis 1998). Incorporating the results of the first eight years of developer-funded fieldwork projects, as well as the fruits of intense aerial photographic study since the early 1980s (largely by Rog Palmer), the picture had altered radically by the late 1990s, there being 69 Iron Age-attributed sites and 76 Roman (including 15 villas). Nevertheless, while a handful of sites had by then been identified on Cambridge's northern and western claylands, the distributions were still strongly weighted in favour of the Cam River Valley and the county's southern downs. (In the north, the map's frame cuts just shy of the Willingham/Cottenham southern fen-edge where David Hall had found an extraordinary number of sites in the course of the Fenland Survey: Hall & Coles 1994.)

In Table 3.3 the site densities reported by Fox and the *Atlas* are compared with the average density-figures of the three evaluation projects (Addenbrooke's/Trumpington, Barrington and Longstanton). If you consider what the latter's figures really imply, their ramifications are staggering. They suggest that within our *c.* 459 sqkm Cambridge-centred study-frame there should, in total be some 1285 Iron Age and 872 Roman settlements; based on the *Atlas'* (admittedly now out-dated) distributions, this implies that only 5.3 and 8.7% respectively of the area's sites are/were known. Though insightful, this, of course, is not a valid reckoning. The study area is not an 'ideal' or uniform land-mass, and it is cross-cut by river valley corridors (and, later, tracks/roads) that would attract settle-

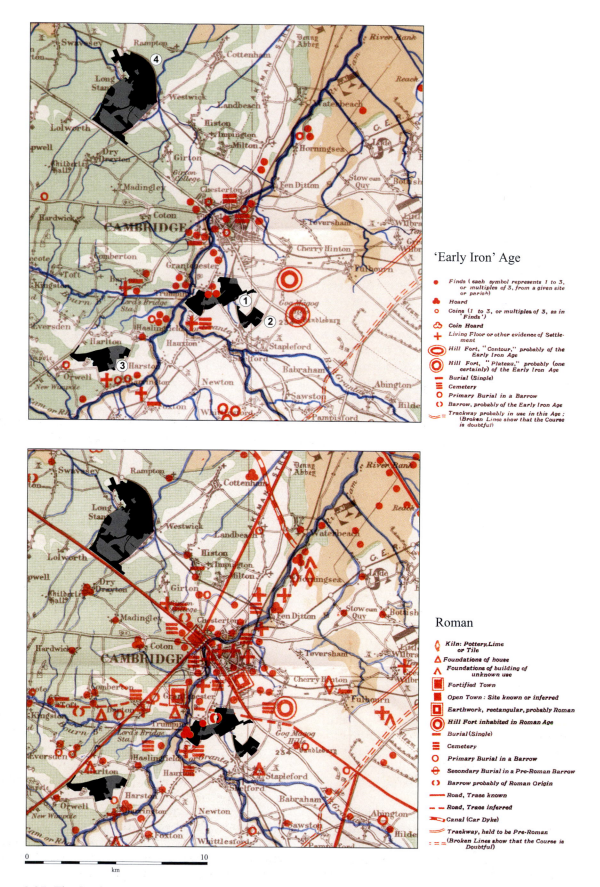

FIGURE 3.25. *The Study Frame (I) - Iron Age and Roman Site Densities: Details from Fox's 1923 maps, with Addenbrooke's/Trumpington Meadows (1), Shelford (2), Barrington (3) and Longstanton (4) evaluation areas indicated.*

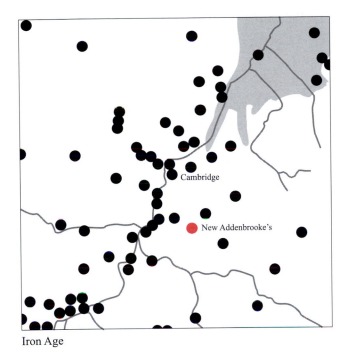

Iron Age

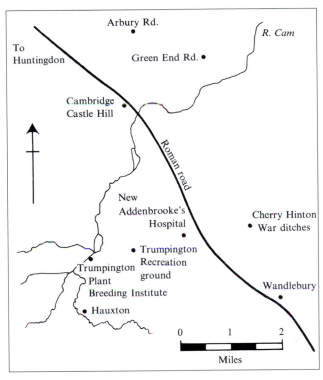

FIGURE 3.27. *Iron Age Site Densities - Davidson and Curtis's map: 'Supposing that all or most of the Iron Age sites in this area have now been located' (1973, fig. 7).*

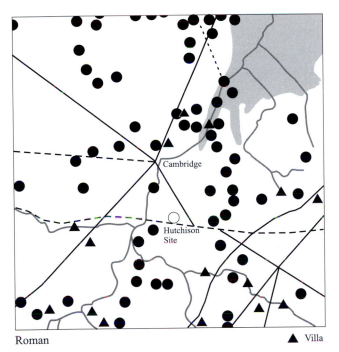

Roman   ▲ Villa

FIGURE 3.26. *The Study Frame (II) - Iron Age and Roman Site Densities: Sites known in 1998 after* An Atlas of Cambridgeshire and Huntingdonshire History *maps (Kirby & Oosthuizen 2000).*

ment. Equally, that given *the choice*, some geologies were clearly avoided is possible. This is, for example, apparent in the terrace-ridge location of most of the Roman settlements at Longstanton, and if the figures are recalculated based on that topographic swathe

alone the Roman densities rise to two sites per sqkm (from 1.4 overall).

These caveats aside, the sheer density of early settlement as indicated by the various evaluation-survey results are nothing less than revolutionary in our basic perception of the past, and this is especially true of the region's claylands (see e.g. Clay 2002; Mills & Palmer 2007). Here it is salient to remember that as little as 25–35 years ago their potential could still be so readily dismissed:

Elsewhere in southern England, Ellison and Harriss (1972) have noted that the catchments of Roman villas tend to include a high proportion of heavy soils suited for grazing cattle, whereas pre-Roman Iron Age and 'native' Romano-British sites concentrate more on light arable soils (Hodder 1982a, 63).

In this context Davidson and Curtis's Plant Breeding Institute paper of 1973 is also relevant, as it represents a brave — if premature — attempt to seriously consider site/landscape densities, in that case Iron Age settlement within the immediate Cambridge region (Fig. 3.27). Clearly undertaken while Davidson was an undergraduate at the University, it directly reflects the palaeo-economic approaches of the day (and acknowledges J.G.D. Clark and Eric Higgs), and the fieldwork was primarily undertaken to obtain faunal and plant remain samples to allow 'for the estimation of the economy of an area during the Iron Age' (Davidson & Curtis 1973, 1). Although their density-interval figures have now been shown to be seriously awry, its conclusions have the benefit of being explicit about their methodological assumptions:

> *Supposing that all or most of the Iron Age sites in this area have now been located,* we can consider the implications if they represent an approximation to the total economic exploitation of this area during that period. ... Not all these sites are of the same type, but a hill-fort and a simple enclosure can be compared in this survey, since they are both bases for economic exploitation. ... *It is clear that there is a regularity of spacing of 1–1¹/2 miles,* and that each is about equidistant from Castle Hill, Cambridge. This distance agrees with present-day estimates for the radius of modern intensive agricultural exploitation, and the spacing from Castle Hill may relate to the early growth and importance of Cambridge (Davidson & Curtis 1973, 11; emphasis added).

Moreover, thinking that the total population of past sites was so low also goes far to explain why so many fairly commonplace settlements such as their site were then scheduled as Ancient Monuments, *apparent* rarity promoting a misguided sense of value.

Comparing the results from the four evaluation projects outlined here makes clear the degree to which *scale is the governing factor* when trying to formulate a 'distributional archaeology', one that allows genuinely comparative results and recovery between projects/areas. Take, for example the Addenbrooke's/Trumpington Meadows environs: at just under 200ha, this undoubtedly represents a massive area — and earlier researchers would have begged for the opportunity to undertake fieldwork at such a scale (and resourcing) — even so, though, it is really too small in itself to distinguish firm patterning. Aside from its two Roman riverside settlements, only one substantive site from each period was found in each of its major topographic/geological zones (see below) and, in order to establish any sense of pattern, extra-survey sources must be drawn upon (stray/early quarry finds, aerial photography and/or earlier excavations), in which fortunately the area abounds. The same would also be true of the Granham's Farm, Shelford and Barrington Quarry results.

Covering an area more than three times larger than any of these, it is only at Longstanton that sufficient data was generated to distinguish 'self-contained' patterning (which is fortuitous as too little work has yet occurred elsewhere on the north-of-Cambridge clays to significantly augment its results and, equally, there is a paucity of local stray finds). Moreover, in the case of Longstanton's surveys, pattern seems all the more apparent due to its more uniform geography, there really only being two landscape zones to contend with: the 'inland' gravel ridge and its flanking claylands (the latter bisected by the line of the Oakington Brook). In other words, had the 'land-mass' area been more varied, an even larger area would have had to have been investigated to achieve a comparable degree of distributional patterning.

In this capacity, given the plethora of findings that developer-funded fieldwork is now annually generating (and whose amassed results can risk seeming chaotic), it is really only with vast-scale landscape evaluation projects such as Longstanton that sites are beginning to be recovered in a sufficiently controlled and uniform manner to yield obvious distributional patterning, which can then serve to frame and illuminate the spate (or 'noise') of smaller scale fieldwork results. In this regard, it can probably be said that comparable-scale fieldwork has only thus far occurred within the greater Cambridge region along the Ouse River Valley and the western fen-edge (and, perhaps, also across the eastern side of the Isle of Ely), and in those areas alone is there a similar control of site/period densities. While certainly seeing large-scale work, to achieve an equivalent degree of patterning, the southern fen-edge, and Cam Valley and southern chalk downlands generally, still need require further 'scale' investigation.

CHAPTER 4

Concluding Discussion — Scattered Evidence

Christopher Evans

The science of archaeology might well be defined as the study of the past distribution of culture-traits in time and space, and of the factors governing their distribution. For the plotting of extinct culture in space-time the cartographic method, of which Dr Fox has here given so masterly a demonstration, is of the utmost value both for popular exposition and as *an engine of research*. An archaeological distribution-map not only exploits the most basic and common quality of all antiquities, *viz.* their geographical position, but by its very existence implies the co-ordination of *scattered evidence* and the establishment of a synthetic relation with their geographical background (Clark 1933, 232; emphasis added).

In the last chapter we moved a long way 'out' from the Hutchison Site — distancing in the provision of context and progressing through ever-enlarging frames of interpretation. This final discussion will, accordingly, have to both consider the implications of the broader survey data and also review the excavations' findings informed by this broader, multi-faceted 'landscape-scale' perspective.

In keeping with volume's mapping-related themes, having already cited data from the *Cambridgeshire Historic Atlas* (Kirby & Oosthuizen 2000), here two other recent atlases will be drawn upon. The first, providing results of other extra-regional Iron Age and Roman landscape surveys, is Jeremy Taylor's *An Atlas of Roman Rural Settlement in England* (2007). The other, a much less obvious source, is Moretti's *Atlas of the European Novel* of 1998; its more general relevance relates to the unexpected connections that mapping can reveal.

Hutchison revisited

As opposed to the sheer quantity of fieldwork and analysis that has been directed towards the Fenland and Ouse Valley over the last 15 years, South Cambridgeshire has not seen the same degree of exposure and excavation. Largely as a result of not having been subject to a comparable scale of recent quarrying (as opposed to earlier coprolite extraction),

the character of its prehistoric landscapes/land-use is less convincingly understood. Equally, contributing to the picture of its apparent landscape stability and settlement continuity (see Chapter 1), nor has the area seen much in the way of palaeo-environmental research; even the excavation of South Cambridgeshire's Roman sites has been relatively small-scale. All of this impacts on what local context can be assembled for the Hutchison Site's findings, but, of course, this is set to change when the main Addenbrooke's/Trumpington environs developments commence.

When trying to elucidate the nature of the Hutchison's Early Neolithic usage, it is relevant that no major 'pit settlements' of the period have been recovered in the south of the county (see Garrow 2006), with the nearest substantive sites of the period being excavated along the southern fen-edge (Mortimer 2005; Gdaniec *et al.* 2008; Evans *et al.* 2006). This being said, evidence has been forthcoming of the Neolithic usage of both the area's riverside terraces and higher chalklands (e.g. Evans *et al.* 1999). Here, two points should be stressed. The first relates to the exploitation of flint and that unlike, for example, in Norfolk or the Sussex downlands, there has been no evidence for formal flint mining *per se* (Barber *et al.* 1999). Instead, at the riverside Babraham Research Campus Site it is clear that large peri-glacial hollows within the gravel and lower chalk terraces were exploited as a convenient source of flint nodules (Armour 2007) and, elsewhere, tree-throws were similarly utilized (McFadyen 1999a,b) Secondly, as is apparent in the Granham's Farm evaluation-survey results, and as dug at the Babraham Road Park-and-Ride Site (Hinman 2001; see also Gdaniec *et al.* 2008 and Pollard 2002), what are presumed to have been large, seasonally wet 'hollows' in higher off-river locations also clearly attracted short-stay activity, and, along with spring-lines, they would have been another much needed source of water (see below concerning water supply and 'shafts').

Relevant to any attribution of the environs-area fieldsystems, what is crucially important of the

FIGURE 4.1. *Bronze Age Fieldsystems: Left, fieldsystem extending through the northern Clay Farm fields (with line of possible later trackway shown in grey-tone); right, cropmark boundaries south of Worts Causeway that clearly correlate with the alignment of the Bronze Age ditches in the County Council's Park-and-Ride Site (Hinman 2001), with '1' indicating the location of later Bronze Age settlement found in the side of the City's anti-tank ditch (Collins 1948; Fell 1949). (Reproduced by permission of Ordnance Survey on behalf of HMSO. © Crown copyright 2008. All rights reserved. Ordnance Survey licence number 100048686.)*

Hutchison Site's later Bronze Age usage is that what appeared to be its sole fieldsystem boundary also ran northwest–southeast and on what seems to have been the period's 'prime' or paramount alignment. This ditch-line's orientation would not match that of the County Council's Babraham Road Park-and-Ride Site (Hinman 2001), which rather ran due east–west. From this, it could be inferred that the main north–south (i.e. 'cardinal') alignment of the cropmark boundaries south and east of the Bell School/2020 Lands is also of this Bronze Age attribution (Fig. 4.1). Admittedly it is difficult to push this dominant-alignment argument too far, as quasi-radial/twisting boundaries are also apparent in that area and the evidence of cropmark systems will invariably be partial. (One suspects that the southern end of the part of the system immediately west beside the Park-and-Ride 'block' — that is also aligned more cardinally and which alone extends well up the flank of the White Hill Down [Fig. 3.17] — is similarly of later Bronze Age date.)

These observations should lead us to reconsider the Bell School 'fossilized alignment' argument. Look

again at Figure 3.8: certainly the Bronze Age-to-Roman boundaries bunch-up there, but the actual orientation of the Roman ditches (northnortheast–southsouthwest) diverges by some ten degrees from that of the post-lines. With the latter essentially running north–south, the evidence could there equally further support that north–south, in fact, was the predominant later Bronze Age axis within the eastern portion of the immediate area. Yet, as attested to by the 'lie' of the Site I triple-circuit enclosure (northwest–southeast), this would not be the only orientation of the period within the larger area. Indeed, if the northwestern Clay Farm fieldsystem is also of Middle/later Bronze Age date, then its axes would not be the same as those in the eastern Addenbrooke's lands and this, thereby, would attest to the simultaneous existence of two (neighbouring) Bronze Age landscape-systems.

The paucity of large-scale investigations within southern Cambridgeshire is perhaps most telling as regards its Bronze Age landscapes, and their understanding is certainly relatively undeveloped when compared to more northern areas of the County (though see Yates 2007, 97–8 for overview). What, for

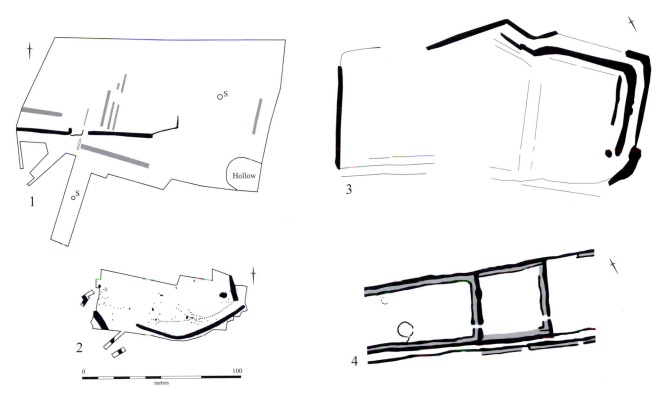

FIGURE 4.2. *Middle/Later Bronze Age Enclosures: 1) County Council's Babraham Road Park-and-Ride Site with main Bronze Age features indicated in black and later features in grey ('S' indicates 'pit shafts'; after Hinman 2001, fig. 4.3); 2) Fulbourn Hospital Site (after Brown & Score 1998, fig. 2); 3) Site I triple-circuit enclosures; 4) Pryor's Newark Road compounds, Fengate (Pryor 1980).*

example, is a typical enclosed settlement of the time in the area (Fig. 4.2): a quasi-circular configuration such as at Fulbourn Hospital (its arcing ditch and post-lines admittedly associated with a straight northwest-southeast oriented ditch boundary; see Chapter 1) or the 2020 Lands Site I 'elaborated triple-rectangle'? Given this, the possibility that the *c.* 100 m diameter embanked ring located south of the 2020 area (and at the end of White Hill Down) might even represent a Mucking- or Springfield Lyons-type Ringwork should be recognized. What, however, can be stated with some confidence based on the survey results is the degree to which the Middle/later Bronze Age seems to mark the initial horizon of obviously permanent settlement. Recent fieldwork elsewhere has shown that there is nothing particularly regionally specific in this, but what is striking is the extent to which the region's more extreme environments were penetrated and, in effect, colonized during the Middle/later Bronze Age. This 'colonization' would range from the enclosure (rectangular) of that date found atop Barrington Ridge to the roundhouse that occurs midway up the side of Clarke's Hill at Granham's Farm, Shelford (further afield it would also include the Striplands Farm Site on Longstanton's 'heavy lands').

Before progressing, we need to briefly consider the character of the early Addenbrooke's environs landscape, especially in the light of Hinman's ritual arguments (2001). While any landscape will be valued and considered somehow distinguished by its inhabitants, on the whole I have yet to be convinced that there is anything particularly 'special' here (for example the existence of a causewayed enclosure adjacent to Wandlebury is certainly not as yet demonstrated). Yes, the area saw 3–5 ring-ditches (including Site XIII's 'circle' at Trumpington Meadows: see Fig. 4.3 concerning ring-ditch excavations in the south of the county), but then so did almost all Fenland Bronze Age landscapes that have been extensively excavated; this was simply how nodal points in the landscape were marked (Evans & Knight 2000; 2001). Equally, the evidence of *The Whole Way* dry valley-/winterbourne-set pit-shaft at Barrington might call into question any generic ritual-shaft attribution of such features. True, with its auroch bone, the shaft at the Babraham Road Park-and-Ride Site may have seen votive-closing. Yet we shouldn't underestimate the problems of early water supply in such 'inland/off-river' landscapes and this has long been debated concerning the possibility of early settlement on high chalk downlands

FIGURE 4.3. *The Cherry Hinton Ring-ditches (TL 491 560): the 1997 excavations looking south. Probably of Early/ Middle Bronze Age attribution, no mortuary interments were recovered in association (of the 20 Middle Bronze Age ring-ditches excavated at Lodge Farm, St Osyth, Essex, cremations were only found in direct association with three; Germany 2007, 38–43, fig. 28); see Malim 1993, Barclay & Williams 1994 and Pollard 2002 for the excavation of ring-ditches and other allied 'monument-types in Southern Cambridgeshire.*

(e.g. Martin 1930). Remember, after all, the degree to which the Hutchison Site was peppered with pit wells, and also the 42 ft depth (12.80 m) of the Roman well excavated at the War Ditches (see Inset, Chapter 2); similarly, the Early Saxon pit-well recently excavated along the north side of Field C was 2.60 m deep (with the watertable being reached at a depth of 1.40 m) and its profile had all the characteristics of a vertical 'shaft' (see *Last Things* Inset). In this vein, might not these various 'shafts' have been seasonal wells or, effectively, run-off water collection points?

The evidence of probable votive later Bronze Age metalwork deposition apparently from the vicinity of the Edmundsoles Site, together with the human remains associated with the causeways of that date at Lingey Fen and the earlier findings of Bronze Age metalwork along this stretch of the Cam, could point to a distinct suite of river-related ritual activity during that period. This may, however, be better thought of as 'watery'- or marsh-related, as it may have occurred as much in relationship to the pocketed fens that earlier dotted the Cam Valley as to the river itself and, in this regard, these activities may well have been directly comparable to Fenland Bronze Age ritual practices

(e.g. Evans 2002a). Yet, of course, the point is that this was not the Fens, and the issue of what recommended and distinguished the broader Addenbrooke's/ Trumpington landscape will be a theme that we will return to once more in this chapter.

In order to further the issue of attributing the broader environs lands fieldsystem, at this point it is worth jumping periods and considering the nature of the Early Roman landscape. Typically, settlement of that time consisted of farmsteads with their attendant infield and/or stock paddocks. While they may be associated with 'big-scale' (i.e. dispersed) wide-interval boundaries, the kinds of extensive dense-interval fieldsystem that are known to be relatively common in the second millennium are not characteristic of the region's Romano-British landscapes. Given this, what do we make of the system extending throughout the Bell School/2020 Lands, which seems to align (northwest–southeast) on the Roman road system and which has generally been dated to that period (though Cra'ster's 1967 enclosure also shared this orientation)? Similarly, what was the relationship between the Hutchison Site's Roman usage and the settlement of that period now know to lie just south of the road (Sites III–V)? True, they may not have been directly contemporary and Site IV would seem to have had settlement continue until at least the third century AD. Though much has been lost through the Hospital's construction, with its settlement apparently extending continuously over perhaps as much as *c.* 25 ha, what the immediate Addenbrooke's landscape of the time seems most reminiscent of is Baldock, Herts. (Stead & Rigby 1986, fig. 3; Bryant & Niblett 1997, 276–8, fig. 27.6), which is held to be a 'minor centre' located at a cross-roads. Whether or not such an appellation is appropriate in this case will have to await future excavation.

It is, nevertheless, certainly essential to note that both the larger Addenbrooke's Roman complex and Site 15/18 at Longstanton are substantially greater in size than the main upper walled extent of Roman Cambridge and exceed the 20ha threshold figures that Taylor applies to urban/proto-urban sites (2007, 50). This is not for a moment to suggest that they themselves were towns (as opposed to ubiquitous 'centres'), but does reflect upon the complexity of the Roman countryside, which to date has seen little problematization within the Cambridge region. Indeed, the existence of these other 'centres' demands that Cambridge's status as a Roman town, at least in Early Roman times, be reappraised. This, however, is beyond the scope of this study and will have to await the second volume in the series, that being specifically concerned with the town's immediate hinterland and recent fieldwork within its bounds (Evans & Lucas forthcoming).

The kind of direct Iron Age-to-Roman continuity seen at the Hutchison Site would now seem to be entirely typical. Though by no means all later Iron Age settlements continued in use into Roman times, very few first-century Roman settlements seem entirely new foundations; in this case, Site XIX at Trumpington Meadows is seemingly an exception to this otherwise near-rule. Site 15/18 at Longstanton could serve as one of many potential examples of such continuity; equally, the two large Iron Age settlements investigated in the Barrington Quarry evaluation also probably continued until Flavian times. The real impact of Romanization in terms of the reorganization of landholdings would generally have to be attributed to the late first/second century AD (e.g. Taylor 2007, 110). In this regard it is unfortunate that at this time we cannot be more explicit about what the establishment of the Phase 5 boundary system at the Hutchison Site related to. Certainly it would seem to mark the end of Roman settlement *per se* on the site itself and reflects the implementation of a larger scale agricultural system whose associated settlement lay at some distance.

It is tempting to relate this development to either the villas known at the Perse School to the north or, southward, that at Shelford, but this cannot currently be demonstrated.

Extending west to the river, the Trumpington Meadows investigations significantly broaden our perspective of the area's Roman land-use (as opposed to what is otherwise Addenbrooke's 'inland' focus). Its Sites XIX and XX may well match the Edmundsoles riverside settlement and clearly attest to a dense network of river-front systems in the south of Cambridgeshire. The excavations at Hinxton, Babraham Research Campus and Bourne Bridge provide other comparable examples (Armour 2007; Mortimer & Evans 1996; Pollard 1996b; Timberlake & Armour 2007). Certainly they point to the fundamental importance of water-borne transportation at the time (which the cutting of the fenward Car Dyke canal further indicates). Of course, by extension, given the apparent Iron Age foundations of so many of these settlements, it would have to be presumed that river-transport was also significant during later prehistory.

Aside from attesting to the fact that Anglo-Saxon settlement extended west into the area of Field C in the 2020 Lands (and reflecting the lingering landscape-influence of Roman roads), the survey-environs data provides little additional direct context for the Hutchison Site's Saxon occupation. Settlements of the period are known at both Trumpington and Grantchester (Alexander & Trump 1972), and in recent years have been excavated both in Cambridge (Dodwell *et al.* 2004) and the south of the county generally (e.g. Gamlingay: Murray & McDonald 2006). Of the latter, what is singularly interesting is that wherever there has been large-scale excavation of Roman riverside sites (such as the afore-listed three), evidence of Saxon settlement has been forthcoming. Yet these are usually of small-scale and of 'Early' date, with Middle Saxon settlements being much rarer.

Finally, we must consider the area's Iron Age, which thus far has been overlooked. In fact, this has been a matter of intentional 'by-passing', as the character of South Cambridgeshire's Late Iron Age arguably still remains *the* issue. Marking the northern limits of the Aylesford-Swarling 'zone' and directly reflecting upon the dynamics of acculturization (e.g. Haselgrove 1982; 1984), it is one entirely specific to the region (alone) and was even distinguished as such by Fox:

> We may now deal with the problems presented by the topographical distribution of pottery of the Aylesford type, of which the pedestal urn is the most striking form, and the rite of cremation. The Aylesford class of wares is in our district

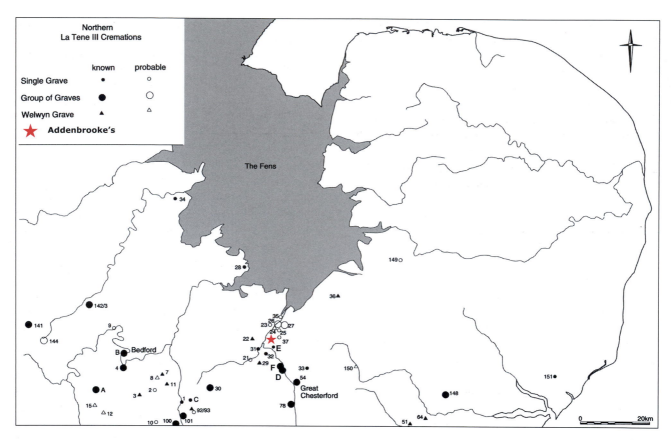

FIGURE 4.4. *Northern Aylesford-Swarling interments, with numbers indicating Whimster 1981 gazetteer entries; A) Salford, Beds.; B) Biddenham Loop, Beds.; C) Norton Road, Stofold, Beds.; D) Hinxton, Cambs; E) Granham's Farm, Shelford; F) Duxford (after Hill et al. 1999 and Whimster 1981). (Reproduced by permission of Ordnance Survey on behalf of HMSO. © Crown copyright 2008. All rights reserved. Ordnance Survey licence number 100048686.)*

commonest in the corn-growing belt, drained by the tributaries of the Great Ouse, extending from Hitchin to Sandy, and in the upper Cam Valley, being found at eighteen sites in these regions. *Typical forms have not up to the present been found in the north-east of our district or in the southern fens ... The most northerly sites at present recorded are Milton and Barnwell. At Peterborough, as Mr Wyman Abbott informed me, they do not occur* (1923, 102; emphasis added).

As discussed in Chapter 2 above, fieldwork subsequent to the 1999 overview concerned with this theme (Hill *et al.* 1999) — such as the recovery of Late Iron Age/Conquest Period cemeteries at Clay Farm, Granham's Farm (Shelford) and Duxford (Lyons in prep.) — would only further reinforce the idea that the Cambridge area marked the northern limits of the Aylesford-Swarling zone: the *borderlands* of this volume's title (Fig. 4.4). Certainly the recovery of coins and brooches of the period in some numbers from the Hutchison Site (in contrast to sites north of the City), further confirms this pattern. Indeed, it is an interesting reflection on how early obvious trait-patterning was identified that, despite having seen an enormous

amount of fieldwork over the last 85 years, the distribution of Aylesford (-Swarling) types essentially remains little changed since Fox's time. Against this, some complications in recent years have emerged, such as what appears to be the status of the Late Iron Age communities at the Camp Ground and Plant Sites at Colne Fen, Earith (see Table 2.46). Nevertheless, the notion that we are seeing *different* Iron Ages in relationship to the degree of Romanizing influence prior to the Conquest — variously the dynamics of acculturization (and, potentially, its intentional rejection) — remains a key point for the region's research.

There is equally the question of just how far back in time the sense of a regional north–south divide can be traced. We know, for example, that the lower/middle reaches of the Great Ouse river valley approximately mark the southern limits of the Middle Iron Age Scored Ware pottery tradition and also broadly correlate with the northern extent of later Iron Age gold coinage distributions (e.g. Haselgrove 1987). This background highlights just how important the forthcoming Longstanton environs fieldwork is, as there is a pressing need to articulate the Iron Age of these 'betwixt' claylands: the swathe between Cambridge South's Romanized 'sphere' and the western fen-edge and South Midlands traditions. It will also afford the opportunity to seriously address the issue of landscape *influx and colonization*, as that is exactly what the evaluation results point to. From tentative forays during the later Bronze/Early Iron Age, there does seem to be a distinct 'arrival' of permanent settlement during the Middle Iron Age. Certainly the mechanism of this expansion — first learning the possibilities of landscapes (in this case coping with heavy soils and an inland locale) through various short-stay exposures and then settling — is a process that would have occurred at different times and places and at times even repeatedly, as certain landscapes could not sustain intense long-term usage (or else other environmental factors intervened); there was clearly an episodic ebb-and-flow of settlement (e.g. the fens and high downlands).

In reference to our borderland theme, and how far the region's divide can be backdated, the importance of the Early/Middle Iron Age Site XV/ Trumpington Park-and-Ride Site cannot be overestimated (its inelegant entitlement belying its status). Site XV suggests some manner of settlement nucleation, and perhaps centralized grain storage, that regionally could only be directly compared to the 'open' pre-defences settlement at Wandlebury. Admittedly, other significant large Early/Middle Iron Age complexes are known, such as those at Fengate or Langwood Farm, Chatteris and, nearer at hand, the larger Greenhouse Farm complex on Newmarket Road, Cambridge (e.g. Cooper 2003; Evans 2003b; Gibson & Lucas 2002), yet in these other instances we cannot be certain of the scale of their settlement and to what degree they reflect the cumulative imprint of shifting foci. Nor do they seem to have had any centralized/mass grain storage capacity, which elsewhere seems a critical impetus towards hillfort construction.

In this vein, the importance of the War Ditches should not be overlooked and that after this volume's archival researches we can, at last, be assured of its plan-form. McKenny Hughes, indeed, got it right from the outset: a unique near perfectly circular (150 m dia.) Early/early Middle Iron Age 'fort'. Now, with full confidence, it can take its place alongside Wandlebury and Arbury — all (near-) perfectly circular and seemingly of the same approximate date (Evans & Knight 2002). Their form is unparalleled elsewhere and to have three such 'great' ringworks cluster together does seem to tell of some 'special' socio-cultural expression, a perceived need for defence and/or a 'declaration of territory' claim. This implies that the Cambridge area was, in fact, also *borderlands* (and possibly contested)

from at least the middle centuries of the first millennium BC. (Located on the eastern edge of the River Cam, the prehistoric earthwork enclosure at Borough Hill, Sawston, *c.* 4.25 km southwest of Wandlebury [Taylor *et al.* 1993], is now also known to be a Iron Age 'hillfort', albeit lowlying [Mortimer 2001]; however, its ovoid plan would distinguish it from the three above-listed 'circles'.)

Distributions and the 'engine of research'

Viewed in a long-term perspective, the amassed evidence from the Addenbrooke's/Trumpington environs does suggest a degree of intrinsic landscape zonation. The sequence of the western Clay Farm fields would seem to represent the 'back-side' of the riverside zone and, if so, it suggests a *c.* 1.5 km wide 'corridor' on this side of its course. Although a relatively minor feature, the eastern Clay Farm low-ground *trough* appears to have had a significant impact and to have divided the eastern lower chalk plain from the riverside area. This is expressed in the orientation of contemporary boundary systems across its respective sides — both in prehistory and during Roman times — with no direct continuity/continuation across this low swathe. Equally, as has already been remarked, this zonation would also extend to background flint densities, with the riverside corridor generally seeing levels twice that of the eastern chalk plain. Of course, certain components cross-cut these zones; particularly, the westward line of the Roman road and the distribution of ring-ditches. Nevertheless, it is again a nice conceit to think that Fox would have fully approved of the idea that a subtle topographic feature — the eastern Clay Farm fields' trough — could apparently have had such a lasting impact in the appraisal/zonation of land in the past.

Enlarging our perspective somewhat, having now explored facets of the area's archaeology it is worth briefly reconsidering its broader topography. This is a departure from most publications where the 'lie of the land' usually remains a topic of the first chapter's scene-setting. Yet, given Fox's geographic-imperative it is appropriate that it again comes to the fore at this volume's end. As is apparent on Figure 4.7, which characterizes Cambridgeshire's relief geography, the Addenbrooke's/Trumpington environs are situated at a marked pinch-point in the landscape. Located adjacent to the southern head-waters of the River Cam proper, it is where the Greensand Ridge in the west and, to the east, the chalklands of the Gog Magog Hills, narrow the valley to *c.* 5 km. Equally, it is here that the waters divide, or rather where the Cam was joined by its three main tributaries: the Bourn Brook in the west, the River Rhee in the southwest and,

Last things

Directly anticipating the publication of this volume and also further fieldwork in the area, in June of 2008 the CAU commissioned a geophysical survey across the grounds of the Long Road Sixth Form College immediately west of the Hutchison Site (Bartlett 2008), its primary aim being to detect the westward route of the Roman road. As shown on Figure 4.5, the results were somewhat disappointing. Although the magnetometry survey shows a hint of a linear anomaly of the line of the road, all that really shows are the faint traces of ridge-and-furrow agriculture (see Fig. 2.45) and, otherwise, modern school ground-related disturbance.

The commissioning of this survey also arose as a result of investigations relating to a diversion of the water main in Field C that had occurred in the autumn of the previous year (Timberlake 2007). This involved trenching along the line of rerouting across the northern side of the field and led to the excavation of a tight cluster of 16 Early Anglo-Saxon pits and a well (Figs. 4.5 & 4.6). While all shared distinct 'dark earth-type' fills, the vertically sided 2.60 m deep well (F.12) extended far deeper than the 0.15–0.85 m deep concave-profiled pits. Although no structures as such were identified, the quantity of domestic refuse recovered

indicates that settlement must have lain nearby. In addition to 685 pieces of animal bone, daub fragments (1500 g), worked stones (including 35 pieces of lava quernstone) and ironworking slag, the latter also included several sherds of fifth- to sixth-century handmade pottery from at least four vessels (two decorated) and four iron knife blades (plus a nail and a square-sectioned tool). The recovery of four sherds of Romano-British pottery and six worked flints attests to earlier activity in the vicinity.

The investigation's economic evidence would accord with the period's findings from the main Hutchison Site excavations, and the one bulk sample analysed from its Saxon features (pit F.2) yielded intensively burnt grains of spelt and possibly emmer wheat, rye and probably hulled barley. The animal bone assemblage was dominated by cattle (50% MNI), with lesser quantities of sheep/goat, horse (both 16.7% MNI), pig (8.3% MNI) and domestic goose (8.3% MNI).

Obviously a component of the Site VI complex (see Chapter 3 above), only further fieldwork will elucidate the true character of this occupation and, appropriate to 'last things', the trench results can only be considered tantalizing. Nevertheless, when combined with the evidence of the Hutchison Site, it certainly suggests that an extensive Early–Middle Saxon settlement lay on either side of the former Roman road.

FIGURE 4.5. *Sixth Form College geophysical survey and location of the Water Main trenching. (Reproduced by permission of Ordnance Survey on behalf of HMSO. © Crown copyright 2008. All rights reserved. Ordnance Survey licence number 100048686.)*

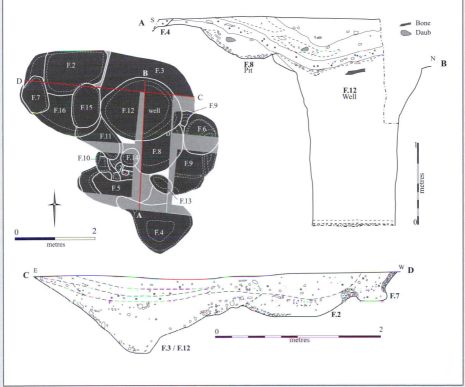

FIGURE 4.6. *The Water Main Early Anglo-Saxon pit cluster: top, photograph from south; below, plan and selected sections (note profile of the well-shaft).*

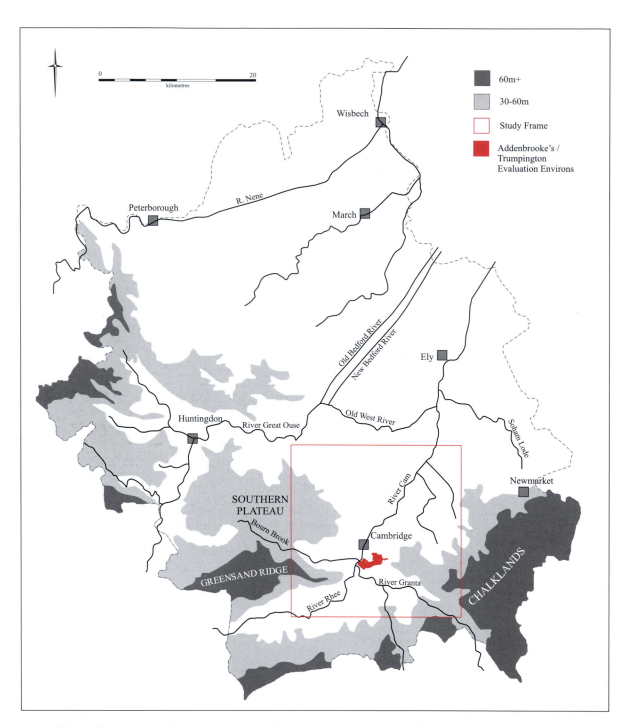

FIGURE 4.7. *Where Waters Join - Cambridgeshire Relief Geography Map (after Sheail 2000). (© Crown copyright and/or data base right. All rights reserved. Licence number 100048686.)*

also from the southeast, the Granta. Presuming that each would have served as 'communication corridors' through the landscape, this then would have been a significant nodal point and somewhere that distant communities interacted. This, for example, may well account for its Bronze Age causeways and metalwork deposition. Similarly, with its 'fanning' tributaries and subsidiary streams the flanking riverside terraces

of the Cam's lower valley lands would have been enormously fertile, which surely contributes to the higher density of settlement, at least during the Iron Age and Roman times. This is certainly not to advocate any kind of strict environmental determinism, as there always will have been a *cultural landscape geography* — variously socio-political territories, communication routes and the cultural appraisal/demarcation of land.

Nevertheless, it is physical geography that would have determined the base-line possibilities of the land's usage in the first place.

Crucial here is that, in the course of this volume's researches, we have managed to dismantle one of its original imperatives: a strict Cambridge-dominated focus, as if *the town* was the thing to explain (i.e. 'the land behind Cambridge' perspective). The recognition that both the larger Addenbrooke's Late Iron Age/Roman complex (a 'minor centre') and the broader Addenbrooke's/Trumpington environs — situated at 'the hub of waters' — variously existed as places in their own right and not just as an adjunct to what was to become Cambridge, can only be heralded as a successful outcome.

When, of course, the Addenbrooke's/Trumpington Meadows survey-environs lands are excavated we fully expect that its site inventory will be greatly nuanced and amended. At this point, however, and harking back to Chapter One's advocacy of field-survey data in its own right, some review is required of the various survey techniques and their respective recovery rates. Certainly it is clear that fieldwalking surface-collection will only register a restricted range of site types. Admittedly, in this case there was a degree of local bias due to the extent of topsoil disturbance incurred through having had the showground sited on the western Clay Farm fields. Yet a wide range of sites identified through trenching failed to register at all on the surface; for example, none of later Bronze/Iron Age attribution registered and even most of the Romano-British settlements' surface traces were extremely low. The latter is surely, in part, due to the fact that the sites of that period seem largely to be of earlier date, which lack the intense surface build-up characteristic of Late Roman sites. Nevertheless, the occupation density of the majority of the sites discovered through trenching (often announced by cropmarks) seems to have been too low to result in any significant ploughsoil register.

This cannot just be attributed to local conditions and comparable biases are apparent in the Fenland Survey results (e.g. Hall & Coles 1994), now seen in the light of almost twenty years' intensive in-depth testing though development-led fieldwork. While in that environment the problems of greater local soil-depth masking have to be accounted for, there, for example, later Bronze Age settlement only rarely registered on the surface as opposed to Middle/later Iron Age sites. This is, of course, ultimately also a product of the different nature of the periods' settlement holdings: Bronze Age occupation was generally more short-lived and subject to shift, whereas ditch-bounded Iron Age sites must reflect longer tenancy and, accordingly, greater surface build-up and fieldwalking trace.

In this context it is also appropriate to draw upon data in Taylor's *Atlas* (2007), in which the results of a series of systematic landscape-scale fieldwalking projects are outlined and their Iron Age and Roman distributions compared. For our purposes here, the findings of three, from a variety of environments, will have to suffice: Raunds, Northants, and Barton Bendish and Loddon in Norfolk (Table 4.1).

Seeing, on average, Iron Age densities of 0.6 sites per sqkm and 0.7 Roman, what is clear is the some two- to four-fold discrepancy between the results of the Cambridge area surveys and the fieldwalking projects (having densities of 1.3–1.5 Roman sites per sqkm, Williamson's Northwest Essex fieldwalking findings are more directly comparable; 1984). Mills' Bedfordshire studies, at least her second area, suggests a similar pattern. Of her 112 cropmark sites there, only 19 (17%) had registered in the course of Hall's fieldwalking (Mills 2007, 140); a nearly six-fold discrepancy, in that case, taken alone the fieldwalking sites would suggest a density of only 0.4 Iron Age/Roman sites per sqkm. This, again, simply indicates that not all sites register as surface scatters. Admittedly, the larger and more dense settlements are the more likely to be known by such techniques, yet, by way of warning, the great Site 15/18 24 ha complex at Longstanton was entirely a new discovery and had never been detected on aerial photographs (though, with hindsight, it was visible on Luftwaffe imagery). This being said, the unpredictability of when/how cropmarks register on heavy soils (e.g. R. Evans 2007) — as well as the greater earlier fieldwork emphasis on the region's chalklands — means that the area's claylands are likely to reveal the bulk of the unknown sites, at least those of Iron Age/Roman attribution.

TABLE 4.1. *Comparative fieldwalking site densities.*

	Raunds (44.6 sqkm)		Barton Bendish (15.7 sqkm)		Loddon (20.8 sqkm)	
	No.	Density (per sqkm)	No.	Density (per sqkm)	No.	Density (per sqkm)
Iron Age	19	0.4	15	0.95	9	0.4
Roman	32	0.7	13	0.8	13	0.6

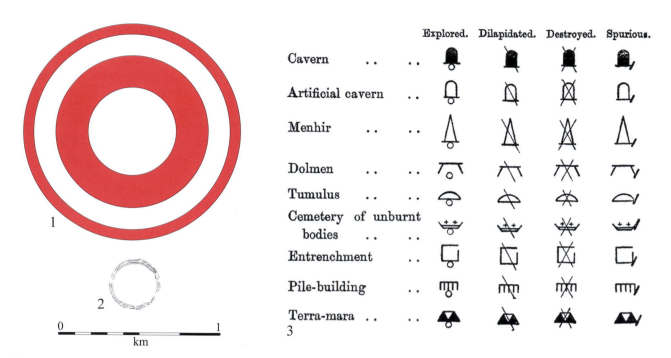

	Explored.	Dilapidated.	Destroyed.	Spurious.
Cavern				
Artificial cavern ..				
Menhir				
Dolmen				
Tumulus				
Cemetery of unburnt bodies ..				
Entrenchment ..				
Pile-building ..				
Terra-mara				

1

2

3

0 ————————— 1
km

FIGURE 4.8. *Dot Languages: 1 & 2) Fox's 1923 map symbol for hillforts shown to reproduction-scale relative to Wandlebury's circuit. Fox did not invent the archaeological distribution map as such, but rather fully realised the potential of distribution plotting in relationship to geographical factors. In demonstration, '3' shows a series of symbols proposed for the international codification of archaeological maps during the 1870s (J. Evans 1876, 433); under the auspices of the Society of Antiquaries of London and the Congress of Archaeological Societies, during the last decades of the nineteenth century a series of county archaeological maps (with accompanying gazetteers) were produced in* Archaeologia *(see Evans 2007, 297, note 115).*

Based, therefore, on the 'lessons' of the broader Addenbrooke's (*et al.*) environs fieldwork, the employment of a battery of evaluation techniques can only be recommended. Trenching alone will largely overlook a range of pre-later Bronze Age scatter sites, while fieldwalking is unlikely to detect a spectrum of feature-based land-use if the accompanying artefacts occur at relatively low densities. Finance, of course, is an underlying issue in all this. The funding available towards survey-stage investigation since 1990 is vastly greater than ever could have previously been envisaged, and the formalization of evaluation-survey fieldwork is one of the major achievements of planning-led development-related fieldwork. It is *a singularly new type of archaeological practice*, arguably one that has seen far greater methodological development over the last 15 years than excavation itself (e.g. Evans 2000a; Hey & Lacey 2001). Through such grand-scale projects within the region, we are, for the first time, beginning to locally grasp a real sense of what were the past's settlement/population densities. The critical difference between today's work and Fox's pioneering study is that, whereas he was largely only able to scrutinize and plot the distribution of stray-finds and earthworks, now it is a matter of *sites* proper.

Again, issues of *dimension and scaling* sit at the heart of this matter (see e.g. Lock & Molyneaux 2006). Looking again at Fox's distribution maps (Fig. 3.25) you realize just how enormous are his various distribution dots: to scale, each of his barrow symbols would be *c.* 30 ha in area and Wandlebury's circuit amounts to 140 ha — respectively an exaggeration of some 330 and 20 times their true size (Fig. 4.8; see Evans 2000b concerning 'The problem with dots'). This does not just relate to the technology of the day's production — hand-annotated (lithographic) basemaps as opposed to today's computer-controlled data — but also the time's interpretative framework. With so little excavation undertaken, of course, earthworks (augmented by the ready logic of prehistoric 'ways' and Roman roads) loomed large in the region's early 'past story'. Moreover, by extension, the southern downlands, with their easily read earthwork-palimpsests (as opposed to the masked fenlands and the presumed heavy forest cover of the clays), came to dominate the story.

Today, with projects like the Addenbrooke's/ Trumpington Meadows, Barrington and Longstanton environs surveys, we are beginning to appreciate the real *settlement fabric of the past*. With, for example, Iron

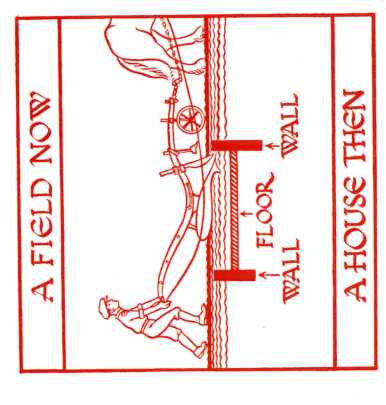

A FIELD NOW

FLOOR

WALL

WALL

A HOUSE THEN

The ploughman often strikes buried foundations, the walls and floors of old houses, farms, churches or castles.

Help to write the history of
Cambridgeshire & the Isle of Ely

YOU MAY FIND THESE

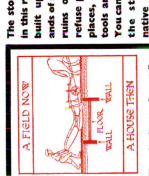

A FIELD NOW

FLOOR
WALL WALL

A HOUSE THEN

The ploughman often strikes buried foundations, the walls and floors of old houses, farms, churches or castles.

OLD POTS

ABOUT 100 A.D.

ABOUT 1500 B.C.

ABOUT 1800 B.C.

ABOUT 1 FOOT HIGH

Old pots can be broken but not destroyed. Their age can be told by their shape and decoration. Sometimes they contain burnt human bones. Report all old pots, even if in fragments.

The story of the past in this region has been built up from thousands of small finds, the ruins of old houses, refuse pits and burial places, broken pots, tools and weapons.

You can help to record the story of your native county by reporting promptly any finds like these you may yourself discover or hear about. They may be important.

IF YOU FIND ANY of the above or any other ancient remains please report it **AT ONCE to:**

**UNIVERSITY MUSEUM
OF ARCHÆOLOGY AND ETHNOLOGY,
DOWNING STREET, CAMBRIDGE.
TELEPHONE : CAMBRIDGE 497.**

MILES C. BURKITT, M.A.
CURATOR

C. H. S. BUSHNELL, M.A., Ph.D.
CURATOR

ISSUED BY THE CAMBRIDGE ANTIQUARIAN SOCIETY

GRAVEL PIT

TOP SOIL

GRAVEL

GRAVEL

BLACK SOIL, FILLING A PIT, DITCH OR POST-HOLE

The side of a gravel pit often shows a black patch of soil. It may be a refuse pit or where a wooden post or an old timber or wattle and daub building stood.

Bones or Small Objects

1000 to 500 B.C. About 600 A.D.

Skeletons are often accompanied by ornaments or weapons and give much information about our ancestors. Such finds should be reported at once.

FIGURE 4.9. *The Strike of the Ploughman – Later 1940s University Museum of Archaeology and Ethnology Poster, with detail right.*

Age and/or Roman settlements generally lying at an interval of *c.* 300–500 m across much of the region — and with comparable densities now also known at the Earith/Haddenham fen-edge and Ely's clays (Evans 2000b) — comes the realization that there simply is/was far more 'past' than has ever been thought possible. Of course, these survey results still require the detailing that can only come through the full excavation of the various projects' sites to determine their exact contemporanity. Nevertheless, the data suggests that during later prehistory and Roman times much of the countryside saw quite high population levels. In fact, recent work at Colne Fen, Earith indicates that densities at that time were broadly comparable to those within the parish during the eighteenth/early nineteenth century (Evans, with Appleby, Lucy & Regan forthcoming).

The recognition of these densities calls for no less than a reappraisal of the entire project of regional archaeology and its excavation practices. It invariably makes individual sites seem less 'special'. Moreover, in terms of such an abiding directive for archaeology as 'the explanation of cultural change', this makes it incredibly unlikely that, for example, *the site* where bronze metallurgy was first adopted or social hierarchy — or whatever — first emerged will ever be found and, instead, *the transmission of influence* is what must be addressed. This, for example, reflects upon the issue raised in Chapter Two concerning how new knowledges of kiln and pottery production were transferred. Yes, if settlements were far-flung such mechanisms as itinerate potters (or, otherwise, metalwork smiths) might be necessary to explain the spread of specialist skills. However, in densely settled landscapes various modes of more casual/near-daily interaction come to the fore; just as it can be imagined that the local influence of an individual, having been away — perhaps serving in the army or as an apprentice — and acquiring new production techniques and/or styles, on their return, could more readily spread through closely knit communities.

Somewhat conversely, the awareness of the proximity of 'site neighbours' and the extent to which we are dealing with *settlement networks* should now also lead to a certain interpretative modesty. The excavation of one site alone is unlikely to provide 'the key' to the period as a whole, and the realization of the density of archaeological sites itself strikingly demonstrates the complexity of past social systems and underlines just what a need there is for greater interpretative sophistication. Although having received little direct attention in archaeology, the situation of neighbours (like kin) is fundamental to any understanding of the operation of past social life.

Finally, it seems appropriate to include within this volume, and indeed conclude it with, a late 1940s University Museum local archaeology poster (Fig. 4.9). Issued in the era of Bushnell and Fell's curatorship, its emphatic 'call-to-arms' tone (i.e. this is what a feature looks like and 'YOU may find THESE') seems to almost hark back to WWII aeroplane-spotting wall-charts. A copy of this poster has hung in my office for the last 15 years; aside from its design qualities, I've always appreciated the sense of collective past effort it conveys: 'Help to write the history of …'. It also well sums up the state of much of Cambridgeshire's archaeology during the era of Fox, which would, in fact, have still been valid up to the 1970s and the advent of Fengate's large-scale fieldwork. Prior to then, excavations were generally small-scale and the recovery of sites was often a matter of noticing features exposed in the sides of quarry pits; indeed, surface finds were the main sources of the County's record — things arising from 'the strike of the ploughman'.

Against this background and ethos, such groundbreaking fieldwork projects as have been outlined here can only mark a threshold in the region's practice and, certainly, today these are exciting times in archaeology. Yet with the results of such projects also comes a crucial challenge, as the multi-faceted complexity of these landscapes thoroughly undermines the ready comfort of 'simple past' stories.

REFERENCES

Abrams, J., 2000. *Prehistoric Fieldsystems at Long Road 6th Form College, Cambridge: an Archaeological Evaluation.* (Cambridgeshire County Council Archaeological Field Unit Report 176.)

Abrams, J. & D. Ingham, 2008. *Farming on the Edge: Archaeological Evidence from the Clay Uplands to the West of Cambridge.* (East Anglian Archaeology Report No. 123.) Bedford: Albion Archaeology.

Adams, R.McC., 1965. *Land Behind Baghdad: a History of Settlement on the Diyala Plains.* Chicago (IL): University of Chicago Press.

Alexander, J. & D. Trump, 1972. *Grantchester 1971: a Preliminary Report on Excavations.* Cambridge and London: Board of Extra-mural Studies.

Alexander, J. & J. Pullinger, 2000. Roman Cambridge. excavations on Castle Hill 1956–1988. *Proceedings of the Cambridge Antiquarian Society* 88.

Alexander, M., N. Dodwell & C. Evans, 2004. A Roman cemetery in Jesus Lane, Cambridge. *Proceedings of the Cambridge Antiquarian Society* 93, 67–94.

Anderson, K., 2007. The Late Iron Age and Roman pottery, in *The ARES Site, Babraham Research Campus Cambridgeshire: AN Archaeological Excavation*, by N. Armour. (Cambridge Archaeological Unit Report 752.)

Anderson, K., forthcoming. The Late Iron Age and Roman pottery, in *Archaeology along the Cambridgeshire Guided Busway*, by M. Collins. Cambridge: Cambridge Archaeological Unit.

Anderson, K. & C. Evans, 2005. *The Archaeology of Clay Farm, Trumpington, Cambridge: Preliminary Investigations.* (Cambridge Archaeological Unit Report 699.)

Armour, N., 2001. *An Archaeological Evaluation at Downing College Sports Field, Long Road, Cambridge.* (Cambridge Archaeological Unit Report 452.)

Armour, N., 2007. *The ARES Site, Babraham Research Campus Cambridgeshire: an Archaeological Excavation.* (Cambridge Archaeological Unit Report 752.)

Atkins, R. & A. Mudd, 2003. An Iron Age and Romano-British settlement at Prickwillow Road, Ely: excavations 1999-2000. *Proceedings of the Cambridge Antiquarian Society* 92, 5–55.

Ballantyne, R.M., 2002. Preliminary assessment of the bulk samples from Whittlesey brick pits, in *Prehistoric and Roman Archaeology at Stonald Field, King's Dyke West, Whittlesey – Monuments and Settlement*, by D. Gibson & M. Knight. Cambridge: Cambridge Archaeological Unit, 61–70.

Ballantyne, R.M., 2005. The botanical assemblage, in *The Saxon and Medieval Settlement at West Fen Road, Ely: the Ashwell Site*, by R. Mortimer, R. Regan & S. Lucy. (East Anglian Archaeology Report 110.) Cambridge: Cambridge Archaeological Unit, 100–113.

Ballantyne, R., forthcoming, in *Hinterlands: the Archaeology of West Cambridge*, C. Evans & G. Lucas. (CAU Landscape Archives/New Archaeologies of the Cambridge Region 2.) Cambridge: Cambridge Archaeological Unit.

Ballin, T.B., 2002. Later Bronze Age flint technology: a presentation and discussion of post-barrow debitage from monuments in the Raunds Area, Northamptonshire. *Lithics* 23, 3–28.

Barber, M., D. Field & P. Topping, 1999. *The Neolithic Flint Mines of England.* Swindon: English Heritage.

Barclay, A.J. & R.J. Williams, 1994. *Four Wentways, Little Abington, Cambridgeshire: Archaeological Evaluation.* Oxford Archaeological Unit.

Barrett, J., 1980. The pottery of the later Bronze Age in lowland England. *Proceedings of the Prehistoric Society* 46, 297–319.

Bartlett, A., 2008. *Long Road College, Cambridge: Report on Archaeogeophysical Survey 2008.* Bartlett-Clark Consultancy.

Bartosiewicz, L., W. Van Neer & A. Lentacker, 1997. Draught cattle: their osteological identification and history. *Annalen Zoologische Wetenschappen* 281, 1–147.

Bass, W.M., 1992. *Human Osteology: a Laboratory and Field Manual.* Columbia (MO): Missouri Archaeological Society.

Baxter, I.L., 2002. Occipital perforations in a late Neolithic probable aurochs (*Bos primigenius* bojanus) cranium from Letchworth, Hertfordshire, UK. *International Journal of Osteoarchaeology* 12, 142–3.

Bayley, J., 1988. Analytical results for the brooches, in Puckeridge-Braughing, Hertfordshire: the Ermine Street excavations, 1971–1972. The Late Iron Age and Roman settlement, by T.W. Potter & S.D. Trow. *Hertfordshire Archaeology* 10, 54–7.

Beedham, G.E., 1972. *Hulton Group Keys: Identification of the British Mollusca.* Buckinghamshire: Hulton Educational Publications.

Biddulph, E., 2005. Last orders: choosing pottery for funerals in Roman Essex. *Oxford Journal of Archaeology* 24, 23–45.

Birchall, A., 1965. The Aylesford-Swarling culture: the problem of the Belgae reconsidered. *Proceedings of the*

Prehistoric Society 31, 241–367.

Bishop, M.C. & J.C.N. Coulston, 2006. *Roman Military Equipment. From the Punic Wars to the Fall of Rome.* 2nd edition. Oxford: Oxbow.

Blinkhorn, P.W., 1999. Of cabbages and kings: production, trade and consumption in Middle Saxon England, in *Anglo-Saxon Trading Centres and their Hinterlands. Beyond the Emporia*, ed. M. Anderton. Glasgow: Cruithne Press, 4–23.

Bloch, M., 1998. Why trees, too, are good to think with: Towards an anthropology of the meaning of life, in *The Social Life of Trees: Anthropological Perspectives on Tree Symbolism*, ed. L. Rival. Oxford: Berg, 39–55.

Boessneck, J., H.H. Müller & M. Teichert., 1964. Osteologische Unterscheidungsmerkmale zwischen Schaf (*Ovis aries* Linné) und Ziege (*Capra hircus* Linné). *Kühn-Archiv* 78, 1–29.

Boon, G.C., 1961. Roman antiquities at Welshpool. *Antiquaries Journal* 41, 13–31.

Boon, G.C., 1991. Tonsor Humanus: razor and toilet-knife. *Britannia* 22, 21–32.

Boon, G.C., 2000. The other objects of copper alloy, in *Late Iron Age and Roman Silchester. Excavations of the site of the Forum-Basilica 1977*, by M. Fulford & J. Timby. (Britannia Monograph Series 15.) London: Society for the Promotion of Roman Studies, 180–86.

Bradford, L.J., 1978. The Cambridge Archaeological Field Group: first report. *Proceedings of the Cambridge Antiquarian Society* 68, 11–13.

Brooks, S. & J. Suchey, 1990. Skeletal age determination based on the *Os Pubis*: a comparison of the Acsádi-Nemeskéri and Suchey-Brooks methods. *Human Evolution* 5, 227–238.

Brothwell, D., 1981. *Digging Up Bones: the Excavation, Treatment and Study of Human Skeletal Remains.* London: British Museum (Natural History).

Brothwell, D., K. Dobney & A. Ervynck, 1996. On the causes of perforations in archaeological domestic cattle skulls. *International Journal of Osteoarchaeology* 6, 471–87.

Brown, R. & D. Score, 1998. A Bronze Age enclosure at Fulbourn Hospital, Cambridgeshire. *Proceedings of the Cambridge Antiquarian Society* 87, 31–43.

Brown, R.A., 1986. The Iron Age and Romano-British settlement at Woodcock Hall, Saham Toney, Norfolk. *Britannia* 17, 1–58.

Brown, S., 2003. *Trumpington: Past and Present.* Stroud: Sutton Publishing.

Browne, D.M., 1974. An archaeological gazetteer of the city of Cambridge. *Proceedings of the Cambridge Antiquarian Society* 65(1).

Brudenell, M., 2004. *Land Adjacent to the Bell Language School, Cambridge: an Archaeological Evaluation.* (Cambridge Archaeological Unit Report 646.)

Brudenell, M., 2007. The prehistoric pottery, in *Past and Present: Excavations at Broom, Bedfordshire, 1996–2005*, by A. Cooper & M. Edmonds. Oxford: Oxbow, 241–264.

Brudenell, M. & A. Cooper, 2008. Post-middenism: depositional histories on Later Bronze Age settlements at Broom, Bedfordshire. *Oxford Journal of Archaeology* 27(1), 15–36.

Brudenell, M. & A. Dickens, 2007. *Trumpington Meadows, Cambridge: an Archaeological Evaluation of a Bronze Age, Iron Age and Romano-British Riverside Landscape.* (Cambridge Archaeological Unit Report 753.)

Bryant, S.R. & R. Niblett, 1997. The late Iron Age in Hertfordshire and the north Chilterns, in *Reconstructing Iron Age Societies*, ed. A. Gwilt & C. Haselgrove. Oxford: Oxbow Monograph 71, 270–81.

Buikstra, J.E. & D. Ubelaker, 1994. *Standards for Data Collection from Human Skeletal Remains.* Columbia (MO): Missouri Archaeological Society.

Butler, C., 2005. *Prehistoric Flintwork.* Stroud: Tempus.

Carter, G.A., 1998. *Excavations at the Orsett 'Cock' Enclosure, 1976.* (East Anglian Archaeological Report 86.) Chelmsford: Essex County Council Archaeology Section.

Cessford, C. & D. Mackay, 2004. *Cambridgeshire Guided Busway: a Series of Archaeological Evaluations.* (Cambridge Archaeological Unit Report 591.)

Chaplin, R.E. & F. McCormick, 1986. The animal bones, in *Baldock: the Excavation of a Roman and Pre-Roman Settlement 1968–72*, by I.M. Stead & V. Rigby. (Britannia Monograph Series 7.) London: Society for the Promotion of Roman Studies.

Clark, J.G.D., 1933. Review: C. Fox 'The Personality of Britain'. *Antiquity* 7, 232–4.

Clark, J.G.D., 1960. Excavations at the Neolithic site at Hurst Fen, Mildenhall, Suffolk (1954, 1957 and 1958). *Proceedings of the Prehistoric Society* 26, 202–45.

Clarke, D.L. (ed.), 1972. *Models in Archaeology.* London: Methuen.

Clarke, D.V., 1970. Bone dice and the Scottish Iron Age. *Proceedings of the Prehistoric Society* 36, 214–32.

Clay, P., 2002. *The Prehistory of the East Midlands Claylands: Aspects of Settlement and Land-use from the Mesolithic to the Iron Age in Central England.* (Leicester Archaeology Monograph 9.) Leicester: University of Leicester Archaeological Services.

Cohen, A. & D. Serjeantson, 1986. *A Manual for the Identification of Bird Bones from Archaeological Sites.* London: Archetype Publications.

Coles, J.M., 1987. *Meare Village East: the Excavations of A. Bulleid and H. St. George Gray 1932–1956.* (Somerset Levels Papers 13.) Thorverton: Somerset Levels Project.

Collins, A.E.P., 1948. An early Iron Age Site on Hills Road, Cambridge. *Proceedings of the Cambridge Antiquarian Society* 41, 76–7.

Connor, A., 2000. *Middle Iron Age Activity at 90 Glebe Road, Cambridge: Further Investigations.* (Cambridge County Council Archaeological Field Unit Report A160.)

Cooke, N., F. Brown & C. Phillpotts, 2008. *From Hunter Gatherers to Huntsmen: a History of the Stansted Landscape.* Oxford & Salisbury: Framework Archaeology.

Cool, H.E.M., 1998. Personal ornaments other than brooches, in *Roman Castleford. Excavations 1974-85*, vol. 1: *The Small Finds*, eds. H.E.M. Cool & C. Philo. Wakefield: Yorkshire Archaeology, 57–61.

Coombs, D., 2001. Metalwork, in *The Flag Fen Basin. Archaeology and Environment of a Fenland Landscape*, by

F. Pryor. London: English Heritage, 255–317.

Cooper, A., 2003. *Cambridge Airport Replacement Terminal: an Archaeological Evaluation.* (Cambridge Archaeological Unit Report 523.)

Cooper, A. & M. Edmonds, 2007. *Past and Present: Excavations at Broom, Bedfordshire 1996–2005.* Oxford: Cambridge Archaeological Unit/Oxbow Books.

Cra'ster, M.D., 1961. The Aldwick Iron Age settlement, Barley, Hertfordshire. *Proceedings of the Cambridge Antiquarian Society* 54, 22–46.

Cra'ster, M.D., 1969. New Addenbrooke's Iron Age site, Long Road, Cambridge. *Proceedings of the Cambridge Antiquarian Society* 62, 21–8.

Cra'ster, M.D., 1982. Further finds from motorway spoil-heaps. *Proceedings of the Cambridge Antiquarian Society* 71, 58.

Crummy, N., 1983. *The Roman Small Finds from Excavations in Colchester 1971–9.* (Colchester Archaeological Report 2.) Colchester: Colchester Archaeological Trust.

Crummy, N., 1997. From bracelets to battle-honours: military armillae from the Roman Conquest of Britain, in *Image, Craft and the Classical World. Essays in Honour of Donald Bailey and Catherine Johns*, ed. N. Crummy. (Monographies Instrumentum 29.) Paris: Éditions Monique Mergoil, 92–106.

Crummy, P,. S. Benfield, N. Crummy, V. Rigby & D. Shimmin, 2007. *Stanway: an Elite Burial Site at Camulodunum.* (Britannia Monograph Series 24.) London: Society for the Promotion of Roman Studies.

Curle, J., 1932. Objects of Roman and Provincial Roman origin found on sites in Scotland not definitely associated with Roman constructions. *Proceedings of the Society of Antiquaries of Scotland* 66, 277–397.

Curwen, E.C., 1937. Querns. *Antiquity* 11(42), 133–51.

Dannell, G. & P. Wild, 1987. *Longthorpe II: The Military Works-depot: an Episode in Landscape History.* (Britannia Monograph Series 8). London: Society for the Promotion of Roman Studies.

Dauncey, K.D.M., 1942. The strategy of Anglo-Saxon invasion. *Antiquity* 16, 51–63.

Dauncey, K.D.M., 1952. Phosphate content of soils on archaeological sites. *Advancement of Science* 9, 33–7.

Davidson, I. & G.J. Curtis, 1973. An Iron Age site on the land of the Plant Breeding Institute, Trumpington. *Proceedings of the Cambridge Antiquarian Society* 64, 1–14.

Davis, N., 1998. Archaeological investigations in Cambridgeshire: a national overview. *Proceedings of the Cambridge Antiquarian Society* 87, 93–6.

Davis, S.J.M., 1987. *The Archaeology of Animals.* London: Batsford.

Dawson, D., 2007. First World War practice trenches in Pullingshill Wood, Marlow: an interpretation and evaluation. *Records of Buckinghamshire* 47(1), 179–90.

Dawson, M., 2000. The Iron Age and Roman periods: a landscape in transition, in *Prehistoric, Roman and post-Roman Landscapes of the Great Ouse Valley*, ed. M. Dawson. (CBA Research Report 119.) York: Council for British Archaeology, 107–30.

Deegan, A., 2007. Archaeology on the Boulder Clay in Northamptonshire: some results from the Northamptonshire National Mapping Programme Project, in *Populating Clay Landscapes*, eds. J. Mills & R. Palmer. Stroud: Tempus, 104–19.

Deetz, J., 1977. *In Small Things Forgotten: the Archeology of Early American Life.* New York (NY): Anchor Books.

Denison, S., 1996. News. *British Archaeology* 16: July 1996.

Dickens, A., 1998. *Barrington Quarry, Barrington, Cambridgeshire: Archaeological Desktop Study and Fieldwalking.* (Cambridge Archaeological Unit Report 276.)

Dickens, A., 2002. *Clay Farm, Trumpington, Cambridge, Archaeological Desktop Assessment.* (Cambridge Archaeological Unit Report 506.)

Dickens, A. 2005. *Trumpington Meadows: Desktop Study, Fieldwalking, Geophysical Survey and Watching Brief.* (Cambridge Archaeological Unit Report 681.)

Dickens, A., M. Knight & G. Appleby, 2006. *Barrington Cement Quarry, Cambridgeshire: Archaeological Evaluation Below Barrington Ridge.* (Cambridge Archaeological Unit Report 715.)

Dobney, K., 2001. A place at the table: the role of vertebrate zooarchaeology within a Roman research agenda for Britain, in *Britons and Romans: Advancing an Archaeological Agenda*, eds. S. James & M. Millet. (CBA Research Report 125.) York: Council for British Archaeology, 36–45.

Dodwell, N., S. Lucy & J. Tipper, 2004. Anglo-Saxons on the Cambridge Backs: the Criminology site settlement and King's Garden Hostel cemetery. *Proceedings of the Cambridge Antiquarian Society* 93, 95–124.

Driesch, A. von den, 1976. *A Guide to the Measurement of Animal Bones from Archaeological Sites.* (Peabody Museum Bulletin 1.) Harvard (MA): Peabody Museum of Archaeology and Ethnology.

Driesch, A. von den & J. Boessneck, 1974. Kritische Anmerkungen zur Widerristhöhenberechnung aus Längenmaßen vor und frühgeschichtlicher Tierknochen. *Saugetierkundliche Mitteilungen* 22, 325–48.

Driver, T.G., 2007. *Pembrokeshire: Historic Landscapes from the Air.* Aberystwyth: Royal Commission on the Ancient and Historical Monuments of Wales.

Drury, P.J., 1988. *The Mansio and Other Sites in the South-eastern Sector of Caesaromagus.* (CBA Research Report 66.) London: Chelmsford Archaeological Trust & Council for British Archaeology.

Edmonds, M., 1995: *Stone Tools and Society: Working Stone in Neolithic and Bronze Age Britain.* London: Batsford.

Edmonds, M., C. Evans & D. Gibson, 1999. Assembly and collection: lithic complexes in the Cambridgeshire Fenlands. *Proceedings of the Prehistoric Society* 65, 47–87.

Eggers, H.J., 1951. *Der Römische Import im Freien Germanien.* (Atlas der Urgeschichte 1.) Hamburg: Hamburgisches Museum für Volkerkunde und Vorgeschichte.

Eggers, H.J., 1966. Römische Bronzegefässe, in *Britannien, Jahrbuch des römisch-germanischen Zentral museum, Mainz* 13, 67–164.

Ellis, R & S. Ratkai, 2001. Late Saxon and medieval village remains at Longstanton, Cambridgeshire, in *Four Sites in Cambridgeshire: Excavations at Pode Hall Farm, Paston, Longstanton and Bassingbourn, 1996–7*, by P. Ellis, G. Coates & R. Cuttler. Oxford: British Archaeological Reports 322, 63–103.

Ellison, A. & J. Harriss, 1972. Settlement and land use in the prehistory and early history of southern England: a study based on locational models, in *Models in Archaeology*, ed. D.L. Clarke. London: Methuen, 911–62.

Erith, F.H. & I.H. Longworth, 1960. A Bronze Age Urnfield on Vinces Farm, Ardleigh, Essex. *Proceedings of the Prehistoric Society* 45, 178–192.

Evans, C., 1989. Archaeology and modern times: Bersu's Woodbury 1938/39. *Antiquity* 63, 436–50.

Evans, C., 1990. *Archaeological Investigations at Swavesey, Cambridgeshire, 1990.* (Cambridge Archaeological Unit Report 4.)

Evans, C., 1991. *Archaeological Investigations at Hatton's Farm, Longstanton, Cambridgeshire.* (Cambridge Archaeological Unit Report 16.)

Evans, C., 1997. Sentimental prehistories: the construction of the fenland past. *Journal of European Archaeology* 5, 105–136.

Evans, C., 1999. The Lingwood Wells: a waterlogged first millennium BC settlement at Cottenham, Cambridgeshire. *Proceedings of the Cambridge Antiquarian Society* 87, 11–30.

Evans, C., 2000a. Testing the ground - sampling strategies, in *The Fenland Management Project: Excavations 1991–1995*, eds. A. Crowson, T. Lane & J. Reeve. (Lincolnshire Archaeology and Heritage Reports Series 3.), 15–21; 23–73.

Evans, C., 2000b. Archaeological distributions: the problem with dots (#3), in *An Atlas of Cambridgeshire and Huntingdonshire History*, eds. T. Kirby & S. Oosthuizen. Cambridge: Centre for Regional Studies, Anglia Polytechnic University, 3–4.

Evans, C., 2002a. Metalwork and 'Cold Claylands': Pre-Iron Age occupation on the Isle of Ely, in *Through Wet and Dry: Essays in Honour of David Hall*, eds. T. Lane & J. Coles. (Lincolnshire Archaeology and Heritage Reports Series 5 and WARP Occasional Paper 17.) Sleaford: Heritage Trust of Lincolnshire, 33–53.

Evans, C., 2002b. *The Archaeology of the Addenbrooke's Environs: a Desktop Essay.* (Cambridge Archaeological Unit Report 497.)

Evans, C., 2003a. *Power and Island Communities; Excavation of the Wardy Hill Ringwork, Coveney, Isle of Ely.* (East Anglian Archaeology Report 103.) Cambridge: Cambridge Archaeological Unit.

Evans, C., 2003b. Britons and Romans at Chatteris: investigations at Langwood Farm, Cambridgeshire. *Britannia* 34, 175–264.

Evans, C., 2007. 'Delineating objects': nineteenth century antiquarian culture and the project of archaeology, in *Visions of Antiquity: the Society of Antiquaries of London 1707–2007 (Archaeologia 111)*, ed. S. Pearce. London: Society of Antiquaries of London, 266–305.

Evans, C. & G. Appleby, forthcoming 2009. Historiography and fieldwork: Wyman Abbott's Great Fengate ring-ditch (A lost manuscript found). *Proceedings of the Prehistoric Society.*

Evans, C. & A. Dickens, 2002. *Longstanton New Settlement, Cambridgeshire: Archaeological Desktop Assessment.* (Cambridge Archaeological Unit Report 489.)

Evans, C. & I. Hodder, 2006a. *A Woodland Archaeology: the Haddenham Project (I).* (McDonald Institute Monographs.) Cambridge: McDonald Institute for Archaeological Research.

Evans, C. & I. Hodder, 2006b. *Marshland Communities and Cultural Landscapes from the Bronze Age to Present Day: The Haddenham Project (II).* (McDonald Institute Monographs.) Cambridge: McDonald Institute for Archaeological Research.

Evans, C. & C. Humphrey, 2002. The afterlives of the Mongolian yurt: the 'archaeology' of a Chinese tourist camp. *Journal of Material Culture* 7, 189–210.

Evans, C. & C. Humphrey, 2003. History, timelessness and the monumental: the oboos of the Mergen environs, Inner Mongolia. *Cambridge Archaeological Journal* 13(2), 195–211.

Evans, C. & M. Knight, 2000. A fenland delta: later Prehistoric land-use in the lower Ouse Reaches, in *Prehistoric, Roman and Saxon landscape studies in the Great Ouse Valley*, ed. M. Dawson. (CBA Research Report 119.) York: Council for British Archaeology, 89–106.

Evans, C. & M. Knight, 2001. The 'community of builders': the Barleycroft post alignments, in *Bronze Age Landscapes: Tradition and Transformation*, ed. J. Brück. Oxford: Oxbow Books, 83–98.

Evans, C. & M. Knight, 2002. A Great Circle: investigations at Arbury Camp, Cambridge. *Proceedings of the Cambridge Antiquarian Society* 91, 23–53.

Evans, C. & G. Lucas, forthcoming. *Hinterlands: the Archaeology of West Cambridge.* (CAU Landscape Archives/New Archaeologies of the Cambridge Region 2.) Cambridge: Cambridge Archaeological Unit.

Evans, C. & D. Mackay, 2004. *Longstanton, Cambridgeshire - A Village Hinterland: Archaeological Investigations 2004.* (Cambridge Archaeological Unit Report 696.)

Evans, C., J. Pollard & M. Knight, 1999. Life in woods: tree-throws, 'settlement' and forest cognition. *Oxford Journal of Archaeology* 18, 241–54.

Evans, C., D. Mackay & L. Webley, 2004. *Excavations at Addenbrooke's Hospital: the Hutchison Site, Cambridge.* (Cambridge Archaeological Report 609.)

Evans, C., M. Edmonds & S. Boreham, 2006a. 'Total archaeology' and model landscapes: excavation of the Great Wilbraham causewayed enclosure, Cambridgeshire, 1975–76. *Proceedings of the Prehistoric Society* 72, 113–62.

Evans, C., D. Mackay & G. Appleby, 2006b. *Longstanton, Cambridgeshire - a Village Hinterland (II): The 2005 Evaluation.* (Cambridge Archaeological Unit Report 711.)

Evans, C., D. Mackay & R. Patten, 2006c. *The Archaeology of Clay and Glebe Farms, South Cambridge.* (Cambridge

Archaeological Unit Report 708.)

Evans, C., M. Knight & L. Webley, 2007a. An island prehistory: Iron Age settlement, 'poverty' and Romanization on the Isle of Ely. *Proceedings of the Cambridge Antiquarian Society* 96, 41–78.

Evans, C., D. Mackay & G. Appleby 2007b. *Longstanton, Cambridgeshire - a Village Hinterland (III): The 2005 Evaluation.* (Cambridge Archaeological Unit Report No. 755.)

Evans, C., with G. Appleby, S. Lucy & R. Regan, forthcoming a. *Process and History: Prehistoric and Roman Fen-edge Communities at Colne Fen, Earith (The Archaeology of the Lower Ouse Valley, vol. I.)* Cambridge: McDonald Institute for Archaeological Research.

Evans, C. with E. Beadsmoore, M. Brudenell & G. Lucas, forthcoming b. *Fengate Revisited: Further Fen-edge Excavations, Bronze Age Fieldsystems & Settlement and the Wyman Abbott/Leeds Archives* (CAU Landscape Archives Series: Historiography and Fieldwork.) Oxford: Oxbow Books.

Evans, J., 1876. Note on a Proposed International Code for Symbols for the use on Archaeological Maps. *Journal of the Anthropological Institute of Great Britain and Ireland* 5, 427–36.

Evans, J., 1893. An archaeological survey of Hertfordshire. *Archaeologia* 53, 245–62.

Evans, J., 1990. The Cherry Hinton finewares. *Journal of Roman Pottery Studies* 3, 18–29.

Evans, J., 1992. Some notes on the Horningsea Roman pottery. *Journal of Roman Pottery Studies* 4, 33–43.

Evans, J., 1998. Belgic pottery and kiln furniture from Swavesey, in *Iron Age and Medieval Activity at Blackhorse Lane, Swavesey*, by J. Roberts. (Cambridgeshire County Council Archaeological Field Unit Report 151.)

Evans, J., 2001. Material approaches to the identification of different Romano-British site types, in *Britons and Romans: Advancing an Archaeological Agenda*, eds. S. James & M. Millett. (CBA Research Report 125.) York: Council for British Archaeology, 26–35.

Evans, R., 2007. The weather and other factors controlling the appearance of crop marks on clay and 'difficult' soil, in *Populating Clay Landscapes*, eds. J. Mills & R. Palmer. Stroud: Tempus 16–27.

Evison, V.I., 1987. *Dover: the Buckland Anglo-Saxon Cemetery.* (Historic Buildings and Monuments Commission of England. Archaeological Report 3.) London: Historic Buildings and Monuments Commission of England.

Farrand, B. & E. Webber, 1776. *A New Display of the Beauties of England; or, A Description of the Most Elegant or Magnificent Public Edifices, Royal Palaces.* London: R. Goadby.

Fell, C.I., 1949. Bronze razor from Hills Road, Cambridge. *Proceedings of the Cambridge Antiquarian Society* 42, 128.

Fitzpatrick, A.P., 1997. *Archaeological Excavations on the Route of the A27 Westhampnett Bypass, West Sussex, 1992.* vol. 2: *the Late Iron Age, Romano-British, and Anglo-Saxon Cemeteries.* (Wessex Archaeology Report no. 12.) Salisbury: Trust for Wessex Archaeology.

Foot, W., 2006. *Beaches, Fields, Streets and Hills: the Anti-invasion Landscapes of England, 1940.* (CBA Research Report 144.) York: Council for British Archaeology.

Ford, H.S., 1987. Chronological and functional aspects of flint assemblages, in *Lithic Analysis and Later British Prehistory: Some Problems and Approaches*, eds. A.G. Brown and M.R. Edmonds. (Reading Studies in Archaeology 2/British Archaeological Report 162.) Oxford: BAR, 67–83.

Ford, H.S., R. Bradley, J. Hawkes & P. Fisher, 1984. Flintworking in the Metal Age. *Oxford Journal of Archaeology* 3, 157–73.

Foster, K., 1881. An account of the excavations of an Anglo-Saxon cemetery at Barrington, Cambridgeshire. *Proceedings of the Cambridge Antiquarian Society* 5, 5–33.

Fox, A., 2000. *Aileen: a Pioneering Archaeologist.* Leominster: Gracewing.

Fox, C., 1918. *Ancient Military Earthworks in the Cambridge District. Buzz!* "B" Company No. 2 Officer Cadet Battalion. Cambridge: University of Cambridge Library holding.

Fox, C., 1923. *The Archaeology of the Cambridge Region.* Cambridge: Cambridge University Press.

Fox, C., 1932. *The Personality of Britain.* Cardiff: National Museum of Wales.

Fox, C., 1947. Reflections on 'The Archaeology of the Cambridge Region'. *Cambridge Historical Journal* 9, 1–21.

Fox C. & T.C. Lethbridge, 1925. The La Tène and Romano-British cemetery, Guilden Morden, Cambs. *Proceedings of the Cambridge Antiquarian Society* 27, 49–71.

France, N.E. & B. Gobel, 1985. *The Romano-British Temple at Harlow, Essex.* Harlow: West Essex Archaeological Group.

French, C.A.I., 2004. Evaluation survey and excavation at Wandlebury Ringwork, Cambridgeshire, 1994–7. *Proceedings of the Cambridge Antiquarian Society* 93, 15–66.

French, D.H., 1972. Excavations at Cass Hasan III 1969–70, in *Papers in Economic History: Studies by Members and Associates of the British Academy Major Research Project in the Early History of Agriculture*, ed. E.S. Higgs. Cambridge: Cambridge University Press, 182–8.

Frend, W.H.C., 1998. Roman kilns at Penfold Farm, Milton. *Proceedings of the Cambridge Antiquarian Society* 87, 45–7.

Frere, D.H.S., 1943. Late Neolithic Grooved Ware near Cambridge. *Antiquaries Journal* 23, 34–41.

Friendship-Taylor, R., 1999. *Late La Tène Pottery of the Nene and Welland Valleys, Northamptonshire.* (British Archaeological Reports 280.) Oxford: Archaeopress.

Fryer, V. 2002. Quantification and assessment of the plant macrofossils and other remains, in Neolithic and Bronze Age occupation in the Yare Valley: excavations at Three Score Road, Bowthorpe, 1999–2000, by J.W. Percival. *Norfolk Archaeological Journal* 44(1), 59–88.

Fulford, M. & J. Timby, 2001. Timing devices, fermentation vessels, 'ritual' piercings? A consideration of deliberately 'holed' pots from Silchester and elsewhere. *Britannia* 32, 293–7.

Gardiner, J. & T. Williamson, 1993. Archaeologies of region, in *Flatlands and Wetlands: Current Themes in East Anglian Archaeology*, ed. J. Gardiner. (East Anglian Archaeology 50.) Dereham: Norfolk Archaeological Unit, 171–81.

Garrow, D., 2006. *Pits, Settlement and Deposition during the Neolithic and Early Bronze Age in East Anglia*. (British Archaeological Report 414.) Oxford: BAR.

Garrow, D., E. Beadsmoore & M. Knight, 2005. Pit clusters and the temporality of occupation: an earlier Neolithic site at Kilverstone, Thetford, Norfolk. *Proceedings of the Prehistoric Society* 71, 139–57.

Gdaniec, K., 1993. *Archaeological Investigations at Fulbourn Hospital, Fulbourn, Cambridge*. (Cambridge Archaeological Unit Report 83.)

Gdaniec, K., M. Edmonds & P. Wiltshire, 2008. *A Line across Land: Fieldwork on the Isleham-Ely pipeline.* (East Anglian Archaeology 121.) Cambridge: Cambridge Archaeological Unit.

Germany, M., 2007. *Neolithic and Bronze Age Monuments and Middle Iron Age Settlement at Lodge Farm, St Osyth, Essex.* (East Anglian Archaeology 117.) Chelmsford: Essex County Council.

Gerrard, C., 1989. *Slate Hall Farm, Cambridgeshire. Stage 1 Archaeological Assessment.* (Cotswold Archaeological Trust Report 8906.)

Gibson, D. & G. Lucas, 2002. Pre-Flavian kilns at Greenhouse Farm and the social context of early Roman pottery production in Cambridgeshire. *Britannia* 33, 95–127.

Grant, A., 2002. Scales of reference: archaeozoological approaches to the study of behaviours and change, in *Bones and the Man: Studies in Honour of Don Brothwell*, eds. K. Dobney & T. O'Connor. Oxford: Oxbow, 79–87.

Green, F.J., 1985. Evidence for domestic cereal use at Maxey, in *Archaeology and Environment in the Lower Welland Valley*, by F.M. Pryor & C.A.I. French. (East Anglian Archaeology 27.) Cambridge: Cambridge Archaeological Committee, 224–32.

Gregory, T., 1992. *Excavations in Thetford, 1980–1982: Fison Way.* (East Anglian Archaeology 53.) Gressenhall: Norfolk Field Archaeology Division.

Grieg, J.R.A., 1991. The British Isles, in *Progress in Old World Palaeoethnobotany*, eds. W. Van Zeist, K. Wasylikowa & K. Behre. Rotterdam: A.A. Balkema, 299–334.

Grigson, C., 1982. Sex and age determination of some bones and teeth of domestic cattle: review of the literature, in *Ageing and Sexing Animal Bones from Archaeological Sites*, eds. B. Wilson, C. Grigson & S. Payne. (British Archaeologioal Reports 109.) Oxford: BAR, 7–23.

Gwilt, A. & C. Haselgrove (eds.), 1997. *Reconstructing Iron Age Societies: New Approaches to the British Iron Age.* (Oxbow Monograph 71.) Oxford: Oxbow.

Haigh, D., 1975. *A Correlation between the Archaeological Sites and Field Names: a Survey of Parishes Along the Line of the Northern and Western By-passes of Cambridge.* Cambridge Collection.

Halkon, P. & M. Millett, 1999. *Rural Settlement and Industry: Studies in the Iron Age and Roman Archaeology of Lowland East Yorkshire.* Leeds: Yorkshire Archaeological Society and East Riding Archaeological Society.

Hall, A., 2001. *An Archaeological Desk-based Assessment of Downing College Sports Field, Long Road, Cambridge.* (Cambridge Archaeological Unit Report 418.)

Hall, D., 1991. Field surveys in Bedfordshire. *Bedfordshire Archaeology* 19, 51–6.

Hall, D.N. & J.M. Coles, 1994. *Fenland Survey: an Essay in Landscape and Persistence.* London: English Heritage.

Hall, D. & J. Hutchings, 1972. The distribution of archaeological sites between the Nene and the Ouse Valleys. *Bedfordshire Archaeology* 7, 1–16.

Halstead, P. & P. Collins, 2002. Sorting the sheep from the goats: morphological distinctions between the mandibles and mandibular teeth of adult *Ovis* and *Capra*. *Journal of Archaeological Science* 29, 545–53.

Harcourt, R.A., 1974. The dog in prehistoric and early historic Britain. *Journal of Archaeological Science* 1, 151–75.

Hartley, B.R. 1957. The Wandlebury Iron Age hillfort excavations of 1955–56. *Proceedings of the Cambridge Antiquarian Society* 50, 1–27.

Hartley, B.R., 1960. Notes on pottery from some Romano-British kilns in the Cambridge Area. *Proceedings of the Cambridgeshire Antiquarian Society* 53, 23–8.

Haselgrove, C.C., 1982. Wealth, prestige and power: the dynamics of Late Iron Age centralization in south eastern England, in *Ranking, Resource and Exchange*, eds. C. Renfrew & S. Shennan. Cambridge: Cambridge University Press, 79–88.

Haselgrove, C.C., 1984. Romanization before the conquest: Gaulish precedents and British consequences, in *Military and civilian in Roman Britain*, eds. T. Blagg & A. King. (British Archaeological Reports 136.) Oxford: BAR, 5–63.

Haselgrove, C.C., 1987. *Iron Age Coinage in South-East England: the Archaeological Context.* (British Archaeological Reports 174.) Oxford: BAR.

Haselgrove, C.C., 1997. Iron Age brooch deposition and chronology, in *Reconstructing Iron Age Societies: New Approaches to the British Iron Age*, eds. A. Gwilt & C. Haselgrove. (Oxbow Monograph 71.) Oxford: Oxbow, 51–72.

Haselgrove, C.C., 2003. The brooch assemblage in wider perspective, in Britons and Romans at Chatteris: investigations at Langwood Farm, Cambridgeshire, by C. Evans. *Britannia* 34, 239–42.

Havis, R. & H. Brooks, 2004. *Excavations at Stansted Airport, 1986–91.* (East Anglian Archaeology Report 107.) Chelmsford: Heritage Conservation and Essex County Council.

Hawkes, C.F.C. & C.I. Fell, 1943. The Early Iron Age settlement at Fengate. Peterborough. *Archaeological Journal* 100, 188–223.

Hawkes, C.F.C. & M.R. Hull, 1947. *Camulodunum.* London: Society of Antiquaries of London.

Hawkes, J., 1951. *A Land.* London: Cresset Press.

Hegarty, C. & S. Newsome, 2007. *Suffolk's Defended Shore: Coastal Fortifications from the Air.* Swindon: English Heritage.

Hermsen, I., 2000. Een opmerkelijke dobbelsteen uit Didam (Gld.). *Westerheem Nr. 4.* August 2000.

Herne, A., 1991. The lithic assemblage, in *Excavations at Grimes Graves, Norfolk*, fasicule III, eds. I. Longworth, A. Herne, G. Varndell & S. Needham. London: British Museum, 21–93.

Heslop, D., 1988. The study of the beehive quern. *Scottish Archaeological Review* 5, 59–77.

Hey, G. & M. Lacey, 2001. *Evaluation of Archaeological Decision-making Processes and Sampling Strategies.* Oxford: Oxford Archaeological Unit.

Hill, J.D., 1995. *Ritual and Rubbish in the Iron Age of Wessex.* (British Archaeological Report 242.) Oxford: Tempus Reparatum.

Hill, J.D., 1997. The end of one kind of body and the beginning of another kind of body? Toilet instruments and 'Romanization' in southern England during the first century AD, in *Re-constructing the Iron Age*, eds. A. Gwilt and C. Haselgrove. (Oxbow Monograph 71.) Oxford: Oxbow, 96–107.

Hill, J.D., 2002. Just about the potter's wheel? Using and depositing Middle and later Iron Age pots in East Anglia, in *Prehistoric Britain: the Ceramic Basis*, eds. J.D. Hill & A. Woodward. Oxford: Oxbow, 143–60.

Hill, J.D., C. Evans & M. Alexander, 1999. The Hinxton Rings - A Late Iron Age cemetery at Hinxton, Cambridgeshire, with a reconsideration of northern Aylesford-Swarling distributions. *Proceedings of the Prehistoric Society* 65, 243–74.

Hillman, G.C., 1981. Reconstructing crop husbandry practices from charred remains of crops, in *Farming Practice in British Prehistory*, ed. R.J. Mercer. Edinburgh: Edinburgh University Press, 123–62.

Hingley, R., 2000. *Roman Officers and English Gentlemen: The Imperial Origins of Roman Archaeology.* London: Routledge.

Hinman, M., 1999a. *Granhams Farm Golf Course - Neolithic to Medieval; the Archaeological Landscape surrounding Granhams Farm, from Nine Wells to Hinton Way, Great Shelford, Cambs: An Evaluation.* (Cambridgeshire County Council Archaeological Field Unit Report 167.)

Hinman, M., 1999b. *Ritualistic Prehistoric Activity and Inhumations on land adjacent to Babraham Road, Cambridge.* (Cambridgeshire County Council Archaeological Field Unit PXA Report 10.)

Hinman, M., 2001. Ritual activity at the foot of the Gog Magog Hills, Cambridge, in *Bronze Age Landscapes: Tradition and Transformation*, ed. J. Bruck. Oxford: Oxbow, 33–40.

Hinman, M., 2003. *A Late Iron Age Farmstead and Romano-British Site at Haddon, Peterborough.* (British Archaeological Reports 358.) Oxford: BAR.

Hinman, M., 2004. *Neolithic, Bronze Age and Iron Age Activity on land adjacent to Hauxton Road, Trumpington, Cambridge.* (Cambridgeshire County Council Archaeological Field Unit Report 706.)

Hinman, M., forthcoming. *Cambridge Park & Ride Sites.* East Anglian Archaeology.

Hodder, I., 1982a. *The Archaeology of the M11: Excavations at Wendens Ambo.* London: Passmore Edwards Museum.

Hodder, I., 1982b. *Symbolic and Structural Archaeology.* Cambridge: Cambridge University Press.

Hughes, T. McK., 1891. On some antiquities found near Hauxton, Cambridgeshire. *Proceedings of the Cambridge Antiquarian Society* 7, 24–8.

Hughes, T. McK., 1904a. The War Ditches, near Cherry Hinton, Cambridge. *Proceedings of the Cambridge Antiquarian Society* 10, 452–81.

Hughes, T. McK., 1904b. On the Potter's Field at Horningsea, with a comparative notice of the kilns and furnaces found in the neighbourhood. *Proceedings of the Cambridge Antiquarian Society* 10, 174–94.

Humphrey, J., 2003. The utilization and technology of flint in the British Iron Age, in *Re-searching the Iron Age: Selected Papers from the Proceedings of the Iron Age Research Student Seminars, 1999 and 2000*, ed. J. Humphrey. (Leicester Archaeology Monographs No. 11.) Leicester: School of Archaeology and Ancient History, University of Leicester, 17–23.

Humphrey, J., 2004. The use of flint in the British Iron Age: results from some recent research, in *Lithics in Action: Papers from the Conference Lithic Studies in the Year 2000*, eds. E.A. Walker, F. Wenban-Smith & F. Healey. (Lithic Studies Society Occasional Paper 8). Oxford: Oxbow, 243–51.

Hurst, J.G., 1976. The pottery, in *The Archaeology of Anglo-Saxon England*, ed. D.M. Wilson. Cambridge: Cambridge University Press, 283–348.

Hussen, C.M., 1983. *A Rich Late La Tène Burial at Hertford Heath Hertfordshire.* (British Museum Occasional Paper 44.) London: British Museum Press.

Hutchinson, V., 1986. *Bacchus in Britain: the Evidence of his Cult.* (British Archaeological Reports 151.) Oxford: BAR.

Hutton, J. & C. Evans, 2007. *NCP Car Park, Addenbrooke's Hospital, Cambridge: Archaeological Investigations.* (Cambridge Archaeological Unit Report 778.)

Hylton, T., 1994. Other non-ferrous objects, in *Bancroft: a Late Bronze Age/Iron Age Settlement, Roman Villa and Temple-Mausoleum*, vols. 1 & 2, by R.J. Williams & R.J. Zeepvat. (Buckinghamshire Archaeological Society Monograph 7.) Aylesbury: Buckinghamshire Archaeological Society, 303–321.

Isler, H.P., 2005. Grabungen auf dem Monte Lato 2004. *Antike Kunst* 48, 103–11.

Jackson, D. & B. Dix, 1987. Late Iron Age and Roman settlement at Weekley, Northants. *Northamptonshire Archaeology* 21, 41–93.

Jackson, R.P.J., 1990. *Camerton. The Late Iron Age and Early Roman Metalwork.* London: British Museum Press.

Jackson, R.P.J. & T.W. Potter, 1996. *Excavations at Stonea, Cambridgeshire, 1980–85.* London: British Museum Press.

Kemp, S., 1993. *Cambridge Southern Relief Road: Archaeological Field Evaluation.* (Cambridgeshire County Council Archaeological Field Unit Report 85.)

Kennett. D.H., 1970 The Shefford burial. *Bedfordshire Magazine* 12(93), 201–3.

Kennett, D.H., 1973. Seventh century cemeteries in the Ouse Valley. *Bedfordshire Archaeological Journal* 8, 99–108.

King, A., 1991. Food production and consumption, in *Britain in the Roman Period: Recent Trends*, by R.F.J. Jones. Sheffield: J.R. Collis, 15–20.

Kirby T. & S. Oosthuizen (eds.), 2000. *An Atlas of Cambridgeshire and Huntingdonshire History*. Cambridge: Centre for Regional Studies, Anglia Polytechnic University.

Leith, S., 1996. *An Archaeological Evaluation at the Perse School for Boys, Hills Road, Cambridge*. (Cambridgeshire County Council Archaeological Field Unit Report A89.)

Lethbridge, T.C., 1948. Further excavations at the War Ditches. *Proceedings of the Cambridge Antiquarian Society* 42, 117–27.

Lethbridge, T.C., 1953. Burial of an Iron Age warrior at Snailwell. *Proceedings of the Cambridge Antiquarian Society* 47, 25–37.

Lethbridge, T.C., 1957. *Gogmagog: the Buried Gods*. London: Book Club Associates.

Lethbridge, T.C., n.d. Autobiography. Unpublished manuscript.

Lock, G. & B. Molyneaux (eds.), 2006. *Confronting Scale in Archaeology: Issues of Theory and Practice*. New York (NY): Springer.

Longworth, I.H., A. Ellison & V. Rigby, 1988. *Excavations at Grimes Graves, Norfolk 1972–1976, fascicule 2: The Neolithic and Bronze Age Pottery*. London: British Museum Press.

Lovejoy, C.O., R.S. Meindl, R.P. Mensforth & T.J. Barton, 1985. Multifactorial determination of skeletal age at death: A method and blind tests of its accuracy. *American Journal of Physical Anthropology* 68, 1–14.

Lucas, G., 1997. Prehistoric, Roman and post-Roman pottery, in *The Archaeology of the St Neots to Duxford Gas Pipeline 1994*, eds. J. Price, I.P. Brooks & D.J. Maynard. (British Archaeological Reports 255.) Oxford: BAR, 49–88.

Lucas, G., 1999. *Roman Pottery Production in Cambridgeshire*. Supplement Report to CUMAA/Crowther-Benyon Fund.

Lucy, S., J. Tipper & A. Dickens, forthcoming. *The Anglo-Saxon Settlement and Cemetery at Bloodmoor Hill, Carlton Colville, Suffolk*. East Anglian Archaeology.

Lyne, M.A.B. & R.S. Jefferies, 1979. *The Alice Holt/Farnham Roman Pottery Industry*. (CBA Research Report 30.) London: Council for British Archaeology

Lyons, A., in prep. *Life and Death at Duxford, Cambridgeshire, from the Middle Iron Age to the Post-Medieval*. East Anglian Archaeology.

Mackay, D., 2002. *Addenbrooke's Electricity Substation: an Archaeological Evaluation*. (Cambridge Archaeological Unit Report 469.)

Mackay, D., 2004. *Elective Care Facility, Addenbrooke's Hospital, Cambridge: A Second Archaeological Evaluation*. (Cambridge Archaeological Unit Report 606.)

Mackreth, D.F., 1988. Excavations at an Iron Age and Roman enclosure at Werrington. *Britannia* 19, 107–19.

Mackreth, D.F., 1992. Brooches of copper alloy and of iron, in *Excavations in Thetford, 1980-1982: Fison Way*, by T. Gregory. (East Anglian Archaeology 53.) Gressenhall: Norfolk Field Archaeology Division, 120–29.

Mainman, A.J. & N.S.H. Rogers, 2000. *Craft, Industry and Everyday Life: Finds from Anglo-Scandinavian York*. (The Archaeology of York 17: The Small Finds.) York: Council for British Archaeology.

Malim, T., 1993. An Investigation of multi-period cropmarks at Manor Farm, Harston. *Proceedings of the Cambridge Antiquarian Society* 82, 11–54.

Malim, T., 1998. Prehistoric and Roman remains at Edix Hill, Barrington, Cambridgeshire. *Proceedings of the Cambridge Antiquarian Society* 86, 13–56.

Malim, T. & J. Hines, with C. Duhig, 1998. *The Anglo-Saxon Cemetery at Edix Hill (Barrington A), Cambridgeshire; Excavations 1989-1991 and a Summary Catalogue of material from the 19th Century Interventions*. (CBA Research Report 112.) York: Council for British Archaeology.

Manaseryan, M.H., K. Dobney & A. Ervynck, 1999. On the causes of perforations in archaeological domestic cattle skulls: new evidence. *International Journal of Osteoarchaeology* 9, 74–5.

Manning, W.H., 1985. *Catalogue of the Romano-British iron tools, fittings and weapons in the British Museum*. London: British Museum.

Margary, I., 1955. *Roman Roads in Britain*. London: Phoenix House.

Martin, E., 1930. Dew-Ponds. *Antiquity* 4, 347–51.

May, T., 1918. On some Early Roman finds from Plesheybury, Essex: in the public Museum at Chelmsford. *Transactions of the Essex Archaeological Society* 14, 227–32.

Maynard, D.J., R. Cleary, R. Moore, I.P. Brooks & J. Price, 1997. Excavations at Foxton, Cambridgeshire, 1994, in *The Archaeology of the St Neots to Duxford Gas Pipeline 1994*, eds. J. Price, I.P. Brooks & D.J. Maynard. (British Archaeological Report 255.) Oxford: BAR, 21–39.

McFadyen, L., 1999a *An Archaeological Evaluation at Heathfields 2, Duxford, Cambridgeshire*. (Cambridge Archaeological Unit Report 326.)

McFadyen, L., 1999b *Archaeological Fieldwalking at Heathfields 2, Duxford, Cambridgeshire*. (Cambridge Archaeological Unit Report 339.)

McOmish, D., D. Field & G. Brown, 2002 *The Field Archaeology of the Salisbury Plain Training Area*. Swindon: English Heritage.

Medleycott, M., forthcoming. *The Roman Town of Great Chesterford*. East Anglian Archaeology Report.

Miller, T.E. & M. Miller, 1982. The M11 western by-pass; three sites near Cambridge: 3 Edmundsoles, Haslingfield. *Proceedings of the Cambridge Antiquarian Society* 71, 41–72.

Mills, J., 2007. Surveying the claylands: combining aerial survey and fieldwalking methods in identifying archaeological sites on 'difficult' soils, in *Populating Clay Landscapes*, eds. J. Mills & R. Palmer. Stroud: Tempus, 132–46.

Mills, J. & R. Palmer, 2007. *Populating Clay Landscapes*. Stroud: Tempus.

Moretti, F., 1998. *Atlas of the European Novel, 1800–1900*. London: Verso.

Mortimer, R., 2001. *The Hillfort at Borough Hill, Sawston, Cambridgeshire: an Archaeological Watching Brief*. (Cambridge Archaeological Unit Report 450.)

Mortimer, R., 2005. *Neolithic, Bronze Age, Iron Age and Romano-British Occupation along the Route of the Fordham Bypass, Fordham.* (Cambridgeshire County Council Archaeological Field Unit Report 816.)

Mortimer, R. & C. Evans, 1996. *Archaeological Excavations at Hinxton Quarry, Cambridgeshire: the North Fields.* (Cambridge Archaeological Unit Report 168.)

Mortimer, R., R. Regan & S. Lucy, 2005. *The Saxon and Medieval Settlement at West Fen Road, Ely: The Ashwell Site.* (East Anglian Archaeology Report 110.) Cambridge: Cambridge Archaeological Unit.

Moss-Eccardt, J., 1988. Archaeological investigations in the Letchworth Area, 1958–1974: Blackhorse Road, Letchworth; Norton Road, Baldock; Wilbury Hill Letchworth. *Proceedings of the Cambridge Antiquarian Society* 88, 35–103.

Murphy, P., 1989. Plant remains, in A Romano-British pottery kiln at Stowmarket, by J. Plouviez. *Proceedings of the Suffolk Institute of Archaeology* 37, 1–12.

Murphy, P., 2003. Plant macrofossils and molluscs, in *Power and Island Communities: Excavations at the Wardy Hill Ringwork, Coveney, Ely,* by C. Evans. (East Anglian Archaeology 103.) Cambridge: Cambridge Archaeological Committee, 84–114.

Murray, J. & T. McDonald, 2006. Excavations at Station Road, Gamlingay Cambridgeshire, in *Anglo-Saxon Studies in Archaeology and History* 13, ed. S. Semple. Oxford: University School of Archaeology, 173–330.

Needham, S., 1995. A bowl from, Maidscross, Suffolk: burial with pottery in the Post Deverel-Rimbury period, in *'Unbaked Urns of Rudely Shape' Essays on British and Irish Pottery for Ian Longworth,* by I. Kinnes & G. Varndell. (Oxbow Monograph 55.) Oxford: Oxbow, 159–71.

Needham, S., 1996. Post Deverel Rimbury pottery, in *Excavations at Stonea, Cambridgeshire, 1980–85,* by R. Jackson & T. Potter. London. British Museum Press, 245–56.

Nenova-Merdjanova, R., 2000. Bronze vessels and the toilette in Roman times, in From the parts to the whole, vol. 2. Acta of the 13th International Bronze Congress, held at Cambridge, Massachusetts, May 28 – June 1, 1996, eds. C. Mattusch, A. Brauer & S. Knudsen. *Journal of Roman Archaeology* supplementary series 39, 201–4.

Niblett, R., 1999. *The Excavation of a Ceremonial Site at Folly Lane, Verulamium.* (Britannia Monograph Series 14.) London: Society for the Promotion of Roman Studies.

Niblett, R., 2001. *Verulamium: the Roman City of St Albans.* Stroud: Tempus.

Novotný, B., 1955. Hrob Velmože Z Počátku Doby Římské V Praze-Bubenči. *Památky Archaeologické* 46, 227–49.

Nuber, H.U., 1972. Kanne und Griffschale. Ihr Gebrauch im täglichen Leben und die Beigabe in Gräbern der römischen Kaiserzeit. *Bericht der Römisch-Germanischen Kommission* 53, 1–232.

O'Connor, T.P., 1991. *Bones from 46–54 Fishergate, York.* Dorset: York Archaeological Trust/Council for British Archaeology.

Oettel, A., 1991. *Bronzen aus Boscoreale in Berlin.* (Staatliche Museen zu Berlin.) Tübingen: Wasmuth.

Oosthuizen, S., 2003. The roots of the common fields: linking prehistoric and medieval field systems in West Cambridgeshire. *Landscapes* 1, 40–64.

Oosthuizen, S., 2006. *Landscapes Decoded: the History of Cambridgeshire's Medieval Fields.* Leicester: University of Leicester Department of English Local History and University of Hertfordshire Press.

Ortner, D.J. & W.J. Putschar, 1985. *The Identification of Pathological Conditions in Human Skeletal Remains.* Washington (DC): Smithsonian Institution Press.

Osborne, M., 2002. *20th Century Defences in Britain: Cambridgeshire including Peterborough and Huntingdon.* Market Deeping: Concrete Publications.

Parker, R., 1975. *The Common Stream.* London: William Collins.

Parry, S.J., 2006. *Raunds Area Survey: an Archaeological Study of the Landscape of Raunds, Northamptonshire 1985–94.* Oxford: Oxbow.

Partridge, C., 1981. *Skeleton Green: a Late Iron Age and Romano-British Site.* (Britannia Monograph Series 2.) London: The Society for the Promotion of Roman Studies.

Patten, R. & C. Evans, 2005. *Striplands Farm, West Longstanton, Cambridgeshire: an Archaeological Excavation.* (Cambridge Archaeological Unit Report 703.)

Pautreau, J.P., 1999. *Antran: un ensemble aristocratique du premier siècle.* Poitiers: Musées et Société des antiquaires de l'Ouest.

Payne, S., 1973. Kill-off patterns in sheep and goats: the mandibles from Asvan Kale. *Anatolian Studies* 23, 281–303.

Peacock, D.P.S., 1982. *Pottery in the Roman World: an Ethnoarchaeological Approach.* London: Longman.

Peacock, D.P.S., 1998. *The Archaeology of Stone: a Report for English Heritage.* London: English Heritage.

Pearce, R.J.H., 1999. Cases Studies in a Contextual Archaeology of Burial Practice in Roman Britain. Unpublished PhD thesis, University of Durham.

Philpott, R., 1991. *Burial Practices in Roman Britain. A Survey of Grave Treatment and Furnishing* AD *43–410.* (British Archaeological Reports 219.) Oxford: BAR.

Pollard, J., 1996a. Iron Age riverside pit alignments at St Ives, Cambridgeshire. *Proceedings of the Prehistoric Society* 62, 93–115.

Pollard, J., 1996b. *Excavations at Bourn Bridge, Pampisford, Cambridgeshire, part 2: Roman and Saxon.* (Cambridge Archaeological Unit Report 165.)

Pollard, J., 2002. The ring-ditch and the hollow: excavation of a Bronze Age 'shrine' and associated features at Pampisford, Cambridgeshire. *Proceedings of the Cambridge Antiquarian Society* 91, 117–32.

Porter, N.T. & E. Porter, 1921. Report on objects of antiquarian interest found in the Coprolite Diggings during 1917 and 1918. *Proceedings of the Cambridge Antiquarian Society* 22, 124–6.

Potter, T.W. & S.D. Trow, 1988. Puckeridge-Braughing, Hertfordshire: the Ermine Street excavations 1971–2. *Hertfordshire Archaeology* 10, 21–9.

Powell, W.R. (ed.), 1963. *A History of the County of Essex,* vol.

III: *Roman Essex. Victoria County History*. Woodbridge: Boydell and Brewer.

Priddy, D. & D.G. Buckley, 1987. An assessment of Essex enclosures, in *Excavation of a Cropmark Enclosure complex at Woodham Walter, Essex, 1976 and An Assessment of Excavated Enclosures in Essex together with a selection of cropmark sites*, by D. Buckley, J. Hedges & D. Priddy. (East Anglian Archaeology 33.) Norwich: Essex County Council Archaeology Section, 48–77.

Pryor, F., 1974. *Excavation at Fengate Peterborough England: the First Report*. (Royal Ontario Museum. Archaeological Monograph 3.) Ontario: Royal Ontario Museum.

Pryor, F., 1980. *Excavation at Fengate, Peterborough, England: The Third Report*. (Royal Ontario Museum Archaeology Monograph 6.) Toronto: Royal Ontario Museum.

Pryor, F., 1984. *Excavation at Fengate Peterborough, England: the Fourth Report*. (Northamptonshire Archaeological Society Monograph 2/Royal Ontario Museum Archaeological Monograph 7.) Leicester: Northamptonshire Archaeological Society/Ontario: Royal Ontario Museum.

Pryor, F., 1996. Sheep, stockyards and field systems: Bronze Age livestock populations in the Fenlands of eastern England. *Antiquity* 70, 313–24.

Pryor, F., 2001. *The Flag Fen Basin: Archaeology and Environment of a Fenland Landscape*. Swindon: English Heritage.

Pryor, F. & C.A.I. French, 1985. *Archaeology and Environment in the Lower Welland Valley*. (Fenland Project, Number 1/ East Anglian Archaeology 27.) Cambridge: Fenland Project Committee/Cambridgeshire Archaeological Committee.

Pullinger, J. & C.J. Young. 1982. The M11 Western By-pass; Three sites near Cambridge: 1 Obelisk Kilns, Harston. *Proceedings of the Cambridge Antiquarian Society* 71, 1–23.

Pullinger, J., V. Heal & A.J. Legge, 1982. The M11 Western By-pass; Three sites near Cambridge: 2 Lingey Fen, Haslingfield. *Proceedings of the Cambridge Antiquarian Society* 71, 25–40.

Ratković, D., 2005. *Roman Bronze Vessels in the Roman Collection of the National Museum in Belgrade*. Belgrade: Narodni Muzej.

RCHM(E), 1959. *An Inventory of the Historical Monuments in the City of Cambridge*. London: Her Majesty's Stationery Office.

Regan, R., 1996. *An Archaeological Evaluation for Smith Kline Beecham, Addenbrooke's Hospital, Cambridge*. (Cambridge Archaeological Unit Report 189.)

Riddler, I. 1998. When there is no end to a good game. *British Archaeology* 31, 10–11.

Roberts, J., 2003. *Hinxton Road, Duxford Post-excavation Assessment and Updated Project Design (PNUM 3303)*. (Cambridgeshire County Council, Report Number PXA44.)

Roberts, C.A. & M. Cox, 2003. *Health & Disease in Britain: from Prehistory to the Present Day*. Stroud: Sutton.

Roberts, C.A. & K. Manchester, 1995. *The Archaeology of Disease*. Stroud: Sutton.

Roberts, K.E., 2004a. The environmental bulk samples from Cherry Hinton, in *Land Adjacent to 63 Church End, Cherry Hinton. An Archaeological Excavation*, by C. Cessford & R. Mortimer. Cambridge: Cambridge Archaeological Unit Report 607.

Roberts, K.E., 2004b. The environmental bulk samples, in *The Cambridge and County Folk Museum, Cambridge: An Archaeological Excavation*, by C. Cessford. (Cambridge Archaeological Unit Report 574.)

Robinson, M., 1995. *Addenbrooke's Island: an Archaeological Evaluation*. (Cambridge Archaeological Unit Report 148.)

Rodwell, W.J., 1978. Stamp-decorated pottery of the early Roman period in eastern England, in *Early Fine Wares in Roman Britain*, eds. G.D. Marsh & P.R. Arthur. (British Archaeological Reports 57.) Oxford: BAR, 225–92.

Rogers, J. & T. Waldron, 1995. *A Field Guide to Joint Disease in Archaeology*. Chichester: Wiley.

Sakař, V. 1970. *Roman Imports in Bohemia*. (Fontes Archaeologici Pragenses 14.) Pragae: Museum Nationale Pragae, Sectio Praehistorica.

Salzman, L.F. (ed.), 1967. *A History of the County of Cambridge and the Isle of Ely*, vol. I. Oxford: Oxford University Press for the Institute of Historical Research.

Schmid, E., 1972. *Atlas of Animal Bones for Prehistorians, Archaeologists and Quaternary Geologists*. Amsterdam, London & New York: Elsevier.

Scott-Fox, C., 2002. *Cyril Fox: Archaeologist Extraordinary*. Oxford: Oxbow.

Sheail, G., 2000. Relief and landforms, in *An Atlas of Cambridgeshire and Huntingdonshire History* (Entry 2), eds. T. Kirby T. & S. Oosthuizen. Cambridge: Centre for Regional Studies, Anglia Polytechnic University.

Silver, I.A., 1969. The ageing of domestic animals, in *Science in Archaeology, A Survey of Progress and Research*, eds. D. R. Brothwell & E. Higgs. London: Thames & Hudson, 283–30.

Slater, A. & A. Dickens, 2008. *Further Evaluation at Clay Farm, South Cambridge. The 2008 Green Corridor Evaluation*. (Cambridge Archaeological Unit Report 826.)

Smith, J.T., 1997. *Roman Villas: a Study in Social Structure*. London & New York (NY): Routledge.

St Clair, L.E., 1975. Teeth, in *Sisson and Grossman's The Anatomy of Domestic Animals*. 5th edition. Philadelphia, by R. Getty. London & Toronto: W.B. Saunders.

St Joseph, J.K., 1965. Air reconnaissance: recent results, 4. *Antiquity* 39, 143–5.

Stace, C., 1997. *New Flora of the British Isles*. Cambridge: Cambridge University Press.

Stead, I.M., 1967. A La Tène III burial at Welwyn Garden City. *Archaeologia* 101, 1–62.

Stead, I.M., 1976. The earliest burials of the Aylesford culture, in *Problems in Economic and Social Archaeology*, eds. G. Sieveking, I.M. Longworth & K.E. Wilson. London: Duckworth, 401–16.

Stead, I.M. & V. Rigby, 1986. *Baldock: the Excavation of a Roman and Pre-Roman settlement 1968–72*. (Britannia Monograph 7.) London: Society for the Promotion of Roman Studies.

Stead, I.M. & V. Rigby, 1989. *Verulamium: the King Harry Lane Site*. (English Heritage Archaeological

Report12.) London: English Heritage/British Museum Publications.

Steele, D.G. & C. A. Bramblett, 1988 . *The Anatomy and Biology of the Human Skeleton*. College Station (TX): A&M University Press.

Stevens, C., 1998. The plant remains, in *Excavation of the Middle Saxon to Medieval Village at Lordship Lane, Cottenham, Cambridgeshire*, by R. Mortimer. (Cambridge Archaeological Unit Report 254.)

Stevens, C., 2000. The plant remains, in *Excavation of the North Field, Greenhouse Farm, Cambridge*, by D. Gibson & G. Lucas. (Cambridge Archaeological Unit Report 354.)

Swan, V.G., 1984. *The Pottery Kilns of Roman Britain*. London: Her Majesty's Stationery Office.

Tassinari, S., 1993. *Il Vasellame Bronzeo di Pompei*. (Ministero per i beni culturali ed ambientali, Soprintendenza Archeologica di Pompei, Cataloghi 5.) Rome: 'L'Erma' di Bretschneider.

Taylor, A., 1977. *Prehistoric Cambridgeshire*. Cambridge: Oleander Press.

Taylor, A., 1997. *Archaeology of Cambridgeshire*, vol. I: *South West Cambridgeshire*. Cambridge: Cambridgeshire County Council.

Taylor, A. 1999. *Cambridge: the Hidden History*. Stroud: Tempus.

Taylor, C. & P.J. Fowler, 1978. Roman fields into medieval furlongs, in *Early Land Allotment*, eds. H.C. Bowen & P.J. Fowler. (British Archaeological Report 48.) Oxford: BAR, 159–62.

Taylor, C., P. Topping & A Oswald, 1993. A prehistoric enclosure at Sawston, Cambridgeshire. *Proceedings of the Cambridge Antiquarian Society* 82, 5–9.

Taylor, J., 2007. *An Atlas of Roman Rural Settlement in England*. (CBA Research Report 151.) York: Council for British Archaeology.

Ten Harkel, L., 2006. *Archaeological Excavations at Castle Street, Cambridge*. (Cambridge Archaeological Unit Report 739.)

Thompson, I., 1982. *Grog-tempered Belgic Pottery of Southeastern England*. (British Archaeological Report 108.) Oxford: BAR.

Thompson, M.W., 1990. *The Cambridge Antiquarian Society, 1840–1990*. Cambridge: Cambridge Antiquarian Society.

Timberlake S., 2007. *Addenbrooke's Hospital Water Main Diversion: an Archaeological Investigation*. (Cambridge Archaeological Unit Report 794.)

Timberlake, S. & N. Armour, 2007. *The Roman Cemetery Site. The Babraham Institute, Cambridgeshire: an Archaeological Excavation*. (Cambridge Archaeological Unit Report 754.)

Timby, J., R. Brown, E. Biddulph, A. Hardy & A. Powell, 2007. *A Slice of Rural Essex: Recent Archaeological Discoveries from the A120 between Stansted Airport and Braintree*. (Oxford Wessex Archaeology Monograph 1.) Oxford: Oxford Wessex Archaeology.

Tipper, J., 2003. *Elective Care Facility, Addenbrooke's Hospital, Cambridge: an Archaeological Evaluation*. (Cambridge Archaeological Unit Report No. 578)

Toller, H.S. 1980. Orsett Cock. *Britannia* 11, 35–42.

Tomber, R. & J. Dore, 1998. *The National Roman Fabric Reference Collection. A Handbook*. London: Museum of London Archaeology Service.

Trotter, M. & G.C. Gleser, 1952. Estimation of stature from long bones of American Whites and Negroes. *American Journal of Physical Anthropology* 10, 463–514.

Trump, D., A.J. Legge & J. Alexander, 1975. *Cambridge, Rectory Farm, Great Shelford, 1975: Interim Report*. Cambridge: Board of Extra-Mural Studies, University of Cambridge/London: Dept. of Extra-Mural Studies, University of London.

Trump, D., A.J. Legge & J. Alexander, 1977. *Cambridge, Rectory Farm, Great Shelford, 1975–77: Interim Report*. Cambridge: Board of Extra-Mural Studies, University of Cambridge/London: Dept. of Extra-Mural Studies, University of London.

Tyers, P., 1996. *Roman Pottery in Britain*. London: Routledge.

Ubelaker, D., 1989. *Human Skeletal Remains. Excavation, Analysis, Interpretation*. Washington (DC): Taraxacum.

Ucelli, G., 1950. *Le Navi di Nemi*. Rome: Libraria dello stato.

UKDFD, 2006. UK detector finds database, Ref. No. 4210. http://www.ukdfd.co.uk.

UKDFD, 2007a. UK detector finds database, Ref. No. 6296. http://www.ukdfd.co.uk.

UKDFD, 2007b. UK detector finds database, Ref. No. 7005. http://www.ukdfd.co.uk.

van der Veen, M., 1996. Plant remains, in *Excavations at Stonea, Cambs. 1980–85*, by R.P.J. Jackson & T.W. Potter. London: British Museum Press, 613–37.

van der Veen, M., 1999. The economic value of chaff and straw in arid and temperate zones. *Vegetation History and Archaeobotany* 8, 211–24.

Voss, H-.U. with M. Erdrich, H. Keiling, J. Parschau, R. Laser, A. Leube, J. Richthoen, E. Schultze & H. Stange, 1998. *Corpus der Römischen funde im europaischen Barbaricum*, Band 3: *Bundesland Mecklenburg-Vorpommern*. (Römisch-Germanische Kommission des Deutschen Archäologischen Instituts zu Frankfurt am Main, Staatliche Museen zu Berlin, Brandenburgischen Landesmuseum für ur- und Frühgeschichte. Deutschland). Bonn: Habelt.

Wait, G.A., 1992. *Archaeological Investigations: New Addenbrookes, Centre for Brain Repair, 1992*. (Cambridge Archaeological Unit Report 74.)

Walker, D.J.C., 2007. Understanding Pottery Kilns. Interpreting Structure and Process through Experimental Archaeology. Unpublished PhD thesis, Nottingham University.

Walker, F.G., 1910. Roman roads into Cambridge. *Cambridge Antiquarian Society Communications* 14, 141–76.

Watts, M., 2002. *The Archaeology of Mills & Milling*. Stroud: Tempus.

Webb, D., 2007. A Patera/Trulleum from Clay Farm, Cambridgeshire: Notes from ongoing research and the development of an online resource. *Lucerna, The Roman Finds Group Newsletter* 34, December 2007.

Webster, G., 2002. Copper alloy mounts, fasteners, studs and pins, in *The Legionary Fortress at Wroxeter. Excavations by Graham Webster, 1955–85*, by G. Webster, ed. J. Chadderton. London: English Heritage, 112–22.

West, S., 1998. *A Corpus of Anglo-Saxon Material from Suffolk.* (East Anglian Archaeology 84.) Bury St. Edmunds: Suffolk County Council Archaeology Service.

West, S. E., 1964. Excavations at Cox Lane (1958) and the town defenses, Shire Hall Yard, Ipswich. *Proceedings of the Suffolk Institute of Archaeology* 29, 23–303.

Whimster, R., 1981. *Burial Practices in Iron Age Britain.* (British Archaeological Reports 90.) Oxford: BAR.

White, D.A., 1964a. Excavations at the War Ditches, Cherry Hinton, 1961–62. *Proceedings of the Cambridge Antiquarian Society* 56, 9–29.

White, D.A., 1964b. Excavations at the War Ditches, Cherry Hinton, 1949–51. *Proceedings of the Cambridge Antiquarian Society* 56, 30–41.

White, L., 1998. *Archaeological Excavation at Cherry Hinton Ring Ditches, Fulbourn Road, Cambridge.* (Cambridge Archaeological Unit Report 247.)

Whittaker, P., 2002a. *An Archaeological Evaluation at 28–30 Long Road, Cambridge.* (Cambridge Archaeological Unit Report 483.)

Whittaker, P., 2002b. *An Archaeological Evaluation at Strangeways Laboratory, Worts Causeway, Cambridge.* (Cambridge Archaeological Unit Report 487.)

Whittaker, P., C. Evans & D. Gibson, 2002. *Granham's Farm, Great Shelford, Cambridgeshire: an Archaeological Evaluation.* (Cambridge Archaeological Unit Report 514.)

Wilkens, I.J., 2005. *Where Troy Once Stood.* Groningen: Gopher Publishers.

Wilkes, J.J. & C.R. Elrington (eds.), 1978. *The History of the County of Cambridge & the Isle of Ely*, vol. VII: *Roman Cambridgeshire.* Oxford: Oxford University Press for the Institute of Historical Research.

Williamson, T.M., 1984. The Roman countryside: settlement and agriculture in NW Essex. *Britannia* 15, 225–30.

Williamson, T., 1987. Early co-axial field systems on the East Anglian boulder clays. *Proceedings of the Prehistoric Society* 53, 419–31.

Willis, S., 1996. The Romanization of pottery assemblages in the east and north-east of England during the first century AD: a comparative analysis. *Britannia* 27, 179–221.

Willis, S., 1998. Samian pottery in Britain: exploring its distribution and archaeological potential. *Archaeological Journal* 155, 82–133.

Wilson, B., 1992. Considerations for the identification of ritual deposits of animal bones in Iron Age pits. *International Journal of Osteoarchaeology* 2, 341–9.

Woods, P. & S. Hastings, 1984. *Rushden: the Early Fine Wares.* Northampton: Northamptonshire County Council.

Woolley, L., 1953. *Spadework: Adventures in Archaeology.* London: Lutterworth Press.

Woudhuysen, M., A. Legge & J. Alexander, 1981. *Excavations at The Hollicks, Rectory Farm, Great Shelford, 1980.* Cambridge: Board of Extra-Mural Studies, University of Cambridge/London: Dept. of Extra-Mural Studies, University of London.

Wright, R.P., 1950. Roman Britain in 1949: I. sites explored: II. inscriptions. *Journal of Roman Studies* 40, 92–118.

Yates, D.T., 2007. *Land, Power and Prestige: Bronze Age Field Systems in Southern England.* Oxford: Oxbow Books.

Young, R. & J. Humphrey, 1999: Flint use in England after the Bronze Age: time for a re-evaluation? *Proceedings of the Prehistoric Society* 65, 231–42.